D1596935

Christianity in Africa
and the African Diaspora

Christianity in Africa and the African Diaspora
The Appropriation of a Scattered Heritage

Edited by

Afe Adogame
Roswith Gerloff
Klaus Hock

continuum

Continuum International Publishing Group

The Tower Building   80 Maiden Lane
11 York Road   Suite 704
London   New York
SE1 7NX   NY 10038

www.continuumbooks.com

British Library Cataloguing-in-Publication Data
A catalogue record for this book is available from the British Library.

ISBN-10: HB: 1-8470-6317-9
ISBN-13: HB: 978-1-8470-6317-5

Library of Congress Cataloging-in-Publication Data
A catalog record for this book is available from the Library of Congress.

Typeset by Newgen Imaging Systems Pvt Ltd, Chennai, India
Printed and bound in Great Britain by Biddles Ltd, King's Lynn, Norfolk

Contents

Part Two: Gender Perspective

Part Three: Charismatic/Pentecostal Perspectives

Part Four: Diasporic Perspectives

List of Contributors

Afe Adogame holds a PhD in History of Religions from the University of Bayreuth, Germany. One of his main research and teaching expertise is on African religions in the diaspora. He is Asst. Professor and currently teaches World Christianity and Religious Studies at the University of Edinburgh, UK.

Olayemi Akinwumi holds a PhD in African History from the University of Ilorin, Nigeria. His recent edited book is 'Intergroup Relations in Nigeria in the 19th and 20th Century'. He is currently a professor and the Dean of Arts, Nasarawa State University, Keffi, Nigeria.

Abraham Akrong, educated at the University of Ghana, the Trinity Theological Seminary, Legon Ghana and Lutheran School of Theology at Chicago. At present Senior Research Fellow and Head of Section of religion and philosophy at the Institute of African Studies University of Ghana, Legon.

Dapo Asaju is a Professor of New Testament and Church History at the Department of Religions, Lagos State University, Ojo-Lagos, Nigeria. He is an ordained priest of the Church of Nigeria, Anglican Communion.

J. Kwabena Asamoah-Gyadu is Associate Professor in Religious Studies and Pentecostal/Charismatic Christianity at the Trinity Theological Seminary, Legon, Accra, Ghana. Asamoah-Gyadu's book "African Charismatics" is published by E. J. Brill, Leiden (2005).

Deji Ayegboyin is a Senior Lecturer in the Department of Religious Studies at the University of Ibadan, Nigeria. His teaching and research focus includes Church History and African Christianity.

Bolaji Olukemi Bateye is a Lecturer in the Department of Religious Studies, Obafemi Awolowo University (OAU), Ile-Ife, Nigeria. She is also a resource person at the OAU Centre for Gender and Social Policy Studies.

Jonathan J. Bonk is the Executive Director of the Overseas Ministries Study Centre, and editor of the International Bulletin of Missionary Research. He took his Ph.D. under Andrew F. Walls at the University of Aberdeen.

Nico Botha is currently Associate Professor in Missiology, Department of Christian Spirituality, Church History and Missiology at the University of South Africa (UNISA). He obtained a Doctorandus in Theology (Missiology) at the University of Utrecht, Netherlands and a Doctor in Theology at UNISA 2005.

Ezra Chitando is Associate Professor in History and Phenomenology of Religion in the Department of Religious Studies, Classics and Philosophy at the University of Zimbabwe.

Deidre Helen Crumbley is Associate Professor of Africana Studies in the Interdisciplinary Studies division of North Carolina State University. In addition to her terminal degree in Anthropology from Northwestern University, Crumbley also holds a Masters of Theological Studies from Harvard Divinity School.

Deborah Gaitskell is a Research Associate of the History Department at the School of Oriental and African Studies (SOAS), University of London. Her published works focuses on gender and Christianity: mission domesticity, African girls' education, and churchwomen's groups.

Roswith Gerloff is an ordained woman theologian. She lectured at the universities of Birmingham, Frankfurt am. Main. and Leeds. She founded the Centre for Black and White Christian Partnership in Birmingham. Her research include Black Christianity and Pentecostalism in Britain, Europe, and Intercultural Theology.

Herbert Griffiths hold a PhD from Leeds University, UK. He lectures in Church History and Church Doctrines at Immanuel Theological College in London. He is an Elder in the Seventh-day Adventist in London, UK.

Ursula Harfst is a pastor of the Protestant Church in the Rhineland. From 2002 to 2005 she served as an associate pastor in a congregation in Duisburg-Hochfeld. From February to September 2008, she coordinated the programme "Cooperation between German and foreign language churches" of the United Evangelical Mission in Germany.

Antipas L. Harris hails from Manchester, Georgia, a second generation African American Pentecostal-holiness ordained minister of fifteen years. He recently completed a DMin degree in Theology at Boston University School of Theology and he is now Assistant Professor of Practical Ministry at Regent University School of Divinity, USA.

Andreas Heuser, theologian and political scientist, Department of Ecumenical Relationship of the Protestant Church in Hesse and Nassau/Germany, and theological advisor in the research department of the Council of Christian Churches of an African Approach in Europe (CCCAAE).

Klaus Hock has been a professor for History of Religions – Religion and Society at the University of Rostock since 1996. His research focuses on Islam and Christian-Muslim relations, African religions, and transculturation.

Alle G. Hoekema studied Theology at the Universiteit van Amsterdam. He holds a Ph.D. from Leiden University (1994). Now he works part time as an assistant professor in Missiology at the Vrije Universiteit in Amsterdam.

Evangelos Karagiannis is Assistant Professor at the Institute for Social Anthropology of the University of Zurich. His research topics are nationalism and ethnicity (particularly in the Balkans) migration, and religious communities.

Nina Glick Schiller is Professor of Anthropology at the University of New Hampshire, USA and a visiting Research Associate at the Max Planck Institute of Social Anthropology, Germany.

Dominique Kounkou is a sociologist based in Sorbonne, Paris. France. He is President of the Council for Christian Communities of an African Approach in Europe (CCCAAE).

Aurélien Mokoko Gampiot earned his PhD in Sociology from the University of Rennes 2, France, in 2003 on 'Kimbanguism from the homeland to the host society.' He published part of his findings in (Paris: L'Harmattan, 2004) and is about to publish a second work on Kimbanguists in France.

Philomena Njeri Mwaura is a Senior Lecturer in the Department of Philosophy and Religious Studies, Kenyatta University, Kenya where she obtained her doctorate. She is currently the President of the International Association for Mission Studies.

Matthews A. Ojo holds a PhD in Theology (Church History) in the School of Oriental and African Studies and Kings' College (University of London) in 1987. He is currently a Professor in the Department of Religious Studies, Obafemi Awolowo University, Ile-Ife, Nigeria.

Richard V. Pierard is Emeritus Professor of History, Indiana State University, and currently scholar in residence at Gordon College, Wenham, Massachusetts, USA.

Benjamin Simon studied Theology and Educational Sciences at the Universities of Heidelberg, Marburg and Pietermaritzburg/RSA. He is currently lecturer at the Makumira University College (Tumaini University) in Tanzania.

Kevin Ward is Senior Lecturer in African Studies in the Department of Theology and Religious Studies at the University of Leeds, UK. He has worked extensively in East Africa and was ordained in the (Anglican) Church of Uganda.

Prologue
Dominique Kounkou

Welcome Speech: President of the Council for Christian Communities of an African Approach in Europe. Hirschluch (09 November 2003)

Your Excellencies, Ladies and Gentlemen;

Dear brothers and sisters who love peace and want to create it in a world in process of reaching a decisive turning point.

Honorable personalities and high Church authorities of Christian communities and of the Council of Christian Communities of an African Approach in Europe.

Dear hosts from the Universities, from culture, religion and politics.

Dear friends of peace who have come from afar to build bridges within our humanity when history left us with an ocean of blood, tears, misery and hatred.

I am honoured to welcome you to the Third International Interdisciplinary conference of the African Christian Diaspora in Europe (CCCAAE) taking place here in the Hirschluch conference centre, not far from Berlin, Germany, on the theme : 'The 1884 Berlin-Congo Conference: the partition of Africa and its implications for Christian mission today.'

This third conference is organized under the auspices of the CCCAAE, Humboldt University (Berlin), Rostock University, and the Hamburg Mission Academy. As president of the CCCAAE I thank these four institutions that worked in collaboration towards the realization of this conference under the best of conditions. In your name, I thank them all. Allow me to thank also those institutes that made possible in one capacity or another, the coming-into-existence of this gathering. Asking forgiveness in advance for anyone I might have forgotten, I wish to thank those present: – the research Institute of Missiology; the Catholic Africa Centre in Berlin; the International Convent of Christian Congregations in Berlin.

This conference would not have been possible, were it not for the long persistent work of the organizational conference team composed of: Dr Roswith Gerloff, Dr Afe Adogame, the General Secretary Alimany Sesay, Professor Andreas Feldtkeller, Pastor Peter Mansaray, Dr Andreas Heuser, Dieudonné

Tobbit and the African Council of Berlin and its president Dr Arthur Kingsley. I am filled with infinite gratitude for the work they have accomplished.

Ladies and gentlemen, dear brothers and sisters, let me tell you we are gathered to enliven a momentum, an event of peace on which we shall build a new Africa and a bridge between Europe and Africa. In 2002, we asked our God for the deliverance of Africa in front of the Reichstag and the location were once the partition of Africa was decided upon; this is not to be separated from the conference we are holding today! It is indeed during the meeting of the Council executive in Berlin in 2002 that both decisions, to pray for the deliverance of Africa and the theme of this conference were taken. By this resolution, we want to undo the destiny of Africa that humans diverted – a destiny turned into the 'black man's burden' according to Davidson Basil.

Healing Memory

We also want to heal the memory of the generations which have given birth to a world marked by hatred. The roots of this lie in the history that divided us Africans so that we now may be united and re-build our continent together. The same history separates us into colonists and colonized, whereas as Africans and Europeans we should be able in spite of our differences to act and co-operate towards an equitable commerce and a more balanced and lasting development.

When Portugal, the oldest occupant on Africa's Atlantic coast, suggested an international conference in 1884, it aimed at a solution to more efficiently control Africa and bury the tensions between the European conquistadores on the black continent. Fourteen countries responded to the invitation then put forward by Germany. It is important to put this into the context of the ensuing geostrategic evolutions of these countries. Among the big powers, we find Belgium, France, Portugal, Great Britain, Italy, Spain, Sweden, Norway, Austria-Hungary, Germany, Denmark and Holland. Does not this group still form the spine of the European Community? Russia also was to show up at the conference and became one of the world powers during the cold war. So did the USA, the Super power today. Finally, Turkey was to be present, yet another country which applied for membership in the EU. Ladies and gentlemen, the political geostrategy of the dominant powers that is, historically speaking, the cause of this convocation, remains the same until today.

Historically, the Berlin–Congo conference lasted a year, from 15 November 1884 to 26 February 1885. It ended with the geometrical partition of Africa. In the following century, the European powers experienced the fever of the industrial revolution, hence the request for raw materials from Africa and the need to create new outlets. Politically, this position still makes sense.

On one hand, the desire to dominate the world crystallizes in the tendency of these political powers gathered at the Berlin–Congo conference to affirm to the world the image of a dominated: Africa. Otto von Bismarck, Chancellor of Germany as the inviting power, pronounced such in his introductory speech, the effects of which live on and assert Africa as eternally dominated. The speech, however, did not lack humanitarian aspects.

Since then, indeed, it has been argued that there were hopeful intentions towards Africa, yet the occidental political actors continued with their control and hence deceived the Africans. In 1885, the argument consisted in putting an end to slavery and to propose humanitarian actions towards Africa. Then it was not yet stated explicitly that Europe needs raw materials from a continent now brought into globalization and turned into a simple outpost.

Churches, too, saw in these actions God's plan to develop a mission, even an 'international right for mission' (Boegner). Thus they abused opinion. The church, in a state of euphoria, did not pay attention to the dangerous balkanization of Africa, and to the fact that this discredited the Christian faith among black people, bringing to despise the church, the Gospel and any white man. At the same time, an indestructible superiority complex was planted in the minds of white people up to the point that it turned into hatred for blacks. One could brush it aside and turn a new leaf, if it were not for the 1884/85 event, its aberrations and unfolding mechanisms that still impact on our world and international relations. Political logic of the past still shapes the present and the future.

I come from Brazzaville, Congo, the region in the south called Pool that is going through a genocide stifled by international opinion. The international community exploits petrol from the Congo. It chooses to support a tyrant who wants to do away with the Pool population. Neither the international community nor the tyrant himself will publicly declare their true intentions. When invited to a joint action to save the Congo, they all excuse themselves by refusing to meddle in internal affairs, an argument backed up by international opinion, which justifies the lack of intervention to stop a dictatorship they put in place. The case of the Congo is not exceptional in Africa and, like in 1885, the church, too, continues to fall into a trap.

Let Us Communicate!

Dear friends, when we re-open the file on the Berlin–Congo Conference after a century, this is not meant to perpetuate the order of political violence and the infernal cycle of political revenge. We aim at a goal: to establish the truth on the trap into which the church as well as the whole of humanity have fallen. This truth can rehabilitate the dignity of political actions in international relations.

This very truth will set us free from the semi-truths which mutilate the image of God and hurt the deepest roots of human beings.

Hence we are asking our experts, through their papers and statements, to explain plainly what really happened at that time in all domains, religious, political, social and cultural. We are also asking for their help in evaluating the consequences, in particular those which keep on disturbing African populations and the relationship between whites and blacks. We wish that, at the end of this conference, the mutual trust between the children of God, whatever their colour, be reborn! In the heart of this planet and the globalization process, we ask God for His gift of forgiveness, peace and reconciliation – a peace the world alone is not able to provide.

We shall look from the past into the future. We will heed the expectations of peace and justice in Africa. We will examine our responsibilities in the face of ignored and forgotten wars, the origins of which are to be found in the decisions of the Berlin–Congo Conference. We will attempt to explore the right way to become actors of peace and progress facing a mutual future. At the end, we have to leave this place each with a dream, transformed into a collective act, aiming at building a new humanity, prosperous and reconciled.

For us, the Holy Spirit enacts Isaiah's vision in which the wolf and the lamb, the descendant of the colonizer and the colonized, live, dwell and work in faith together. For Africa, we call upon the reconstruction of spaces of prosperity where humans become true citizens endowed with the power for decision-making and empowered to determine their lives. Hence we will contribute to better our children's lives. May the Holy Spirit enlighten our work and lead us towards new divine paths yet untouched by human intelligence. Dear friends, instead of fighting and getting into wars, may we enter the life-giving dialogue! I thank you and wish you God's speed.

Introduction

Contemporary studies in anthropology and sociology of religion speak of 'religions on the move', referring to processes of transmigration and transculturation, which unleash dynamic, reciprocal, transitory and multidimensional creations in shaping a poly-contextual world. This implies that religions have to be regarded as cultural and spiritual phenomena whose 'taken-for-granted' essence has resulted from transcultural and transnational processes of mutual influence, interaction and continuous adaptation to new environments, developments and encounters. The emphasis here is on 'a new model of understanding religion which emphasizes process and practitioners over form and content' (C. Yawney). Religions, including different forms of Christianity, respond to ever changing circumstances and play a role in constructing and re-constructing, even 'inventing' cultural and national identities.

The continent of Africa, with its traumatic experience of the transatlantic slave trade as an unprecedented mode of forced exile, and the development of accelerated intercontinental African migration in the context of globalisation in the second half of the twentieth century, is a case in point. Africa herself has gone through numerous phases of internal and external migration which also has effected the arrival and settlement of larger or smaller African migrant groups in Europe and the Americas – and, in fact, the presence of religious traditions quite alien to western established religions.

Today, the western world is therefore faced with the arrival of so-called 'indigenous' religions in cross-fertilisation with contextualized Christian interpretations on its own shores. Moreover, it is compelling to acknowledge that these current manifestations are 'not new' but have had precursors in a multifaceted history. This applies to African, Caribbean, Latin American and Asian histories with their respective unique experiences. For Africa, in particular, it was the 'Berlin–Congo Conference 1884/85' which enabled the European powers to partition the continent not according to its natural, human, geographical and cultural boundaries but to their imperial interests, yet which also set in motion unforeseen developments.

The historical circumstances surrounding this Congress and its aftermath have generated both intended and unintended consequences and implications for Christian mission in contemporary Africa, and also within the spiritual maps of the globe. Africa was divided not only into artificial geographical boundaries to facilitate political subjugation, economic exploitation and expropriation, but, in a sense, the partition transcended geographical, political and economic terrains to include religious divisions. African philosophies, cultures and indigenous religions were suppressed, ignored and often ridiculed. At the aftermath of the historical event, the various European missionaries became largely streamlined along the new boundaries on the levels of nationality and denominational affiliation.

In the transmission process, Western denominationalism which coloured European Christianity became one of the discreditable legacies of mission-oriented Christianity in Africa. Yet, the indigenous communities on the grassroots of diverse regions – caught up in the tensions between imperial powers and the quest for freedom, socio-cultural control and resistance to domination, the colonial face of mission, and the tenacity of religion as understood by Africans – continued to shape people's identities, developments and expressions in the struggle for survival and human dignity. Hence, the complexity of 'contemporary' transmigratory processes from and to Africa must be considered in the light of this history of Western colonial expansion and the Western missionary movement; and vice versa the turbulent history from the end of the nineteenth century is also discovered as facilitating a global transformation of modern Christianity not only in the South, but now also affecting the northern hemisphere. Cross-cultural transplantation from either side, and the capability of Christianity to re-interpret faith in diverse contexts, have forged an understanding in which traditions and activities overlay one another, overlap, blend, create new forms on the margins and therefore challenge the validity of all boundaries, exclusivist doctrines and centres.

The relative success story of Christianity in Africa and African Christianity is not unconnected with its translatability and vernacularization, or what some African Christians describe as 'power-in-participation' in the Spirit. Especially, the language factor is central to the contextualization of Christianity in Africa. The place and role of indigenous agencies therefore become crucial in this respect. Christian demography in Africa has been further transformed with the emergence of African Instituted Churches (AICs) and of Pentecostal and Charismatic Christianity into the religious landscape. As religious space is now increasingly being contested with the encounter and interaction among these brands of Christianity, and the interface between them and Islam and other religions, this generates a further level of action and reaction, suspicion and tension. On the other hand, this intra- and inter-religious encounter produces a certain degree of mutual influence and accommodation, even respect and mutual acceptance at the same time. For instance, it has become fashionable in a sense to talk about the 'pentecostalization' of indigenous and mission churches.

This is reflected in the global stature of contemporary African Christianity. It portrays how world Christianity must be realised in local contexts, as local contexts are now reckoned as the qualifier of world Christianity, both in Africa and in diasporic movements. While the significance of Africa as one of the new Christian centres of gravity cannot be underestimated, we should equally be attentive to the ways in which African Christianity has joined other religious traditions in the religious diversification of western societies. As an example, the claim of a 'reverse-mission' or the re-missionization of Christianity in the secularized west is fast becoming a major feature of their evangelistic strategies and mission agendas. With the conscious appropriation of new media technologies, participation in both theological and public discourses, the engagement in intra- and inter-religious links and networks, these varieties of African Christianity are systematically inserting themselves into global religious landscapes.

From 1997, a number of 'African Christian Diaspora Consultations' took place in Britain, Sweden, Germany and Switzerland of which two (Leeds and Cambridge) attempted to develop instruments and mechanisms for affirming the significance and implications of this religious development particularly for contemporary Europe. In 2003, as a follow-up, scholars of religion, historians, social scientists and theologians together with religious practitioners from the African Diaspora, in the continents of Africa and America gathered at the Hirschluch conference centre near Berlin to look particularly into the Berlin–Congo Conference and its implications for Christian mission under the title: 'The Berlin–Congo conference 1884/85, the partition of Africa, and implications for Christian Mission today'. Alongside with both Humboldt and Rostock Universities, the conference gained its impetus from the newly founded Council of Churches of an African Approach in Europe (CCAAE).

The aims of this conference were: to examine the historical and socio-political consequences of the partition of Africa for the continent and the African Diaspora, highlighting issues such as migration, racism and sexism; to look critically into the political role the Christian mission played in colonizing Africa, as well as, into the paradigm shift in mission locally and globally; to inquire into the significance of diverse indigenous movements (not least pentecostal) emanating from the two-thirds world in their struggle for survival in dignity, as well as their interaction with religious and secular European institutions; and in all these aspects explore the practical consequences, not least giving Black women a prominent place in the proceedings. Also, to avoid any misinterpretation and further exploitation, the gathering was based on direct mutual encounter between renowned African scholars and resource persons and representatives of African churches. Since colonial languages still dominate, the medium of communication had to be English and French.

This edited book is the outcome of this consultation's diverse considerations, with each author standing for her or his own local context, experience, perspectives and interpretation. So it may not present a comprehensive overview but can serve as a pointer to future discoveries and discourses that may contribute to a deeper understanding of the rapid transformation of the Christian faith, a new paradigm in mission, instruments for overcoming racial and cultural barriers, and strategies for promoting intercultural, ecumenical and inter-religious dialogue.

Among questions to be asked are: To what extent can African Christianity serve as a catalyst in the transmission of Christianity in a context of growing religious pluralism and ethnic diversities worldwide? How and to what extent does African Christianity mark a turning point or serve as a challenge to developments within and outside world Christianity? How, in response to secularism's critique of religion as such, can it contribute to peacemaking in an increasingly polarized world and help, as the Welcome speech by Dominique Kounkou suggests, 'to heal the memory of generations', and 'aim at building a new humanity, prosperous and reconciled?' Will the claim of a 'next Christendom', perceived in some circles, as a reliance on the power of the Holy Spirit remain a mirage or are we effectively witnessing the radical transformation of Christianity or even of religion generally?

The book is divided into four main parts: Part One deals with the historical antecedents and ensuing developments surrounding the Berlin–Congo 1884 Conference and shows how this singular historical event has visited wide ranging political, social, economic, cultural but also significant religious implications for contemporary world Christianity. It points to the ambivalent nature and aspects of mission to Africa; the inaptly uneven distribution of knowledge about its distinctive place in both human and Christian history; the struggle for liberation and a new role of church and religion in the process of such a transformation; with case studies such as African Anglicanism, Baptist contributions, among others. The part also engages in missiological discourses and practical consequences, as contributions take on theological issues that confront African and western Christianity alike. It delves into such issues as deconstructing colonial mission in favour of gospel transmission by cultural means, and the focus on incarnational and holistic approaches.

Part Two explores gender discourses that have become central to the understanding of African Christianity within the wider purview of global Christianity, pointing to the affirmation of female leadership against continuing religio-cultural and sexual male hegemony; the 'rebirth' of African theology in view of the HIV/AIDS pandemic and the shaping of new religious identities and landscapes in response to power relations and artificial boundaries.

Part Three on Charismatic/Pentecostal perspectives examines the varied ways in which they have contributed to the shaping and transformation of African Christianity; the social changes, both local and global, stimulated through indigenous enterprises and transnational religious networks Africa as laboratory for 'Churches of the Spirit' that carry a potential for the renewal of contemporary Christianity; the new charismatic movements as catalysts for closer identification with the spiritual and physical needs of Africans, but also in dire need of a more consistent social, political and economic critique; and the lived-out existence in the diaspora grounded in the conviction that our universal humanity counts more than any singular nation state.

Part Four on diasporic perspectives tackles specific socio-political and cultural issues that shape the transmission and adaptability of Christianity in Africa and the African Diaspora. It starts with a discourse on diaspora religions, pointing to their hybridity or dynamic character, an 'open space' created by such movements. It explores the change of the mission paradigm in diasporic Seventh-day Adventism. Most importantly, it investigates the influence of worldviews and cosmological traditions on Africans in migration; the colonial politicization of religions versus a contemporary evangelistic impulse; case studies on Black Seventh-day Adventist and Kimbanguism; and the problems inherent in negotiating one's identity in adapting to new environments.

The volume concludes with contributions calling for a new ecclesiology, and presents examples and strategies for ecumenical intercultural dialogue between established churches and new religious communities in the European west.

Afe Adogame (Edinburgh),
Roswith Gerloff (Leeds) and
Klaus Hock (Rostock),
February 2008

Part One

Historical Developments

Chapter 1

Political or Spiritual Partition: The Impact of the 1884/85 Berlin Conference on Christian Missions in Africa[1]

Olayemi Akinwumi

The free public exercise of all forms of Divine worship, and the right to build edifices for religious missions belonging to all creeds, shall not be limited or fettered in anyway whatsoever.[2]

Introduction

The decision by Bismarck to call the Berlin conference in 1884 was to resolve all crises associated with the Western interest in Africa, during the scrambling or the mad rush for colonial possessions. All the concerned powers met in Berlin and resolved, without reference to the Africans, to partition the continent among themselves. This is the political partition. More than that however, the decision taken at the conference had significant impact on the spread of Christianity in the continent. It led to the partition of Africa into different Christian groups. In other words, it led to the promotion of sectarianism in Africa. As Africans were not involved in the Berlin conference, so also they had no opportunity of choice when they were confronted with these missions supported, indirectly by the colonial governments. This is why Roman Catholic mission became widespread in the French colonies, while Anglican became popular in English colonies. The chapter argues that spiritual partition went alongside with the political partition. This is reflected in the map of Christianity in Africa.

The 1884/85 Berlin conference, without doubt, is one of the significant events that took place in the history of the world. It was in this conference that Africa, erroneously referred to as the 'Dark Continent', was partitioned among the European powers. The partition was done without any African representative in attendance and without any consideration of the historical and cultural background of the people involved. The continent has continued to suffer from the consequences of this conference two centuries after. The list of woes is long: civil and boundary wars. This political theme is however not the focus of this chapter. Rather the object of this chapter will be on the impact of the 1884/85 conference on Christianity in Africa. This is an area that is yet to attract sufficient scholarly attention. I argue in this chapter that the conference institutionalized denominationalism and sectarianism in Africa. In other words, what happened in Berlin was also spiritual partition. The European imperial powers, represented by their colonial officers, began to encourage their own denominations in their various areas of influence. Denominations that have been fully established in some African regions before the conference suddenly lost out to the others supported by the colonial government. The conference also put to an end to interdenominational co-operation between the various missions in Africa and thus began the rivalry between the missions. This chapter also argues that most of the crises within Christianity today in Africa, whether inter and intra-denomination, have some roots in the past.

This chapter is divided into three major sections. The first section will focus on the pre 1884/85 period, and the second and third sections will deal with the Berlin conference and the impact of the conference on the missions in Africa. This chapter, I hope will generate scholarly interest and contribute to the knowledge on Christianity in Africa.

Pre 1884/85 Era: The Missionaries and the Spread of Christianity in Africa

As pointed out by Bolaji Idowu, it is not specifically clear when Christianity came to Africa.[3] With reference to Edwin Smith, it must have got to Africa very early in its history. According to Smith, 'the early period of her (African) history, the church has never been absent from Africa. Christian communities existed in Africa long before they were found in the British Isles and Northern Europe.'[4] Christianity in this period was however only restricted to certain areas, especially areas with proximity to the Middle East and the coastal settlements in the continent.

The first concerted effort to introduce Christianity to the continent was carried out by the Portuguese in the fifteenth century. Portugal, at this time, had emerged as a marine power. Expeditions were sponsored and supported by the king to different areas of the globe. The expeditions were motivated not only by economic gains, but also inspired by religious zeal.[5] As a result of their effort, most of the coastal cities in West and East Africa had come under the influence of Catholicism, the official religion of the State. Some of these areas included Cape Verde, Elmina, Sao Tome, Delagoa, Natal, Mombasa and Benin. Alan Ryder, who has written a seminal work on the Benin and the Europeans, wrote on the attempt by the Portuguese to convert the 'Oba' (king) of Benin and his subjects to the Catholic faith by inducing him with the economic advantages attached to the conversion. According to Ryder, the king was told that his conversion and subsequent baptism 'would bring him (the king) guns as well as grace'.[6] One would like to add at this point that Christianity was only professed by the royal courts in Africa in this period because of what they stood to benefit from it, as seen in the example of the Oba of Benin above.

The Portuguese were not the only nationals involved in spreading Christianity in Africa. The Spanish,[7] the Germans and the Dutch were equally active in the continent. However, their efforts at this initial stage were not successful. Albeit, it should be mentioned that missionary work was carried out half-heartedly. The following reasons could be attributed to this: One, the missionaries only concentrated on the coastal population, especially the ruling elites. Two, they were few in numbers and with limited funds; three, most of them could not cope with the local climate and politics; four, the belief in some quarters in Europe that it was not necessary to convert Africans and five, most importantly, economic interest was more prominently in their minds. By the end of the eighteenth century, Christianity was yet to be established in the continent.[8] An English sailor who visited Warri at the end of the eighteenth century summarized the state of Christianity in Nigeria:

> we were much surprised to see, placed on a rude kind of tablet, several emblems of the Catholic religion, consisting of crucifixes, mutilated saints, and other trumpery. . . . A large wooden cross, which had withstood the tooth of time, was remaining in a very perfect state, in one of the angles formed by the two roads intersecting each other. King Otoo's subjects appeared to trouble themselves very little about religion of any kind.[9]

The early nineteenth century witnessed a renewal or missionary revival in the continent by the foreign missions. This revival was as a result of 'the abolition of slave trade and the resurgence of missionary work in Europe.'[10] As a result of the abolition, more men were released to participate in evangelization, especially the freed slaves. Indeed, by the second half of the century, the missions had succeeded in planting Christianity in Africa. Their success could be attributed to the following: the change in the methods of evangelization, employment of more missionaries and indigenous people to preach the gospel, availability of more funds and co-operation between the different denominations in the continent. The co-operation that existed between the denominations will be further discussed below.

As mentioned above, the nineteenth century witnessed the 'invasion' of the continent by the Catholic and Protestant missions. According to Idowu, 'all branches of the Church in Europe vied in holy rivalry to spread the Christian faith'.[11] The Catholic missionaries, mostly the French and later by the Irish and the Italian missionaries spear headed the Christian 'crusade' to Africa. Indeed, the record buttresses the fact that all the Catholic missionaries in all the regions at the beginning of the nineteenth century were French. These missionaries belonged to different groups like the Holy Ghost Fathers, the White Fathers and Sisters, and the Lyon Mission. Due to the effort of these missionaries Catholicism became entrenched in Africa.

The Protestants on the other hand were equally active in Africa in the nineteenth century. Different Protestant missions became committed to spreading the 'gospel' to Africa. Some of these missions included the Church Missionary Society (CMS), the Berlin Missionary Society, the Basel Evangelical Missionary Society, the Nordic Mission, the American Missionary Society, the Methodists, the American Presbyterians, the Salvation Army and the Africa Inland Mission. Two of these missions, the Berlin Missionary Society and the North German Mission in Bremen deserve to be mentioned for two reasons. One, the 1884/85 Conference took place in Germany, and two; because of their success in Africa. Both missions were very fervent and committed to spreading the gospel to Africa. Between 1800 and 1827 for example, the mission in Berlin was said to have sent about eighty missionaries to West and South Africa. So also was the Mission in Bremen. Indeed, the history of Christian missions in Africa would be incomplete without mentioning the German contributions.

One of the points raised above was the co-operation that existed between the missions. It was one of the major reasons for the success of Christianity in the continent. As a result of this interdenominational co-operation in Africa, German missionaries were happy to serve under the Anglican or the Church Missionary Society, an English outfit. Most of the CMS or Anglican missionaries in Nigeria were Germans. They included Revs. C. A. Gollmer, (he came from Württemberg), David Hinderer and also G. F. Buhler.[12] So also were missionaries from Basel. In Sierra Leone, in spite of the fact that it was an Anglican Mission that was first established there, the mission did not grow until the German missionary, Gustav Nyländer came in 1806 to lead the mission. Indeed, Basel served as a depot for Christian activities in Africa. The co-operation came to an end after the 1884/85 conference when most of the powers insisted on promoting the mission from their respective homes. The attitude created discord between the missions. It marked the beginning of rancour among the missions.

Before the 1884/85 conference we have a picture of the continent painted with different missions in co-operation and in one spirit to preach and to convert Africans to Christians. The Catholics were established in the West, East, Central and South Africa. The Protestants were equally represented in all regions of the continent. Christianity, at this period, could be said to have germinated in the continent.

The 1884/85 Berlin Conference

The nineteenth century also marked the scramble or what is referred to as the mad rush for colonies in Africa. The European powers began to establish claims on the different parts of Africa to primarily protect their economic interest. In the vanguard for establishing colonial claims were the European traders who felt that their economic interest was likely to be jeopardized if their home governments did not do anything to protect their interest. Bismarck, the German chancellor, reluctantly accepted to have colonies in Africa on behalf of Germany to protect the country's economic interest. A scholar has rightly asserted this:

> Bismarck would not have become interested in the occupation of any colonial territory had he been sure that occupation of the same territory by England or other countries would not have resulted in restrictions on trade. The seizure of territory was intended to protect Germany's overseas market[.][13]

Because of the tension created as a result of the quest to establish claims in Africa, especially between the powers (Britain and France, Germany and Britain and France and Germany), Bismarck called for a conference to resolve all issues pertaining to colonial possession in Africa. Other reasons he gave for the conference in his opening remarks to the delegates at Wilhelmstraße, his official residence in Berlin, and venue of the conference included, 'to regulate the conditions most favourable to the development of trade and civilization in certain regions of Africa'; 'to assure all nations of the advantage of free navigation on the two chief rivers flowing into the Atlantic ocean (the Congo and the Niger)', 'to obligate the misunderstanding and disputes which might in future arise from new acts of occupation on the coast of Africa', and 'to further the moral and material well-being of the native population'.[14]

From November 15, 1884 to February 26, 1885, the conference deliberated on these various issues. Present at the meeting, including the contesting European powers, were the host country, Germany, England, France, the United States, Belgium, Spain, Netherlands and Russia.[15] At the end of the meeting, the continent was partitioned among these various powers. In West Africa, Britain had Nigeria, Ghana (formerly Gold Coast), Gambia and Sierra Leone. Germany had Togo, while France had most of the countries. These included Benin (formerly Dahomey), Niger, Chad, Ivory Coast, Senegal and Mali. In East Africa, Britain had Kenya and Uganda, while Germany had Tanganyika (now Tanzania as a result of the unification of Tanganyika and Zanzibar). Southern Africa and Central Africa were shared among the powers, including Portugal. Germany lost its former territories, Togo, Cameroon, Tanganyika and Namibia as a result of its defeat in the First World War.

One of the major decisions taken was the need for physical presence of the colonial powers in Africa rather than mere declarations of interest or influence by the powers. In this sense many missions acted as mere agents of imperialism on behalf of their governments. The CMS missionaries for example saw the whole Nigeria as British colony, which should not be penetrated by any other power. For example, in Nigeria, the Catholic influence in Yorubaland which was promoted by the Society of African Missions of Lyons, was discouraged by the British missionaries and government. This was contrary to the decision on missionary activities taken at the conference that all religious missions should exercise all forms of worship and right to build edifices without any restriction or hindrance whatsoever.[16]

The 1884/85 partition had tremendous impact on the missionary activities in the continent. Ogbu Kalu pointed out the negative impact of the conference on Christianity in the continent. He wrote that the Berlin conference 'introduced virulent forms of European nationalism into the continent' and that 'the mission churches embellished this spirit with denominational stripes'.[17] This was because of the recognition and support granted by the various colonial governments to the various missions which had origin from the home countries. The action led to the breakdown of interdenominational co-operation that existed between the missions in Africa and also divided the countries along denominational lines. The action has led some African countries been classified today as either Catholic or Protestant countries. It has also led to the diminishing status of some missions which did not have official status. Also, some missions became divided into two as a result of the political partition. An example could be seen in West Africa where the Wesleyan Minha community was cut into two parts; a section came under the French Togo, while the second came under the British Gold Coast (now Ghana). Status of missions like this and the others that did not have official recognition diminished. Finally, and very importantly, it marked the beginning of competition between the missions, between the Catholics and Protestants on one hand, and on the other hand, between the different Protestant missions. The competitive spirit was aptly expressed by a Catholic father in Nigeria in 1907. The Catholic Father was quoted to have said that 'we have been in an atmosphere of war and of conquest, war with the Protestant . . . war with the pagans, war with enemies in different forms'.[18] In Tanganyika, the German Governor also made reference to the rivalry between the different missions in the region in 1908. According to the Governor:

The White Father and the Herrnhuters (that is, Moravians) . . . no longer fight with fictional occupation of giant stretches of country by means of outposts consisting mostly of a single coloured 'helper' or 'catechist' but through an encroachment upon the established mission sphere of the opposing confession. . . . It is regrettable that many missions, despite all declarations against Islam, combat the other Christian confessions much more than Islam.[19]

The statements above demonstrated the hostility and division among the Christian missionaries during the colonial period.

Catholicism became the official mission in all the countries that came under French colonial influence. In the Senegambia region, Catholicism became integrated with the French colonial presence there. In Ivory Coast, the French Governor, Binger, wrote official letter, in his capacity as the Governor, to the Catholic mission in Planque, Lyon to invite the mission to the state.[20] In Congo, Leopold II only gave official recognition to the Catholic missions, especially the Catholic missions from Belgium. First, the Flemish Scheut Fathers were invited to take over the Catholic mission from the French Catholic Fathers, who migrated out to the French Congo. By 1890, the Scheutists were joined by the Belgian Jesuits, Trappists and Sacred Heart Fathers. All these Catholic missions were granted free land to establish their missions, granted subsidies and were offered free transport for their personnel and goods. As a result, Catholic Mission became more entrenched in Congo than the Protestants.[21] In the Portuguese colonies too, Catholicism was promoted above all other missions.

Colonial governments with Protestant background also promoted their missions to the disadvantage of Catholics. In the areas under the British influence, CMS or Anglican Mission was officially recognized by the other missions. In Buganda, (now in Uganda), the CMS missionary, who was posted to the kingdom presented two letters of introduction to King Mutesa I. One of these letters was from the Foreign Office in London.[22] In Gold Coast (Ghana), the Governor of the colony, MacLean, officially welcomed the CMS missionary, Thomas Birch Freeman to the colony. In Sierra Leone, another British colony, the CMS received annual subsidy of about £500.[23] In Nigeria, although almost all the missions were established in the region, the CMS was given more recognition. As a result, the Anglican Church became more established in many parts of the country, especially in the West. In recognition of the assistance of the British colonial government to the Anglican mission, the leader of the CMS in Hausaland (northern Nigeria), Rev. Miller, wrote to commend Lugard when he left the North in 1906. He wrote:

> The Committee felt that by your resignation they are losing a friend in the field upon whose kindly consideration and fair-minded treatment they have always been able to rely. They have desired me to express to your Excellency their grateful recognition of the sympathy and help extended by you to the society and its missionaries when most needful and valuable.[24]

In the colonies under the German control, especially in Togo, the Bremen Mission took advantage of the imposition of German rule there to establish their post. In Tanganyika, the Leipzig Mission established firm control of the region, while in Namibia, the German missionaries actually paved the way for the establishment of the German colonial control of the region. These missions in all the German colonies left as a result of the First World War. These colonies became mandated territories. As a result of this change, missions associated with the new colonial governments in these mandated territories became the most popular in the territories.

By the late nineteenth and early twentieth centuries, new dimensions had been introduced to the history of Christian Missions in Africa. This is the emergence of indigenous Christian Missions or African Independent Churches in Africa. These churches were largely a reaction to European domination of church leadership. They were also a reaction to how the Europeans disdained the African ways of life, some of which had nothing to do with religion, including Christianity. The AIC characteristically set out to champion the propagation of Christianity among Africans under African leadership and to nurture a sort of African Christianity, a Christianity that would mirror the Christian message with the African eyes as distinct from a Western-orientated Christianity. These Churches marked the beginning of what is called Africanizing Christianity without however tampering with the doctrines and teaching of Christianity.[25]

The following could be said to be the negative impacts of the partition on the spread of Christianity: it stopped the interdenominational co-operation between the missions; it led to the rivalry between missions, in some cases open conflicts between some missions; it led to the recognition of some missions over the others and the diminishing status of others; and it laid the foundation for further fragmentation of Churches in Africa.

Post-Partition Development

The post-partition era did not fare better in terms of division in Christendom in Africa. The first decade after independence continued to witness intense rivalry between the mission and the African Independent Churches (AICs). Indeed, it could be said that political independence spurned the AICs into action as more and more churches began to emerge and continue to gain more converts at the expense of the mission churches. Olowo confirms the above thus:

> while attendance at the orthodox churches are falling, spiritual churches are swelling in numbers . . . the Celestial and the Cherubim and Seraphim churches show a massive increase in membership.[26]

Some of these AICs however were established along ethnic lines. In Nigeria, the Aladura churches (that is the Cherubim and Seraphim and the Celestial Church of Christ) are predominantly Yoruba churches. The Brotherhood of the Star and the Cross (under Olumba) is predominantly associated with the Efik in the erstwhile Eastern region of Nigeria. The post-independence era also witnessed fragmentation among the AICs. The struggle for leadership position and control of resources contributed to this. The Cherubim and Seraphim before the end of the first decade of independence have divided into many factions with different names. The popular ones included the Cherubim and Seraphim Movement, Cherubim and Seraphim Society, the Sacred Order of Cherubim and Seraphim.

The new trend today is the emergence of Pentecostal or Born-Again churches everywhere in Africa. The churches are more or less American in operation. They are well organized and their leaders are more educated. Apart from the above, the churches emphasize more on prosperity. This has attracted more people to these Pentecostal churches. According to Isichei, this is not surprising. 'The Gospel of prosperity', as she called it, 'promises a miraculous escape from unemployment and poverty'.[27] The proliferation of these churches has further divided Christianity in the continent. The Pentecostals are against the orthodox churches – the Catholic, Anglicans, Presbyterians and Methodists which had created different areas of influence in the continent. The Pentecostal churches are however winning more members than the orthodox churches.[28]

Conclusion

The 1884/85 Conference had tremendous impact on Christianity in Africa. It accelerated fragmentation in Christendom in Africa with the support of the various colonial powers that occupied Africa. These colonial powers laid the foundation of the present division, what I have termed spiritual division in the continent. The emergence of the AICs and the Pentecostal churches in the last century has complicated the division, disunity and fragmentation in the continent. Areas of influence created by the orthodox churches in the late nineteenth and early twentieth centuries have been challenged by the Pentecostal churches. Effort to unite all the Christian missions against militant Islam has not always succeeded because of the rivalry between these mission churches. Until the issue of disunity and rivalry is resolved, churches in Africa will continue to speak in many voices.

Notes

[1] This chapter was written when I was still at the Freie Universität, Berlin, Germany as a research fellow courtesy of the Alexander von Humboldt fellow. I thank the Alexander von Humboldt Foundation for the award.
[2] This is one of the terms of the General Acts of the Berlin Conference. Quoted in Henderson, Lawrence W., *Angola: Five Centuries of Conflicts* (Ithaca: Cornell University Press, 1979), 111.
[3] See Idowu, E. Bolaji, 'The Predicament of the Church in Africa', in: Baeta, Christian G. (ed.), *Christianity in Tropical Africa* (Oxford: Oxford University Press, 1968), 417.

4 Smith, Edwin, *The Christian Mission in Africa* (London: International Missionary Council, 1926), 8.

5 Sundkler, Bengt and Christopher Steed, *A History of the Church in Africa in Africa* (Cambridge: CUP, 2000), 44.

6 See Sundkler and Steed 2000: 48 and Ryder, Alan, *Benin and the Europeans 1485–1879* (London: Longmans, 1969), 46.

7 Pope Alexander VI (Borgia), a Spaniard had in 1493 divided the world into two for the purpose of evangelization. He assigned the West to Spain, while the East was handed over to Portugal.

8 For details see Groves, Charles P., *The Planting of Christianity in Africa* (London: Lutterworth Press, 1948); Ryder, Alan, 'Portuguese Missions in West Africa', *Tarikh 3*, No. 1 (1968), 14–22; Falola, Toyin, *Violence in Nigeria: The Crisis of Religious Politics and Secular Ideologies* (Rochester: University of Rochester Press, 1998), Chapter One. and Falola, Toyin, *The History of Nigeria* (Westport: Greenwood Press, 1999), 40.

9 See Adam, John, *Remarks on the Country Extending from Cape Palmes to the River Congo* (London: Whittaker, 1823), 124–25.

10 Idowu 1968: 47.

11 Ibid.

12 See Akinwumi, Olayemi, *Colonial Contest for the Nigerian region 1884–1900: A History of the German Participation* (Münster: LIT Verlag, 2002).

13 See PRO/FO 84/1815 in Akinwumi 2002: 16.

14 See Wesseling, Hendrik L., *Divide and Rule: The Partition of Africa, 1880–1914* (Westport, Conn.: Praeger, 1996), 114–15.

15 Ibid.

16 Quoted in Henderson 1979: 111.

17 Kalu, Ogbu, 'Experiencing Evangelicalism in Africa: An Africanist Perspective', in: Falola, Toyin (ed.), *Ghana in Africa and the World* (Trenton: Africa World Press, 2003), 344.

18 Omotoye, Rotimi, '*Ecumenism in Nigeria*' (Mimeo, n.d.).

19 Von Rechenberg, quoted from Isichei, Elizabeth A., *History of Christianity in Africa: From Antiquity to the Present* (Grand Rapids: William B. Eerdmans Publishing Company, 1995), 231.

20 Sundkler and Steed 2000: 196.

21 See Reardon, Ruth Slade, 'Catholic and Protestants in the Congo', in: Baeta, Christian G. (ed.), *Christianity in Tropical Africa* (Oxford: Oxford University Press, 1968), 85–86. See also Falola, Toyin, *Nationalism and African Intellectuals* (Rochester: University of Rochester Press, 2001).

22 Idowu 1968: 424.

23 Ibid.

24 Crampton, Edmund P. T., Christianity in Northern Nigeria (London: Geoffrey Chapman, 1976).

25 Adekunle, Julius O., 'Christianity', in: Falola, Toyin (ed.), *Africa* (Durham: Carolina Academic Press, 2003), 585.

26 Olowo, Bola, 'God or Mammon?', *West Africa* (August 1990), 13–19, 2274.

[27] Isichei, Elizabeth A., *History of Christianity in Africa: From Antiquity to the Present* (Grand Rapids: William B. Eerdmans Publishing Company, 1995), 336.

[28] The Pentecostal churches are more organized, their leaders are more educated, and most importantly, many of these Pentecostal churches have international connection to the Western world, especially the US.

Chapter 2

Ecclesiastical Cartography and the Invisible Continent[1]

Jonathan J. Bonk

There is a natural assumption that maps offer objective depictions of the world. The message of this book is that they do not, and that the innumerable ways in which they do not, serve to place maps as central and significant products of their parent cultures.[2]

For [post-Columbus] cartographers, maps became ephemera, repeatedly redrawn to new information. The sea monsters and ornamental flourishes disappeared to make way for new landmasses of increasingly accurate shape.[3]

Africa as Terra Incognita

Among the better-known medieval maps is the Hereford Mappa Mundi, *c.*1300, a striking example of historical and theological projection onto an image of the physical world. The map provides an abundance of European and Mediterranean detail, and is congested with familiar towns and cities from Edinburgh and Oxford to Rome and Antioch. It is onto this familiar terrain that all of the significant historical and theological events are projected – the fall of man, the crucifixion and the apocalypse. As for the rest of the world, the greater part of Africa and Asia blurs into margins featuring elaborately grotesque illustrations of prevailing myths and savage demonic forces.[4]

The Catalan World Map some two centuries later was likewise more revealing of European ignorance than of actual geography. 'The strangest geographical feature', Whitfield notes, 'is the shape of Africa: at the extremity of the Gulf of Guinea, a river or strait connects the Atlantic with the Indian Ocean, while a huge land-mass swells to fill the base of the map. No place-names appear on it'.[5] The continent is replete with dog-headed kings, and paradise is located in Ethiopia. Beyond the gates of Europe, the laws of God and nature were apparently suspended, and anything was possible. This map represented, in Whitfield's words, 'a powerful, dramatic but not a logical, coherent picture of the world'.[6]

While considerable cartographic clarity has since been achieved in the realm of geography and culture, ecclesiastical 'maps' on the other hand, continue to badly misrepresent, under-represent or simply ignore the actual state of affairs in much of the world, especially Africa. Among the most astonishing religious phenomena of the twentieth century has been the growth of Christianity in Africa. Yet, strangely, even the most recent attempts by mainline church historians to help seminarians and church leaders locate themselves and find their way in the terra firma of contemporary world Christianity take scarcely any note of Africa. In 2002, for example, Westminster John Knox Press published Randall Balmer's 654-page 'Encyclopedia of Evangelicalism'. The author of this volume, far from apologizing for his conspicuous lack of reference to African or any other non-Western subject matter, 'readily acknowledges' in his Preface that 'the volume is weighted heavily toward North America'.[7] Africa is represented by a token smattering of Western mission agencies such as the Africa Inland Mission.

Equally unsatisfactory is the 'Biographical Dictionary of Evangelicals', published in late 2003.[8] This 789-page cornucopia of information on evangelical figures from the 1730s to the present indeed 'brims with interest while providing reliable historical information', as the inside flyleaf attests, yet only a single black African – Samuel Adjai Crowther – merits inclusion. 'Geographically', the Introduction explains, 'the scope is the English-speaking world, understood in its traditional sense as the UK, the USA, Canada, Australia, New Zealand and South Africa. . . . [but] In general', the editor continues, 'my goal has been to include those figures that would be of interest to scholars, ministers, ordinands, students and others interested in the history of evangelicalism'.[9]

Since cartographic studies are as much the 'cause' as the 'result' of history, continued reliance on such antiquated maps ensures the ongoing confusion of Christian guides attempting to locate themselves and their protégés ecclesiastically. Thus, despite the very modest results accruing from the prodigious efforts of nineteenth century missionaries like David Livingstone, Robert Moffat, Mary Slessor and C. T. Studd, these names are household words today; contrarily, while Christian numerical growth in Africa has burgeoned from an estimated 8 or 9 millions in 1900 to some 380 millions in 2003,[10] scarcely anything is known about the persons chiefly responsible for this astonishing growth – African catechists and evangelists.[11]

That such a state of affairs should persist despite world Christianity's quantum demographical, spiritual and intellectual shift from the North to the South and from the West to the East is partially explained by factors delineated by Andrew Walls in his 1991 essay, 'Structural Problems in Mission Studies'. Despite the global transformation of Christianity, Walls notes, not only do Western syllabuses fail to adequately register this phenomenon, but they 'have often been taken over in the Southern continents, as though they had some sort of universal status. Now they are out-of-date even for Western Christians. As a result, a large number of conventionally trained ministers have neither the intellectual materials nor even the outline knowledge for understanding the church as she is'.[12]

But might not this troubling lacuna in the existing reference corpus be partially due to an absence of basic reference tools providing convenient access to non-Western Christian data that instructors, desperate to keep pace with ordinary teaching demands, require? I believe this to be at least partially so. Since the new maps have not been created, the old maps must serve. The story of the church in Africa thus remains mere desiderata – a footnote to the story of European tribes, the religious expression of the West's 500-year ascent to world military, economic and social hegemony. Africa remains 'terra incognita', a blur on the margins of world Christianity's self-understanding.

Since the greatest surge in the history of Christianity occurred in Africa over the past 100 years, and continues its breathtaking trajectory into the twenty-first century, it is both disappointing and alarming that yet another generation of Christian leaders, scholars and their protégés, relying upon existing 'up-to-date' reference sources, will learn virtually nothing of this remarkable phenomenon, or of the men and women who served and who serve as the movement's catalysts. Africa remains 'the dark continent', not due to an absence of light, but because the lenses through which the religious academy peers are opaque, rendering Africa invisible.

Why this should be so is not surprising, given the challenges associated with documenting the lives of persons who, even if literate, leave scarcely any paper trail.[13] But it underscores the troubling tendency of the global Christian reference corpus to perpetuate the illusion of the West as the axis upon which the Christian world revolves. To the notion that it is otherwise, ecclesiastical cartographers today seem as impervious to the factual verities as was the Catholic Church to the once radically new – but correct – cosmology of Copernicus. The fact is, there are no base-line reference tools to which one might turn for information on those whose lives and activities have produced in Africa a Christian revolution unprecedented in the history of our globe.

Project Luke: The Dictionary of African Christian Biography[14]

From 31 August to 2 September of 1995, a scholarly consultation of modest proportions was hosted by the Overseas Ministries Study Centre in New Haven. It was convened to discuss the need for an 'International Dictionary of Non-Western Christian Biography. Volume I: Africa, or An Oral History Christian Biography Register for Africa'. The official announcement issued by participants at the conclusion of the consultation summarized the *raisons d'être* and 'modus operandi' of the envisaged 'Dictionary':

A team of international scholars is planning a *Dictionary of African Christian Biography*. While the 20th-century growth and character of Christianity in Africa is without historical precedent, information on the major creative and innovative local figures most vitally involved is virtually absent from the standard scholarly reference works.

The Dictionary will cover the whole field of African Christianity from earliest times to the present and over the entire continent. Broadly inter-confessional, historically descriptive, and exploiting the full range of oral and written records, the Dictionary will be simultaneously produced electronically in English, French and Portuguese.

The Dictionary will not only stimulate local data gathering and input, but as a non-proprietary electronic database it will constitute a uniquely dynamic way to maintain, amend, expand, access and disseminate information vital to an understanding of African Christianity. Being non-proprietary, it will be possible for material within it to be freely reproduced locally in printed form. Being electronic, the material will be simultaneously accessible to readers around the world.

Contributors will be drawn from academic, church and mission communities in Africa and elsewhere. The Dictionary will not only fill important gaps in the current scholarly corpus, but will inform, challenge and enrich both church and academy by virtue of its dynamic and internationally collaborative character.[15]

The prescience of this announcement has been born out by subsequent developments, for the enterprise has crept steadily forward since then, so that today more than 100 research institutions, seminaries and university departments in 20 African countries have joined the effort to produce a baseline, biographical memory base by formally identifying themselves as *Dictionary of African Christian Biography* (*DACB*) Participating Institutions. It is hoped that by 2010 an additional 100 African educational and research institutions will officially join in the task of researching and recording the stories of their continent's church fathers and mothers.

The contours of the dictionary

Chronologically, the 'Dictionary' spans 20 centuries of Christian faith on the African continent, thus counteracting the notion that Christianity in Africa is little more than the religious accretion of nineteenth and twentieth century European influence. 'Christianity in Africa', Fr John Baur aptly reminds his readers, 'is not a recent happening, nor it is a byproduct of colonialism – its roots go back to the very time of the Apostles'.[16] As I write, a significant proportion of the stories appearing in the database feature subjects who lived and died prior to the thirteenth century. Some 378 names have been associated with the 'Ancient Church' section of the database, while some 160 of the over 500 subjects associated with Orthodox 'Ethiopia' lived prior to the twelfth century, as did a majority of the 226 Coptic subjects identified as Egyptian.

Ecclesiastically, likewise, since Christian expression in Africa does not readily lend itself to standard Euro-American tests of orthodoxy, the 'Dictionary' aims at inclusiveness rather than exclusiveness.[17] Thus, for example, key figures associated with such heterodox organizations as the Church of Jesus Christ of Latter-Day Saints or the Watch Tower Bible and Tract Society, as well as those in sometimes highly-controversial African-Initiated churches, are included on the basis of their 'self-definition' as Christians.[18]

Inclusion criteria are as broad and as flexible as possible. In general, those persons deemed at local, regional, national or denominational levels to have made a significant contribution to African Christianity, and whose stories are indispensable to an understanding of the church as it is, will be included. While main entries are generally restricted to subjects who are African either by birth or by immigration, non-African subjects such as foreign missionaries, whose contributions to African church history are regarded by Africans themselves to have been significant, are also included. Similarly, while a majority of the subjects will be confessed Christians, some non-Christians are included, if they are deemed to have played a direct and significant role in the regional or national development of Christianity.

Linguistically, dictionary entries now appear in English, with some in French. Swahili and Portuguese entries are beginning to make appear. The plan is for the database to become available in the five languages most broadly under-stood across Africa where the Christian presence is notably vital: English, French, Portuguese, Swahili and Arabic. Since the material is non-proprietary, there is nothing to prevent a research institute, academic department or enter-prising individual from translating the stories into any language, but the intention is to receive stories in any one of these five working languages, and to have each story translated into the other four languages.[19]

A data collection template has been designed to ensure a measure of uni-formity in the cognitive fields around which the details of each subject's life are arranged.[20] Insofar as such data as birth dates are actually available, these are included. Otherwise, an attempt is made to link the birth of a subject to a particular period or an auspicious event. Wherever possible, published as well as oral sources of information are utilized. While documentation can pose a serious challenge, the standards commonly employed by those working in the field of oral history are utilized.[21] The database comprised two levels of informa-tion: one, the '*Dictionary*' itself, is accessible on-line and on CD-ROM; the other, the Dictionary's working database, is accessible only to the editors. The former contains information on figures who, if not deceased, are advanced in years; while the latter stores information on still active subjects who are likely to merit inclusion in the database someday.

The choice and arrangement of African subject names has always been a peculiar challenge, as Norbert C. Brockman points out in the foreword to his earlier *An African Biographical Dictionary*: 'Names have symbolic and even descriptive meanings among many African groups, and a person may be known by several names, not to mention a wide variety of spellings. . . The order of names familiar in the West is not always used, nor are 'family names' a universal custom in Africa'.[22] But in the case of the *DACB*, this problem is ameliorated by the nature of the medium itself. Being an electronic database, Dictionary CD-ROM users are able to access the information in a variety of ways, including any of the subject's names, ecclesiastical affiliations, countries of residence and citizenship, languages, ethnic group, and so on. Similarly, the problem of evolving and changing country or region nomenclature is resolved by the medium itself, enabling one to access, say, the life of a first century subject by searching by name, by country (e.g. Egypt), or by category (e.g. Ancient Church). For those accessing the Dictionary on the World Wide Web, the process is even more efficient. Simply typing the name of the biographical subject – say, Biru Dubalä – into Google will bring up the Ethiopia Index page of the '*DACB*'.

The dictionary's modus operandi[23]

The project's data collection network is not hierarchical but lateral – a kind of 'spider's web', with OMSC as the nexus for as many data collection centres as might emerge. The web already extends to numerous points across Africa. Some 94 seminaries, university departments and research centres in 20 countries have joined the enterprise as participating institutions, formally agreeing to actively promote the research and writing of the stories of persons deemed to be of significance to any adequate comprehension of the 'how' and 'why' of the Church in a given locale. In some instances, the research and writing of a story is a requirement for graduation. This information is organized and written in conformity to standard *DACB* guidelines. Duly designated liaison coordinators then send these stories either directly to the coordinating office in New Haven, or to one of four *DACB* offices in Ghana, Zambia, South Africa and Nigeria.[24] The New Haven office is responsible for entering the stories into the database.

Both the legitimacy of the subject and the accuracy of the story are safeguarded by associating the names of the participating institution, the liaison coordinator, and the author, with each biographical entry. Once each year, participating institutions receive the updated CD-ROM version of the dictionary, whose contents can be freely used – with attribution – in the preparation of syllabi, supplementary readings, or booklets. No restriction is placed on making copies of the CD-ROM.

Biographical subjects – now numbering more than 3,100 – are identified on the basis of their perceived local, regional, national, or continental or denominational significance. No subject is excluded if, in the opinion of communities of local believers, his or her contribution is deemed singular. In addition, printed materials of all kinds – church and mission archives, church histories, mission histories, denominational histories, doctoral and masters' theses, in-house denominational and mission society magazines, as well as existing reference tools and biographical dictionaries – have been and continue to be culled with a view to discovering the identities and stories of key African Christians.

Publication and distribution

The Dictionary is being produced as a web-based resource and distributed as a CD-ROM in its annually updated form to all African participating institutions. The advantages of electronic publishing are such that academic publications and reference works are increasingly appearing in digital form. But as an African proverb wryly observes, 'the darkest place in the house is beneath the candle', for another, darker side to the rosy inevitability of electronic publishing was likewise identified a decade ago. Information available only in digital form can quickly find itself rendered passé, prisoner to a technology that is both expensive and doomed to rapid obsolescence. This point was eloquently made by Jeff Rothenberg, a senior computer scientist in the social department of the RAND Corporation in Santa Monica, California:

> Although digital information is theoretically invulnerable to the ravages of time, the physical media on which it is stored are far from eternal . . .. The contents of most digital media evaporate long before words written on high-quality paper. They often become obsolete even sooner, as media are superseded by new, incompatible formats – how many readers remember eight-inch floppy disks? It is only slightly facetious to say that digital information lasts forever – or five years, whichever comes first.[25]

Rothenberg goes on to remind readers that digital information requires sophisticated, expensive, and rapidly evolving hardware and software for its storage and retrieval. Twenty-two centuries after its composition, the Rosetta Stone, he notes, is still readable; Shakespeare's first printed edition of Sonnet 18 (1609) is still legible nearly 400 years later; digital media, on the other hand becomes virtually unreadable within a decade. It is for reasons such as this that consideration is being given to producing a printed version of the dictionary, in abridged and rigorously edited form, to be distributed to all participating institutions sometime after 2010.

From the very beginning, the *DACB* has maintained that publishing rights should be freely granted to churches, denominations, national or international publishers wishing to produce a printed version of the entire electronic database or printed versions of any portion of the database deemed useful to them.

Were the 'Dictionary' to be conceived as a proprietary, profit-making venture, it is highly doubtful whether it could gain significant Africa-wide circulation. Purchasing such a database would be out of the question for most Africans, making their stories unavailable to Africans themselves. The cost of producing and distributing the dictionary in its annually updated, non-proprietary CD-ROM form is borne by the project management office in New Haven.

Awareness of the *DACB* continues to grow. We are learning that the *Dictionary* is increasingly utilized by instructors who require their students to get into the habit of using the database for their African Church History assignments. As virtually the only central source of information on African Christian biography, the *DACB* website is experiencing steady and growing traffic, as Table 2.1 indicates.

Furthermore, the *DACB* has become a stimulus for similar data gathering initiatives elsewhere. The Centre for the Study of Christianity in Asia (Trinity College, Singapore) is using the *DACB* as a model to produce an Asian Christian biographical database, as are The Don Bosco Centre in Shillong, India, and the Trinity Methodist Church in Selangor Dural Ehsan, Malaysia.

Table 2.1 *DACB* Website traffic from April 2005 to March 2006

Month	Total page views	Daily average page views	Quarterly average page views
2005			
April	27,877	929	
May	25,768	831	
June	28,525	951	
Quarterly Total	82,170		904
July	29,530	952	
August	30,654	989	
September	30,099	1,003	
Quarterly Total	90,283		981
October	35,457	1,144	
November	27,156	905	
December	23,345	753	
Quarterly Total	85,958		934
2006			
January	23,908	771	
February	26,348	941	
March	37,500	1,207	
Quarterly Total	87,756		973

In September 2003 I was officially notified that an editorial team consisting of members of the Contextual Theology Department of the Union Biblical Seminary and co-ordinated by Dr Jacob Thomas, supported by an all India Council of Advisors, has likewise embarked on a biographical project modelled after the *DACB*, but focusing on the Indian sub-continent. 'The inspiration for this project', reads the public announcement, 'comes from . . . the *Dictionary of African Christian Biography* (DACB@OMSC.org). The *DICB* [*Dictionary of Indian Christian Biography*] project is grateful for the partnership by which there is mutual encouragement and sharing of relevant ideas'. Since 2005 OMSC has served as hosting institution and 'incubator' for *The Biographical Dictionary of Chinese Christianity*.[26]

Conclusion

Among the several ongoing challenges facing the dictionary, an obvious one is the uneven volume and quality of its country, language and denominational content. It is readily evident that while the numbers of stories in English are relatively plentiful, with French-language entries lagging far behind, the languages representing the other three lingua franca of Africa are still scarcely represented. This is due to neither oversight nor neglect, but to the linguistic limitations of the principals involved, and to the fact that the Dictionary reflects only those stories that have been submitted. Not *DACB* facilitators in New Haven, but participating institutions and their duly designated liaison coordinators in Africa, are the key to researching and writing dictionary entries.

Added to this is the somewhat patchy quality of the stories. Anyone browsing the *DACB* will at once be struck by the patchiness of both the quality and consistency of the nearly 1,000 biographies that currently make up the database. Some of the stories are a mere one or two sentences in length, while others run to several thousand words. While scholarly exactitude marks some of the entries, many stories have been contributed by persons who are neither scholars nor historians. But since this is a first-generation tool; and since the stories are non-proprietary, belonging to the people of Africa as a whole; and since, finally, it is assumed that 'some' memory is better than total amnesia, the inchoate quality of some of the entries is to be expected, tolerated and even welcomed. This being a first-generation memory base – an attempt to ensure that there is some kind of memory to which scholars and leaders of subsequent generations will have access – it will remain for another generation to redress the weaknesses and deficiencies inherent in the present dictionary.

The stone scrapers and blades of our Paleolithic forbears, deemed to be functionally deficient in our age, were nevertheless the survival tools of another. It is inevitable that any early tool should, by the standards of a later generation, be regarded as primitive and somewhat unsatisfactory. But lest this truism stifle the creative process, the reminder that it is often just such inadequacies that spark disgruntled users to develop better ones is reassuring.

The *DACB*'s approach to story research, writing and publication is predicated upon the active cooperation of African participating institutions. Not all of the 94 different educational institutions and research centres formally identified with the project have submitted stories to the *Dictionary*. An effort is being made to encourage incorporation of biographical research and writing assignments into the syllabi of appropriate university or seminary courses, utilizing the standards provided by the *DACB*.

Annual *DACB*-related trips to Africa since 1999 have taken me to scores of universities, seminaries and research centres in Kenya, Ethiopia, Uganda, Zambia, Ghana, Nigeria, South Africa, Namibia, Egypt, Tanzania and Malawi. Journeys to Sudan, Mozambique and Angola are contemplated in the near future. A total of 101 academic centres in 19 African countries are presently registered as official participating institutions, contributing to a steady flow of biographical materials for the Dictionary. In addition, the *DACB* has co-sponsored a series of one-week oral history workshops in Kenya, Zambia, Madagascar, attracting faculty members and academic researchers from scores of African countries. Increasing numbers of African churches and academic institutions are cooperating by encouraging their members and students to research and produce the raw narratives from which the database is being created. Finally, the *DACB* is actively co-operating with the International Association of Mission Studies to circulate an archives manual designed specifically for non-Western institutions.[27]

Maverick economist E. F. Schumacher once stood on a street corner in Leningrad, trying to get his bearings from a map provided for him by his Russian hosts. He was confused, because while there was some correspondence between what the map registered and what he could see with his own eyes (e.g. the names of parks, intersecting streets.), several enormous churches looming in front of him were nowhere indicated on his map. Coming to his assistance, his guide pointed out that while the map did indeed include some churches (pointing to one on the map), that was because they were actually museums. Those that were not museums were not shown. 'It is only the "living churches" we don't show', he explained.[28]

Africa clearly has a distinctive and growing place in Christian history, yet many parts of the African Christian story are too little known, not least within Africa itself, and in Western Christian consciousness, the continent continues to be regarded as a forbidding and dangerous mass, known chiefly for its capacity to generate the stuff of which newspaper profits are assured: rampant corruption, political dysfunction, recurring famine and genocidal civil wars. A parallel and more significant reality, comprised a richly diverse and thriving range of Christian congregations whose churches serve as centres of human normalcy, integrity and hope, escapes notice. The *Dictionary of African Christian Biography*, the fruit of inter-African and international cooperation, is offered as a modest first step in bringing our ecclesiastical maps up to date.

Notes

[1] Versions of this article have appeared in two journals. See Bonk, Jonathan, 'Ecclesiastical Cartography and the Invisible Continent', *International Bulletin of Missionary Research*, 28(4), (October 2004), 153–58 and idem, 'Ecclesiastical Cartography and the Problem of Africa', *History in Africa, 32*, (2005), 117–32.

[2] Whitfield, Peter, *The Image of the World: 20 Centuries of World Maps* (San Francisco: Pomegranate Artbooks in association with the British Library, 1994), viii.

[3] Landes, David S., *The Wealth and the Poverty of Nations: Why Some are So Rich and Some are So Poor* (New York: W. W. Norton, 1998), 99.

[4] Whitfield 1994: 20–21.

[5] Ibid: 26.

[6] Ibid: 26.

[7] Balmer, Randall, *Encyclopedia of Evangelicalism* (Louisville and London: Westminster John Knox Press, 2002), vii.

[8] Larsen, Timothy (ed.), with consulting editors D. W. Bebbington and Mark A. Noll, and organizing editor Steve Carter, *Biographical Dictionary of Evangelicals* (Leicester, UK, and Downers Grove, Illinois: InterVarsity Press, 2003).

[9] Ibid: 1.

[10] Barrett, David B. and Todd M. Johnson, 'Annual Statistical Table on Global Mission: 2003', *International Bulletin of Missionary Research*, 27(1) (January 2003), 25.

[11] Isichei, Elizabeth A., *History of Christianity in Africa: From Antiquity to the Present* (Grand Rapids: William B. Eerdmans Publishing Company, 1995), 98–99.

[12] Walls, Andrew F., 'Structural Problems in Mission Studies', *International Bulletin of Missionary Research*, 15(4) (October 1991), 147.

[13] Even a figure as significant as William Wadé Harris, hailed in 1926 as 'Africa's most successful evangelist' in consequence of his astounding impact upon the establishing of the Christian faith among the peoples of the Ivory Coast 'left no writings except half a dozen short dictated messages' See Shank, David A., 'The Legacy of William Wadé Harris', *International Bulletin of Missionary Research, 10*(4) (October 1986), 170.

[14] From Lk. 1.1–3.

[15] The consultation, hosted by the Overseas Ministries Study Center in New Haven, Connecticut, was underwritten by the Pew Charitable Trusts' Research Enablement Program (REP).

[16] Bauer, John, *2000 Years of Christianity in Africa* (Nairobi, Kenya: Paulines Publications, 1994), 17.

[17] In a personal letter dated 9 April 1998, Professor J. F. Ade Ajayi observed that 'the issue of just who is and who is not' a 'Christian' is not always so clear cut in Africa as it is in some parts of the world. A well-educated woman, for example, 'moved from the Christ Apostolic Church to Jehovah Witness without necessarily realizing that she had thereby lost her initial focus on Christ'. Inclusion is the

DACB's operative principle, on the assumption that end-users can exercise their own exclusion criteria.

[18] A. F. Walls identifies six persisting continuities within the varied emphases characteristic of Christianity across time: (1) worship of the God of Israel, (2) the ultimate significance of Jesus Nazareth, (3) the activity of God where Christians are, (4) Christian membership in a community which transcends time and space, (5) use of a common body of Scriptures and (6) the special uses of bread, wine and water. In instances where a subject's ecclesiastical orthodoxy might be doubtful, these criteria will be employed. See Walls, Andrew F., 'Conversion and Christian Continuity', *Mission Focus, 18*(2) (1990), 17–21.

[19] Since professional translation costs are prohibitive, the rendering of all biographical entries into the five stipulated languages must be voluntary – perhaps undertaken by religious studies or history departments.

[20] These simple guidelines have gradually evolved into Bonk, Jonathan and Michele Sigg, *An Instructional Manual for Researchers and Writers* (New Haven: *Dictionary of African Christian Biography*, 2004); available at: http://www.dacb.org/guidelines-writers.html, a 64-page booklet that elaborates the essential techniques of oral history as well as providing examples of a range of stories already appearing in the dictionary.

[21] While there are no major problems in academia with research into oral tradition, a number of standard, common-sense guidelines need to be observed: (1) Oral data needs to be collected openly in an open forum where it can be challenged or augmented; (2) What it told to the researcher must be told and repeated to others in the same area for cross-checking; (3) Oral traditions may provide a variety of points-of-view on the subject; (4) Oral tradition will be used to augment written sources, and vice-versa. One of the advantages of an electronic database over a published volume is the possibility of including a field for unsubstantiated complimentary (or even contradictory) anecdotes relating to the subject. Such anecdotal information provides texture and depth of insight into the subject, or at least into peoples' perceptions of the subject.

[22] Brockman, Norbert C., *An African Biographical Dictionary* (Santa Barbara, Denver and Oxford: ABC-CLIO, 1994), vii: 'provides sketches for 549 prominent sub-Saharan Africans from all periods of history'.

[23] The dictionary is not finance-driven. Its stories are the result of African ingenuity and enterprise, rather than a questionable byproduct of foreign funds.

[24] The *DACB* initially explored setting up an Arabic language coordination office in conjunction with the Global Institute South at Uganda Christian University, but now anticipates locating the facility in Khartoum – the heart of Christian Arabic-speaking Africa.

[25] Rothenberg, Jeff, 'Ensuring the Longevity of Digital Documents', *Scientific American, 272*(1) (1995), 42. According to the National Media Lab (www.nml.org), 'CD-ROMs have a certified lifetime of 10 years. . . . [while] magnetic tape is good for 5 to 20 years, conventional CDs up to 50 years, and archival microfilm for 200 years. The longevity champ . . . [is] acid-free paper . . . [which] should last for 500 years'. Furthermore, 'Print . . . avoids what University of Michigan data expert John Gray calls 'the problem of unstable technology'–the likelihood that media will outlive the devices that can read them'. See Wildstrom, Stephen H.,

'Bulletin Board: Data Life Span', *Business Week* (17 June 1996), 22. The Rosetta stone, dated to March 196 BC, in the ninth year of Ptolemy V, is a dark-grey-pinkish granite stone (originally thought to be basalt in composition) measuring $114 \times 72 \times 28$ cm^3 on which is inscribed writing in Egyptian and Greek, using three scripts, Hieroglyphic, Demotic Egyptian and Greek. Because Greek was well known, the stone was the key to deciphering the hieroglyphs. See http://www.crystalinks.com/rosetta.html.

[26] See the Website: http://www.bdcconline.net/

[27] Smalley, Martha Lund and Rosemary Seton, compilers, *Rescuing the Memory of Our Peoples: Archives Manual* (New Haven: International Association for Mission Studies [IAMS], 2003). The manual is freely available in PDF form in English, French, Swahili, Mandarin and Portuguese at: http://www.omsc.org/Links.htm.

[28] Schumacher, E. F., *A Guide for the Perplexed* (New York: Harper & Row Publishers, 1977), 1.

Chapter 3

Colonization in Africa: The Local and Global Implications for Christianity in Contemporary Nigeria

Deji Ayegboyin

Introduction

Measured on the time-scale of history, the colonial period was but an interlude of comparatively short duration. But it was an interlude that radically changed the direction and momentum of African history.[1]

Colonization of Africa, in the real sense of it, may be placed within the second segment of the second phase of modern colonialism, (1880–1914).[2] Marxist and underdevelopment theorists insist that this intrusion into the history and development of Africa fundamentally changed the course and subsequent development of Africa.[3] Some African scholars conclude that most African countries' undying problems have deep roots in this event.[4] Of course, there are scholars, including Africans who 'regard the colonial impact as skin-deep with some positive effects'.[5]

What is Colonialism?

Colonialism is both a system and an ideology. As a system, it refers to the occupation and domination of a weak country by a more powerful nation. As an ideology colonialism accentuates the benefits of the system primarily to the mother country. Thus, colonialism is a direct form of influence and control of a colonized territory to the extent of establishing political and economic institutions that seek to achieve essentially the economic needs of the colonial power. By colonization of Africa we refer to the occupation and control of Africa by European powers namely, Spain, Portugal, The Netherlands, France, Britain, Belgium, Germany and Italy between the close of the nineteenth and the twentieth centuries. During this period, the British Empire was by far the largest and most diverse, followed by France and others.

Objectives of Colonialism

The stimulus behind the control of different parts of Africa remains contentious. Some authors attribute the reason simply to the dynamics of advanced
capitalism, emphasizing Europe's need for raw materials and outlets for its
surplus capital. Others call attention to strategic and diplomatic impetus,
noting the 'tendency of European leaders to treat colonies as pawns in a global
chess game'.[6] The colonialists, on the other hand, have advanced ostensibly
laudable reasons to justify the colonial systems they created. R. Robinson
and J. Gallagher illustrate the representative psyche of British imperialism
thus:

> They . . . were sure that their ability to improve the human condition
> everywhere was as tremendous as their capacity to produce wealth. . . .
> Expansion was not simply a necessity without which industrial growth might
> cease but a moral duty to the rest of humanity.[7]

Other European countries have equally advanced reasons to validate their
colonial adventure in the continent. They claim that colonization which
brought to their colonized territories numerous economic, health, technological and educational benefits was at considerable costs and virtually on charitable
grounds.

It is interesting to note that in the notional justification for European colonization of Africa silence was observed on the economic grounds for the scramble
for Africa. Adu Boahen quotes Gam and Duignan who maintained that:

> the imperial system stands out as one of the most powerful engines for
> cultural diffusion in the history of Africa; its credit balance by far out weighs
> its debit account.[8]

It may be recalled that in his 'Wealth of Nations' Adam Smith had advocated
that Christianity would be a useful institution in the colonization of hostile
societies. Smith's views were published in 1776 at the time when European's
interest in colonialism was increasingly becoming clear. Evidently, the Christianization of the African Continent was one of the means by which Europe
hoped to regenerate Africa which was then referred to as the 'Dark Continent'.
The great commission to spread the gospel to all nations must have motivated
some to enter various African regions. Because of the support of Christian
missions, home countries and governments gave moral, material, financial,
legal support and protection to the missionaries. Consequently, Christians
influenced colonial policy makers.

Some hold that another factor behind the drive for colonies was 'the need to
release pressure caused by population growth which resulted in social unrest in
European cities. It was hoped that emigration of people would reduce poverty

and crime at home. Some African writers categorize the sole goal of colonialism as trade or commerce'.[9] Indeed, ruling nations sought economic benefits from their colonies. 'They moulded the economies of their colonies to fit their own needs'.[10] Mercantilism made it mandatory for colonies not to compete by manufacturing their own goods. They were also expected to trade only with their mother countries. Walter Rodney contends that 'Colonialism had only one hand – it was one-armed bandit'.[11]

With the advancement of industrialization in Europe, the colonization of Africa was vigorously pursued on grounds of controlling trade routes or regions that were of economic, political or military importance. This led to power politics in the struggle for supremacy. As a result, the colonizing activity was characterized by aggression and violence. The greedy manner of the process of colonization gave rise to the description of the scene as the scramble for colonies in Africa.[12]

Methods of Colonization

Colonization of the African continent was achieved through several means. Some of the colonies were established through the commercial means. Chartered companies, acting with the authority of the British government, played significant roles in the establishment of British colonies in Africa. In the case of Nigeria, the Royal Niger Company (RNC) made treaties with traditional chiefs along River Niger and River Benue as well as the coast of the Atlantic Ocean. The RNC established an administration with a small army of African soldiers to ensure that there was an effective protection of life and property at the trading posts and along the banks of Niger and Benue.

Sometimes colonies were established by military means. Colonization by means of chartered companies was not possible in establishing colonies that were far away from the coasts and navigable rivers. In such cases naval power and military force were employed to establish colonial rule. The use of sea power and military force assisted the British to complete the annexation of Nigeria in 1914. That year the three entities: the colony of Lagos, the Southern Protectorate and Northern Protectorate were amalgamated to form the colony called Nigeria under the administration of the first governor-general, Lord Lugard.

Partition and Occupation

Towards the end of the nineteenth century, the 'colonizing activity of Africa' was characterized by aggressive competition and greed. The dissension which this scramble triggered off would have resulted in a continental war. As Europe was sitting on this volcano which was about to erupt, Portugal proposed the Conference of European powers to settle the disputes brewing over the European activities in the Congo region. Otto von Bismarck, Chancellor of the new German Empire, agreed to host the meeting of 14 nations to discuss territorial disputes in Africa. The Conference was held in Berlin from November 1884 to February 1885 and it was attended by representatives from a number of European nations including the United Kingdom, France, Germany, Spain, Italy, Belgium, the Netherlands and the United States. Interestingly enough, Africans were not invited to this conference in which the partition and occupation of their continent by European nations was the major point of discussion. This total exclusion of Africans from the conference suggests *ab initio* that Africans were not to be favoured by the policy decisions of the Berlin Conference.

The Berlin Conference produced the Berlin Act with a number of provisions to safeguard Colonial activities in Africa. We shall mention two provisions which we consider relevant to our discussion. Article 34 of the Berlin Act, which is often referred to as the 'doctrine of spheres of influence', stipulated that any European nation that took possession of an African coast or declared a protectorate over an African coast or territory 'should notify the signatory members of the Berlin Act in order to have such a claim ratified'. This article dealt with the extent of influence over a territory. According to it, the possessions of a coastal region connoted the ownership of its hinterland. Article 35 which outlined the so-called 'doctrine of effective occupation' stipulated that the nation that occupied a coastal territory should provide enough evidence that it possesses authority to protect life and property of the people in the region and open avenues for free trade and free transits. This agreement made absolute occupation of colonies a crabby business.

Administration of Colonies in Africa

Administration of colonies in Africa differed from one European nation to another. However, the distinctive types of administration were those of France and Britain. France's colonial administration was called 'assimilation'. Based on this principle France administered her colonies by direct rule. As a result, French government did not make use of the existing traditional institutions such as traditional kingship and council of elders.[13]

Britain, on the other hand, governed her colonies by 'indirect rule'. She made use of the existing traditional chieftain structure. Traditional chiefs governed their peoples under the guidance and supervision of British officials. To some extent indirect rule retained African culture and civilization distinct from British culture and civilization.[14] Belgium's most important colony was Congo Kinshasa (now Democratic Republic of Congo – DRC). The King of Belgium, Leopold II, originally acquired Congo in 1885 as his personal property. Belgian Congo was ruled so badly that Belgian government took it over in 1908. Belgian Congo was ruled directly from Brussels which refused the

Congolese any share in the administration of their country. Belgium's administration of Congo may well be termed 'dictatorial' rule.

By 1914, each of the major European powers had established a 'Colonial Office' attached to a home government. Although the European civil service was made up of only a few Europeans, the European officials controlled a large number of indigenous subordinates referred to as 'obedient servants' or 'humble servants' as evident in colonial correspondences. The European civil servants were, therefore, referred to as 'the steel frame' of the colonial administration in Africa. In their administration of colonies in Africa, colonial powers depended largely on the power of the armed forces and the police with the backing of the courts and prisons. Any opposition to any colonial policy was severely dealt with promptly.

In colonies in Africa, colonial powers introduced their own languages – English, French, German, Portuguese, Flemish, Dutch, Spanish, Italian – as well as their laws, education and medical services. By and large they suppressed African cultural values, beliefs and practices altogether on grounds that they were cruel and violent. Even the Africans who had been well educated locally and in European educational institutions and could speak and write European languages accurately were still regarded as inferior. In this case, the denial of equality was seen as a matter of racial inferiority. Soon, many Africans realized that Colonialism was a great cultural, economic and political evil that must be quickly terminated everywhere on the African continent. As a result, anti-colonial movements and rebellions burst open in the name of African nationalism. Nationalists fought colonialism through violent demonstrations, protests, strikes and uprisings by the masses and militia. They demanded self-government which was eventually granted by colonial governments at various times.[15]

Why Nigeria?

Nigeria is the platform from which we will look on Africa as we discuss the local and global implications of colonialism on the church. The reasons for this are obvious: Nigeria is the most populous country in Africa. It is a country of immense physical and human diversity with an economy which is the largest in black Africa. Many countries in Africa look up to Nigeria to provide leadership on the continent.

Implications of Colonialism for Christianity in Nigeria

The proponents of colonialism maintain that it benefited not only the ruling nations but also the colonized people. Some hold a contrary opinion. Evidently, the implications of British colonization of Nigeria for the church can best be described as mixed. It is also obvious that there is an intricate and indispensable correlation between the local and global effects of colonialism on the contemporary Church in Nigeria.

Positive implications

Benefits of Western education

Colonial rule in Nigeria has brought important and lasting changes made possible through the benefit of Western education. That the missionaries helped to build the church is a fact that cannot be denied. It is also true that the 'selective' education given to the Africans is regarded in some circles as an instrument of imperialism, that is, to make the Africans more serviceable to the colonial master. Be that as it may, it is obvious that Western education has had far reaching effects on the church. In the leadership of the church today there is much preference for the well-educated clergy. Even in the Indigenous African Churches where in the past, seniority by age and possession of the charisma were the primary criteria, today the pendulum swings more in the direction of the learned. There are many examples to cite: One of the most obvious to recall is the 'election' of Dr Enoch Adeboye, a University don, as the General Overseer of the Redeemed Christian Church of God by his spiritual father, Rev. Akindayomi. Another is the most recent consecration of Dr Rufus Oshitelu as the Primate of the Church of the Lord (Aladura). Quite a number of the founders and leaders of virtually all denominations in Nigeria today are educated. This has helped many to break new grounds not only at the local but at the global levels. Today, most of the chief executives in the church have epithets which show that they are not leading local but international organizations. Most Rev. Dr Rufus Oshitelu is described as 'The Primate of the Church of the Lord (Aladura) Worldwide'. Others include Archbishop Prophetess, Dr Dorcas Olaniyi, and Founder of the Agbala Daniel Church. (Worldwide); Archbishop (Dr) Margaret Idahosa is the President of the Church of God Mission (International). Outside Nigeria, there are educated Nigerians leading international organizations. These include among others: Her Grace Most Rev. Onyuku-Opukuri Fidelia, the Archbishop of Born Again Christ Healing Church, (International), and Most Rev. Father Olu Abiola of Aladura Church (International) in London.

Provision of lingua franca

There are obvious values in the promotion of indigenous mother tongues in the new culture outgrowth. Today, many linguists are advocating for the resuscitation and recognition of local languages and dialects (including dead ones).[16] As Babalola argues:

> To every right thinking Nigerian the mother tongue should be a personal possession of great importance to which (Nigerians) they have a strong and deeply-felt loyalty, it gives them emotional roots in the community of speakers of the language. The mother tongue is the carrier of communal tradition and is the vehicle of acculturation[.][17]

However, as Babalola admits, there is no Nigerian language which is spoken as a mother tongue by more than 50 per cent of the total population. Consequently, English is crucial for administrative and professional unity in the polity. Kloos notes that in the use of language one can observe the growing importance of English as a veritable pan-human language.[18]

Colonialism made possible the spread and usage of English, French, Spanish and Portuguese, to name just a few which are more popular, all over the continent. These languages, which are more universal than the African dialects, have enabled more people to communicate with others who are outside their own local or ethnic groups. In all these colonies, as Boahen observes, the mother tongue of the colonial power either in its pure or pidgin form, became the official and business language and in many cases the main means of communication between the numerous linguistic groups that constitute the population of each colony. It is significant to stress that except in North Africa, Tanzania, Kenya and Madagascar, these languages have remained the official languages.[19]

The implication of the lingua franca for Christianity in Nigeria today is obvious. Colonial languages have facilitated the spread of Christianity in all states in Nigeria. Just as missionaries pushed further and further inland during the colonial era, many Nigerian missionaries especially from the Deeper Life Bible Church and the Redeemed Christian Church of God, are being trained to be at least bi-lingual (particularly in French and English) in order to assist them penetrate into the continent of Africa and beyond. Apart from denominational outreaches there are organizations such as the Nigerian Evangelical Missions Association (NEMA) – which has a membership of over 90 missions' agencies and denominations with more than 3800 active missionaries in 38 countries around the globe. Today, the NEMA is reckoned to be the first of its kind in the African continent.

Acceleration of Christian global network

With the ending of colonial rule many people from former colonies migrated to the countries that once ruled them. Many Nigerians have gone to live in the United Kingdom. Ambassador Howard Jeter postulates that 'Nigerians now represent one of the largest groups in the African Diaspora and one of the most well organized entities'.[20] Igbo and Yoruba associations flourish particularly in Britain and the United States. The churches in Nigeria are seizing the opportunity of the emphasis on organized and institutional co-operation between Africa and the Diaspora to accentuate their presence abroad. New Religious movements from Nigeria endeavour to establish congresses in Europe and America. Thus, new local churches consider it a matter of pride to hold conventions in the big cities abroad. Even though membership of virtually all of these movements is made up of Africans, this development adds some elements of reputation, recognition, and acceptability to these movements. A number of these African Churches like World Soul Winning and Evangelistic Ministry (WOSEM), World of Faith Outreach International Centre (WOIC), United Brethren in Christ Church (UBC) etc. are listed in 'Christliche Internationale Gottesdienste – Ein Wegweiser, 2003–2004'.[21]

On the other hand, some African Christian leaders have come to Nigeria from Europe and America to set up their ministries and non-governmental organizations with global connections, especially in terms of foreign funding. Their styles of dressing, preaching, healing, teaching and interest in tele-evangelism have had some impact on the churches at home. On the whole these interactive relationships have brought about local and global goodwill, and co-operation among ministers. Besides, institutional co-operation between Africa and the Diaspora is not just to unite on 'an ad-hoc basis' around a specific cause as has happened in the past. The challenge now is to create institutional links that join Africa and the Diaspora in addressing the chronic problems that have deeply affected either or both of them.

Urbanization

Another important beneficial effect of colonialism is urbanization. As Afigbo rightly notes, urbanization 'was not unknown in pre-colonial Africa'[22] but there is no doubt that as a result of colonization the spread and pace of urbanization was greatly accelerated. Besides, as Caldwell also observes, because of the provision of hospitals, pipe-borne water, sanitary facilities, better housing and increase in employment opportunities in the big towns in the colonies, urbanization increased.[23] The population of most already existing towns and new ones grew by leaps and bounds. Today there is unduly much concentration of churches, particularly by the charismatic and neo-pentecostal movements in the urban areas. Indeed, as Kalu notes, the church in Nigeria is mostly an urban phenomenon. He stresses, 'all religious forms are exploding in numerical strengths and have gained voice in the public space'.[24] Incidentally, most if not virtually all African churches in Europe and America are also in urban areas such as Hamburg, Frankfurt, London, New York, Washington, Amsterdam etc. Quite a number of these African churches abroad get round the problem of affordable space to meet by converging in parking garages and out of way places to worship on Sundays.

The rise of Ethiopian and African Indigenous Churches

Colonialism led to nationalist feelings and resistance movements. This in part gave birth in the religious field to Ethiopian and African Indigenous Churches. The Ethiopian Churches came first from the tail end of the nineteenth century and the early part of the twentieth century. In Nigeria they include: The Native Baptist Church (1888), the United Native African Church (1891), the African Church (1901), the Christ Army Church (1915) and the United African Methodist Church, Eleja (1917). The Ethiopian Churches were established to demonstrate the Africans' rejection of Euro-American leadership while keeping still to the shape and pattern of the established church from which they seceded.[25] From the early twentieth century the African Indigenous Churches emerged. These strands of development of Christianity were constructed on models which were distinct from the Western historic churches. David Barrett argues that these reflect another form of rebellion. It was revolution against a Christianity that had become over Europeanised.[26] Prophecy, healing, divination and revelation feature in these churches. Their impact has changed the face of Christianity in the World. Before the close of the twentieth century they had become vibrant, influential and shared international religious experience. All the primary indigenous churches founded between 1920 and 1947, such as the Christ Apostolic Church; the Cherubim and Seraphim Movement, the Church of the Lord (Aladura) and the Celestial Church of Christ have branches all over Europe and America. From the 1980s the African led Charismatic churches have also taken Western Europe by storm.

Ecumenical efforts

Andrew Walls remarked:

> Perhaps the largest issues for the Church of Christ in the twenty-first century will be ecumenical . . . (and that) Africa, Asia and Latin America will be the leading theatres of mission, and it is hoped of theological activity.[27]

Walls wondered whether each Church will develop along its own local lines through its own local resources, so that in the end there are welters of local Christianities with no fellow-feelings. In Nigeria, because of overt attempts to Islamize the country, there are moves more than ever before for the churches to work and walk in harmony. Various ecumenical groups have been founded. These include the Christian Association of Nigeria (CAN), the Christian

Council of Nigeria (CCN), the Pentecostal Fellowship of Nigeria (PFN), the Organization of African Instituted Churches (OAIC), etc. These have taken cue from what is happening on the world Ecumenical scene. They have not only embarked on ecumenical activities at the local levels; a number of the groups have undertaken various forms of ecclesiastical and ecumenical affiliations with American and European Christianity. In Europe and America, ecumenical groups aimed at fostering unity among African led Churches are springing up. Some of these include International Ministerial Council of Germany – a ministerial networking drawing together immigrant pentecostal charismatic churches;[28] 'Afrikanerseelsorge', which aims at uniting all African congregations in Hamburg under one umbrella and to work with the German congregations;[29] Council of Christian Communities of an African Approach in Europe, Federation of African Churches in Brussels, Conference of African Churches in Switzerland, etc. Apart from these, there are inter church networks in which African churches participate. These include 'Samen Kerk in Nederland' and Gift of Africa to Europe (GATE) an organization of essentially independent and African churches which are active in the field of 'evangelization in Europe'.[30] The main task of 'Afrikanischer Christenrat Hamburg' looks laudable: It says in part:

> For us ecumene is not just theory but practice. We try to give ecumene a concrete shape in our everyday lives. Ecumene is communication, reconciliation and liberation from the walls that have been erected by the scatteredness of Christianity.[31]

Negative implications

Resentment against the Church

While it is true that there are positive effects, even greater, some argue, are the negative implications. The first implication of colonialism is the resentment which some have against the church. The harshest critics of colonialism are also the critics of the church. They maintain that just as the colonialists dominated the political institution so also did the missionaries dominate the church. The colonization of the land was seen to have been extended into the church. Reasons for this proposition are many. The Church in Africa appeared to have been founded to care for the colonialists and the merchants. Most of the legislations of the time were made to protect the foreign identity of the church. Besides, there was cultural antagonism in the church. Examples of this abound. Bishop Ajayi Crowther suffered insults and humiliation. Although he was consecrated Bishop yet he was not accorded the dignity of that position. It may be recalled that in one of Townsend's petitions he contended that no matter the worth of an African Bishop he would lack the respect and influence necessary for such a high office.[32] Also, the affairs of the church were determined and managed by the European clergy at home and abroad.

Consequently, Africans were denied the opportunity to exercise their competence in the administration of the churches. Young and sometimes inexperienced European missionaries were imposed on the African clergy. This policy of racial discrimination was and is still frowned upon by some youths who have turned their back on the church. They insist that the church was used as an instrument of imperialism and that Christianity is the religion of the oppressor. They argue that an institution that preaches love but practices racism and segregation must be rejected. In the diasporas many white churches are said to discriminate against African led churches. Many of them refuse to allow the Africans, who for lack of space need rooms to meet in white churches building in the afternoons. Because of these reasons, some young Africans, mostly students refuse to identify with the church. They prefer to call themselves, communists, Marxists, agnostics, African traditionalists and even atheists.

Institutionalization of denominationalism

We have said elsewhere that in Nigeria, 'there are so many varieties of Christianity that using the plural "Christianities" may perhaps better capture the Christian landscape'.[33] The reason seems obvious: Christianity in Nigeria is a 'widely scattered family of denominations, all of them professing some kind of faith in Christ'. These differences are reflected in the liturgy, church government and models of worship which were brought by different denominations. Sometimes, the contentions and hostility between various denominations were transferred unto the mission fields. These denominational shades that attended the planting of Christianity marked the beginning of divisions in Nigerian church life. For example, the deep division between Protestants and Roman Catholics was exhibited in Eastern Nigeria. Here, the Catholics and Protestants presented 'two rival social groupings struggling with each other for positions of power and influence'. Ekechi describes what happened in that part of Nigeria as 'scandal of interdenominational rivalry'.[34] Some missionaries realized that the denominationalism which they introduced was an accident of history which should not have been transferred to the mission field. In 1911, Mr A. W. Wilkie warned his fellow Protestant Missionaries in Nigeria in this memorable statement:

> We are not here primarily to establish in Africa, Presbyterianism, or Methodism or any other ism, but to preach Christ and take a lowly place, under the guidance of Holy Spirit of God, in laying the foundation of a Church, which will not be foreign to Africa.[35]

From the above it is evident that the roots of denominationalism in Africa should be traced to the denominational jealousies, biases, contentions and misconceptions forced on the people in the mission fields.[36] It will be thorny to sustain the credibility of the Church unless African Christians are willing to overcome the stigma that Christianity was allied to colonization.

Problems of governance

It is impossible to disagree absolutely with those who offer a persuasive argument to the effect that many problems of governance, power and authority in Africa are derived from colonial patterns of a mixture of direct and indirect rule. Colonial powers introduced what they called 'democratic form' of government in the colonies in Africa but they gave their subjects very little democratic training in preparing them for independence. Colonial rulers gave them selective education, little political knowledge, imposed metropolitan structures and superimposed Western forms and conceptions on the subjected societies.[37] The political implications for African nations have been painful and agonizing in African politics today.

Besides, colonial masters instituted artificial boundaries, which forcefully united distinct ethnic groups, which do not share linguistic, religious and symbolic identities. In some cases homogeneous groups that share a strong sense of solidarity based on common language, history and culture were divided. Also, because colonial administrators maintained a superiority stance over those they ruled, when eventually the local elites took over the instruments of governance 'they maintained the hierarchical posture, concerned about securing the obedience of their people' who could be deceived and exploited.[38] Africa has experienced many social and political upheavals as a result of this history. In Nigeria, the church in the North has not known much peace. The whole of the 1990s was marked by various kinds of religious extremism ranging from massacre of people to the destruction of hundreds of places of worship because of some un-wise political decision taken by some state Governors.

Inter-religious conflicts

The prevalent inter-religious conflicts in Nigeria today may be seen in part as a transcription of the inter-ethnic wars insinuated by slave dealers in order to facilitate human trade and the forced amalgamation of the state. The oneness of Nigeria remains to be effectively established. Tekena Tamuno wonders why the 1914 Amalgamation and the British officials who inspired it left many questions unanswered. Tamuno quotes the minutes of C. Strachey (of the Colonial office) who expressed reservations:

Sir Lugard's proposals contemplate a state in which it is impossible to classify. It is not a unitary state. It is not a confederation of states. If adopted, his proposals can hardly be a permanent solution – the machine may work passably for sufficient time to enable the transition period to be left behind, by which time the answer to the problem Unitary versus Federal State – will probably have become clear.[39]

'To keep Nigeria one' is still a big task. The tension between the mosque and the church in Nigeria is a cause for concern. Conflicts between the two religions are the major cause for instability in Nigeria today. Instability would certainly hamper the progress of missions in evangelism in the 'unreached' places in the North.

Dependence syndrome

Some African scholars have observed that a 'typical feature of the colonial economy was the total and deliberate negligence or discouragement of indus-trialization and the processing of locally produced raw materials and agricultural products in most of the colonies'.[40] This deliberate act, as it were, gave birth to what some have termed 'dependence syndrome' or better still 'the Equiano Caliban complex'.[41] That is the tendency to look towards Europe, east or west for spiritual, political and economic 'salvation'.

The reason for this, according to Adu Boahen, is that:

Whatever colonialism did for Africans in Africa, given its opportunities, its resources and the power and influence it wielded in Africa, at the time, it could and should have done far more than it did.[42]

In the church, the missionary served as a school master who refused to allow his student to stand for himself for fear that he might begin to think for himself. The African is expected to remain a child who looks towards Europe and America for spiritual and economic salvation. And so in the political, economic and religious arena some level of childishness still prevails.

Delay in the indigenization of the church

Just as the colonialists dominated the land, so also did the missionaries dominate the church. Most legislations of the time were made to protect the foreign identity of the church to the detriment of the African congregation. The church was highly Westernized and there was utmost disregard and lack of respect for the African culture. The Lambeth Conference condemned almost everything African. It condemned African mode of burial, wedding, recreation and virtually everything. In some congregations, African converts were compelled to wear European dresses during worship and ultimately to imbibe the European culture and way of life. Consequently, the missionaries failed to encourage the indigenization of Christianity. It never occurred to them that Christianity could be expressed in non-Western forms. They insisted that Christianity must remain forever Western. The average African emotional response to the Ultimate Being was condemned as satanic. Colonial ideology did not only try to domesticate Christianity, imperialization of the symbol of Christ was deeply rooted in Africa. It was in consequence of these prejudices that the African Indigenous Churches emerged to introduce a branch of Christianity that is rooted in African traditional culture.[43] Today, not only the AICs in Nigeria are pragmatic in contextualizing Christianity in African culture, the Mission Churches are now more practical in their response to the problems of their African congregation. They have come to the realization that missionary Christianity with European cultural manifestations is too foreign to meet some of the pressing demands of the Nigerian. The regret of some is that this realization has come rather late.

Denigration of the status of women

Boahen observes rightly that one of the regrettable social impacts of colonialism was the deterioration that it caused to the status of the woman in Africa. Indeed, women were inhibited from joining most of the activities introduced or intensified by colonialism such as Western education, cash crop farming and other lucrative job opportunities. The colonial rule, Iliffe confirms, 'was indeed a man's World'.[44] It is true enough that long before colonization of Africa several African societies adopted the patrilineal structure, but as La Ray Denzer points out in her study of three West African Women under colonialism:

> The constraints of European patriarchal policy reinforced the patriarchal structure of traditional and Muslim African societies, with the result that the wide variety of women's indigenous political institutions were rapidly stripped of their former authority and status.[45]

Layiwola explains that decline in the status of women's indigenous institution was accelerated because the form of urbanization that colonialism presented tended to put emphasis on men's wage labour while women and wives were appendages to these labourers in the service of Colonial masters. Thus, the economic and social security guaranteed to women in traditional societies were lacking in the urban slums that expanded under colonialism.[46] This negative stance against women is noticeable in the church in Nigeria. In spite of the fact that the mission churches preach the equality of sexes, men usually hold the principal positions of authority. The Bishops, Reverend Ministers, Pastors and Choir leaders are expected to be men. One of the revolutions caused by the AICs has to do with the elevation of women's status in the church. The AICs in Nigeria emulated by the Neo-Pentecostals have been exceptional in encouraging women to participate in the ministry of the church. Today, both at home and abroad, African women hold positions of leadership as founders, co-founders, Reverend- mothers, Bishops and Archbishops. It is not surprising that there are usually more women societies, prayer groups, hospitality associations and welfare unions than men's in the AICs.

Conclusion

This chapter has discussed the objectives of colonialism, methods of colonization, partition and occupation of colonies to prepare the ground for an evaluation of the implications of colonialism for Christianity in Nigeria. The chapter emphasized that there are both negative and positive dimensions to the impact of colonialism in Africa in general and Nigeria in particular. From the discussions so far it is clear that the church in Nigeria cannot fully break away from the effects of colonialism and the fanciful balloon known as globalization. There is a way out. The church in Nigeria should have a judicious blend of what is best in the African culture and integrate into the new paradigm of global civilization.

The second crucial issue to raise is what may be termed the re-colonization of the Nigerian state by the local political elites. It is over four decades now since Nigeria became independent of Britain. One wonders whether we should continue to blame Britain for our social, political, economic and religious woes. The church in Nigeria must rise up to wage a relentless war against greed, religious violence, ethnic hostility, political instability and above all corruption which have made some to wonder whether Africa has fared better after decolonization.

Notes

[1] Boahen, Adu, 'Colonialism in Africa: Its Impact and significance', in: Boahen, Adu (ed.), *General History of Africa VII, Africa under Colonial Domination 1880–1935* (Heinemann: University of California Press, 1985), 783–806.

[2] Modern European Colonialism may be divided into two overlapping phases. In the first phase (from 1515 to 1800), Western Europe led by Spain and Portugal expanded into the West Indies and the Americas. In the second phase, Great Britain was one of the European countries which spearheaded expansion into Africa, Asia and the Pacific.

[3] Their views are well expressed in Rodney, Walter, *How Europe Underdeveloped Africa* (London and Dar es Salaam, Tanzania Publishing House, 1976).

[4] See for example Tamuno, Tekena, *Nigeria: Its People and Its Problems* (Lagos: FGP, 1991).

[5] Boahen quotes J. F. A. Ajayi as consistently maintaining that the impact of colonialism has been exaggerated and that it id not cause any break in continuity. See Boahen 1985: 806.

[6] 'Colonies and Colonialism', in: *Microsoft Encarta Encyclopedia* CD-Rom, 2001.

[7] Robinson, Ronald and Gallagher, John, *Africa and the Victorians: The Official Mind of Imperialism* (London: Macmillan, 1967), 1.

[8] Boahen 1985: 783.

[9] See for example Nyang, Sulayman, 'Christianity and Westernization in Africa', *A Current Bibliography on African Affairs, 18*(1) (1985–1986): 43.

[10] Rodney 1976.

[11] See *The Oxford Interactive Encyclopedia* CD Rom, (Oxford: TLC Properties Inc., 1997).

[12] Ibid.

[13] Instead of 'yours sincerely', colonial official letters ended as 'yours obedient servant' or 'your humble servant'. This was part of the general colonial orientation in which the local people were purposely intended to be servants of the colonial power, but never to be masters.

[14] See Kalu, Ogbu, *The History of Christianity in West Africa* (London: Longmans, 1980), 182.

[15] Kloos, Peter, 'The Dialectics of Globalisation and Localization', in: Staring, Richard, Steenbergen, Bart van, and Wilterdink, Nico, (eds), *Globalization, Inequality and Difference, Consequences of Transnational Flows* (Oxford: Rowman and Littlefield Publishers, 1999), 281–97.

[16] Babalola, Adeboye, 'African Renaissance: Making the New Culture grow well out of the old', in: Ogude, Peter (ed.), *Towards an African Renaissance. Occasional Publications of Nigerian Academy of Letters, 2*(2), (2002) 1–53.

[17] Babalola, Ibid, and Kloos 1999: 281–97.

[18] Boahen 1985: 797.

[19] See 'Missions Charter', Nigeria Missions Newsletter. A Publication of Nigeria Evangelical Missions Association (NEMA), 1(3) (May, 2003) 1–5.

[20] Jeter, Howard, '"Reaching out to the African Diaspora": The Need for Vision', Remarks of the American Ambassador at the Nigerian Institute of International Affairs, Lagos, Nigeria, March 2002.

[21] Ein Wegweiser 2003–2004, Places, Times and Languages of Worship for Foreign Language Christian Fellowships in Berlin and Brandenburg (Berlin: WDL Verlag, 2003).

[22] Afigbo 'The social repercussions of colonial rule: the new social structures', in Boahen 1985: 878.

[23] Caldwell, 'The social repercussions of colonial rule: demographic aspects', in Boahen 1985: 472f.

[24] Kalu, Ogbu, 'Pentecostal and Charismatic Reshaping of the African Religious Landscape in the 1990', *Mission Studies, XX* (2003): 1–39.

[25] Ayegboyin, Deji and Ishola, Ademola, *African Indigenous Churches: A Historical Perspective* (Lagos: Great Heights, 1999).

[26] Barrett, David B., *Schism and Renewal in Africa* (London, OUP, 1968).

[27] Walls, Andrew, 'Christian Scholarship in Africa in the Twenty-first Century', *Journal of African Christian Thought, 4*(2) (Dec. 2001): 44–52.

[28] See Handbill of International Ministerial Council of Germany: (n.d.): 1.

[29] Joachim Stelzner (red.) *Wer wir sind und was wir tun. Kulturelles und Kommunales Assenheim.* Niddatal, 2003: 6

30 'Report about African Christians in the Netherlands' (n.d.), 2.Please see 'The Position of African Christians in the Netherlands', Chapter 24 in this volume.

31 Wer Wir Sind: 2.

32 Omoyajowo, Justus A. (ed.), *Makers of the Church in Nigeria* (Lagos: CSS, 1995): 100.

33 Ayegboyin, Deji and Asonzeh, Franklin, 'Taxonomy of Churches in Nigeria: A Historical Perspective', *Orita: Ibadan Journal of Religious Studies, 34*(1&2) (2002): 68.

34 Ekechi, Felix K., 'Scandal of Inter-denominational Rivalry', in: Kalu, Ogbu (ed.), *The Nigerian Story* (Ibadan: Day Star, 1970): 305–6.

35 Ayegboyin, Deji, 'Rediscovering and Fostering Unity in the Body of Christ: The Nigerian Experience', in: Ishola, Ademola and Deji Ayegboyin (eds), *Rediscovering and Fostering Unity in the Body of Christ: The Nigerian Experience* (Lagos: Wellspring, 2000). 21.

36 Oshitelu, Gideon A., 'The Ecumenical Movement: A Historical and Theological Perspective', in: Ishola, Ademola and Deji Ayegboyin 2000: 67f.

37 See Munoz 2002: xxii.

38 Gifford, Paul, *African Christianity: Its Public Role* (Indiana: IUP, 1998).

39 Tamuno 1991.

40 See Boahen 1985: 202.

41 Ogude, S. E., 'Globalisation and African Development: Options for the 21st Century', *Annals of the Nigerian Academy of Letters 2* (2002): 53

42 Boahen 1985: 805.

43 Ayegboyin and Ishola 1991: Chapter 17.

44 Quoted by Boahen 1985: 803.

45 Quoted by Layiwola 2001: 127.

46 Ibid.

Chapter 4

The Role of the Churches in the Struggle for Liberation in Southern Africa: A Thematic Survey

Ezra Chitando

Introduction

The partitioning of Africa following the Berlin–Congo conference had massive implications for the continent. The conference, held between 1 November 1884 and 26 November 1885 under the German Chancellor Otto von Bismark, ushered a new era when European powers divided the continent with the sole purpose of exploiting Africa's resources. For Southern African countries, this gave rise to settler colonialism, racism and oppression. The ideology of European supremacy reigned supreme, while Africa laboured under the 'Dark Continent' label. Significantly, in most parts of Africa the introduction of Christianity had coincided with the process of colonization. This has led to the popular African critique of missionaries as the drumbeaters of colonialism.

This chapter examines the participation of churches in liberation struggles in South Africa and Zimbabwe. While recognizing the peculiar and complex nature of each country's history, the chapter utilizes insights from comparative religion to identify similarities and differences in the participation of the churches in the struggle in the two countries. Through an analysis of selected themes in Southern African church history, the chapter highlights the extent to which religion both shapes and is shaped by politics and other contextual realities. The first section outlines the introduction of Christianity in South Africa and Zimbabwe. The second section highlights similarities in how the churches addressed racism and oppression in the two countries. The third section examines some of the salient differences in the responses of the churches in these countries. An interpretation of how the churches could become agents of social change in Southern Africa is provided in the fourth section.

The Scramble for Resources and Souls
in Southern Africa: An Overview

The history of the implantation of Christianity in Africa has been recounted in a number of studies. Such undertakings include in-depth studies by some of the leading authorities on the subject, particularly in the late 1990s.[1] Other researchers have endeavoured to locate the impact of Christianity on the African imagination.[2] These narratives are helpful in their exploration of the complex manner in which Christianity was brought to African shores. A review of these works illustrates the challenges associated with such exercises.[3] This chapter recognizes the controversies and contestations surrounding the retelling of the story of Africa's encounter with Christianity, particularly the question of its expansion on African soil.

A number of themes have dominated the debate on the introduction of Christianity to Africa. These include the role of missionaries in the colonization process, with most African intellectuals accusing Christianity of complicity in the theft of African resources. Other researchers have sought to disengage Christianity from colonialism. The contribution of African evangelists has also been debated, alongside the question of the role of women in the rapid expansion of Christianity in Africa. While no scholarly consensus has emerged on these issues, it remains valid to observe that the coming of Christianity to Africa had remarkable consequences for the continent. A historian of religion observes that the history of religions in Southern Africa has been indelibly affected by the encounter between Christianity and indigenous religions.[4] A new religion had been brought to the African landscape and a scramble for African souls had started. This study appreciates the challenges related to the writing of African church history but does not seek to debate the main issues.

The history of the church in South Africa began with the coming of the Dutch (1652), the French Huguenots (1668) and the early German settlers a little later.[5] It was from these early beginnings that Christianity was able to expand and later become a significant player in the history of the country. As was the case in Zimbabwe, earlier Catholic initiatives had not made much headway, and it was the Protestants who led in the efforts to convert Africans. The Dutch Reformed Church became the established church and the close association between church and state was born. The nineteenth century missionary movement generated increased interest in the evangelization of Africans. Various missionary bodies began sending their members to South Africa in efforts to win African souls. The dynamic nature of Christianity in South Africa implies that its political, social and cultural history is doubly rich.[6] While the Christian presence in Zimbabwe predated the Pioneer Column of 1890, it is important to observe that the growth of Christianity became notable after the establishment of the colonial state. It therefore remains true that "the colonial occupation of

1890 fully opened the way for missionary activities in Zimbabwe".[7] It is this close association between missionary efforts and the colonial enterprise that has led to the emergence of a hostile African intellectual opinion against Christianity. African creative writers, philosophers and theologians have protested against what they regard as the collusion between missionaries and colonial agents. In the case of Zimbabwe, the Pioneer Column of the British South Africa Company had Anglican and Catholic missionaries, symbolically illustrating the close connection between the two undertakings.

The missionaries who brought Christianity to Southern Africa shared common assumptions with colonial agents. The Berlin–Congo Conference of 1884/5 and the World Missionary Conference held in Edinburgh in 1910 were both informed by the notion of the superiority of European culture over that of non-Europeans. While the meeting in Berlin partitioned Africa politically, the one in Edinburgh led to the spiritual division of the continent. Although there were some conflicts between missionaries and colonial agents, in most cases the shared cultural base mitigated the differences. In addition, denominational rivalries were only felt at a later stage as missionaries from different denominations often established cordial relations in the initial phase. Thus:

> Missionaries themselves, quite often regardless of their denominations or nationality, found themselves as birds of a feather flocking together in a strange and sometimes hostile environment. But as soon as they started gaining some success with the native peoples, particularly the chiefs and the kings, signs of competitiveness and open hostilities emerged. With the second stage of evangelization of Africans, the era of denominationalism and religious competitiveness dawned in Africa with Africans influenced by one missionary society developing hostile or negative spirits against their counterparts.[8]

Both colonialism and denominationalism sought to recreate and rename the African. In South Africa and Zimbabwe, conversion to Christianity was often thought of as being conversion to European values and tastes. As many African theologians have noted, African cultural values were regarded as primitive and backward, with the convert being exhorted to take up a completely new identity. One symbolic gesture that underlined this transformation was the taking up of a new name. In both countries, converts were expected to adopt a biblical or European name to mark the transition to a new worldview. Culture-bound names were denounced as the past that had to be swept away by the cleansing power of the gospel. The various denominations interpreted conversion to Christianity as making a total break with the past.

The division of the two countries into distinct missionary zones led Africans to take up new identities on denominational lines, alongside accentuating ethnic consciousness. Although accusing missionaries of inventing tribalism in Southern Africa might be stretching the point, it should be admitted that ecclesiastical boundaries tended to create new definitions of space. In Zimbabwe, the translation of the Bible into the vernacular led to specific dialects being identified with specific regions, giving rise to the phenomenon of ethnically based churches. In addition, colonial boundaries disregarded traditional African states, while missionary translations of the Bible had the consequence of heightening ethnic consciousness amongst Africans.

The introduction of Christianity and colonialism into Southern Africa led to confrontations over resources, particularly land. African souls and land appeared to be high on the agenda of those who conquered Africa. Christianity became powerful by virtue of its association with colonial agents, effacing all other competitors from the public sphere. In South Africa and Zimbabwe, the civilizing mission of European powers operated in tandem with the saving mission of the missionaries. For many Africans, the churches in Southern Africa had become an intricate cog in the colonial machinery. This was confirmed by the participation of the churches in the displacement of Africans from their ancestral lands. Missionary bodies were happy to receive large tracts of land from the colonizing powers, frustrating African communities in the process.

The churches in Southern Africa are heavily implicated in the land question in the region. Colonial conquest entailed the removal of blacks from fertile territories and consigning them to rocky spaces. Colonialists and missionaries accessed the prime land, banishing blacks to overcrowded Bantustans or reserves. Land is therefore a strategic theme in Southern Africa, as the Berlin conference was essentially about redrawing African space. Thus, land is 'the place where struggles for domination and control have been played out, it is the place where black people of this continent have been made landless in the land of their birth'.[9] Unfortunately, the churches got entangled in the land question in Southern Africa when they accepted fertile land that had been taken by force from Africans. The partitioning of Africa had now moved to another level where 'sacred spaces' had been created in the form of Christian villages. In Zimbabwe, such mission stations included Chishawasha for the Catholics and Epworth for the Methodists. Africans who continued to stay at these mission stations lost their right to the land and were at the mercy of the missionaries. African cultural practices were banned, and speedy evictions followed those who transgressed the many rules that governed life within these mission farms.

In both South Africa and Zimbabwe, the reality of settler colonialism had a direct impact on the character of Christianity. While some African countries experienced indirect European control, Southern Africa had to endure settler colonialism. The European presence in these countries was quite significant, while the oppression was brutal. For the Africans who were at the receiving end of the unjust system, Christianity was an ideology that lubricated the process of externalizing Africa's resources. It is therefore not surprising that

African traditional spirit mediums were instrumental in the 1896/7 African uprisings in Zimbabwe. Christianity was denounced as an oppressive religion, while indigenous spirituality was utilized to defend African resources.

Given the political and cultural context that shaped the coming of Christianity to Southern Africa, it is not surprising that the churches found themselves at the centre during the struggle for liberation. The quest for freedom by blacks harnessed the churches to be the very arena for the struggle. The guiding ideologies of white supremacy, such as apartheid in South Africa and racial segregation in Zimbabwe, were buttressed by Christian ideas. The Dutch Reformed Church gave moral credence to the apartheid policies of the National Party from 1948 to the attainment of majority rule in South Africa in 1994. When blacks sought to shake off the yoke of oppression, the churches could not remain indifferent. It became necessary for the churches to take sides with the oppressed black majority and to undermine the racist regimes. Although the churches often had conflicting positions concerning the legitimacy of the struggle, the majority later came to realize that the quest for freedom could not be delayed any further. The following section seeks to identify similarities in the responses of the churches to the struggle for liberation in South Africa and Zimbabwe.

A Shared Vision: Churches and the Struggle in South Africa and Zimbabwe

As the preceding section illustrates, the churches were part of the colonization process in many instances. However, in both countries some missionaries like John White protested against colonial excesses from very early on. They sought to separate their task from that of the colonizers. Some missionaries criticized the notion of European superiority and sought to ensure that blacks could advance in all the spheres of life. This was particularly true in the field of education where missionaries played an important role. In both countries, missionaries were significant players in the field of education. They established schools where blacks could get quality education, although social apartheid might have prejudiced black students. Thus:

> Certainly educational institutions like Lovedale, Marianhill, Healdtown and Saint Matthews gave black South Africans better education than was available elsewhere on the continent until the 1950s and were agents of change. Founded by the Presbyterians in 1824 in the eastern Cape, Lovedale was open to all races and denominations. During the nineteenth century this was not uncommon in the Cape, for mission schools there were not segregated, though government schools were for Whites only. At Lovedale, Black and White pupils at school ate at separate tables and slept in separate dormitories, but attended classes together.[10]

In South Africa and Zimbabwe, one of the most significant contributions of the churches to the liberation struggle may be identified as the nurturing of black nationalists. It was the mission-educated African nationalists who posed a serious challenge to racism and white dominance. In South Africa Albert Luthuli, Robert Sobukwe and others had received their education at the hands of the missionaries. In Zimbabwe, leading nationalists like Joshua Nkomo, James Chikerema, Robert Mugabe and others owed their education to the churches. It was these African nationalists who led the struggle for independence, often citing the Christian teaching that all human beings were created as equal before God. Mission schools were therefore instrumental in shaping the convictions of black political leaders in Southern Africa. Christian values of equality and justice galvanized the black struggle for freedom. African nationalists owed their vision of a democratic, just and free nation from Christian teachings. They gained confidence to speak against racial discrimination, and called upon the churches to live up to the ideals of Christianity by condemning apartheid. Thus:

There is no doubt that Christianity shaped the struggle against apartheid; Christian ideals served as an ethical critique of apartheid; as a source of righteous anger that inspired action, and as a wellspring of confidence in eventual victory. Christian values of resistance leaders inspired and shaped black political protest over the twentieth century and in no small measure were instrumental in ushering in a new democratic era.[11]

The appeal to Christian values and principles by black nationalists was meant to undermine the appeal to the same values by settler regimes. White minority regimes in Southern Africa justified their racism and grip on power by claiming that they had divine mandates to rule over blacks. The Nationalist Party tinted the ideology of apartheid with Christian theological ideas, while Ian Smith claimed to be defending Christian civilization in Zimbabwe. State theologies were designed to ensure the hegemony of white minorities in the two countries. It was dangerous for leaders of the various denominations to challenge such abuses of the religion. However, individuals like Trevor Huddleston in South Africa and Ralph Dodge in Zimbabwe were prophetic in their attacks of racist regimes. While they were persecuted for their commitment to the ideals of equality and justice, they remained steadfast.

Most historians of Christianity in Africa have overlooked the role of indigenous clergy in the struggle for liberation in Southern Africa. By the 1950s, many mainline churches had ordained black ministers of religion. As they struggled to overcome income disparities between black and white clergy, as well as to fight institutional racism, they became aware of the need to transform society. In Zimbabwe, ordained Christians like Ndabaningi Sithole, Abel T. Muzorewa and Canaan Banana became focal points of the liberation struggle. However, when the tactics changed to armed conflict, these individuals were overtaken by more radical and militant personalities like Mugabe. Similarly, in South Africa individuals like Desmond Tutu, Frank Chikane and others were at the centre of the resistance movement. Although they were predominantly male due to the coalescence of African and Christian patriarchal ideologies, they provided leadership to the liberation movements.

Southern African churches were also empowered to contribute to the struggle by external bodies such as the World Council of Churches (WCC), through its Program to Combat Racism. Introduced in the 1970s, the program had a special fund that was designed to support humanitarian and educational programmes administered by liberation movements such as the African National Congress (ANC) of South Africa and the Zimbabwe African National Union (ZANU) in Zimbabwe.[12] While these grants generated a lot of controversy in the two countries, they enabled the churches to render practical support to the struggle for independence. Those who opposed these grants felt that they allowed the churches to support violence by the liberation movements. On the other hand, those who applauded the program to combat racism averred that the grants were meant to alleviate suffering and to promote education. Many denominations in Southern Africa were sharply divided over the program. However, the connection of the Southern African churches to the larger global ecumenical movement facilitated greater publicity of the racial discrimination in the region. International pressure against white minority regimes increased and activists felt protected.

Exiled Christians in both South Africa and Zimbabwe were also actively involved in the quest for freedom. In the historiographies of the liberation struggles in both countries, it has remained difficult to balance the contributions of exiles and those who remained behind. Exiled Christians mobilized resources in the host countries and sought to increase awareness of the brutality that blacks had to endure at the hands of racist regimes. A telling example is how South African and Zimbabwean exiles in Sweden played an important role in challenging the Swedish activists to play a more direct role in the struggle. It is also important to note that several influential activists in the Swedish solidarity movement had a background in the church.[13]

While this chapter has tended to dwell on the mainline Protestant churches, it is important to recognize the contributions of the Catholic Church to the struggle in Southern Africa. Liberation movements engaged in considerable rhetoric associated with Marxist principles, making the Catholics hesitant to support them.[14] However, the Catholic social teachings on justice were critical in mobilizing its members to resist apartheid. In the two countries, Catholic leaders were at the forefront in denouncing racial discrimination. They refuted the claims of white minority regimes to be divinely ordained, and called upon their followers to resist oppression. In Zimbabwe, the Catholic Commission for Justice and Peace unmasked the atrocities of the government. Catholic mission stations were also in the line of fire, with many priests and nuns being harassed for their support of the guerrillas. However, it requires a longer narrative to detail the activities of the Catholics in the two countries.

African Independent/Indigenous/Instituted/Initiated Churches (AICs) are often marginalized in Southern African church histories. While the history of religions approach seeks to understand the multiple modes of expression of the various religions, a doctrinal approach has dominated Southern African church history. There is a tendency to exclude AICs from discussions on churches and their contribution to the struggle in Southern Africa. Consequently, most studies dwell on the achievements of the Catholics and the Protestants, effectively writing off AICs from the liberation struggle. This is unfair since Ethiopian churches – AICs that broke away from Protestant denominations – had close links with the movement towards black political liberation. It is significant to observe that, 'In 1912 Ethiopian church leaders were actively involved in the formation of the South African Native National Congress, which would later become (in 1952) the African National Congress.'[15] Members of AICs also contributed to the attainment of majority rule in the two countries in various ways. Crucially, AICs empowered Africans in Southern Africa to recognize that it was possible to operate outside the control of whites and to be successful in such ventures.

Indigenous churches in Southern Africa offered a profound challenge to the assumptions of the Berlin–Congo conference and nineteenth century missionary activities. They equipped their followers with ideological ammunition that they used to question the doctrine of white supremacy. In Zimbabwe, the African Apostolic Church preached the message of the 'Recreation of Africa' where Africans would be free to chart their own destiny.[16] They also gave their members alternative space to exercise leadership skills, outside the patronage of whites. Some AICs members fuelled the nationalist fervour in the 1960s, calling upon Africans to boycott the stifling economic system and to invest in the informal sector. They also encouraged Africans to affirm their cultures and to be confident of their abilities. Although many declared themselves to be apolitical, their rhetoric was in favour of the liberation struggle.

Although the churches were significant players in the struggle for liberation in Southern Africa, the story of their participation is fraught with contradictions. Different denominations often had different attitudes to the struggle at different historical moments. Members of the same denomination could be found on different sides of the political divide. This was particularly pronounced amongst the Protestants, whilst the hierarchical structure of the Catholics gave some form of uniformity to its responses. However, many striking similarities can be discerned from the South African and Zimbabwean contexts. Following the successful introduction of Christianity at the height of colonial occupation, church-state partnership thrived. There was general agreement between the missionaries and colonial officers, although some missionaries challenged colonial excesses. The church also played a key role in the education of African

nationalists, as well as providing courageous leadership to the resistance movement. Although the story of the participation of the churches in the struggle in
Southern Africa is fraught with contradictions, it should be acknowledged that
on the whole the churches succeeded in redeeming themselves in the eyes of
most Africans. The following section seeks to highlight some of the salient
differences between the responses of the churches in the two countries.

The Churches and Southern African Struggles: Notes on Internal Differences

Although South African and Zimbabwe church histories have a lot in common,
given the shared historical experiences, a number of differences can be noted
regarding the participation of the churches in the quest for freedom. One of
the major factors lies in the nature of the struggle for liberation in the two
countries. In Zimbabwe, a full-scale liberation war was waged in the 1970s,
ulminating in the attainment of independence in 1980. In South Africa civil
disobedience became a preferred strategy of fighting the apartheid regime,
although acts of sabotage were also committed. The emergence of a mass movement against apartheid enabled the black church leaders to have a more direct
approach to the struggle than in Zimbabwe where the guerrilla war raged on in
the rural areas.

The churches in South Africa benefited from ideological clarity, particularly
with the emergence of the Black Consciousness Movement and black theology
in the 1960s and 1970s. While the apartheid policies sought to find theological
support through the Dutch Reformed Church, black theology helped to expose
its limitations. South African black theology provided a new interpretation of
the role of Christianity in an oppressive context. It challenged the ideology of
apartheid and equipped blacks to challenge the civil religion of the white Dutch
Reformed Church. The Christian Institute was significant in the emergence of
black theology and it led the way by analysing the economics of apartheid and
exposing the structural injustice that it created.[17] Although the churches in
Zimbabwe developed some helpful theological reflections, they did not generate a consistent theological trend. Black theology in South Africa brought
together the history of racism in the introduction of Christianity, the appropriation of theological themes by white minority regimes, as well as suggesting the
most effective black response. It challenged the ideology of apartheid and
sought to empower blacks in their confrontation with the oppressive state. John
Parratt has offered a helpful summary of these developments, and it is necessary to cite him at length. He writes:

It is unhappily true that Christianity has seldom been free from the taint of
racism, latent or overt, not least in the Reformed tradition; it is also true that

the missionary expansion into Africa was all too often characterized by a curious paradox in that, while preaching the equality of all before God, it nonetheless tended to elevate white Christians into superior beings. In South Africa, however, this hardened into a political dogma, which found its religious mythology in the conception of the Voortrekkers of themselves as the elect of God, set apart to possess the Promised Land by dispossessing the heathen African, and it had its ecclesiastical outworking in the racial units that constituted the Dutch Reformed Church. Black theology, then, is essentially the theological response to the dehumanization of blacks that resulted from the ideology of apartheid.[18]

The nature of the struggle in Zimbabwe also had a bearing on the contribution of the churches, as I have argued above. The vicious armed liberation struggle led to the death of many Christians. In a number of instances, the guerrillas killed members of the various denominations on suspicion of being 'sell outs.' Guerrillas often attacked Christianity as a foreign religion and encouraged blacks to return to indigenous beliefs and practices. They also regarded missionaries as agents of imperialism and forced Christians to denounce 'the white Jesus'.[19] On the other hand, agents of the settler regime also persecuted Christians who actively supported the liberation struggle. Many Christians therefore found themselves in the middle of a painful and demanding war.

Indigenous churches in Zimbabwe tended to have a more direct involvement in the liberation struggle. Their predominantly rural character meant that there were located where most of the fighting was taking place. Zimbabwe's AICs are concentrated in the rural areas, such as the Zionists in the southern provinces and the Apostles in the eastern provinces. It was in these rural areas that members of AICs used their powers of healing to attend to injured freedom fighters. Some of their prophets also used their spiritual powers to offer guidance to the guerrillas. Although Marthinus Daneel[20] uses fiction to make his point, his work highlights the contributions of the AICs to the struggle in Zimbabwe.

Despite these differences, churches in both countries became sites of struggle. In both countries, most denominations had an ambivalent attitude, moving from close association with the settler state to a period of open confrontation. Interpretations of Christianity became contested, with the state promoting versions that furthered its interests, while its critics promoted theologies of liberation. It was difficult for churches to preach the gospel of neutrality amidst so much conflict. As international opinion hardened against racism in Southern Africa, many denominations began to criticize the white minority regimes and contributed to social transformation. The following section briefly locates the importance of the churches as agents of social change in the region.

Churches as Agents of Social Change
in Southern Africa: Some Observations

The preceding sections have shown the extent to which Christianity has been involved in the history of Southern Africa. Though often in contradictory ways, the churches have been agents of change in the region. By supporting liberating movements, churches laid the ground for co-operation with future black nationalist governments. While the Berlin–Congo Conference of 1884/85 took place at a time when European supremacy was taken for granted and facilitated the spread of Christianity, the post-colonial African condition calls for new models of interaction between Africa and Europe. Communities that waged struggles for liberation may no longer accept racism and paternalism.

Churches in Southern Africa are being called upon to continue playing a meaningful role as new challenges have emerged. Despite the celebrations of independence, poverty, HIV and AIDS, drought and other social ills continue to haunt the region. If religion is to play its positive role of promoting abundant life, churches in Southern Africa have to be seen on the frontlines. Black nationalist governments have tended to concentrate on making promises while the majority languish in poverty. In South Africa, the ruling elite has sent contradictory signals on its policy on HIV and AIDS, while whole communities succumb to the effects of HIV and AIDS. In Zimbabwe, the pandemic has wreaked havoc, while scarce resources have been committed to speculative ventures such as participation in the war in the Democratic Republic of the Congo. Southern Africa is at the centre of the HIV and AIDS storm, but the churches struggle to be relevant. In both countries, the shared nationalist vision between the black nationalists and church leaders threatens to stifle the prophetic voice of the churches.

Despite the rhetoric on globalization and the new world order, Africa remains marginalized and exploited by the 'principalities and powers' of this world. The spirit that precipitated the partitioning of Africa has not been jettisoned in Europe and North America. Africa continues to be relegated to footnotes in global affairs, only being retrieved to whet appetites for exotic materials. Images of Africa in Europe remain largely negative,[21] with the continent being reduced to an arena for war, disease and death. Churches in Southern Africa need to remain vigilant as the struggle did not end with the attainment of majority rule. The education of the poor, support for vulnerable groups and advocacy work should remain high on the agenda. As they did during the liberation struggle, churches should continue to support the new struggle for dignity by Africans.

Conclusion

The Berlin–Congo Conference of 1884/85 set into motion events that had massive consequences for Africa. In Southern Africa, a new religion that brooked no rivals was introduced at a time when African resources were being externalized. Christianity became the spiritual wing of colonialism in the eyes of many Africans. However, the churches began to side with Africans as they struggled against racist regimes in South Africa and Zimbabwe. This chapter has highlighted the contributions of the churches to the struggle in Southern Africa. It has noted a number of similarities and differences in the participation of the churches in the quest for freedom in the two countries. While the colonizing European powers were responsible for the humiliation and subjugation of Africans, Christianity is now called upon to fulfil a new role. By supporting the post-colonial African struggles for wholeness of life, churches in Southern Africa can begin writing a new chapter in the history of religions in the region.

Notes

1. Hastings, Adrian, *The Church in Africa, 1450–1950* (Oxford: Clarendon Press, 1997); Isichei, Elizabeth, *A History of Christianity in Africa: From Antiquity to the Present* (Grand Rapids: Eerdmans, 1995); Sundkler, Bengt and Christopher Steed, *A History of the Church in Africa* (Cambridge: Cambridge University Press, 2000).
2. Maxwell, David and Ingrid Lawrie (eds), Christianity and the African Imagination: Essays in Honour of Adrian Hastings (Leiden: Brill, 2002).
3. Ojo, Matthews, 'The Study of African Christianity in the 1990s', *Religion, 30,* (2000): 185–89.
4. Chidester, David, *Savage Systems: Colonialism and Comparative Religion in Southern Africa* (Charlottesville: University of Virginia Press, 1996).
5. De Gruchy, John W., *The Church Struggle in South Africa* (Second edn) (Grand Rapids: William B. Eerdmans Publishing Company, 1986), 1.
6. Elphick, Richard and Rodney Davenport (eds), *Christianity in South Africa: A Political, Social and Cultural History* (Cape Town: David Phillip, 1997).
7. Verstraelen, Frans J., Zimbabwean Realities and Christian Responses: Contemporary Aspects of Christianity in Zimbabwe (Gweru: Mambo Press, 1998), 4.
8. Waruta, Douglas W., 'Towards an African Church', in: Mugambi, Jesse N. K. and Laurenti Magesa (eds), *The Church in African Christianity: Innovative Essays in Ecclessiology* (Nairobi: Initiative Publishers, 1990), 33.
9. Philpott, Graham, 'Land is Storied Space: The Church and Land in Southern Africa', *Bulletin for Contextual Theology in Africa 5/3,* (1998): 4–5, here p. 4.
10. Hope, Marjorie and James Young, *The South African Churches in a Revolutionary Situation* (Maryknoll, New York: Orbis Books, 1981), 21.
11. Graybill, Lyn S., *Religion and Resistance Politics in South Africa* (West Court, CT: Praeger, 1995), 125.
12. Banana, Canaan S., The Church and the Struggle for Zimbabwe: From the Programme to Combat Racism to Combat Theology (Gweru: Mambo Press, 1996), 209.
13. Sellstrom, Tor, *Sweden and National Liberation Movements in Southern Africa* (Vol. 1) (Uppsala: Nordiska Afrikainstitutet, 1999), 38.
14. McKenna, Joseph C., *Finding a Social Voice: The Church and Marxism in Africa* (New York: Fordham University Press, 1997).

[15] Oosthuizen, Gerhardus, 'Indigenous Christianity and the Future of the Church in South Africa', in: Walsh, Thomas G. and Frank Kaufmann (eds), *Religion and Social Transformation in Southern Africa* (St. Paul, Minnesota: Paragon House, 1999), 157–73, 160.

[16] Chitando, Ezra, 'The Recreation of Africa: A Study of the Ideology of the African Apostolic Church of Zimbabwe', *Exchange, 32(3)* (2003): 239–49.

[17] Walshe, Peter, Church Versus State in South Africa: The Case of the Christian Institute (London: C. Hurst and Company, 1983), 193.

[18] Parratt, John, *Reinventing Christianity: African Theology Today* (Grand Rapids: Eerdmans, 1995), 156.

[19] McKenna 1997: 158.

[20] Daneel, Marthinus, *Guerrilla Snuff* (Harare: Baobab Books, 1995).

[21] Palmberg, Mai, (ed.), *Encounter Images in the Meeting between Africa and Europe* (Uppsala: Nordiska Afrikainstitutet, 2001).

Chapter 5

Deconstructing Colonial Mission – New Missiological Perspectives in African Christianity

Abraham Akrong

Introduction

The origins of the modern missionary movement coincided roughly with the Western European imperialistic project. However, the pietistic revivalist spirit that nurtured the modern missionary movement was an enthusiastic and optimistic zeal that sought to turn the 'pagan' societies outside Western Christendom into Christian societies through the influence of Christian civilization.[1] But the spread of the Gospel under the aegis of the Western European imperialistic project got the missionary movement entangled in the colonial aspirations of the Western world.[2] This created the conditions for the missionary enterprise to be imperceptibly co-opted into the colonial project which sometimes had to play the role of the cultural and spiritual double of colonialism. The identification of the Christian mission with the 'civilizing mission' of the colonial project generated paradigm for mission which skewed the liberating message of the Gospel and made the Christian experience in Africa more alienating and exclusive because of the accommodation of Christianity to European culture.[3]

Fortunately, African traditional culture and religion which provided the spiritual ecology for the planting, nurture and growth of Christianity also created a new paradigm for African Christianity which inspired and nurtured a protest movement against the 'babylonish captivity' of Christianity in Africa. The various protest movements of African Christianity that resisted the domestication of Christianity were able to bring new perspectives about Christianity that made it possible for African Christians to liberate Christianity and deconstruct its colonial images and paradigms. The result is a different understanding of Christianity that has made it possible for African Christians to appropriate Christianity as a liberating, life-transforming religion of salvation which can help many desperate people in Africa to deal with the existential raptures and structural violence that continue to define their lives. At the centre of this liberated Christianity is a radical paradigm shift nurtured by African traditional spirituality, which has given a place for the questions and concerns shaped by African culture and worldview.

The purpose of this paper is to follow the critique of African Christianity of missionary Christianity and to explore the missiological implications of the new paradigm in African Christianity for the deepening of our common understanding of God's mission in Christ for our salvation. The classical mandate for mission has been Matt. 28.18–20: 'All authority on earth has been given to me. Therefore go and make disciples of all nations, baptizing them in the name of the father, the Son and the Holy Spirit and teaching them to obey everything I have commanded you'. This mission mandate affirms that mission begins with God sending Jesus Christ his son as a way by which God presents himself to humankind (*missio Dei*). The authority to make disciple is a self-authenticating authority because disciples are made in the name and by the authority of God in Christ. The Gospel of John uses such concepts as abundant life and light to express the multidimensional and multifaceted aspects and goals of salvation.[4] Therefore when the goals of making disciples is extrapolated from the larger multifaceted dimensions of salvation in Christ, the mandate for mission often becomes susceptible to ideological manipulations especially those associated with empire building and other hegemonic and domination projects, as the modern history of missions demonstrates.

The Constantine empire-building project gave way to the post Augustinian belief that Western Christendom constituted the millennia Kingdom of Christ. Medieval Christendom passed on this Christendom ideology to the Holy Roman Empire, then to the colonial empires of Spain in the Americas, then to Western European (mainly Protestant) colonial empires of Britain, France, Germany and America. The Protestant powers of Britain, Germany and the United States took over the political messianism of Western Christendom. Together with the Christian faith, Western civilization with its Eurocentric superiority spread to the colonial people who later became Christians. The modern history of Western Christianity and its alliance with colonialism created the impression that the Christian claim to universality also implies Western European conquest and superiority. The theological problem it created for Western mission is how to interpret the universality of Christ as savior of the world without invoking the images of Western European domination and exploitation. This means the interpretation of the universality of Christ without invoking the dominating and hegemonic images of empire-building which often created a link, though false, between Western domination and the universality of Christ in the minds of the victims of colonialism.

The emerging issues for post-colonial African missiology is how to de-ideologize and de-imperialize the mission of God in Christ from its colonial and its Eurocentric bondage, which on most occasions did hamper the universal appeal of God's message of salvation in Christ. The task of post-colonial

African missiology is to re-appropriate and re-interpret the universality of Jesus Christ and his message from the point of view of the stories and experiences of African Christians within the context of their own culture and spirituality.

Critique of Colonial Missiology

The co-option of the universal symbols of Christianity as a function of colonial empire-building was made possible by the fabrication of an imperial theology based on an exclusive and a narrow interpretation of the Judeo-Christian concept of covenant. In this exclusive and narrow interpretation of covenant, election was understood as a special vocation of Western Christendom in God's economy of salvation. This allowed Western Christendom to develop the idea that it has been elected to spread Christianity and civilize the rest of the world in anticipation of the kingdom of God as, for example, one finds in the nationalistic poems of Kipling. This imperial theology for empire-building led to the mutation and transformation of theological concepts into ideological categories for political domination. The result was the 'domestication' of God's covenant of grace with all humanity in Christ, the 'territorialization' of the kingdom of God, the 'politicization' of evangelism, and the 'imperialization' of the symbol of Christ.

The domestication of God's covenant of grace

The idea of covenant relationship is fundamental to the concept of nation-hood in the West. The belief is that those whose ancestors were related to God's covenant with Abraham have a special relationship and blessing from God through the covenant with Abraham. This implied a special election of the descendants of the Abrahamic covenant to a unique function in God's economy of salvation of the world. This election thus gave a privileged position and a special status to the elect as agents in preparing for the advent of the kingdom of God. The exclusive theology of the covenant provided the theological foundation for the construction of the Western colonial ideology of 'manifest destiny'.

The stereological implication of the ideology of 'manifest destiny' meant that salvation was to the elect first and foremost by right, and those outside the covenant can only be saved by proxy through their incorporation into this special covenant identified with Western Christendom. This meant that for outsiders to be saved, they must cease to be who they are and become exactly like those in the privileged position of the elect. This created the category of those outside the covenant as infidels and pagans who can justifiably be treated as less than human. These were the ideological blinders that allowed Western Christendom to completely brush aside the disturbing moral issues raised by the atrocities of the transatlantic slavery, the conquistadores and colonialism. Within the scheme of 'manifest destiny' those outside the covenant like Africans and the Native Americans were regarded as the wards of the West who had to be brought into civilization through slavery, conquest or colonial domination. The morality of conquest and colonialism were not questioned because they were seen as justifiable of ways bringing those outside the covenant into the orbit of civilization and salvation.[5]

The territorialization of the kingdom of God

The territorialization of the kingdom of God is the direct consequence of the domestication of God's covenant of grace with humanity. Consistent with the covenant theology of empire building, the territorial expansion (conquest and colonialism) of the Western Christian nations was viewed as the instrument for the spread of the Christian civilization that will usher in the kingdom of God. Thus the missionaries saw either pax Britannica, pax Teutonica or pax Americana as part of the realization of the 'manifest destiny' of the West ordained by divine providence.

Politicization of evangelism

If empire-building was the prelude to God's kingdom, then evangelism was seen as the means of the spread of Western culture, which in the scheme of the Western view of salvation was a process, which could prepare those outside God's covenant with Christendom for salvation. The precise point of convergence between the interests and goals of both mission and colonialism was the 'civilizing mission' of Christendom believed to be a divine mandate in the scheme of the civilization and salvation of the world. Within this scheme the mandate to go and make disciples was easily interpreted to mean Westernization of the rest of the world which will give them access to salvation.

The imperialization of the symbol of Christ

The imperial ideology that provided the context for mission was able to fashion an image of Christ which was consistent with the political theology of empire-building. Christ was invariably constructed as a conquering hero of Western domination which often made the Christ of mission indistinguishable from the popular image of European conqueror. Jesus Christ was constructed as the hero of Western Imperialism in order to give justification for the colonial empire-building project.[6] The manipulation of the Gospel of Jesus Christ to fit the colonial project contradicted the very nature of the teachings of Christ who taught us to preach about God's righteousness with love and not by the sword of domination.

The aggregate effect of colonial mission made it possible for the cultural and social and economic integration of Africa into the orbit of colonial and neo-colonial political economy. Colonial mission in this sense has created deficits that we must address in our discussion of new paradigms of mission. The integration of the economies of Africa into the global capitalist system has put the African continent into a progressive impoverishing process that continue to distort the socio-economic structures that can support the most minimum quality of life. The crisis in Africa today is about socio-economic structures that can create conditions that will improve the quality of life of the people. Externally, Africa is subjected to global capitalist exploitation and internally, to the violent exploitation of their own political leaders. This colonial debt must be addressed in any discourse on missiology today. The first step towards dealing with this colonial debt and rehabilitating mission as the carrier of the good news that transforms live must start with the elimination of the dichotomies created by the old missionary paradigms between: evangelism and humanization, conversion and social action, and mission and development.

The political debt of colonial mission can be addressed when our mission agenda includes social justice and a participatory democratic process, which can empower everyone to be active players in the society. The cultural debt of colonial mission was the acculturating process of both mission and colonialism, which attempted to reduce African culture to isolated pockets of past memory. Enculturation should therefore be a visible part of our mission agenda today in order to give space for everyone to express his or her experience of God in a joyful meaningful way. Finally, the anthropological debt which has produced what can be described as anthropological poverty brought about by the alienating and acculturating structures perpetuated by the cultural imperialism must be addressed by making culture an object study in missions. The effect of cultural imperialism that leads to acculturation is not only about domination of space and bodies but also the defeat of the soul through the non-recognition of the 'other' as a person.[7] The colonial and missionary structures of Europeanized education meant that to be Christian and educated one must be accommodated to the culture of domination. The effect of this is the de-legitimatization of African culture that defines the humanity of Africans. This debt can only be paid when mission recognizes the value of the other, and the equal dignity of the culture of the other.[8]

Paradigms in African Theology

There are three complementary and inter-related strands in African theology today. We have the contemporary modern theology in its various schools and confessional theologies together with versions of liberationist theologies in the academia. However by far the hottest debate in African theology is whether

African theology should be acculturation or liberation.[9] Interestingly, while the theological debate rages on in the academia, the most important paradigm shift is coming from the theologies of what could be described as new movements in African Christianity inspired by the African pentecostal and neo-pentecostal appropriation of Christianity within the context of African spirituality.

The very early period of the twentieth century experienced great impulses for the Africanization of Christianity in Ghana. This impulse was given expression in the life and work of a group of African prophets – Harris, Oppong and Swanson, who felt called by God to lead their people to the Christian faith as African preachers sent to their own African brothers and sisters. Some of these prophets founded their own churches. Others became itinerant preachers who converted many Africans for the missionary churches. The other impulse for the Africanization of Christianity or the interpretation of Christianity from the perspectives of African spirituality was influenced by what might be described as the fall-out from the Azusa Street experience mediated mainly by African American pentecostals through their tracts and magazines. This cross-fertilization of African spirituality with the pentecostal experience from Azusa gave birth to a number of what has been described as African Indigenous Churches (AICs). Indeed some of the AICs in Ghana were initially nurtured by pentecostal spirituality from the Azusa street experience.[10] Historically, the AICs are the oldest and earliest expression of African protest against the missionary cultural imperialism. The spirit that inspired the movement of the AICs was a cultural protest against the domestication of Christianity by missionary Christianity. The explosion of African spirituality that has been lying dormant in the missionary churches gave birth to an African protest movement that was able to rescue Christianity from Western cultural imperialism and also reclaim African culture for the church in Africa.

The AICs movement was quick to point out, on biblical grounds, the continuities between Christianity and African culture which in their eyes qualify African culture to be both a 'praeparatio evangelii' and also a credible and legitimate vehicle for mediating the salvation message of Christianity for the African society.[11] The significance of the AICs for African theology and mission is that the movement was able to resist the attempt by missionary Christianity to exclude legitimate concerns and aspiration of African Christians from the salvation message of Christianity. The AICs was thus able to demonstrate that African concerns hitherto marginalized by missionary Christianity were legitimate questions for which the Gospel has answers. The appropriation and re-interpretation of the Christianity from the perspectives of African spirituality and on biblical grounds constituted the point of departure for the theology of the AICs. This is precisely the theological revolution that has given Christianity a fertile African soil on which an authentic African message of salvation can be nurtured.[12]

The protest movement of the AICs which rescued the Christian message of salvation from its bondage to Western culture led to the discovery of the truth about Christianity as a universal message of salvation addressed to all human beings in all circumstances, according to the questions and concerns which each group brings from its cultural backgrounds.[13] The shift in the hermeneutic circle initiated by the AICs movement was able to widen the scope of the soteriological appeal of the Christian message for African Christians because it made it possible for Christianity to address real life issues that are of utmost concern for African Christians: healing, protection against evil spirits and witches, abundant life, etc.

Missiological Perspectives in African Christianity

Enculturation and liberation

The debate between enculturationists and liberationists in African theology today is about the approach to theological hermeneutics, whether the focus of African theology should be liberation or enculturation. Other paradigms like the theology of reconstruction, or transformation, are attempts to find a paradigm that can bring a comprehensive perspective to church theology to enable the African church to deal with its numerous problems. All the paradigms, theories and methodologies proposed can add something to this quest for a comprehensive framework that may guide the African church to deal with the daunting problems facing the African society. However, the attention focused on paradigms and methodologies though helpful is not addressing the central issues of the goal of the mission of the church in Africa. The issue is what should be the contribution of African theology to the communication of the Gospel of salvation to the many African Christians who are desperately seeking answers to their problems.

One of the tragedies of post-independent Africa is the poor quality of life of the majority of the people whose lives are dominated by violence, wanton destruction of life, political oppression, economic strangulation, cultural alienation and despair. These are the realities and issues that are defining and shaping the life of African Christians. The focus of mission understood in its wider connotation as God's mission to the world in Christ should be about bearing witness to the promise of abundant life or fullness of life in Christ. Abundant life or fullness of life in this sense is about the quality of life that befits human beings created in the image of God. This in real terms means to humanize all those whose humanity have been violated, abused or destroyed by demonic socio-economic structures.

The debate between theologies of enculturation and liberation are clear indications of a crisis in the dominant missionary theological discussion that had controlled African theological reflection and praxis. The underlying assumptions behind this debate, however, do not adequately address the nature of the crisis in African society, which calls for a new paradigm. Precisely because of this neglect, the debate creates the impression that one can or must make a choice between enculturation and liberation as independent or alternative variables in African theological hermeneutics. But this way of viewing theological hermeneutics in Africa theology introduces a dangerous bifurcation between socio-political factors and cultural factors. The choice between liberation and enculturation, even if it were possible, will limit the scope and perimeters of the ability of African theology to contribute solutions to the complex problems of the African society. And to subsume the complexities of the problems in Africa today under some general theory of socio-political analysis or culture will be a very narrow view of the problems of the African society especially the pressing issues in the recent social history.

The truth, however, is that one cannot have enculturation without the liberation of the African soul and personality from the bondage of the 'colonial mentality' that continues to enslave the African mind. In the same way, liberation as a socio-political hermeneutic cannot ignore the layers of acculturation processes that have distorted the African personality and accentuated the spiritual and identity crises of the African society. Enculturation or recovery of authentic traditional culture and liberation must be part of a dialectics of a transformation theology that can address the complex challenges of the African society.

Acculturation or the domination of traditional culture by Western culture has historically been a function of the colonial and missionary axis of Western European Imperialism. This means liberation must also lead to cultural authenticity and creativity that will give us the freedom and courage to deal with those aspects of traditional culture that continue to enslave the African mind and anachronistic practice which continue to prevent the African society from an effective participation and engagement with the modern world.[14] The liberation perspective must be a critical one which while it criticizes those negative aspects of our culture also affirms the live-giving and life-transforming aspects of our culture that can contribute to the transformation of African society. Similarly, the enculturation perspective must critically evaluate the socio-political process today and isolate those aspects of our present socio-political and economic problems that have traditional cultural dimensions. This must include the leadership crisis in Africa that has contributed to some of Africa's socio-political problems today, the one-party dictatorship, military adventurism, civil wars and genocides, the culture of political corruption, etc.

The missionary perspectives in African Christianity today must be a direct consequence of the rehabilitation of Christianity in Africa by deconstructing the colonial and Eurocentric image of Christianity through a process that can define Christianity as a liberating life-giving and life-transforming religion of salvation. This means that mission in Africa must be reconceptualized to

bring out a new liberative evangelism that includes humanization, enculturation, liberation and transformation. This demands that we overcome the old
dichotomy of evangelizer and the evangelized and rather view mission as an
opportunity for the transformation of relationships, by the encounter with the
'Other' through whom we allow God to transform us by sharing and bringing
different insights into the propagation of the good news. This implies among
other things that the expression of evangelism must be the product of culture
itself rather than a reproduction of European cultural perspectives of mission.
The new perspective of mission should be 'God', 'people' and 'transformation'
instead of the old mission order of 'God, power and 'domination'.

Abundant life

Traditionally, mission has been the institutional way of managing the propagation of the Gospel, and evangelism and missiology the various theological
perspectives that governed the mission enterprise. The goal of mission in
the new paradigm should be the same as Christ bringing abundant life in
the midst of poverty, violence, oppression and insecurity. This will make the
command 'to go and make disciples of all nation' an invitation to new life
possibilities in Christ in whom God is reaching out to all human beings. This
invitation means that all people must be able to be the people of God without
passing through the mediation of other people, because all humanity is constituted by the creative love of God.[15] In Jesus Christ we find a union of proclamation
and hope. Jesus Christ addressed the people as they are and provided definite
solutions to their problems. The proclamation of the kingdom of God is a
message of radical hope that sees God as Lord and giver of life and as the one
who makes transformation possible. In the ministry of Jesus he attended to the
most deeply felt needs, suffering and existential raptures like illness discrimination, slavery, fear of demons, legalism and ritualism. This means that mission
must address the radical hope of the people because Jesus Christ was deeply
concerned with existential raptures that tore people into shreds and rend the
social fabric. Jesus Christ healed the sick, attended to the needs of the poor and
public sinners and defended the marginalized and the socially non-existent.
Jesus felt the pains and heard the cries of the people and there was no cry
for help he ignored.[16]

Mission from the perspective of African Christianity means producing
the kind of evangelism capable of delivering the people from the agonies of
their history, produced by structural violence that continue to dehumanize
them and induce pain and suffering. This is possible because Jesus Christ is
the one who liberates us from the human blemishes in which sin is concretized,
by offering us higher form of social personal and divine relationships. The message of Jesus begins concretely with people. This is what makes the message
truly universal because it starts from the very concrete human condition and

needs; Jesus met people where they were in their natural, cultural and existential context. His message of salvation did not have any acculturating mechanism
that alienated people from their culture or demanded that they should be
'non-persons' in order to benefit from the Gospel. In his pedagogy, Jesus established a dialogical relationship with the people on their own terms. He never
employed power as mediation for the propagation of the reign and the message
of God. He relied on persuasion and argumentation based on common sense.
He witnessed to his version of new life by the witness of his life, his devotion
to others, his boldness in denouncing religious falsehood and his fearless
confrontation of his ideological opponents.[17]

The evangelization method of Jesus Christ is therefore a critique of all reproduction of the Gospel based on domination and the use of political and cultural
power. This implies a mission praxis in which the missionary is converted to
the native, and together the native and the missionary are then converted to
Christ. Once conversion is to Christ, the goal of mission is attained because the
conversion becomes a channel of transformation of relationships.[18] The result
will be the emergence of local Christian communities as one of the faces of the
Christian Church of Christ in the power of the Holy Spirit in history.

The Holy Spirit in human history

The Holy Spirit is ever present in human history. This fact helps to save
missionaries from the arrogance that often tempt them to behave as if it was
they, the missionaries, who first introduced the concept of God to the natives.
The Holy Spirit helps us to appreciate the fact that God is always ahead and
present in local cultures preparing the place for the arrival of the missionary as
part of God's universal plan of salvation. The Holy Spirit is ever present in
human history impelling the dynamics of life and growth.[19] This activity of the
Holy Spirit opens the church to new mission frontiers hitherto unknown.

All cultures maintain an implicit reference to the transcendence, and the
Holy Spirit is revealed in the quest for the infinite reason for existence, infinite
desire for community and eternal life which has endured till today as testimony
to the presence of the Holy Spirit in various cultures. The resistance to the
Spirit where new cultural expressions of Christianity appear was the 'sin' of
missionary Christianity because it saw itself as the full realization of the will of
Christ and the fulfilment of the messianic promise. This was the triumphalistic
arrogance of Western Christendom that resulted from its alliance with colonialism. The Holy Spirit refuses to allow the Gospel to remain in '*illo tempore*'
because to reduce the Gospel to once and for all expression is to condemn
our selves to cultural slavery. The Spirit in its own way is raising prophets
from new Christian communities to lead the way to new and challenging expressions of the Gospel. The Spirit is at work in Christian communities, as at the
Pentecost, to make it possible for everyone to hear the Gospel in his or her own
tongue and cultural idioms.[20]

A new image of Christianity

At the centre of African missiology is a new image of Christianity as religion that is capable of equipping people to deal with the challenge of daily life and other numerous mundane concerns. The emphasis on the emerging perspectives of mission in the new movements in African Christianity is an invitation to us to view mission as an ongoing event that gives us space to feel the presence of God in our lives by the power of the Holy Spirit. Here the Holy Spirit is experienced as God's presence with his people in God's mission in Christ. The Holy Spirit is therefore not just a third person of the Holy Trinity that can be tamed and marginalized through categories of theology and ecclesiology. Instead the Holy Spirit is a cosmological reality for life, liturgy, politics, prayers, healing and wholeness.[21] The Holy Spirit is the experience of the creative power of God that gives us healing, liberation and transformation that empowers us to change our relationships, and our cultural and socio-political structures so that we can create a community that is able to support the kind of quality of life promised to believers.

The pneumatological focus of African Christian missiology comes from impulses that are deeply embedded in traditional spirituality which view human existence in terms of the concrete expression of spiritual essence.[22] For most African Christians then the experience of Holy Spirit as healer, comforter and transformers is the most concrete expression of the truth of God's presence with humanity in Christ. The experience of the Holy Spirit becomes a palpable and creditable proof of God's abiding presence with us and his promise to take care of us as father, because through Christ we have become sons and daughters of God. The status as sons and daughters of God in Christ elicits a life of praise, which we joyfully celebrate in worship and service to our neighbours. Worship and service to neighbours then become gratitude for the abiding presence of God with us in the Spirit.[23]

The constant celebration of God's presence in the liturgy transforms us into agents of change in the power of the Spirit, because in the act of worship we are empowered to participate in the creative transformation, taking place in our communities. This message of transformation in inter-personal relationships means sharing with the world the gift of reconciliation and peace-making that enable us to re-build communities even those torn apart by wars and civil strife. The possibilities of transformation of relationships made possible by the gifts of reconciliation and peace-building becomes the most eloquent expression of Christian witness to love in action. This Christian love is one of the few avenues of reconciliation left in our communities which are engulfed by violence, civil wars, ethnic strife and destruction.

For Africans the mission agenda must include the building of communities and the strengthening of social relationships with the hope of creating what Martin Luther King Jr calls the 'beloved community': A community of love and compassion in which everybody will have the opportunity to fulfil their life's aspiration; a community that works constantly to create the conditions that will improve the quality of life of the people. The goal of mission must essentially be about improving the quality of life for people in community in the widest sense: personal, spiritual, cultural, socio-political and economic dimensions of life. At the end of the day the difference that mission should make is about the quality of life of the people.

Conclusion

The pneumatological focus of African missiology firmly locate mission in God's mission to humanity in Christ: the type of mission whose goals are abundant life or the fullness of life that befits human beings created in the image of God. The recovery of the incarnation as the centre of mission allow us to focus on the different ways in which God's gift are given to us in the service of God and our neighbours. Mission in the incarnational mode makes the holistic mission of Jesus Christ the paradigm for mission. This means that mission must deal with all aspects of life including personal relationship with God, relationship with family, community, society and people of other faiths because at the centre of this perspective of mission is the transformation of all relationships that reflects the values of the kingdom of God. This holistic vision of mission can help us overcome the dichotomies and polarities that have bedevilled missiology, especial between personal salvation and social action evangelism and development.

Wholeness of life brings the issue of quality of life and social justice to the agenda of mission. This view of mission focuses attention more on how to mediate the transforming power of the Gospel rather than the management of the process of winning souls, which has historically made missions prone to colonial ideological manipulations. In the heyday of the colonial era, mission was co-opted into the empire-building ideology of colonialism. In the contemporary world, mission is imperceptibly allowing itself to be co-opted into the structures of multilateral organization whose affluence at the local level are creating problems for the witness of the church. Since the missionaries are often seen as just another group of experts or consultants of either a multinational co-operation or multilateral organization because of their lifestyle, they are not significantly differentiated from the other representatives of the North. The perception of the missionary as just another representative of the affluent North in the South comes with all the divisions and symbols that separate the affluent North from the poor South. For this reason the emerging mission perspectives of African Christianity challenges our partner churches to move to a new paradigm of mission in which there are no sending nor receiving churches but rather the common sharing of experience, knowledge, insights and available resources at the service of the transforming mission of God in Christ. This vision of mission will save the mission enterprise from the trappings of globalization labels that divide God's people into the rich North and the poor South, or the developed North and the underdeveloped South. These labels and divisions are new powerful labels that can co-opt mission at the service of financial capital which is becoming the new God of globalization.

Notes

[1] Escobar, Samuel and Driver, John (eds), *Christian Mission and Social Justice* (Scotdale, Pennslyvania: Herald Press, 1978), 18.
[2] Akrong, Abraham, 'The Historic Mission of the African Independent Churches', *Research Review New Series 14*(2) (1998): 58–67.
[3] Ibid.
[4] Akrong, Abraham, 'An Akan Christian view of Salvation from the Perspective of John Calvin's Soteriology', Ph.D. Dissertation (Chicago: L.S.T.C, 1991), 31.
[5] Hiebert, Paul, 'Are We Our Brothers Keepers?', *Currents in Theology and Mission* 22(5) (1995): 331–42.
[6] Ibid.
[7] Boff, Leonardo, *New Evangelism* (New York: Orbis Press, 1990), xii.
[8] Ibid., xi.
[9] Martey Emmanuel, *African Theology: Inculturation or Liberation* (New York: Orbis Press, 1994).
[10] Larbi, E. Kingsley, *Pentecostalism: The Eddies of Ghanaian Christianity* (Accra: Pentecost Press 2000). 100.
[11] Akrong 1998: 59.
[12] Ibid.
[13] Barrett, David, *Schism and Renewal in Africa* (Nairobi: Oxford University Press, 1968), 127.
[14] Cabral, Amilca, *Liberation and African Culture* (Guinea Bissau: Information Services, 1973), 53.
[15] Boff 1990: 73.
[16] Ibid.: 76.
[17] Ibid.: 80.
[18] Bosch, David, *Transforming Missions* (New York: Orbis Press, 1990), 303.
[19] Akrong 1991: 230.
[20] Boff 1990: 86.
[21] Gerloff Roswith, 'The Holy Sprit in the African Diaspora: Spiritual Cultural and Social roots of Black Pentecostals', in A. H. Anderson and W. H. Hollenweger (eds), *Pentecostals after a Century* (Sheffield: Sheffield Academic Press, 1999), 67–86.
[22] Akrong 1991: 171.
[23] Ibid.: 231.

Chapter 6

Baptists in Africa: A Missionary Church in Action
Richard V. Pierard

The intention of this chapter is to identify some aspects of the work of the Protestant denomination known generically as the Baptists, specifically as it occurred in Africa. To be sure, a number of groups use this name, and they are anything but homogeneous. The differences among them reflect the historical and missionary origins of the different groups together with the impact of indigenous conditions and leaders.

Who Are the Baptists?

Scholars are not in agreement as to when the movement began. Some maintain that the spread of the Radical Reformation's Anabaptists, also known as Mennonites, resulted in the founding of the first Baptist congregations in England in the early-seventeenth-century. Others insist that the Baptists were one strain of Puritan independency and they originated in England without significant Mennonite influence. Many Baptists in the past (and some today) go so far as to say that the first Baptist church was founded in Jerusalem by Jesus Christ and that true Baptists existed throughout Christian history, in the form of 'heretical' groups (such as the Donatists, Albigensians and Waldensians) which were in tension with the established Catholic church. To describe the distinctives of the Baptists is not easy, because there are so many differences among them. There are high-church and low-church Baptists, that is, some are quiet, liturgical types while others are emotionally enthusiastic, 'shouting' Baptists. Some have educated and formally ordained clergy, while others use essentially lay preachers. Some allow women to exercise leadership roles and others keep women in a subordinate position.

However, the great majority of Baptists share some common features. The first is a strong emphasis on individual conversion to Christ – one is not born a Christian; he or she becomes one through faith in Christ. This experience of personal salvation or the 'new birth' is an act of grace and is symbolized in baptism and the Lord's Supper. Second is the teaching of believers' baptism.

They believe that the only valid baptism in the eyes of God is that of a mature person declaring one's testimony of conversion as he or she enters the waters of baptism. This must be done by immersion because only in that way can a person properly and publicly declare faith in the risen Christ. It is essentially a reenactment of the death, burial and resurrection of Christ. This practice sets the baptized believers apart from the world and enables them to covenant together in common confession of the name of Jesus.

The third distinctive is congregational church polity. Those who have placed themselves under Jesus Christ will bond together in free local congregations and together they seek to obey Christ in faith and in life. Under his Lordship they democratically determine their membership and leadership, order their worship and work, and carry out personal evangelism and social action. Each congregation is an independent, self-governing community. It does not accept dictation from any authority above the congregation or outside agency. A congregation may join with others in an association or even a convention, and by this means participate in the larger Body of Christ of whose unity and mission they are proudly a part, but this voluntary, cooperative action does not involve the surrender of congregational autonomy. Baptists are a 'free church' people who reject established churches, and avoid hierarchical or connectional churchly structures.

The fourth feature is that they follow the authority of the Holy Scriptures in all matters of faith and practice. Every believer has the right to read and interpret the Scriptures according to his or her own free action, but under the Lordship of Christ. This involves the rejection of formal creeds and outside pressures upon them to interpret the Bible in accordance with what others expect them to do. Baptists commonly label this 'soul liberty' or 'soul competency', that is, every person has the right and responsibility to deal directly with God without the imposition of a creed, the interference of clergy, or the intervention of civil government.

The fifth distinctive is religious freedom. Baptists demand complete independence from the state and reject all forms of state interference in their activities. This liberty must be available to all people, not just themselves. Caesar is not Christ and Christ is not Caesar. Each individual needs to be free to make choices about faith and commitment unfettered by any outside agency, whether it is the state or an ecclesiastical hierarchy supported by the state. Hence they are staunch advocates of the separation of church and state, or more precisely, religion and government.

Many of the characteristics mentioned here mark other Christian groups as well, but the Baptists hold all of these together in a way that is loyal to the traditions of Reformation Christianity, without at the same time becoming sectarian. For the most part, they are aware that they are only one part of the family of Christ's church on earth, and they will seek in different ways to lend support to the totality of the church's work as the witness to the kingdom that Jesus proclaimed.[1]

Obviously, there are often deviations from these principles. Some churches have very authoritarian pastors or leadership groups, usually in the form of deacons. In the southern United States of America after the Civil War, the churches that belonged to the Southern Baptist Convention became a 'de facto' establishment and they tried to impose their religious values on the whole community. Today in the United States there are many Baptists looking to the government for handouts to support their charitable enterprises, and the George W. Bush administration has shrewdly exploited this situation to win their support for its policies.

Baptists as a Missionary People

Johann Gerhard Oncken, who founded of the German Baptist movement in 1834, popularized the phrase 'every Baptist a missionary'. The Baptists trained at his Hamburg seminary were generally skilled craftsmen, and they fanned out through Germany and Central and Eastern Europe living by the labour of their hands and engaging in aggressive evangelism. Often clashes resulted with leaders of the established churches who attempted to stop their missionizing efforts.

In England the Baptists founded a foreign missionary society in 1792, and in the following year sent out its first missionary to India, William Carey. To be sure, they were hardly the first group to engage in organized missionary work. This had gone on since the foundation of the early church in the Mediterranean region, and before long missionaries had carried the Christian message into western and central Asia and even as far as India and China. By the early Middle Ages most of Europe had been evangelized, and later Roman Catholic missionary orders like the Franciscans and Jesuits laboured in the Americas, Africa, India and East Asia. The Baptists were not even the first Protestants to engage in missionary work. During the eighteenth century the Halle Pietists and the Moravians, or Unity of the Brethren, set examples of creative involvement in spreading the Gospel which inspired other Protestants in Britain and North America to engage in missionary work.

The American Baptists launched their own missionary society in 1814 which they named the Triennial or General Convention, and sponsored the work of Adoniram Judson in Burma and many others. When in 1845, the southerners broke with the national society over the issue of slavery and formed a separate denomination, the Southern Baptist Convention (SBC), they also created a mission society of their own. The northern body renamed itself the American Baptist Missionary Union (ABMU), and it carried on an aggressive program of overseas evangelism similar to that of the British Baptist Missionary Society.

This generalization about the Baptist missionary impulse does not hold true in all cases. There were strict Calvinists in both British and US American Baptist circles who opposed foreign missionary work in general. They believed that God would save those whom he had chosen and their human efforts might interfere with the divine work. Others felt that the creation of mission societies was unbiblical; these bodies were usurping the role of the local churches in carrying out the divine command to evangelize the world.

The Beginnings of Baptist Missions in Africa

Individuals in the African Diaspora undertook the first Baptist missionary efforts in Africa. In 1815 William Crane, a white Baptist from New Jersey who had moved to Virginia and opened a night school for young black men, organized the Richmond African Baptist Missionary Society. Among his students were two African American Baptists who had been born in slavery but had purchased their freedom, Colin Teague (c. 1780–1839) and Lott Carey (c. 1780–1828).The group succeeded in raising sufficient funds to enable Teague and Carey to go to Liberia, the settlement for the 'repatriation' of former slaves that the American Colonization Society had recently founded. Carey formed the Providence Baptist Church and soon became first governor of the colony who had African heritage.[2] Teague, who had moved on to Sierra Leone, returned to Liberia after Carey had been killed in an accidental gunpowder explosion, and assumed leadership of the church. His successors promoted both missionary work and the resettlement of American blacks in the colony, but little financial support was received from America. The Lott Carey Baptist Foreign Mission Convention, founded by African Americans in 1897, has perpetuated the tradition that originated here.

The larger Triennial Convention began sending some white missionaries to West Africa, but their health quickly failed and the undertaking remained in the hands of the indigenous converts. After the split over slavery, the northern Baptists soon withdrew completely from Africa and turned over the work there to the Southern Baptist Convention Foreign Mission Board. The SBC soon shifted its attention from Liberia to Nigeria, and began working among the Yoruba in the 1850s. The African effort languished during the Civil War but was revived in 1872. The southerners used both white and black missionaries, the best known of the latter being William W. Colley (1847–1909) who laboured in Liberia under the SBC and then took the lead in forming the Baptist Foreign Mission Convention in 1880, the first national level missionary association of black Baptists in the United States. The northern Baptists' society, now known as the American Baptist Missionary Union, cooperated with the black Baptists by providing some financial support for their missionaries. Meanwhile, the SBC work in Nigeria, centred at Ogbomoso, became its major enterprise in Africa and was its only field there until after World War II.

An important missionary effort of the Diaspora was the one that British Baptists in Jamaica launched. This built upon the initial endeavour of two former North American slaves, George Liele and Moses Baker, who had come to the island in 1783 and founded an indigenous Baptist work. They asked for assistance from the Baptist Missionary Society (BMS) when the planters opposed evangelizing the slave population, and the first workers arrived in 1814. Together with the African American missionaries, the trio of Thomas Burchell (1799–1846), James Philippo (1798–1879), and William Knibb (1803–1845) established churches among the blacks and plunged wholeheartedly into the struggle against slavery. The Baptists contributed significantly to the passage in 1834 of the Emancipation Act abolishing slavery throughout the Empire, and to securing an end a few years later to the apprenticeship system that kept the former slaves in de facto bondage. The BMS also laboured in Trinidad and other West Indian islands.[3]

In 1842 the Jamaican Baptist Association gained independence from the BMS, opened Calabar College to train clergy, and formed the Jamaica Baptist Missionary Society that worked in Africa with the existing BMS mission on the island of Fernando Po and in Cameroon. Founded in 1841 by John Clarke (1802–1879), the mission drew heavily on Jamaicans such as Joseph Merrick (1818–1849) who did important work in Bible translation. Although deeply motivated by missionary zeal and welcomed by whites who wrongly assumed that the 'repatriated' Jamaicans would thrive in the difficult African climate, the mission lacked sufficient support and ended by 1853. However, the main BMS work in Cameroon, led by Joseph Jackson Fuller (1825–1908), born in slavery in Jamaica, and Alfred Saker (1814–1880) from England, was more successful. They translated the Bible and developed a Christian community among the Douala people.[4]

However, after a few years the mission had not prospered as well as the BMS had hoped, and when the Germans established colonial rule over Cameroon in 1884, the BMS decided to leave. They turned the enterprise over to the Protestant Basel Mission, which after a few years decided to invite the German Baptists to assume responsibility. The latter formed a board in 1898 and operated it as their major field. When the Allies in World War I expelled the German missionaries, Carl Bender (1869–1935), an American citizen, was allowed to stay and he preserved the work from complete destruction. German missionaries eventually returned, and with their ethnic counterparts in the North American Baptist Conference, laboured in British West Cameroon. The Paris Evangelical Mission administered the Baptist field in French-ruled Cameroon. By the end of colonial rule in 1961 three separate Baptist denominations had emerged in the country.[5]

Another major effort originating out of the Diaspora was the missions in Africa sponsored by the National Baptist Convention, USA. This was the first black Baptist denomination in the country, and it had been created by several regional African American groups that came together in 1895. It utilized the Baptist Foreign Missionary Convention as its board. The primary activities were in West Africa, mainly Liberia, but a few workers did serve in South Africa and Nyasaland (Malawi).

After World War I, the European imperial powers effectively curtailed the number of black missionaries from all denominations in Africa, both those serving under white boards and those of the North American black churches. The attitude was that an African American presence there upset the status quo and caused unrest among the indigenous people. One example universally cited was that of John Chilembwe, a Yao from Nyasaland, who was converted under the ministry of a radical independent missionary, John Booth. He was taken to the United States in 1897, studied at a National Baptist college in Virginia, and with black Baptist support from America set up his own operation, the Providence Interior Mission in the Shire highlands. A great champion of justice for Africans, he led a revolt against British rule in Nyasaland in 1915 and was killed by colonial forces.[6]

The Congo Missions

In 1877 Robert Arthington (1823–1900), a wealthy English Baptist businessman and possibly the leading missionary philanthropist in the nineteenth century, had the vision of a chain of mission stations across Africa. He gave the BMS Committee funds for a reconnaissance of the Congo basin, and two missionaries who had already served in Cameroon, Thomas Comber (1852–1887) and George Grenfell (1849–1906), were engaged for the effort. The fact that Grenfell, who would soon become the leading personality in their work there, had taken an African wife was an embarrassment to the board back in London. However, news about this was suppressed as much as possible, because he was much too valuable to the cause to be dismissed.

In the early 1880s, they transported a steamer overland to the navigable stretch of the Congo River and established a new mission there. After a few years of intense work, they and others were able to establish a struggling African church. Meanwhile, the American Baptists became involved in the Congo. In 1884, H. Gratton Guiness turned the Livingstone Inland Mission that he had created at the same time the British Baptists had begun their work in another part of the Congo, over to the ABMU. Soon they too had a prospering church.

It was only a matter of time until the missionaries were drawn into the international controversy over the brutal atrocities perpetrated in the Belgian King's Congo Free State, which had been created at the Berlin Conference of 1885. This was a business enterprise passing itself off as a political entity, and from the very beginning in no way benefiting the Africans. The ABMU missionaries, who worked in the Equator District where the greatest atrocities occurred, began in 1893–1894 to send home letters and reports protesting against the abuses and infringements of the Africans' rights. They were alarmed by the policies of terror (including brutal whippings, the cutting off of people's hands, and actual murders) that were used to intimidate the Africans and to force them to work for the rubber companies to which Leopold had granted concessions in the territory.[7] On the other hand, the British missionaries tended to support the Congo State against its critics, as they had established a more congenial relationship with its authorities.[8]

The ABMU missionaries, particularly the Englishman John B. Murphy and the Swede E. V. Sjöblom who both served under the board, kept up the drumbeat of criticism. At first their reports just appeared in the missionary periodicals, but by 1895 the secular press had begun to run statements and interviews from the expatriate Christian workers in the Congo about the atrocities. Sjöblom was particularly forceful in condemning the situation there, while George Grenfell was more defensive. To counter the critics, Leopold appointed a 'Commission for the Protection of the Natives', which was comprised of six missionaries, including three Catholics and the BMS's Grenfell and Holman Bentley. The commission's powers were restricted, none of its members served in the region where the rubber atrocities were mainly occurring, and it essentially accomplished nothing. The Congo State responded to the criticism by trying to control the activities of the missions, and a brief lull in the conflict followed.

In 1902, the journalist E. D. Morel launched his celebrated campaign for Congo reform, and the situation rapidly heated up again as a wave of humanitarian criticism swept across Europe. This finally led to an erosion in the good relations between the Congo State and the British missions. The Council of the Baptist Union, responding to a proposal by the prominent Baptist social activist John Clifford, agreed in April 1903 to join in a united appeal to the British government to take action to enforce the Berlin Act against the abuses of Leopold. Although some BMS missionaries were supplying Morel with information about abuses, Grenfell dragged his feet until the report of the momentous fact-finding tour of Roger Casement, the British consul in Boma, revealed the full extent of the atrocities. He then turned against the Congo State and resigned from the Commission for the Protection of the Natives. Still, the general secretary of the BMS, Alfred H. Baynes, was reluctant to align his agency on the side of Congo Reform, and only after his resignation did the BMS belatedly embrace the cause. The society's General Committee finally on 17 October 1905 called on the British government to intervene.[9]

The American Baptists had meanwhile toned down their criticism, partly because of their contacts with the English, but an American Presbyterian missionary, William M. Morrison, informed his ABMU colleagues about the desperate situation in the region where he worked. This resulted in the unleashing in the United States of a new wave of attacks on Leopold's administration, and public opinion was aroused. The ABMU even called on the US government to intervene.[10] Leopold's attitude toward the mission societies hardened and he tried to neutralize their impact, but a Commission of Enquiry which he had appointed to examine the charges made against the Congo State administration found that they were valid. Its report essentially led to the end of his rule in the Congo, and in 1908 the Belgian state formally annexed the territory. However, thanks largely to reports supplied by the BMS, the British government withheld recognition of the annexation until 1913 in order to keep pressure on the Belgians to end the continuing system of forced labour and heavy taxation.[11]

In the twentieth century the Belgian Congo was a major mission field for the BMS and the ABMU's successor, the American Baptist Foreign Mission Society, and would continue to be so after independence. At the same time, other Baptist societies from the United States initiated ministries there as well.

The Americanization of the African Missions

This is a huge topic in itself. Following World War I, the centre of gravity in the Western (or northern) Protestant missionary outreach shifted from Great Britain to the United States, and after World War II the American involvement and influence was overwhelming.[12] A concomitant feature of this development was the rapid growth of faith missions, which, in contrast to the denominational mission boards, required their personnel to raise their own financial support. This resulted in a new kind of missionary, one who was skilled in fund-raising at home and could make impassioned appeals for money. On the field, such people tended to be more simplistic than the traditional missionaries in their approach to proclaiming the Gospel. Many of them were less educated and informed about the culture of the peoples among whom they worked, and accordingly they were condescending toward the indigenous Christians, thus perpetuating a practice that has haunted Western missions from the very beginning.

Another development was an explosion of missionary work by the Southern Baptists, while the work of the Northern American Baptists suffered a precipitous decline. The missions of the SBC were well-funded and quickly developed an extensive infrastructure. They were much less ecumenical in their outlook and more inwardly institutional in character. The Southern Baptist mission churches formed 'conventions', as opposed to the 'unions' that characterized the linkages of British and other American Baptist mission churches, and they operated in their own narrow world of cooperative work.

The fundamentalist takeover of the SBC leadership in the 1980s/early 1990s had a dramatic impact on its Foreign (now International) Mission Board. One was a dramatic shift of emphasis in evangelism and church planting to the missionaries themselves rather than equipping indigenous Christians to carry out these tasks. Second was forcing all missionaries to sign the Baptist Faith and Message confession, including the controversial sections added in 1998 and 2000 which required wives to submit to their husbands and restricted the ordained clergy to men. Women could no longer perform pastoral ministry in Southern Baptist churches, and they were systematically squeezed out of teaching posts at the theological seminaries. All missionaries serving under the International Mission Board were required to sign the statement. In 2003 those who refused to sign or would do so only with reservations were dismissed from their service.

When the fundamentalists leading the SBC were unable to gain control of the Baptist World Alliance, the international organization that links over 200 Baptist unions and conventions around the world, they formally withdrew their membership from it. Their announced future plans were to use their missions to create a new and separate global network of Baptist churches, but the effort so far has been unsuccessful. The Southern Baptists had engaged in a similar tactic with the International Baptist Theological Seminary in Zürich, Switzerland. When they could no longer control that agency which their mission board had founded in 1948, they cut off all of their funding to it. The European Baptist Federation responded by assuming ownership of it, moving it to Prague, Czech Republic, and operating it as a European institution completely without formal SBC support.

Conclusion

Baptist groups have been major players in the rich and fascinating story of African Christianity and the African Christian Diaspora. They contributed significantly to the spread of the faith in Africa which is well on the way to becoming, numerically speaking, the most Christian of all the continents in the world, and also in the Caribbean. It is an experience of sharing and cooperation, both between indigenous Africans and those in the Diaspora, and between Westerners and Africans. It manifests itself modern mission, especially of Baptists migrating from the Congo to the continent of Europe, and of descendants of Native Baptists to Britain. It is this kind of cooperation and interaction that has made Christianity truly a global faith.

Notes

[1] 'Toward a Baptist Identity: A Statement Ratified by the Baptist Heritage Commission [of the Baptist World Alliance] in Zagreb, Yugoslavia July, 1989', in Brackney, William H. and Ruby J. Burke (eds), *Faith, Life, and Witness* (Birmingham, AL:

Samford University Press, 1990), 146–49; Shurden, Walter B. *The Baptist Identity: Four Fragile Freedoms* (Macon, GA: Smyth & Helwys, 1993).

2 See Fitts, Leroy, *Lott Carey: First Black Missionary in Africa* (Valley Forge, PA: Judson Press, 1978); Idem, *The Lott Carey Legacy of African American Missions* (Baltimore, MD: Gateway Press, 1994).

3 Stanley, Brian, *The History of the Baptist Missionary Society 1792–1992* (Edinburgh: T. & T. Clark, 1992), 68–105.

4 Ibid.: 106–114; Russell, Horace O. *The Missionary Outreach of the West Indian Church: Jamaican Baptist Missions to West Africa in the Nineteenth Century* (New York: Peter Lang, 2000).

5 Kwast, Lloyd E. *The Discipling of West Cameroon: A Study of Baptist Growth* (Grand Rapids: Wm. B. Eerdmans, 1971); Weber, Charles W. *International Influences and Baptist Mission in West Cameroon: German-American Missionary Endeavor under International Mandate and British Colonialism* (Leiden: E. J. Brill, 1993).

6 Shepperson, George and Thomas Price, *Independent African: John Chilembwe and the Origins, Setting and Significance of the Nyasaland Native Rising of 1915* (Edinburgh: Edinburgh University Press, 1958).

7 Torbet, Robert G. *Venture of Faith: The Story of the American Baptist Foreign Mission Society and the Woman's American Baptist Foreign Mission Society 1814–1945* (Philadelphia: Judson Press, 1955), 325–36.

8 Slade, Ruth M. *English-Speaking Missions in the Congo Independent State 1878–1908* (Brussels: Académie Royale des Sciences Coloniales, 1959) focuses more heavily on the British Baptist Mission; while Lagergren, David, *Mission and State in the Congo: A Study of the Relations between Protestant Missions and the Congo Independent State Authorities with Special Reference to the Equator District, 1885–1903* (Lund: Glerup, 1970) looks mainly at the American mission and its Swedish-born worker E. V. Sjöblom.

9 Stanley 1992: 137–38; Lagergren 1970: 307, 320–29.

10 Lagergren 1970: 311–12; Torbet 1955: 326.

11 Stanley 1992: 138–39.

12 Pierard, Richard V. 'The Pax Americana and the Protestant missionary movement', in Joel A. Carpenter, and Shenk R. Wilbert (eds), *Earthen Vessels: American Evangelicals and Foreign Missions, 1880–1980* (Grand Rapids: Wm. B. Eerdmans, 1990), 155–79.

Chapter 7

The Empire Fights Back – The Invention of African Anglicanism

Kevin Ward

African Anglicanism – a Contradiction in Terms?

We do not choose our names. Some of us are proud of our names. Others feel resentful and wish our parents had given the matter a bit more consideration. Christian churches are sometimes named after great theological themes: Catholic, Evangelical, Pentecostal, Aladura. Some remember important founders: Luther, Kimbangu, the Bamalaki of Uganda. Some point to important organizational principles: Reformed, Methodist, Congregational. The Anglican Communion seems peculiarly unfortunate in being saddled with a particular place. Anglicanism is, after all, simply another word for 'English'. How can a communion be truly worldwide with such a parochial name? How can it be truly 'local' in Ghana or Uganda, Barbados or Brazil? Some churches have solved this conundrum by abandoning the term 'Anglican' altogether in their title. And so, on the model of the 'Church of England', we have the 'Church of the Province of Southern Africa' or simply the 'Church of Uganda'. In colonial days Ugandan Anglicans belonged to the 'Native Anglican Church' – a strange contradiction this: 'native' and 'English'? The Anglican Church in Sudan calls itself the Episcopal Church: but the use of this term may seem just as problematic as Anglican. On the other hand, the Church of the Province of Kenya has recently decided officially to return to the use of the Anglican term: it is now the Anglican Church of Kenya.

People learn to live with their names, to triumph over them. It is generally better to be open about our past than to try to hide it. Anglican Christians in Africa cannot realistically hide the fact that their history is intimately bound up with a colonial history. Anglicanism was and remains strong wherever British rule was exercised. It was and remains weak in parts of Africa which were not at some time British. *'Anglicane? Qu'est que c'est. Vous êtes chrétiens? C'est une secte, ou quoi?'* asks a local in Lubumbashi when asked the way to the Anglican

Church.[1] The surprising thing may be that there is an *église anglicane* in the Congo Democratic Republic or Rwanda or Madagascar.

The British Empire has more Muslim subjects than the Ottoman and Persian empires combined, boasted one Anglican missionary in Cairo in 1909. 'Who would doubt the issue of this glorious conflict?' he concluded, confident that Islam would wither away under the combined onslaught of Christian mission and colonial rule.[2] But he himself was to live to see the disadvantages of British colonial rule in Palestine when he became Bishop in Jerusalem, with a largely Arab membership. Few missionaries could be sanguine about the connection between Anglicanism and colonialism in Africa in the era of the independence struggle of the 1950s. Yet, there can be little doubt that belonging to the 'dini ya Queeni' (the religion of Queen Victoria and her successors) did have a certain prestige throughout the colonial period. Anglicanism easily fitted into an 'establishment' mentality. If Christianity and 'power' (political/ educational/cultural) went together, then Anglicanism was a form of Christianity which had lots going for it.

In Britain the Anglican Church was and remains the established Church within England. It ceased to be the established church in Ireland in 1867 and in Wales in 1922. It has never been the established church in Scotland. It has never been an established church in Africa. The fact that the Britain had a second establishment (the Presbyterian Church in Scotland), and that in Ireland it increasingly had to take into account a Catholic majority meant that the established Church of England was from the start definitely not for export. Colonial establishments in Canada and the Caribbean, legacies of the eighteenth century, were dismantled. Britain took seriously the agreements of the Congress of Berlin about freedom of religion in the colonies. Although there were complaints about undue favouritism towards Anglicans, the British were careful to maintain neutrality. They were particularly sensitive to aggressive evangelism in predominantly Muslim areas; and (as Adrian Hastings has said) were particularly careful not to offend Catholic missions.[3] Nevertheless, Anglicans were perceived to be the official church in the colonies. In 1914 Yoswa Kate denounced the cathedral at Namirembe in Kampala as a ssabo (traditional shrine) of the English traditional religion.[4] The cathedrals of Nairobi and Salisbury were even more closely identified with the colonial administrations. But, in these areas there was a further complication: the presence of a substantial settler community meant that Anglicanism was perceived not only as the church of the government, but as the church of the settlers. In fact in Kenya and Southern Rhodesia there were, in reality, two Anglican churches (the settler and the native), united only at the very top, in the person of the (white) bishop. It was an apartheid situation. In Kenya the 'native' church was ten or more times bigger than the settler church, but the representation on the diocesan synod was thoroughly stratified racially: there were equal numbers of delegates from the settler and African communities (and often white mission-aries were appointed to represent them in any case). Two issues for the forging of an African Anglicanism emerge from this:

1. The need to 'speak for ourselves' through proper representation on decision making bodies. Anglicans may have a good record in training a local African clergy, but they were much slower in devolving real power to Africans. They led the way in the appointment of Bishop Samuel Ajayi Crowther as Bishop in 1862. But from his death in 1891 to the 1950s, no African diocesan bishop was appointed in any African country.
2. The need to create an appropriate, indigenous African Anglicanism. This could not be created by the missionaries, though they could either hinder or encourage the process. It was the achievement of African themselves.

In the Caribbean, the Anglican Church in the eighteenth century had been almost exclusively a settler church. Missionary efforts had been feeble, and obstructed by settlers who feared a Christianized slave population. Only in the era of emancipation was there a panic change of mind: Christianity was then seen as useful for creating a docile work force. But it was too late for Anglicans to participate really convincingly in the great evangelistic work undertaken by African Caribbeans themselves. Anglicans had failed to plant, and Baptists and Methodists reaped a harvest which they themselves had sewn. Nevertheless, an African Anglican church did emerge throughout the Caribbean.[5] By the mid-nineteenth century it was a church struggling to find a black voice. The case of Robert Gordon is instructive.[6] A son of black Creole parents, he was brought up a Methodist, but at 17 became a catechist in the Church of England in Kingston, Jamaica. He sought ordination in the 1850s. The bishop did not refuse, but suggested that he should train as 'a missionary to Africa'. Gordon was suspicious that this implied that there was no place for a black priest in Jamaica. He found his way to England and then sent as a missionary to the Huron in Canada, working among ex-slave refugees from the USA. He was ordained deacon.

Returning to Jamaica, a new bishop again told him to go to Africa, refused to ordain him as a priest but did offer him a job as a teacher. This he refused. He returned to England, where in 1872 he wrote a tract 'The Church in Jamaica – why it has failed'. Surprisingly he persisted in claiming an Anglican identity. He justified this because, he said, 'the contempt for blackness' in Jamaican society would persist 'as long as institutions of undeniable power such as the Anglican church continued to be white in structures of authority and command'. So by the end of the nineteenth century, the ordination of black clergy for work in the West Indies became common. A particularly interesting example is Alexander McGuire from Antigua. He worked for many years as an Episcopa-lian priest in New England before serving in his native Antigua. In the early

1920s, he joined Marcus Garvey's Universal Negro Improvement Association. He possibly hoped that the Anglican Church might become the church of choice for this movement, but in this he was disillusioned, and went on to establish his own 'African Orthodox Church', of which he became the first Bishop.[7] Bishop Alexander was to have an impact in South Africa and in East Africa. In Uganda, it was reading about this church in Garvey's newspaper 'The Negro World' that led to the protest of Reuben Mukasa Spartas. At the end of the service in the Native Anglican Church in Bombo, he announced that he was forming a new church for all 'right-thinking Africans', 'all who are proud to be African and do not want to be houseboys in their own homes'.[8]

West Africa

In contrast, in West Africa, Anglicanism was, from the beginning, closely associated not with the plantocracy and slave owning, but with emancipation and dignity. Wilberforce was an Anglican. Anglicans were centrally involved in the creation of Sierra Leone as 'a province of freedom'. Fourah Bay College in Freetown became the nursery for a vibrant, intellectual movement, in which English culture and civilization and English Christianity were seen, not as alien and oppressive. It was not something to be denied Africans on racial grounds. It was to be embraced and employed for the regeneration of Africa. It produced a generation of African Christians, perfectly at ease with the Anglican Church: the church of Bishop Samuel Crowther, of Bishop James 'Holy' Johnson, of Herbert Macaulay. It played a part in the formation of Pan-Africanism. One of the intellectual pioneers was the black American Episcopalian priest, Alexander Crummell.[9]

In Nigeria, Anglicanism, as John Peel has shown, was a powerful force, a catalyst, in the creation of a renewed Yoruba national identity, as the Rev. Samuel Johnson's great work of cultural retrieval, 'History of the Yoruba', shows.[10] The very survival of this key work is a miracle: sent to England for publication in 1897. But a CMS advisor felt that the 647 pages manuscript was 'prolix' and 'the subject matter so very unimportant both from a secular and a religious point of view that I have no what to recommend'. The society then 'lost' the manuscript. In 1901 Johnson died and his brother, Dr Johnson, reconstructed the work from the notes and drafts. Completed in 1914, it was again sent to England – but this time the ship was captured by the Germans, and ended up in America, where it languished until, in 1921, it finally was published.[11]

The increasing racism within British colonial and missionary thinking by the end of the beginning of the twentieth century meant that West African Christians had to struggle to assert their dual identity as English/Anglican Christians and Yoruba or Igbo or Sierra Leonians. The elites did succeed. They created a confident Nigerian Anglican culture, expressed, for example, in the Ransome Kuti family, connected to David Olubi, the first locally born Yoruba priest: the educationalist I. Ransome Kuti, Funmilayo Ransome-Kuti (1900–1978), his wife, a women's campaigner, their son the popular singer Fela Kuti (with his hedonistic life style and scores of wives not perhaps a good Anglican), and the Nobel prize winner Chinua Achebe.[12] But if a family like this shows the importance of the Anglican Church, the fact that it is so often seen as a church of the educated, the powerful, the elites, is a drawback.

In Liberia, William Wade Harris served for many years as an Episcopal Church teacher among his own Grebo people. In Liberia tensions between an African American elite and the native people led Harris to raise the British flag as a protest! Then he embarked on that remarkable evangelistic campaign across Liberia, Cote d'Ivoire as far as Ghana, preaching in English, but offering a less exclusive, alienating form of Christianity for all, which resulted in an independent church.[13] In Nigeria, the Anglican Church was much more successful than in Sierra Leone or Liberia by appealing to a wide spectrum of society. Aladura churches often began as prayer groups within the Anglican Church. They were not able to stay under the Anglican roof, however, the evangelistic zeal of Nigerian Anglicanism has, nevertheless, made it the strongest single church in Nigeria – its 17 million members challenging the Church of England as the largest church of the Anglican communion.[14]

Southern Africa

Unlike West Africa, Anglicanism in Southern Africa has been dominated by its considerable white constituency. Even in the black church, it has been the white missionaries from England who have tended to dominate the scene. Yet, the Church of the Province of Southern Africa has a strong record of witnesses against apartheid: Trevor Huddleston, Michael Scott, Bishop Ambrose Reeves, Hannah Stanton, etc. Those who have gained international fame for their protests in the 1950s and 60s have tended to be English missionaries, the exception being Alan Paton, a white South African, and Steve Biko, a Xhosa. Apart from Biko, only recently have the lives of African Anglican political activists been 'remembered' and recorded: for example, Nancy Goedhal's work on James Calata, an Anglican priest and ANC chairman in the Ciskei.[15]

Attention has also begun to focus on the evangelistic and pastoral work of African bible women by Debbie Gaitskill. Biko is an important figure, especially for his emphasis on the need for black South Africans to struggle to assert their own identity. Work has been undertaken on the indigenous spiritual movement among Zulu Anglicans, pioneered by Philip Mbatha and (Bishop) Alphaeus Zulu: the 'Iviyo lofakazi bakaKristu', the Legion of Christ's Witnesses.[16] In Zimbabwe the Vigil movement of communal night prayer, worship and

Eucharist, grew out of the Chimurenga (liberation movement) among Anglican and other Protestant churches.[17] From the 1980s, on the political scene, Bishop Desmond Tutu, the first black bishop of Cape Town (elected 1976) did become internationally recognized. His work was important, not only for the fight against apartheid, but for repositioning the Anglican Church in South Africa at the forefront of prophetic witness by African church leaders.[18]

But I want to draw attention briefly to an earlier period, in the former German colony of South West Africa (Namibia). Compared to the Lutheran churches of Namibia, Anglicans are a small community there. In front of the parliament building in Windhoek is an impressive statue of a priest, standing with other heroes of the independence struggle. He is Fr Theophilus Hamutumpangela, an Ovambo Anglican priest from Ovamboland, in the north of Namibia. At mass in his parish of Christ the King in 1954, he preached a seminal sermon against the intimidation, violence and daylight robbery perpetrated by the South African security forces on Ovambo migrant labourers returning home from their contrasts in the mines of the Rand in South Africa. He invited people to stay behind to voice their grievances, and then smuggled a letter through Angola, addressed to the United Nations. The UN took up the case. Other letters followed in which the awfulness of the migrant labour contract system was exposed. The authorities were infuriated. They banned Hamutumpangela from his homeland and exiled him to Windhoek. Here he was an important figure, with Sam Njoma, in the formation of the SWAPO (the South West African Peoples' Organization), which was to mount the armed struggle against South African occupation of Namibia, and to lead to independence in 1990. Herman Toivo ya Toivo, educated at St Mary's Anglican school in Odibo, is another important Anglican figure from the freedom struggle.[19]

East Africa

West African Anglicanism can be characterized as the free embrace of a Christian civilization shaped by 'English' values'. South African Anglicanism has been characterized by a tortuous black African struggle for political and cultural integrity. In East Africa a distinctively African Anglicanism emerged much earlier. Much of this was due to the remarkable case of Buganda. There Anglicanism emerged from the 1890s as the unofficial established church, the church of the Kabaka and the traditional elites (as opposed to the new elites of say the Yoruba). The process of cultural reappropriation and recreation evidenced by the works of Sir Apollo Kaggwa and Hamu Mukasa invite comparisons with the role of Anglicans among the Yoruba. But here the writing was in Luganda, not English. There was a strong sense of the incorporation of Anglican Christianity into an existing culture, transforming and re-envisioning it, but not making something new. Here Anglicanism became, not the religion of the Queen of England, but the religion of the Kabaka, and of the other Ugandan rulers. Such an appropriation was not without problems, but it did produce a very strong, vibrant, self-confident and distinctively Ugandan form of Anglican Christianity.[20]

The other vastly important phenomenon in East Africa has been the Balokole movement, the East African Revival. This began as an assertion of a distinctively African form of Evangelical revivalism promoted by Baganda Christians in Rwanda. It profoundly influenced the Anglican Church in Uganda, Rwanda, Burundi, Congo and Sudan. It penetrated deeply into the Lutheran church in Bukoba (which was already strongly conscious of an early Anglican influence on its own history in then 1890s).[21] It permeated the life of the Anglican, Presbyterian and Methodist churches of Kenya. Unlike the Aladura churches of Nigeria, this movement of the spirit remained strongly attached to an Anglican identity, even when radically critical of the nominalism and dead 'orthodoxy' which they found in the church. The Balokole movement was the first group in East Africa to embody in practical terms the equality between black and white which was so difficult to realize in colonial society. In that sense it strongly undermined the intellectual and political premise of racial inequality on which colonialism was based.[22]

Anglicanism in East Africa has also been characterized by a flexibility and responsiveness of African cultural sensibilities. In the 1929 female circumcision crisis, Anglicans lost far fewer members than those Protestant churches which embarked on a vigorous campaign against female circumcision. The question of female genital mutilation remains a deeply sensitive and difficult issue. In 1929 the decision to focus on this issue was widely seen by the majority of Kikuyu Christians as part of a wider cultural aggression which would undermine Kikuyu identity.[23]

In Zaire in the 1970s, Mobutu's attempts to regulate and control the many independent churches, caused many groups to seek communal membership of the Anglican church as providing a congenial home for their practice of Christianity.[24] But one has to say, that it has been this willingness to adapt even more to local sensibilities which has been one of the strong criticisms of the new pentecostal movement which is at the moment a powerful force throughout Africa and not least in east Africa.

Gay Issues

Pentecostalism is a challenge to Anglicans in all parts of Africa. It is also being absorbed into the Anglican church. Pentecostalism is a youth movement, and wherever the Anglican church takes seriously its youth work, it is open to charismatic forms of Christianity, beginning in the late 1960s in secondary school Christian and Scripture Unions, especially in West and East Africa.

This is one reason for the present crisis in worldwide Anglicanism over gay issues. People have spoken of the stance of the Archbishop of Nigeria, Peter Akinola, and of the Ugandan bishops, as a refusal to let the West set the agenda; the assertion of a more conservative, biblically based evangelical Anglicanism of the south over the liberal, secular North. There is some truth in this. But it is, of course, much more complicated. It can also be seen as an example of neo-colonialism – the utilization of African Anglican leaders by anti-gay conservative groups within the churches of North America, Australia and Britain, to form an anti-liberal coalition. It ignores the tremendous complexity of the issues of sexual morality (polygamy, experimental marriages, promiscuity, exploitation of women etc.) which the African churches have always wrestled with, but without being able to impose a single 'Christian', never mind 'African' ethic. I suspect that the criticisms of the compromises of Anglican Christianity in these areas by the pentecostal movement is one important reason for the difficulty of East and West African Anglican leaders to accord the same flexibility and pastoral sensitivity to gay issues which they recognize in other forms of human sexual relationships. In contrast South African Anglican leaders see gay issues as part and parcel of the struggle to overcome structures of apartheid and oppression, and have responded very differently.[25]

Conclusion

African Anglicanism was never formally part of a church establishment. But it tended to prosper in areas where it had a strong sense of alliance with government – in colonial times, primarily the British authorities. It helped in the transformation of elite structures and to create new social forms of establishment. But in so doing it also became strongly rooted among the rural peasantry in those areas where it was strong and vibrant. Anglicanism also developed forms of critique of government which it continued into the era of independence. Archbishop Tutu in South Africa and Bishop Henry Okullu in Kenya, both in their own ways mounted effective forms of opposition to political authoritarianism. In Uganda, Archbishop Janani Luwum's involvement in opposing Amin led to his death as a martyr. In the academy, the establishment of African theology as an effective discipline was pioneered by Anglicans such as Harry Sawyer in West Africa and John Mbiti in East Africa.

If Anglicans traditionally have felt naturally more comfortable in situations where they have influence, they have also expanded beyond those spheres: into Mozambique and Angola, and into the Congo Democratic Republic. In the CDR and also, dramatically, in Sudan, recent years have seen a remarkable flourishing of Anglican Christianity, in times of civil war and the collapse of central government. Here new forms of Christianity, little influenced by a European missionary inheritance, and arising from a sense of local or regional identity, have found congenial expression in the Anglican/Episcopal Church. African Anglicanism is characterized by a strong evangelistic impulse, not least in areas such as Northern Nigeria and Sudan, where it competes with African Islam. Its greatest successes also continue to be in rural areas. In the towns it faces strong competition from pentecostal churches. Some older leaders bemoan the loss of Anglican urban youth to these churches. But Anglicanism has also adapted, with its own forms of charismatic worship and appeal, to a youth culture. In this sense, Anglicanism is part of the general pentecostalization of African Christianity over the last two decades.

African Anglicans now constitute more than half the membership of the worldwide Anglican Communion. Nigeria has over 17 million members. The Anglican Church of Uganda claims about 40 per cent of the population – a higher percentage than England![26] For long this numerical strength was hardly reflected in the structures or thought of the Anglican Communion, which remained dominated by the theological and ethical concerns of Northern Anglicans. Some have seen the present crisis in the Anglican Communion over homosexuality as a 'revenge' of the African Church, whose voice was for too long discounted – the empire striking back in religious terms at the secularism and atrophied faith of the West. But, the present crisis can also be seen as part of an American culture war 'by proxy', in which conservative Episcopalians, long disillusioned with the development of their church have finally found in the Anglican church of Africa and elsewhere, allies for their struggle.[27] What is certain is that the debate on homosexuality is not one which has arisen from within Africa itself, though it does draw attention to an issue which African Christians cannot evade, as modern forms of gay identity become part of an African social scene. Marriages, family life, sexuality, have long been part of the contested landscape of African (and Anglican) Christianity, and the issue of homosexuality can be seen as one aspect of that debate. The worldwide Anglican crisis has served to stifle that debate within Africa, rather than to illuminate it. But there are long-held values of tolerance and moderation within African Anglicanism which potentially will be of great value for African Christians generally as they evaluate this new aspect of sexual being and conduct.

Notes

1   Naish, Tim, 'Anglicans?', in: Wingate, Ward, Pemberton and Sitshebo, *Anglicanism A Global Communion* (London: Mowbray, 1998), 161–65.
2   Quoted in Shehata, Samy, 'An Evaluation of the Mission of the Episcopal Church in Egypt from 1918-1925', MA dissertation, University of Birmingham, n.d. [probably late 1990s], 12.
3   Hastings, Adrian, 'The clash of Nationalism and Universalism within Twentieth-Century Missionary Christianity', in: Brian Stanley (ed.), *Missions, Nationalism, and the End of Empire* (Grand Rapids: Eerdmans, 2003), 15–33.

4 Welbourn, Fred, *East African Rebels* (London: SCM, 1961).

5 Dayfoot, A. C., *The Shaping of the West Indian Church 1492–1962* (Kingston: University of the West Indies, 1999).

6 For details of Gordon's life and work, cf. Stewart, Robert, *Religion and Society in Post-Emancipation Jamaica* (Knoxville: University of Tennessee, 1992).

7 Burkett, Randall K., *Garveyism as a Religious Movement* (Metuchen: Scarecrow, 1979), 71–74.

8 Welbourn 1961: 77–112.

9 Dunn, D. Elwood, *A History of the Episcopal Church in Liberia 1821-1898* (Metuchen: Scarecrow, 1992).

10 Johnson, Samuel, *The History of the Yorubas* (London: Routledge, 1921 [reprinted 1966]).

11 Peel, J. P. D. *Religious Encounter and the Making of the Yoruba* (Bloomington: Indiana University Press, 2000).

12 For the Ransome-Kuti family see Johnson-Odim, Cheryl, and Mba, Nina, *For Women and the Nation: Funmilayo Ransome-Kuti of Nigeria* (Chicago: University of Illinois, 1997).

13 Shank, David, *Prophet Harris* (Leiden: Brill, 1994); Haliburton, G. M., *The Prophet Harris* (London: Longman, 1971).

14 Adogame, Afe, and Omoyajowo, Akin, 'Anglicanism and the Aladura Churches in Nigeria', in: Wingate, Ward, Pemberton and Sitshebo, *Anglicanism: A Global Communion* (London: Mowbray, 1998), 90–97.

15 Goedhals, Nancy, 'African Nationalism and Indigenous Christianity: A Study in the Life of James Calata (1895–1983)', *Journal of Religion in Africa*, 31 (1), 2003: 63–82.

16 Shorten, Richard, *The Legion of Christ's Witnesse* (Cape Town: University of Cape Town, 1987).

17 Presler, Titus, *Transfigured Night: Mission and Culture in Zimbabwe's Vigil Movemen* (Pretoria: UNISA, 2000).

18 Du Boulay, Shirly, *Desmond Tutu* (Grand Rapids: Eerdmans, 1988); Pieterse, Hendrick (ed.), *Desmond Tutu's Message* (Leiden: Brill, 2001).

19 Grotpeter, J. J., *Historical Dictionary of Namibia* (Metuchen: Scarecrow, 1994), 191.

20 Kiwanuka, S. M., *A History of Buganda* (London: Longmans, 1971); Taylor, John V., *The Growth of the Church in Buganda* (London: SCM, 1958).

21 Sundkler, Bengt, Bara Bukoba, *Church and Community in Tanzania* (London: C. Hurst, 1980).

22 Ward, Kevin, 'Tukutenereza Yesu' in: Nthamburi, N., *From Mission to Church* (Nairobi: Uzima, 1991), 113–44; St John, P., *Breath of Life* (London: Norfolk Press, 1971); Kibira, Josiah, *Church, Clan and World* (Uppsala: Gleerup, 1974).

23 Murray, Jocelyn, 'The Kikuyu Female Circumcision Controversy', PhD dissertation, University of California, 1971; Ward, Kevin, 'The Development of Kenyan Protestantism', PhD dissertation, University of Cambridge, 1976.

24 Important recent work on Anglicanism in the Congo Democratic Republic includes the PhD dissertations of Ande, Georges Titre, 'Authority in the Anglican Church of Congo', PhD dissertation, University of Birmingham, 2003; and Wild-Wood, Emma, 'Migration and Identity: the Development of an Anglican

Church in North-east Congo (DRC), 1960-2000', PhD dissertation, University of Edinburgh, 2004.

[25] Ward, Kevin, 'Same-Sex Relations in Africa and the Debate on Homosexuality in East African Anglicanism', *Anglican Theological Review, Illinois, 84.1* (Winter 2002): 81–112.

[26] For worldwide Anglican statistics, cf. *The Church of England Yearbook 2004* (London: Church House, 2004), 334–87.

[27] I am grateful to a Ugandan Anglican friend working in the States, Rev. Benjamin Twinamaani, for alerting me to some of these issues. However, the interpretation I give here is mine.

Chapter 8

Imperial War-Zones and Frontiers of Conversion

Andreas Heuser

Africa until recently was laying before us as an unfathomable,
unsubstantial, black clod of earth.

Walter Beck 1938[1]

I am walking and I am tired, walking and tired,
I am going to that land of perfection.

Isaiah Shembe 1932[2]

Imperial Topography and Conversion

The period between 1880 and 1920 indulged in almost unparalleled cartographic energy to visualize the historic transformations of the colonial era in
Africa. The colonial expansion initiated a virtual boom in the production of
new maps to demonstrate the authority to construct and project territories. Two
events reveal the cartographic narrative of the time span under review. The
1884/1885 Berlin–Congo Conference set the guidelines for the colonial revision of spatial imagination. Its cartographic acts defined, divided and distributed
African terrain to establish a political, social and cultural hegemony. A generation later, the first World Missionary Conference in Edinburgh 1910 ventured
the same gesture of strategic power by drawing maps on a global scope. The
congress was infused by a pathetic formula to christianize the world within one
generation. In order to enable such an eruptive change in religious demography, the Conference constructed a rather simple taxonomy that distinguished
between 'missionized' and 'not yet missionized' spheres.

Both the Berlin and Edinburgh conferences display a spatial paradigm
that reduced the social, geographical or historical complexity of African
societies. The metropolitan topography established clear-cut definitions, it
separated inside and outside and animated the lust of covetous 'imperial eyes'

(M. L. Pratt) to conquer, classify and ultimately to contain the plural, diverse environments of the peripheral 'Other'. While the secular rhetoric of alterity localized the Otherness as an absolute difference, religious vocabulary interpreted its incorporation into history as an act of salvation. Seeking to tame the 'Dark Continent' with its raw religious materials, the occidental monopoly of meaning turned the religious landscape into a battlefield. It legitimized the invasion of that 'unfathomable, unsubstantial, black clod of earth' with the blessings of a superior Christian civilization.

In the portrayal of the 'Self' and the 'Other', cultural and social identities appear to be homogeneous. In order to stabilize European identities, internal breaks and diversities in the image of the undisciplined and uncivilized 'Other' are fading away. Entangled in the spirit of imperial mapping, the evangelizing predictions at the World Missionary Conference in Edinburgh ignored that the African continent experienced a tremendous demographic change. In the period between the Berlin and Edinburgh conferences mass conversions to Christianity took place. Such eruptions were left almost unnoticed at the Edinburgh meeting. The report of the conference refrained from a detailed description of this striking religious transformation.[3]

The explanatory failure of the World Missionary Conference echoes a revealing lacuna in African comparative religion. For Hastings the phenomenon of social conversion to Christianity in the period roughly between 1880 and 1920 as a whole 'remains one of the most decisive, unexpected and still inadequately understood chapters within the Christian history of Africa'.[4] Keeping this warning in mind, the following approach focuses on the subject of conversion in Southern Africa or, more precisely, in Natal. On global terms, Natal happened to be the region with the densest net of missionary presence at the time. Nonetheless, the Christian population remained marginal for decades. Significantly, 'conversions spread rapidly after 1890, so that by 1910', Etherington estimates, 'the conversion of the entire black population to some form of Christianity appeared to be only a matter of time'.[5] Etherington thus narrows down the core period of conversion in Southern Africa. The argument presented here is that the phenomenon of social conversion during this period relates mainly to the South African War, 1899–1902, and its aftermath. The AICs surfaced as cardinal actors in the processes of religious change which, as pointed out by Hastings, were 'often hardly, if at all, distinguishable from a primary movement of mass conversion'.[6]

Frontiers of War Transformed into a 'Land of Prophets'

Currently, advocates of the so-called 'spatial turn' in historiography revision the connections between space, the 'Other', and power. They perceive the border as the privileged place to localize social innovations and to measure impulses of cultural dynamics. Hence, Karl Schlögel defines historiography properly as a science of the border. In a play of German keywords, he designs the border as 'Ursprungsort des Originalen und Originellen' (genuine place of origins and originals).[7] This contradicts all imperial illusions to create razor-like territories of unequivocal identity that reduce to silence the more dynamic options of communication at the border that has become the starting point to interpret history. In terms of comparative religion, it may emerge as a spatial category of mixing symbolic structures. Earlier on, David Chidester invoked the hermeneutic horizon of the border in the formation of Southern African comparative religion. His focus lies on the frontier as a space of intercultural contact providing seminal notions of comparative religion. Following Chidester, the religious discoveries at the frontier depend on a specific historic dynamic with different types of colonial and post-colonial balance of power creating different mental landscapes with divergent conceptualizations of African and Christian religions.[8]

Even though Chidester links religious discourses with political transformation, he ignores a socio-historic context of crucial impact on the history of religion in Southern Africa: the South African War of 1899–1902 between the two Boer Republics (Orange Free State and the South African Republic/Transvaal) and Great Britain. This war developed into one of the fiercest conflicts in colonial history. Ending with British colonial hegemony over the subcontinent the turmoil entered the cultural memory of Africans as the 'War of the Whites'. Nonetheless, the 'War of the Whites' affected the African population on a wide scale by heavy tolls in human lives, large-scale expropriations of land and forced removals. Additionally, the 'War of the Whites' featured one historical novelty, the mass-internment of civilians in numerous 'concentration camps' laid out in frontier zones and at railway lines.[9] In short, Africans experienced the long lasting destabilizing effects of a colonial conflict that left behind a 'blood-soaked South Africa',[10] as commented in popular religious pamphlets.

Social historians characterize the experience of African victims of war as an 'introverted quietism' that paralysed the social consciousness of a whole generation.[11] However, the observation of a renowned contemporary political analyst, Sol Plaatje, disagrees with the thesis of an amnesia of social and individual identity. Roaming the scorched earth in post-war South Africa, Plaatje describes a fundamental change in the religious landscape. In retrospective, he defines South Africa in 1916 as the 'land of prophets'.[12] Obviously, the experiences of violence and migration, of social seclusion and material deprivation induced a search for a new explanatory religious frame. It gave rise to a new religious movement of African 'prophets'.[13]

A few years later, Plaatje's observation of a 'land of prophets' was forged into terminology. In the early 1920s, mission-educated members of the African 'intelligentsia' again invented the term 'Church Indepentism'. With this classic designation, African theorists of religion hinted at a diversification of African

Christianity that had taken place. The invention of the term AICs reversed a cultural mapping that dominated the jargon of missionary Christianity in South Africa. For decades missionary circuits applied the idiomatic repertoire of denial defining AICs as 'separatists' and 'sects' or coined them as a 'New Heathendom amongst the natives'.[14] The new term instead integrated these churches into the legitimate representations of Christianity in Africa, on the one hand. On the other hand, they conceptualized AICs as a self-styled African Church tradition, as a new religious movement in its own right.[15] Spatial historiography, in conclusion, calls the border the genuine place of innovations, with hybridity considered its thriving force. It is obvious that the indwelling ambiguity of all mentioned spatial metaphors subvert the static intentions of the imperial borderline, praising diffusion instead of division. The border as a contact zone is the exemplary location to prove the fluid character and the plurality of religious spaces. In contrast to the metropolitan viewpoint, then, it is the marginal border that becomes the creative center of meaning. In Southern Africa, the border appears in the most dramatic form as a frontier of the 'War of the Whites'. Notwithstanding its epochal signature, this colonial war does not appear prominently in the literature on the genesis of AICs.[16] Yet, at the colonial fronts of war, in overcrowded islands of peace, in gated communities of refugee camps, the symbolic, ritual and spiritual concepts of a new brand of African Christianity were shaped.

Itinerant Prophecy and Gated Communities

AICs defied the unequivocal cartographic code of political settings. Those African 'prophets' transformed colonial boundaries into the spatial ambiguity of sacred landscapes. The founder generation of AICs is characterized by a constant trespassing of boundaries. The spirit of movement is an almost defining feature within the collective memory of AICs. To put it in somewhat oppositional terms: whereas the Christianity of the missionaries sought a stabilizing effect in the secured arena of the mission station, AICs adherents developed a pilgrimage spirituality of non-recognition of territorial spheres of influence.

One typical example of itinerant prophecy is given with the praise song of Isaiah Mdliwamafa Shembe, the founder of the widely known 'Ibandla lamaNazaretha' (Nazareth Baptist Church, NBC). Shembe's praise song is full of historical allusions which document his charismatic authority in a condensed language. Shembe, who converted during the South African War to Christianity, is seen as constantly on the move, as repeatedly transgressing borders to open up unexpected paths of life. The memorizing style of poetry and metaphors portrays Shembe as:

Our wild man . . . whom nobody can ever hold back.
He is thin like a staff and gaunt like a grasshopper.

He has become slim because of the evil world. . . .
(He) who looks slender, but whose horn is more dangerous than that of any other bull.
Our leader into the land of happiness.[17]

In terms of religious history, such 'sacred journeys' (R. Werbner) reverse the frontiers drawn alongside the colonial expansion. During the nineteenth century, African religious imagination conceptualized African–European power relations with a novel version of creation myths. The Southern African frontier still embattled, those myths distributed spheres of power to colonizers and colonized and allocated the sea to Europeans, and the land to Africans.[18] At the turn of the twentieth century the spatio-religious concept of colonial history took another subversive form. Already, the mythically re-conquered land was not far from being turned into holy ground. Now, at the closed frontier the experience of inferiority turned into the counterpraxis of movement. A wide range of hymns composed by Shembe is stimulated by the search for the 'land of happiness'. Driven toward the desired 'heterotope', Shembe repeats the pilgrimage motif on and on. 'I am walking and I am tired, walking and tired, I am going to that land of perfection'.[19] There is certainly a fatigue in Shembe's lyrics which deals with the fact of colonial boundaries. Yet, the religious zeal contests the delineation of territorial power.

The Southern African land policy found its climax in the frontiers of the colonial 1913 Land Act, which strictly divided 'European' from 'African' domains. The Land Act, the first law complex of the Union of South Africa, distributed only 7.3 per cent of the total property rights on land to African Reserves. It is common knowledge that the land question plays a major role in the expansion of AICs. Likewise, the symbolic meaning of the Land Act illustrates a demonstration of power to fence in the mobility of the African population. We find similar technocratic political acts to encapsulate African communities already around the turn of the nineteenth and twentieth centuries. With the creation of gated communities the frontiers of the 'War of the Whites' denied the pilgrimage mentality of 'prophets'.

Concentration camps became one staging area for the spread of AICs. In the overcrowded camps many Africans, former evangelists and preachers as well as lay members in mission churches, had their coming out as church leaders. Inspired by African American missionaries who had only recently arrived in South Africa, they distanced themselves from their former churches and encouraged evangelizing activities in the camps. In their activities those evangelists responded to the felt existential need of pastoral care. They offered crisis intervention despite death sanctions by the war administration. As they themselves were part of 'gated communities' throughout the years, they were held in high esteem. In contrast, representatives of the mission churches privileged their pastoral work in the Boer camps, and only reluctantly and far too late showed their presence in African camps. What followed was a process of disillusionment on the African side. When the camps slowly became evacuated in the post-war era, many former mission converts turned away from their mother churches and spread the messages of an independent church into the countryside. Some of them used their organizing talents to figure as leaders of a new movement. A further implication credits those roaming 'prophets' as comparative religionists themselves.[20]

The gated communities, in all their tragedies, provided the historic scene for actions that remind us of Marc Augé's notion of 'non-lieux'. They were provisional, temporary, indefinite places, yet in all their fluidity they facilitated exchange. The principle at work in 'non-lieux' is density and communicative condensation. Thus 'non-lieux', often located at the margins of society, become central providers of impulses which make them a 'lieu', a place *in statu nascendi*.[21] Schlögel accentuates the quality aspects of 'non-lieux' and defines them as generic 'hot places' of meaning. They are the 'hot spaces' of events, 'playrooms, in which those things are forming and are prepared for decision, which otherwise are sanctioned and certified'.[22] With the concentration camps, the escalating frontlines of the South African War and the immediate post-war era produced such hot zones.

Asylum and Exile

Before the foundation of the Union of South Africa in 1910, each Province pursued its own religious policy, ranging from a more liberal stance in the Cape Province to a very rigid order in the former Boer republics and Natal. The Natal border became a strategic tool in the expansion of AICs. Natal not only felt the consequences of the South African War; adding to the social erosion of the post-war era was the Bambatha uprising in 1906. AICs preachers were many in Natal, and colonial authorities stamped them as a political movement under religious disguise. The 'wandering prophets who preach under the canopy of heaven' aroused suspicion as they 'assemble anywhere and every-where'. Apparently being 'under no European control' they held 'all night sessions, weekly and monthly sessions'.[23] In such agitation, colonial admini-strations found any reason to open files which indexed AICs as a subversive 'Black Peril'.[24] Obviously, their outreach was enormous, bluntly imagined as a contaminating 'strain of bacillus'.[25] To find measures of control, Natal was the Colony most inspired to prolong the concept of gated communities. Counter-balancing the whole movement meant to declare a state of emergency:

> Undoubtedly, the best way to deal with these . . . leaders is to remove them right out of the Colony to some other part of the world . . . If it is not possible, . . . the next best thing would be to remove them from their present surroundings and associations, and so to break up and scatter their respective cliques or communities.[26]

It is telling that these strategic options of a Colonial administrator originated in Southern Natal, the very border region with the densest network of AICs preachers. The statement remained singular. Nevertheless, it anticipates two policies of movement control which the colonial apparatus later implemented. Colonial archives display the most popular prophetic figures frequently as 'scurrilous fanatics' or 'rogues'. Such labels, partly grounded in the misunderstanding of AICs' religiosity, prepared two features with an inherent expectation of the decline of AICs. Those were the strategies of deportation and removal.

First, the 'free lance' prophets were sent to the so-called 'land of the North'. The 'land of the North' outside the Colony of Natal is identified in the oral history of AICs as functioning like a far away exile with almost no colonial infrastructure. Notwithstanding, this 'wilderness' later on became a prime target area for succeeding prophets. As pilgrims they sought spiritual legitimacy from their exiled predecessors before they continued in their own mission.[27] The second colonial arrangement was to remove troublesome prophets on a permanent basis. This strategy referred explicitly to the spiritual and liturgical praxis of those 'lunatics.' Authorities engaged in a debate of how to 'pathologize' the movement. They declared its leaders psychologically insane. Now, those African 'prophets', of whom Sol Plaatje would become proud a decade later, were categorized as 'madmen' to be ultimately silenced in mental asylums. In 'special cases' the official strategy chose a combination of two forms of detention: it could alternate between repeated imprisonment and asylum intervals.[28]

The release from custody did rather add to the fame of prophets who continued to be most active in the 'non-lieux' of the border areas. The most protected borders of Natal changed into a genuine 'lieu' of the appearance of AICs as a popular form of Christianity. In face of all administrative verdicts the border produced acts of disobedience. The hinterland adjacent to the Natal border evolved as a safe place to develop missionary tactics. Often treated as illegal or as *personae non grata* in Natal, AICs evangelists used the demarcation line as a demonstration for religious tolerance. Sometimes border rivers became the places of mass conversion and public baptisms. Occasionally the separating intention of the border even got ridiculed: While their congregation assembled at the Natal side, the undesired prophet would preach over the border, from the more liberal side of the Cape Colony. Thus, the frontier became a mechanism of interference.[29]

Symbolic Interventions and Ritual Inversions

The choreography of salvation was shaped in in-between spaces of 'intervention'.[30] Spaces of intervention emerged in regions located either in the most embattled former zones of war or in areas just beyond the frontline. They were considered islands of peace and usually overcrowded by a massive influx of migrants and refugees. The destabilizing effects were felt for years. In the drastic words of a colonial commandant, those areas were 'the dumping ground for all kinds of strangers, dissenters and ill-doers', supported by 'temporary visitors' who infiltrated the area from other provinces. Those 'strangers' were representatives of the so-called Ethiopian Churches – the first generation of church independency – evangelists of mission churches, who were inspired by the messages of African American churches, as well as a quite autonomous group of 'Zionists', who stood in close contact with revival movements within South Africa and the USA. State officials became concerned about the trans-national networks of this mixed group whose theological profile disclosed patterns of 'wicked doctrines'. In their message they built on the mistrust against European rule that had badly affected the African population. But even more challenging to colonial observers was that the main expression of Christian belief shifted from ortho-doxy to ortho-praxy and took on the new form of ritual coherence and symbolic language.[31]

Ritual activity was widespread and African 'prophets' performed with 'terrible noise and much talk'. Missionary observers perceived a ritual anarchy and a symbolic order that resembled only from afar the known rites. Evangelists of mission churches, sent to interrogate the leaders of this movement, reported back some of its main ritual features. Baptism was done in a confusing liturgical frame which intended, so they heard, to 'wash away' the initial 'baptism of the Whites'. To demonstrate the rupture with mission Christianity, mass baptisms by immersion took place. In the drama of conversion women played a significant role. They acted in the public sphere more prominently than in mission churches at that time. Women headed music bands and dance groups on their pilgrimage through the countryside. Their strange habits added to the 'wild characters' of the movement. Clothed in 'brown plush', and wearing 'walking-sticks with colorful strings and spangles' in hands, they sang new hymns and enacted formerly heretic dance. But they claimed the heritage of their former church tradition, too, and mastered the hymns of old, now orchestrating them with drums and in different melodic style.[32] Believers showed more visual symbols: For liturgical purposes they were clad in white gowns like those select few who are saved in the biblical apocalypse; blessed water and purifying ashes represented the state of personal integrity. Dreams and visions affirmed the sanctity of their lifestyle. Conversion was interpreted in new modes of symbolic expression and accompanied by innovative ritual praxis. This form of Christianity attracted, it seemed, mission Christians and many 'heathen' alike.[33]

With healing by faith, there appeared another impetus in the matrix of religious change, which was fairly uncommon within contemporary mission Christianity. Healing occurred in a dense atmosphere of communal fasting and individual prayer. It was combined with exorcism in the name of Jesus Christ and the gift of speaking in tongues to cast off evil forces – a praxis of healing that affirmed colonial officers in their 'madness' – discourse about the movement. To them the display of 'loud mouthings full of sound and fury' meant 'nothing to any rational mind'.[34] However, for their followers the whole ritual set of healing signified the charisma of the movement. With healing as one of the basic participation rites, AICs eventually reached a breakthrough in their church history.[35] Symbolically, healing as well as the other ritual enactments stand for a continual struggle to foster a purified realm free of affliction, a haven of peace and a place impregnable to enemies. Interestingly enough, the African 'prophets' inverted the colonial motif of 'gated communities', as they carved out a protected sanctuary to facilitate their control over adversity, or over the semantics of war and militancy. In conversion theory such an area of association is positively seen as 'encapsulation'.[36] Encapsulation may prevent movement and distraction; it may discourage contact with a former set of social relations. But encapsulation also allows for the creation of sacred space by fusing 'deviant' rituals, enhancing distinct rhetorical styles, and fostering new relationships. Thus, encapsulation maximizes conversion experiences as 'porous boundary experiences'.[37]

Theoretical Conclusions

The historical context of conversion in Southern Africa leads, with Vansina, to the cultural praxis of a 'community living the drama of its own existence'. According to him, this drama is performed in ritual and symbolic action 'that constitutes the heart of religion'.[38] With his argument, Vansina may have opened up a new interest in the ritual and symbolic matrix of African religion. However, discussing theories of ritual change, Catherine Bell recently maintained that up to now 'the emergence of alternative paradigms of ritual action and shifts . . . is not well understood'.[39] Repeating a general observation that ritual praxis tends to resist innovation often 'more effectively than other forms of social custom', Bell mentions in passing 'unstable circumstances' favoring ritual inventions.[40] In support of Vansina, ritual praxis appears thus as a historically formed phenomenon, and the need for ritual innovation indicates an eroded set of cultural imagery to express individual or social identities. The replacement or re-interpretation of ritual expressions, however, also suggests the recovery of a fragmented consensus.

This conceptual sentiment can be backed by the symbol theory of Ernst Cassirer. According to him, cultural praxis may be understood as symbolically mediated praxis. Symbolic forms constitute systems of orientation that structure the routine of social life. The structural logic of symbols again is a basic element for social actors. Symbols, in this interpretation, do not only mirror or imitate the 'drama of existence', they are also veritable 'organs', used to constitute new meaning or to restructure a given environment.[41]

One characteristic 'organ' became visible in the discussion of interventions used by AICs in 'blood-soaked South Africa': AICs refer to the main religious surroundings by offering symbolic and ritual inversions. Such inversive operations like the washing away of the baptism of the Whites, or the exorcism of evil spirits in the name of Jesus Christ are dialectic in nature. On the one hand, they demonstrate the potential of the incorporated tradition. On the other hand, the absorbing power of inversions signals that negative experience can be turned into positive. This aspect of coping with powerful outside forces makes ritual inversions a significant element in the renewal of religious conventions. Consequently, inversive praxis is also directed against the religious environment to provide alternative options of thought. Matthew Schoffeleers describes this ambiguous relation of religious continuity and renewal: 'The outside, threatening, cruel, or unexpected situation or element can be incorporated into a worldview if it can be made to contrast complementarily with the inside, secure, old and routine areas of existence'.[42]

In this light, the principle of inversion appears as a religious activity to check the asymmetrical power relations that were obvious during and after the South African War. Such an interpretation is supported by evidence from African religious history, where inversive activity often arose with vigor in the contexts of death and affliction. In a general sense inversions testified to a high potential to control social and ideological eruptions. AICs counterbalanced the so-called 'War of the Whites' not only by simple inversions or reversals of roles – they indicated an ethical imperative for reform visible in the new dimensions of African Christianity such as healing. In view of the gravity of contemporary experiences, African prophets undermined Southern African frontiers by mimicry[43] for the dissemination of religious knowledge. They adopted a religious language with which they appropriated 'heathen' imagery as well as the 'religion of the "dominant" Whites'.

To sum up, AICs inaugurated the new religious landscape in three dimensions: They re-framed the 'non-lieux' of colonial 'gated communities' into 'lieux' of alternative meaning; they socialized a different religious identity by an array of inversive praxis; and they fashioned a new net of social relations stemming from the hybridity of imperial war zones. This, all combined, facilitated conversion to Christianity in a blood-soaked South Africa.

Notes

[1] Beck, a German ethnographer, in a review of the travel enterprises of Leo Frobenius (quoted in Heinrichs, *Hans-Jürgen, Die fremde Welt, das bin ich. Leo Frobenius: Ethnologe, Forschungsreisender, Abenteurer* (Wuppertal: Hammer, 1998), 60).

[2] From hymn no. 190 composed by Isaiah Shembe, founder of the Nazareth Baptist Church (cf. Heuser, Andreas and Hexham, Irving (eds), *The Hymns and*

Sabbath Liturgy for Morning and Evening Prayer of Isaiah Shembe's amaNazarites (Lewiston: Edwin Mellen, 2005), 131–32.

³ In view of Southern Africa the report only asked in passing whether the missionary societies were prepared to cope with the situation on organizational terms; World Missionary Conference (ed.), *Report of Commission I: Carrying the Gospel to All the Non-Christian World* (Edinburgh: Oliphant, Anderson & Ferrier, 1910), 228–230.

⁴ Hastings, Adrian, *The Church in Africa 1450–1950* (Oxford: Clarendon, 1994), 478.

⁵ Etherington, Norman, 'Christianity and African Society in Nineteenth-Century Natal', in: Duminy, Andrew and Guest, Bill (eds), *Natal and Zululand from Earliest Times to 1910* (Pietermaritzburg: Shooter and Schuter, 1989), 275–301, here p. 296.

⁶ Hastings 1994: 530.

⁷ Schlögel, Karl, *Im Raume lesen wir die Zeit. Über Zivilisationsgeschichte und Geopolitik* (München: Hanser, 2003), 145.

⁸ Chidester, David, *Savage Systems. Colonialism and Comparative Religion in Southern Africa* (Cape Town: University of Cape Town Press, 1996) differs between a 'frontier-, an imperial-, an apartheid-, and a post-apartheid-comparative religion'.

⁹ The life in African camps took a heavy death toll. At the end of the war 31 camps were established with over 60,000 people in the Freestate alone. For a brief summary of the effects of the war on the African population, cf. Heuser, Andreas, *Shembe, Gandhi und die Soldaten Gottes. Wurzeln der Gewaltfreiheit in Südafrika* (Münster: Waxmann, 2003), 147–52.

¹⁰ Quoted in Oosthuizen, Gerhardus C., *The Birth of Christian Zionism in South Africa* (KwaDlangezwa: University of Zululand, 1987), 17.

¹¹ Trapido, Stanley, 'Putting a Plough to the Ground: A History of Tenant Production on the Vereeniging Estates, 1896–1920', in: Beinart, William, Delius, Peter and Trapido, Stanley (eds), *Putting a Plough to the Ground* (Johannesburg: Ravan, 1986), 336–72, here p. 347.

¹² Plaatje, Solomon T., *Native Life in South Africa (1916)* (New York: The Crisis, 1987), 206.

¹³ A number of veteran prophets in Southern Africa claimed to having received their visionary calling during the war, cf. Sundkler, Bengt B., *Zulu Zion and some Swazi Zionists* (London: Oxford University Press, 1976), 61 and Heuser 2003: 149, 277.

¹⁴ Quoted in Heuser 2003: 127. Such quotes, dating from the 1920s, can be followed up from around 1900 well into the 1940s.

¹⁵ South African theologian and politician, John L. Dube, invented the term 'Church Indepentism' in 1922 in a Zulu speaking publication (Heuser 2003: chapter 4). For this etymological reason, I prefer the term African 'Independent' Churches against a variety of alternative options like 'Initiated' or 'Instituted' Churches.

¹⁶ Papini, Robert, 'The Nazareth Scotch: Dance Uniform as Admonitory Infrapolitics for an Eikonic Zion City in Early Union Natal', *Southern African Humanities, 14* (2002): 79–106 takes a fresh approach to AICs-historiography, concentrating on

the pre- and the post-war periods. Further exceptions are Campbell, James T., *Songs of Zion. The African Methodist Episcopal Church in the United States and South Africa* (New York: Oxford University Press, 1995); and Cuthbertson, Greg, 'African Christianity, Missionaries and Colonial Warfare in South Africa at the Turn of the 20th Century', in: Daneel, Marthinus L. (ed.), *African Christian Outreach, I: The African Initiated Churches* (Pretoria: Daan Roux Printers, 2001), 143–64. Most historians still concentrate on the Bambatha rebellion or on the 1913 Land Act as the main socio-historic context for the expansion of AICs.

[17] The praise song appeared in the Zulu weekly newspaper *Ilanga lase Natal*, 20 July 1928.

[18] Cf. Chidester 1996: 118–77.

[19] Hymn no. 190 of The Hymnbook of the Nazareth Baptist Church (cf. Heuser and Hexham 2005: 131–32).

[20] James Campbell (1995: 165–66) has first hinted at the significance of African concentration camps for the spread of the African Methodist Episcopal Church. For the rise of African church leaders like W. Leshega in African camps, see Heuser 2003: 274–80.

[21] Augé, Marc, Orte und Nicht-Orte. *Vorüberlegungen zu einer Ethnologie der Einsamkeit* (Frankfurt: Fischer, 1994) gives some modern examples of model 'non-lieux', such as airports, train stations or rest houses.

[22] Schlögel 2003: 296.

[23] Provincial Archive Natal/Pietermaritzburg (PAN): CNC 96 2155/12/30, *Magistrate Port Shepstone*, 22 September 1915. This file compiles documents from 1904 to 1930.

[24] For the treatment of AICs in colonial archives, cf. Claasen, Johan W., 'Independents made Dependents. African Independent Churches and Government Recognition', *Journal of Theology for Southern Africa, 91* (1995): 5–34. Kamphausen, Erhard, *Anfänge der kirchlichen Unabhängigkeitsbewegung in Südafrika. Geschichte und Theologie der Äthiopischen Bewegung, 1872–1912* (Frankfurt: Peter Lang, 1976), 248–52 provides ample background information on the 'Black Peril' issue.

[25] Quoted by Heuser 2003: 127.

[26] PAN: SNA I/1/343 1935/1906: Magistrate Port Shepstone, 23 June 1906.

[27] Details in Heuser 2003: 193–97. The territory in question is Maputaland bordering Mozambique, where the famous 'blind Johane' was banned.

[28] An example is given with Zandile Nkabinde (cf. Heuser 2003: 111–12). In Natal colonial officials referred frequently to 'Law No. 1/Section 1, 1868 (Lunatics)' Another prominent case is that of Nontetha Nkwenkwe, cf. Edgar, Robert R. and Sapire, Hilary, *African Apocalypse: The Story of Nontetha Nkwenkwe, a Twentieth-Century South African Prophet* (Johannesburg: University of Witwatersrand Press, 1999).

[29] PAN: SNA I/1/468 2437/1910: Report by Delihlazo, 19 December 1911.

[30] Cf. Bhabha, Homi, *Die Verortung der Kultur* (Tübingen: Stauffenberg, 2000), 10.

[31] Provincial Archive Orange Freestate/Bloemfontein (PAO): VAB CO 619 2324/1, Reports by Commandant Ross, *Witzieshoek*, 1909. The region around Wakkerstrom was another birthplace of AIC, cf. Sundkler 1976: 43–67.

[32] Illustrations of such happenings are given in HMBl 70, 1–2/1923: 36; HMBl 53, 11/1906: 341.

[33] HMBl 50, 3/1903: 38; HMBl 52, 6/1905: 85. For more details, cf. Heuser 2003: 142–77.

[34] Quoted in Ranger, Terence O., 'Religious Movements and Politics in Sub-Saharan Africa', *The African Studies Review*, 29/2 (1986): 1–69, here p. 55.

[35] Following Fernandez, James, 'Inter-Ethnic Recruitment in African Religious Movements', *Journal for African Studies*, 2/2 (1975): 131–47, here pp. 142–43. He describes healing in AICs as a central rite to recruit followers from various cultural backgrounds.

[36] Rambo, Lewis, *Understanding Religious Conversion* (New Haven: Yale University Press, 1993), 103–08.

[37] McKnight, Scott, 'Missions and Conversion Theory', *Mission Studies*, 20/2 (2003): 118–39, here p. 132.

[38] Vansina, Jan, 'Religion et Sociétés en Afrique Centrale', *Cahiers des Religions Africaines*, 2/2 (1968): 95–107, here p. 107 (my translation).

[39] Bell, Catherine, *Ritual Perspectives and Dimensions* (New York: Oxford University Press, 1997), 242.

[40] Ibid.: 211.

[41] Cassirer, Ernst, *Wesen und Wirkung des Symbolbegriffs* (Darmstadt: Wissenschaftliche Buchgesellschaft, 1994), 79. Cassirer's symbol theory (brought together with Giddens' social theory of structuration) provides the hermeneutical categories in the study of 'cultural spaces and spatial culture' by Hauser-Schäublin, Brigitta and Dickhardt, Michael (eds), *Kulturelle Räume – Räumliche Kultur. Zur Neubestimmung des Verhältnisses zweier fundamentaler Kategorien* (Münster: LIT, 2003).

[42] Schoffeleers, J. Matthew, *River of Blood. The Genesis of a Martyr Cult in Southern Malawi, c. A.D. 1600* (Madison: Wisconsin University Press, 1992), 148.

[43] Bronfen, Elizabeth and Marius, Benjamin, 'Einleitung', in: Bronfen, Elizabeth and Marius, Benjamin (eds.), *Hybride Kulturen. Beiträge zur anglo-amerikanischen Multikulturalismusdebatte* (Tübingen: Stauffenberg, 1997), 1–29, here p. 13 defines mimicry in line with Bhabha as a cultural means in colonial settings to transform the dominant layers of power from inside.

Part Two

Gender Perspective

Chapter 9

Paradigmatic Shift: Reconstruction of Female Leadership Roles in the New Generation Churches in South-Western Nigeria

Bolaji Olukemi Bateye*

Introduction

Female leadership and gender perceptions in the context of selected New Generation Churches (NGCs) a.k.a. Pentecostal churches in Nigeria are examined in this chapter. It presents a paradigmatic shift by highlighting significant attitudes of NGCs in contrast to imported mission teaching and praxis in promoting patriarchal domination. The chapter adopts the historical critical and feminist hermeneutical methods in directing its inquiry. Questionnaires were administered that were structured to reveal the current thought of the NGCs on the vital issues in question.

There is a significant occurrence among the women in Pentecostal churches in Nigeria today that reflects a paradigm shift. A greater number of Pentecostal women are seen as rejecting the stereotyped passive traditional and supportive roles of women as characterized by most mission churches for support of active female leadership roles in the churches. The denominational-church set-up form is central in the culture of African Christians and its various shades of interpretation of the Bible inform the tradition of African Christians, especially among the Yoruba of south-western Nigeria. Accordingly the stance of a particular denomination towards women has an influence on the gender relations of it members and by implication the larger society.

The Context of New Generation Churches in South-Western Nigeria

What are the NGCs? The genesis of the NGCs lies in the context of the advent of Christianity in Yoruba land of south-western Nigeria. Christian activity in

Yoruba land was clearly distinguished among the Egba in Abeokuta in 1846.[1] The early twentieth century marked the zenith of European powers and was characterized by racism and chauvinism.[2] The Berlin Congo conference of 1884 brought about the partition of Africa whereby European powers had carved out portions of Africa and consolidated them into colonies. This process of colonization left a baneful effect on the continent. It caused what Adewoye has termed, a ritualistic attitude on the part of many Africans toward things European: a kind of mental slavery which makes many Africans look upon other races as inherently superior and regard their experience as wholly and automatically transferable to Africa's needs and aspirations.[3]

The advent of Christianity in Yoruba land had a positive impact with regard to the establishment of schools, hospitals and welfare centres. There was also however the promotion of the Nigerian Pentecostal missions. Matthews Ojo asserts that: 'colonialism gave impetus to Christian missions'.[4] Nevertheless, there was also the promotion of negative attitudes toward African culture and beliefs. The missionaries saw a lot of what they considered to be social evils in Yoruba culture especially regarding polygamy and idolatry. Quoting Professor Ayandele, J. O. Akao has these allegations to level against the white missionaries:

> Missionary activity was a disruptive force rocking traditional society to its very foundations denouncing ordered polygamy in favour of disordered monogamy, producing disrespectful persons and detribalized children through the mission schools, destroying the high moral principles and orderliness, of indigenous society through denunciation of traditional religion without an adequate substitute and transforming the mental outlook of Nigerians in a way that made them imitate European values slavishly whilst holding in irrational contempt valuable features of traditional culture.[5]

Furthermore Akao did not mince words in castigating the organizational pattern of the mission Churches. This is because according to him:

> Right form the 19th century the home based Missions virtually controlled the missionaries in the 'field' and through them the offshoots of the young Churches. It was Europe that dictated the methods of operation, policy and administration of these churches. Their attitude towards the young Churches was that of a teacher to his infant pupils for whom decisions had to be taken.[6]

The castigation of the attitudes of the mission churches on African cultural practices did not end there. It was also observed that just as colonialism came to offset the equilibrium in the socio-cultural set-up of some African societies, especially those of the Yoruba, patriarchal religions of the West came in the cloak of colonialism. Christianity had unwittingly initiated what was tantamount to the destruction of African spiritual and cultural values.

Many ponder and ask like Betty D. Govinden, 'What good is a colonized, unfertilized, passive, silent smothered laity of men and women'.[7] Empowerment is multifaceted and it was discovered that the same religion that preached liberation could also be an agent and instrument of subordination, especially by re-enacting inherited Western Christian values of separation and inequality. The Bible was used authoritatively by the Western orthodox Churches to silence women and prevent them from assuming administrative pastoral roles in the Church hierarchy. There was therefore ambivalence in the stance of Western Christian mission pertaining to women. On the one hand they claimed to liberate and empower women, while on the other hand there was a rigid rejection of women from taking up leadership roles in the Church and in some cases even the larger secular Western society.[8] Black and white males who served in leadership positions also imbibed Victorian attitudes that restricted women to servitude.

Over a period of time the co-existence of Western and African cultures not only in Nigeria but also throughout the black African continent brought about the emergence of New Religious Movements (NRMs). Harold W. Turner defines them as:

A historically new development arising in the interaction between a tribal society and its religion . . . involving some substantial departure from the classical religious traditions of both cultures concerned in order to find renewal by reworking the rejected traditions into a different religious system.[9]

So much scholarly work has been done on missionary impact and New Religious Movements in Nigeria in the last 150 years. Notable among these are the works of Ade Ajayi (1965), Oduyoye (1967), Ayandele (1970), Kalu (1978), and Rosalind Hackett (1987). These works concur that the NRMs in Nigeria have forged new paths for themselves, experimenting with and breaking traditions. Furthermore Engelbert Beyer has classified some of the NRMs in Nigeria according to their respective origins thus: Movements based on Holy Scripture which are therefore Christian or derived from Christianity; Some NRMs derived from other religions such as Hinduism (Ibadan-Bodija Road), Eckankar (in Universities), Buddhism or traditional religions. Some of them adopt elements of Christianity in a syncretic way; Sects based on a distortion of the genuine idea of religion representing a return to paganism, for example, Sat guru Maharaji (Ibadan–Lagos Expressway and Awolowo Avenue, Bodija). Jesus Oyingbo (Lagos, Maryland); Sects of agnostic nature, for example, The Grail Movement (Lagos, Ilupeju, Ibadan, Awolowo Avenue, Bodija).[10]

The NRMs of Christian origin, which is otherwise called 'African Churches or Ethiopian churches', actually began in the nineteenth century as a breakaway from the mission churches. Part of their grouse against the mission churches was that they wanted to be governed by Africans for the evangelization of their race. The African independent, Pentecostal/Charismatic and Evangelical fall under these categories. They all have unique characteristics and each has its emphasis on the belief in the Christian ethos and worship.

To prevent a rigid demarcation of the 'field' the term NGCs is intentionally used to include the Pentecostal churches. Scholars are increasingly recognizing the emergence of these newer Pentecostal and charismatic churches in the African ecclesial experience. They have been termed the 'third response 'to white cultural domination and power in the church.[11] The contemporary ecclesial scene in Nigeria is marked by the Pentecostal style churches. Many of them are relatively newly established and among these groups are those that are categorized according to Rosalind Hackett as: the 'new generation' or 'new breed' churches. They are distinguished not by their denominational labels and heritage, but rather by their commitment to a 'full gospel', highly evangelistic, Bible-centred, not forcibly, but leaning toward, literalist religious orientations. They readily distinguish between those who subscribe to such a worldview- often referred to as 'born-again' -and those who do not. The latter may be disparagingly labelled as 'deal Christians' or 'unsaved'.[12]

Matthews Ojo on the other hand, sees them as responding to the needs and aspirations of Nigerians amidst the uncertainty of their political life and of their constant and unending economic adjustments.[13] Allan Anderson argues that these 'newer Pentecostal churches are a continuation of the earlier Holy Spirit movements in a very different context, they have all responded to the existential needs of the African worldview'.[14] They are so called because of the acclaim and appeal they make to the younger generation and most especially to women'. It is believed that in these churches, unlike in the mission and historical churches women occupy a significant and reasonable space and time. Indeed they are all related. Below are outlined some of the observable trends that account for the popularity of this brand of Christianity: belief in divine healing; care for welfare of members; liturgical emphasis on salvation and holiness; musical attraction; role of women in significant positions; and their attractiveness to the youths.

Most of the NGCs especially ordain women as pastors, deaconesses, evangelists or elders. Those churches founded and led by women are specifically classified under this category. This is not because Nigeria has not recorded women occupying significant positions in African churches but because the phenomenon of female leadership in the churches appears to be an upsurge that is spreading like wild fire in the Nigerian ecclesial experience. Their peculiar disposition on women is of particular interest as it provides the opportunity of examining the nature of gender relations in an African setting.

Influence of Female Religious Leaders on the Attitude of Female Congregational Members

Change according to Lynell Bergen Dyck 'is both threatening and frightful. This is because it touches us at the heart of our self-awareness. So much of what we are in our world or who we perceive ourselves to be and how others perceive us, are tied to our gender'.[15] To think of change in our gender roles is therefore very frightening. Nevertheless change is inevitable. Our major concern here on the NGCs is the attitude of their followers about women in the Ministry. This study has two approaches to this problem and is based on selective sampling of opinion of the members concerned. The first presents a survey of the influence of female religious leaders (Church founders of the NGCs purposely selected for this inquiry), on the attitudes of their female members. The second is a survey of attitudes of the NGCs promoting female leadership. The responses were drawn from their female congregational members.

Selective sampling of opinions of women congregational members in selected churches led by female religious leaders in Yoruba land (i.e. female church founders) by means of questionnaire were used to determine typical viewpoints of such women. Questionnaires were sent to randomly selected women congregational members totalling 180 respondents in six churches itemized A–F in different Yoruba states as follows.[16]

Church category	Church name and founder
A	Christ Miracle Christian Centre, Akure founded and led by Pastor/ Prophetess Remilekun Batire
B	The Last Days deliverance Ministry International Iloo, Ilesha founded by Pastor Bola Taiwo (a.k.a. Iya Tolu Sako Igbala)
C	Agbala Daniel Church with headquarters at Ibadan founded by Archbishop Dorcas Siyanbola Olaniyi. (The Ile-Ife branch of the church was used for the purpose of this survey).
D	Power Pentecostal Church a.k.a. Agbala Olorun kii Ba Ti (Power of God Never Fails), Okota Lagos, founded by Bishop Bola Odeleke
E	Erinmo Great Temple Church, Ori Iyanrin Road, Abeokuta founded by Rev. Apostolic Mother Olufunmilayo Lawanson
F	Christ the Messiah Church, Ilorin, founded by Prophetess (Dr) G. I. Aimila.

Of the 180 questionnaires that were disseminated, 111 (about 62%) were returned which may be conceived as reasonably high. The questionnaire structured on a 'yes', 'no' and 'uncertain' answers contained 18 questions and was demarcated into four different themes viz.:

1. Hermeneutics of the Bible on behalf of women;
2. Women's self-image and identity;
3. Career prospects for women in ministry; and,
4. Gender relationship within the church and society.

For purpose of analysis the 'yes' responses on the questionnaire were extracted and grouped to form tables under their respective themes that corresponded to the question concerned (See Tables 9.1, 9.2, 9.3 and 9.4). Analysis of respondents' answers to the questionnaires of each of the four themes follows:

(i) Hermeneutics of the Bible on behalf of women. The survey revealed that a majority of respondents were positively influenced by the female religious leaders' hermeneutics of the Bible on behalf of women (Table 9.1). More than 50 per cent of the sample approved that women could be preachers, were in support of women as pastors and approved of the ordination of women to the priesthood. In spite of the general consensus, variations and different shades of opinion are noticeable on the affirmation of women reflecting the image of God. While Churches C and D have more than 70 per cent rating, Churches A, B and E have 60 per cent and again Church F has only 50 per cent rating. It appears that the issue of equality between men and women is more controversial than that of women reflecting the image of God. Nevertheless, but for a singular exception Church-category F there is a general consensus of agreement on the issue of equality. The evaluation of Church-category F is surprising and difficult to account for. It could be that the overwhelming Muslim presence in their locality (Ilorin) influenced these women. Church-category D on the other hand also stands out from the rest. Its high rating (90%) could be on

Table 9.1   Hermeneutics of the Bible on behalf of women in the selected churches ('yes' responses in percentages)

Church category	Women alongside men reflect the image of God	Women are not inferior but equal to men	Women should be ordained to the priesthood	Women can be preachers	Women can be pastors
A	69.2	57.7	61.5	69.2	76.9
B	60.0	60.0	73.3	80.0	73.3
C	77.8	66.7	55.6	77.8	64.0
D	81.8	54.5	81.8	81.8	72.0
E	68.2	81.8	68.2	63.6	54.5
F	52.6	47.4	73.7	73.7	58.4

Table 9.2 Women's self-image and identity in the selected churches ('yes' responses in percentages)

Church category	Self-worth	Pride	Fundamental human rights	Liberating your attitudes on issue of gender	Morals
A	73.0	42.3	54.0	58.1	69.2
B	67.0	60.0	67.0	60.0	60.0
C	72.0	56.0	61.0	56.0	72.0
D	64.0	54.5	64.0	72.7	64.0
E	64.0	50.0	68.2	55.0	61.0
F	63.1	52.6	68.4	57.9	70.0

account of the enlightenment of belonging to a cosmopolitan and predominantly Christian society such as Lagos. What is significant concerning the issue of ordination, preaching and pastoring of women is that Church-category F has the second highest rating in support of women preachers. This could testify to the personality and impact of the church founder.

(ii) **Women's self-image and identity.** The influence of female religious leaders on the issue of women's self-image and identity received an overall positive consensus from the women (Table 9.2). Self-worth has the highest rating while pride has the lowest. It is significant that Church-category A, records less than 50 per cent impact with regard to pride. Investigation as to why this should be, revealed that the founder Pastor/ Prophetess Remilekun Batire places emphasis on the submission of women to husbands and their humble disposition. Another significant observation is the highest rating on the issue of morals belonging to Church-category F (74%). Perhaps the reason for this is the necessity of this church in a Muslim environment to be seen as projecting the strict attitude of the Christian faith towards sexual misconduct and polygamy. Such signals would send a message to Muslim converts that are all too conversant with teenage and early marriages.

(iii) **Career prospects for women in the ministry.** As with the issues dealt with above, there is an overall positive response to the influences of female leaders on the women concern (Table 9.3). The highest consensus of the women is evidenced on the issue of creating opportunities. It can be presumed that such religious leaders encouraged the right attitude of mind towards opportunities in their followers. It could however not be verified as to whether such opportunities were with respect to provision of jobs or instilling into the minds of the women that the sky was the limit as far as careers for women were concerned. Church-category's A and D each had a below 50 per cent approval rating on the issue of discipleship. These Churches had a constant high rating on other issues and no plausible reason could be found for this apparent deviation.

Table 9.3 Career prospects for women in the ministry ('yes' responses in percentages)

Church category	Encouragement (sharing life experiences and women's stories)	Setting examples (role model)	Creating opportunities	Mentoring	Discipleship
A	61.5	58.0	69.2	50.0	43.0
B	67.0	60.0	67.0	67.0	53.3
C	50.0	67.0	72.0	55.6	61.0
D	54.5	54.5	72.7	54.6	45.0
E	50.0	68.1	68.0	59.0	59.0
F	52.6	63.2	63.1	57.6	57.6

Table 9.4 Gender relations within the church and society in the selected churches ('yes' response in percentages)

Church category	Empowering women	Liberating women from oppressive socio-economic norms	Gender equity
A	73.0	61.5	69.2
B	73.3	67.0	67.0
C	72.0	77.8	66.6
D	72.7	63.4	54.6
E	72.1	72.1	63.6
F	78.9	68.4	62.0

(iv) Gender relations within the Church and society. The influence of female religious leaders on gender relations strikes a positive chord with the woman in question (Table 9.4). Their positive influence on the empowerment of woman records the highest rating of approval on the issue addressed, over 70 per cent. Church-category F once again comes to the limelight with 74 per cent. Arguably this is on account of its Muslim environment. It is observed that the influence of female leaders as concerning the empowerment of women in their congregation receives the highest rating on the themes addressed. It was also observed that the woman concerned had a high consensus of agreement on the positive influence of female religious leaders to liberating woman from oppressive socio-cultural norms. This even received a higher rating of agreement than that of gender equality.

Attitude of New Generation Churches Promoting Female Leadership towards the Role of Women in Church and Society

The second survey is focused on eliciting information on the impact of female religious leaders as opinion moulders and shapers of their followers (see Tables 9.5.1–9.5.5). The population targeted for this survey consists of women congregational members, male congregational members and ordained male ministers. These are designated under A, B, C respectively in Tables 9.5.1–9.5.5, while the specific questions are provided under the serial numbering in each Table. This population covers a whole spectrum of personalities ranging from the semi-illiterate to the highly literate. Of the 324 questionnaires that were sent out 249 (i.e. 76.9%) were returned which is similar to the cases of those treated earlier signify a high turnout.

The questionnaire administered contains a set of 20 questions on 'YES', 'NO' and 'UNCERTAIN' choice answers. The questions were arranged randomly in the questionnaire, and were grouped under five different themes for analysis viz.: I. Women in politics; II. Women in business; III Women in church leadership positions; IV. Women's changing roles in church and society and V. Influence of female religious leaders on followers thought patterns.

For purposes of analysis, the 'yes' responses were extracted and grouped according to the foregoing themes, divided in Table 9.5.1–9.5.5 below:

Table 9.5.1 Women in politics

	A	B	C	D
Would you vote a woman for President?	41.6	54.5	43.8	46.6
Would you vote a woman for Congress?	64.5	63.6	64.6	64.3
Would you vote a woman for legislature?	72.9	60	61.5	65.5
Can women understand politics as well as men?	43.7	47.7	49.2	46.4

Table 9.5.2 Women in business

	A	B	C	D
Do you approve of women entering business and professional positions traditionally open only to men?	63.5	61.4	46.2	58.2
Can women run business as well as men?	75.0	67.0	53.0	66.7
Do women have as good a chance as men to become an executive?	53.1	57.0	58.5	55.8

Table 9.5.3   Women in church leadership positions

	A	B	C	D
Can women fulfill pastoral roles effectively?	71.8	65.5	67.6	68.7
Do you approve of women serving as Minister?	73.9	68.8	69.2	70.7
Does the Bible support women serving in Pastoral roles?	67.7	57.0	60.0	61.8
Can women run church-related business as well as men?	72.9	54.5	53.8	61.5

Table 9.5.4   Women's changing roles in church and society

	A	B	C	D
Do you favour or oppose most of the efforts to strengthen and change women's status in society?	78.1	57.0	47.7	62.7
Do you think attitudes toward women in the ministry will change significantly within the next 2 years?	76.0	67.0	70.7	71.5

Table 9.5.5   Influence of female religious leaders on thought patterns

	A	B	C	D
Has your church changed your opinion about the low status of women in the Church and society?	61.5	58	50.8	57.4
Has your Church given you enlargement on women leadership roles in the Church?	69.8	52.5	63.1	65.5
Has your Church shaped your views on gender relationships outside the Church?	68.8	69.3	60	66.7
Do you think that your Church has improved women's self-esteem?	77.1	71.6	75.2	74.7
Do you think that your Church has improved women's self-esteem?	64.6	73.9	69.2	69.1

Analysis of Affirmative Responses: Tables 9.5.1–9.5.5

It should be noted that in the table above, only affirmative responses are taken into consideration (that is out of 249 questionnaires sent out, only those who say yes to questions asked were considered). The population selected for this consideration was classified into three groups namely: women congregational members, male congregational members and male ordained ministers. The survey was geographically balanced among the NGCs in Yoruba land. It was also structured in such a way as to document the responses from small, medium and large churches. A general trend of the overall responses shows considerable departure from the normal attitudes toward women. Should this survey reflect a fair sampling of the NGCs then attitudes toward women in ministry, church and society have changed significantly.

In spite of this success story, attitudes towards women in politics can be considered relatively low in comparison to other themes. This is because the total number of affirmative responses was only 46.5 per cent to the question as to whether they can vote a woman as President. The same also tallies with the question as to whether or not women can understand politics as well as their male counterpart. The belief is that although a woman may not be able to play the Nigerian politics according to its rules yet they can conveniently found and lead churches. While there was a low response for having a female President and consequently women's chances in politics is less in comparison to men, there was however the willingness of voting women into congress and state legislature. These recorded 64.3 and 65.5 per cent, respectively.

The total response on women in business was fair. The chances of women becoming executives according to this response however are very slim. On women in church leadership, it has been advocated by religious leaders that we are in the biblical last days, and there is a divine mandate for women to wake up from the norm. The trend shows that women respondents had the highest scoring for women in ministry. While the researcher is not pretending to be surprised by this turn out yet the overall total number of respondent was high. In all, a total number of 68.7 per cent agreed that women could pastor effectively. This supports the observation made during the course of fieldwork by this researcher. The trend however shows a lower ranking by the ordained male ministers if they are to choose between employing equally trained women in ministry. This attitude is also said to be common in the private sector and government offices. Many often claim that they receive lower input from a female staff than the male. However this observation could be biased.

A departure from the above norm was however recorded under the influence of female religious leaders on their thought patterns. A reasonable majority (65%) claimed they had been more enlightened on women leadership roles in the church. Also 76 per cent respondents attested to women's self-esteem as being commendably impacted by this group of female leaders. In all 69.1 per cent agreed that the Church has had an influence on their gender relationship. It is not therefore surprising to record that as many as (72%) agreed that women's' roles in Church and society would change for the better within the next 25 years.

Conclusion

The debate about the place of women especially in leadership roles is plagued by prejudices and cultural factors. A central problem of this study has been to verify the impact of female religious leaders on their followers in the NGCs in south-western Nigeria. For this purpose questionnaires were administered to fathom the attitudes of the congregations of such leaders toward female leadership in the Church and larger society. The findings indicate that the female religious leaders in question influence their followers on various issues relating to gender. This influence has been such as to signify a paradigmatic shift in these Churches by the women themselves from the traditional views on women that deny their acceptance in taking up such roles.

It was discovered that a greater proportion of the NGCs members are supportive of the advance of women in taking leadership roles in the Church and larger society. They go a long way in creating opportunities for women's self-expression. In all, the NGCs are seen to be significant in promoting and encouraging female leadership both in the church and society at large. Accordingly, the attitude as to what a woman's place in the church should be is being revolutionalized. The previous notion that women's roles be restricted to the overseeing of general welfare Sunday school and ethical matters is being reconstructed. There is a new image and identity for the women. There is a new construct for women's roles that put them at parity with the men in most of the NGCs. Women are being encouraged to utilize their full potentials and seek careers to official ministry in the church previously denied them.

In all what emerged amounted to a paradigmatic shift in significant attitudes of the NGCs from the stereotypic notions of imported missions' teaching promoting patriarchal domination. The implication of acceptance of female leadership is that, by questioning the mission or historical churches' attitude towards women in leadership roles. Women are emboldened to question the hitherto unassailable Western ideological prejudices (sexism) imposed on them especially through tradition and colonialism.[17]

Notes

[1] Webster, J. B. *The African Church Among the Yoruba 1888 – 1922* (Oxford: Clarendon, 1964), 1.

[2] Bosch, D. J. *Transforming Mission* (Maryknoll: Orbis, 1991), 302.

[3] Adewoye, O. 'ECOWAS and the Challenge of Neo- Colonialism' in Naiwu Osahon (ed.), *Third World First: Review of Art and Letters of Committed Africans* (Lagos: Third World, 1978), 50.

[4] Ojo, M. A. 'The Dynamics of Indigenous Charismatic Missionary Enterprises in West Africa', *Missionalia*, 25(4) (1997): 537–61. Internet edition in http://www.geocities.com/missionalia/ojo.htm (See also Ojo, M. A. 'The Charismatic/Pentecostal Experience in Nigeria', *Journal of African Christian Thought*, I(2) (1998): 25–32 and Ojo, M. A. 'Pentecostalism, Public Accountability and Governance in Nigeria', a paper presented for discussion at the workshop on *Pentecostal-Civil Society Dialogue on Public Accountability and Governance*, Monday, October 18, 2004 at the Agip Recital Hall, MUSON Centre, Onikan, Lagos).

5   Akao, J. O. 'Is the Mission of the Church still understood in Western Terms?' in Mercy Amba Oduyoye (ed.), *The State of Christian Theology in Nigeria 1980–81* (Ibadan: Daystar, 1986), 6.

6   Ibid.

7   Betty D. Govinden 'In Search of our Own Well' in R. A Musimbi and J. N. Nyambura (eds), *Groaning in Faith: African Women in the Household of God.* (Kenya: Acton, 1966), 124.

8   Langley, Myrtle. *Equal Woman: A Christian Feminist Perspective.* (Southampton Marshalls, 1983), 58.

9   Turner, H. W. *Bibliography of New Religious Movements in Primal Society.* (London: Collins, 1978), 698.

10 Beyer, E. *New Christian Movement in West Africa: A Course in Church History.* (Ibadan: Sefer, 1988), 58.

11 Kalu, O. 'The Third Response: Pentecostalism and the Reconstruction of Christian Experience in Africa, 1970–1995'. *Journal of African Christian Thought, 1*(2) (1998): 25–32.

12 Hackett Rosalind, 'Charismatic/Pentecostal Appropriation of Media Technologies in Nigeria and Ghana'. *Journal of Religion in Africa, XXVIII*(3) (1998): 262.

13 Ojo, M. A. op cit. See also M. A. Ojo. 'The Charismatic/Pentecostal Experience in Nigeria'. *Journal of African Christian Thought, I*(2), 1998): 25 – 32.

14 A. Anderson, 'The Globalization of Pentecostalism' paper delivered at the Commission Meeting of the Churches' Commission on Mission. 14–16 September 2002, Bangor/Wales. (see also Allan Anderson, 'Pentecostal Churches and the Concept of Power' and 'The Pentecostal Gospel, Religion and Culture in African Perspective', 2001: 1–21).

15 Lynell Bergen – Dyck 'The Role of Women in AICs', in Ghana Consultation on AICs. 2001.

16 Interviews with the FRLs in question were carried out during the course of field work and participant observation in the selected congregations from 1997 to 2000. This formed the major bulk of my doctoral thesis, Bateye, B.O. 'Female Leaders of New Generation Churches as Change-Agents in Yoruba land', Unpublished Ph.D. Thesis. Department of Religious Studies, Obafemi Awolowo University, Ile-Ife, 2001. The six churches selected for this study were founded and led by females and categorized as follows: The Last Days Deliverance Ministry International Iloo, Ilesha founded by Pastor Bola Taiwo; Agbala Daniel Church headquarters at Ibadan founded by Archbishop Dorcas Siyanbola Olaniyi (Ile-Ife branch was also used for the purpose of this survey); Power Pentecostal Church (a.k.a) Agbala Agbara Olorun Kii ba ti (Power of God Never Fails.), Okota Lagos, founded by Bishop Bola Odeleke; Erinmo Great Temple Church, Ori Iyanrin Road, Abeokuta founded by Rev. Apostolic Mother Olufunmilayo Lawanson; Christ Miracle Christian Center, Akure founded by Pastor/Prophetess Remilekun Batire; Christ the Messiah Church, Ilorin founded by Prophetess (Dr) G. I. Aimila.

17 Bolaji Bateye 'Reclaiming A Lost Tradition: Nigerian Women in Power and Resistance' in D. O. Akintunde and Helen Labeodan (eds.) *Women, Religion, Culture and Lawmaking in Africa* (Ibadan: Sefer, 2002. 80. pp. 79–91).

Chapter 10

From Holy Ground to Virtual Reality: Aladura Gender Practices in Cyberspace – An African Diaspora Perspective

Deidre Helen Crumbley

The stage opens with the appearance of missionaries. . . . While the missionaries with Christianity implore the colonial subject to lay up his 'treasures in Heaven where neither moth nor rust doth corrupt', the trader and concessionaires and administrators acquire his mineral and land resources, destroy his arts, crafts, and home industries.[1]

Contexts: Church Independency Movements in Africa and Its Diasporas

The Berlin conference of 1884 galvanized two 'scrambles' for Africa captured in the quotation above. European nations scrambled for control of African land and resources, while a patchwork of European and American churches scrambled for African souls. Consequences included the colonization of Africa and the exportation of its people into an involuntary African Diaspora for their labour and expertise.[2] Religious consequences included a reservoir of institutional, symbolic and ritual fodder that peoples of Africa and African descent drew upon to reinvent the faith of their rulers.

Among the Yoruba of Nigeria, this religious reformulation occurred in two waves of church independency, much as it did among African Americans in the United States. The first represented a primarily institutional secession from missionizing churches of the dominant group; the second, a cultural secession from their symbolic and ritual content.[3] First wave churches among African Americans, exemplified by the African Methodist Episcopal Church (AME, 1816) and AME Zion (1820), emerged in the context of chattel slavery, 'segregated Sabbaths', and anti-abolitionism.[4] Nigerian 'African Churches' arose against a backdrop of British colonialism and nationalist resistance to the exclusion from high-church office.[5] AME and AME Zion varied little in liturgy, doctrine, or organizational structures from the Methodist Episcopal Church from which they seceded. Embracing middle class respectability, they distanced themselves from emotive worship styles and 'cornfield ditties' of slave religion.[6] Correspondingly, African Churches such as the United Native African Church (1891) and the African Church Bethel (1901) affirmed Christian orthodoxy, distancing themselves from 'stone age' African religious traditions.[7]

On both sides of the Atlantic, a second wave of autonomous Afro-Christian churches arose with intimate historical ties to Holiness-Pentecostalism. The African American 'Sanctified' tradition that emerged in the early-twentieth-century was shaped by both African derived and 'evangelical Christian [traditions] that became normative for the vast majority of Black Christians'.[8] African-derived plantation religion included practices of conjuring, herbal preparation, divining and religious dance; evangelical Christianity culminated in the 'gift of tongues' in 1906 at the Azusa Street Mission in Los Angeles, an interracial African American founded mission. Here, Black, Baptist pastor Charles Mason received the gift of tongues and later established the Church of God in Christ (COGIC). It ordained ministers, Black and White, was the first Pentecostal church to be incorporated in America, and between 1909 and 1914, there were as many White as Black COGIC congregations. With the invasion of 'Jim Crow' racial segregation into American Pentecostalism, however, the Assemblies of God emerged in 1914 as a separate White denomination.[9]

In Nigeria, first wave African Churches were followed by African Instituted Churches (AICs) such as the Aladura, 'owners of prayer', which selectively blend Christian and Yoruba religious traditions. Aladura churches vary but share the centrality of intercessory prayer; divine healing; spiritual opposition to witchcraft; holy water; prophecy; music and movement central to worship; and greater female leadership roles than in mission churches.[10] On both sides of the Atlantic, some second wave churches reproduced gender asymmetry of older mainline churches; others rejected them. Among African Americans, female leadership is patchy, reflecting a tension between the gender-equalizing impact of American racial practices and the tradition of the Black church as a racism-free zone that privileges Black leadership.[11] For example, the Church of God in Christ (COGIC) prohibits the ordination of women.[12] However, Ida B. Robinson, founded Mount Sinai Holiness Church, established 84 churches, built schools and set up missions abroad.[13]

Similarly, in Aladura, gender practices range from prohibiting female ordination to female ordination within gender-symmetrical institutional structures. The gender practices of the three Aladura churches studied here have spread with them also into Europe and the Americas over the last three decades. These gender practices may be observed not only in urban centres of America, Britain and Germany but also may be tracked through cyberspace at church maintained websites.

Focus, Aim and Methodology

The central question here is, What do Aladura websites communicate about gender practices, and what are their implications for the study of AICs in the Diaspora? Internet-mediated data and images are considered in light of germane Aladura literature, 4 years of uninterrupted fieldwork in Nigeria, and ongoing communication with Aladura on the continent and in America. This study grew out of the intersection between anthropological fieldwork and autobiography. First, the sex of a researcher shapes fieldwork options, in that having a female body and complying with menstrual taboos affected how data was collected. Second, the author was raised in a female led African American Instituted Church (AAIC), a Sanctified storefront church established during the migration of African Americans from the rural South to the urban North between World Wars I and II. In this church, and in the Black community in which the author was raised, female leadership was normative, heightening her awareness of digressions from it among certain Aladura. This article consists of three sections beyond the introduction. First, gender practices of each case-study churches are outlined, followed by an exploration of their respective websites. The conclusion summarizes these findings, then revisits the comparative AIC/AAIC perspective that opened the paper.

Aladura Gender Practices

Aladura churches vary in ritual and symbolic content. For example, in the Christ Apostolic Church, religious dance is accompanied by drumming and clapping, but regular street clothing is donned for Sunday worship. Revelation is constrained by Biblical primacy, and burning candles are not central to worship. In the Church of the Lord (Aladura), white robes are worn, candles and holy water are used, prophecies are taken seriously, and members dance and clap to music and drumming. In the Celestial Church, shoes are removed when white gowns are worn, prophecy is central, only white candles are burned, ritual baths are important purification rites, and clapping while worshiping is forbidden. Similarly, Aladura gender practices vary dramatically, reflecting different institutional histories, organizational strategies and leadership styles.[14] In each of the three Aladura churches examined below, women are, to varying degrees, included as well as excluded from arenas of political and ceremonial power.

Christ Apostolic Church gender practices

Christ Apostolic Church (CAC), the oldest of the three case studies, emerged as an 'egbe', a voluntary association, within St Savior's Anglican parish, when the 1918 worldwide flu epidemic swept through the Yoruba area of south-western Nigeria. CAC was established, not by a charismatic founder, but by a body of male and female civil servants and educators, including Mrs. Sophie Odunlami, a schoolmistress. This new religious institution absorbed the charisma of the prophet-healer Joseph Babalola into its incipient bureaucracy. Before emerging as an autonomous institution in 1941, CAC was briefly affiliated with two White evangelical denominations in America and Britain, respectively, where 'evangelical' refers to Protestant traditions that privilege manifesting in-dwelling spirit and personal sanctity.[15] These early loose affiliations may account for CAC's ecumenical reticence, a tendency to refer it itself as 'Pentecostal' rather than 'Aladura', and prohibition against female ordination.

The organizational strategy of CAC can be described as a decentralized hierarchy. It has functioned as a consensus-based bureaucracy tempered by notions of 'brotherliness', and CAC has always tried to avoid 'taking a brother to court'. The challenge in any growing institution is how to balance inclusivity with institutional structures. This tension has recently resulted in the emergence of two competing executives, requiring the intervention of the court to decide which one actually heads CAC.[16] Still, CAC continues to expand, and women have been its backbone.[17] Women, however, are excluded from ordination as pastors, a biblically based policy sanctioned by 1 Tim. 2. 11–15 (KJV) that exhorts women to 'learn in silence with all subjection' and they 'shall be saved in childbearing'. CAC supports the procreative aspect of female lives as 'maternities' or birthing centres are attached to large CAC assemblies, and special prayer services are available to women who are barren. Maternities are staffed by professionals trained at the Ede School of Midwifery, established and supported by 'Obirin Rere', Good Woman Society, a national 'egbe' responsible for Babalola Girl's school.

Some women hold the office of 'evangelist'; others have played key roles in CAC expansion, such as Mama Ogunranti who planted 'assemblies' throughout Nigeria, in Britain and the United States. When renowned TV and radio evangelist Mrs. Bola Odeleke, established successful ministry in Lagos with its own maternity, the CAC executive ordained her husband as minister in charge. When he died, however, Mrs. Odeleke refused to accept another pastor and broke with CAC.[18] Still, many CAC women continue to work within church structures, and the 2003 seminary graduation program lists several women as class officers.[19] There are no prohibitive menstrual rituals; however, CAC women must speak from outside the chancel area.

Church of the Lord Aladura gender practices

Josiah Ositelu, who founded the Church of the Lord Aladura (CLA) in 1930, envisioned CLA as 'both an African and a worldwide church'.[20] This became a reality when, during his theological training abroad in the 1960s, the second Primate Emmanuel Adejobi, through his colleague and friend Dr Rev. Harold Turner, was introduced to both the Archbishop of Canterbury and the head of the World Council of Churches (WCC).[21] From its inception, women played key leadership roles in CLA. In 'The Early Diary of the Church of the Lord', the late Primate Adejobi documents the entry of women into the ministry as early as the 1930s, and their role in church expansion. In 1959, female ordination was formalized by 'divine injunction' for perpetuity.[22] CLA seminary founder Primate Adejobi established a precedent of male and female student body co-presidents. He publicly celebrated CLA female ordination during a WCC convention, and criticized gender practices of Roman Catholics, the oldest European church, for reducing women to servants, while his young African instituted church ordained women. Furthermore, Article VI section three of the CLA constitution states that both 'The Apostle/Rev. Mother Superior . . . administers the churches under his/her jurisdiction'.[23] Further-more, although all primates have been male, as Primate Adejobi pointed out to the author, the constitution does not prohibit women from the post.

Female ordination in CLA is accompanied by prohibitive menstrual rites. These have been explained as universal symbolic expressions of gender inequity designed to restore social norms that privilege men.[24] They also have been inter-preted as unique expressions of particular worldviews.[25] For example, in West Africa, they have been explained as expressions of awe before the unpredictable and potentially dangerous power of menstrual blood to also create life.[26] Fur-thermore, the notion of 'menstrual ritual practices' has been proposed to expand interpretation beyond negative connotations of the word 'taboo'.[27]

Whether a ritualized reminder of male domination, an expression of cosmo-logical awe, or a combination of these, menstrual rites constrain ritual performance of ordained CLA women. Menstruating women must sit outside the sanctuary, and until they are postmenopausal, women are prohibited from performing the sacraments of burials, marriage, baptism and communion.[28] Having a female body adds conditionality to ordination but does not exclude CLA women from 'the priesthood of all believers'. Still, it is forbidden that 'a woman to be the ultimate arbiter of doctrine' in CLA.[29]

Celestial Church of Christ gender practices

Before his call, Samuel Bilehou Oshoffa was a carpenter. A Yoruba native of Francophone Porto Novo, Republic of Benin, he founded the Celestial Church of Christ (CCC) in 1947 as a church where Africans could experience miracles and no longer depend on 'fetish priests'.[30] Celestial tenets or 'rules and regula-tions' are understood as divinely revealed through the founder.[31] Three of the twelve directly forbid women and men from sitting together during worship, prohibit menstruating women from the church compound, and exclude women from the altar and leading a worship in the sanctuary.[32] Yet, Celestial women have embraced evangelism, pioneering CCC parishes in Nigeria and abroad. Exclusion from ordination did not prevent Mrs. Adebola Sodeinde, a well educated and traveled Lagos businesswoman, from becoming the 'right arm' and 'spiritual daughter' of the founder, who referred to her as 'a man'.[33] Both men and women scale the Celestial ladder of 'anointments' via prophetic or non-prophetic hierarchies.[34] The female hierarchy stops abruptly at the 'Superior Senior' rank ('Superior Senior Prophetess' or 'Lace Superior Senior Elder Sister'), the rank just below the level where ordained anointments begin for males. The Celestial Church also provides special clinics for the pregnant or barren women, and women can 'live' in the Church compound for protracted periods of 'abo' or protection, when pregnant.

Cyber-Propagation of Aladura Gender Images

Aladura churches with their holy grounds established throughout West Africa are now international 'religions on the move'.[35] In America, a half million African immigrants were admitted into the United States between 1992 and 2002; the largest group was over 75,000 Nigerians.[36] The three churches in this study have spread across the world and into the virtual reality of cyber space. The gospel was propagated country by country in the past, but, in this digital age, it takes only a nanosecond to access CAC, CLA, or CCC websites to learn about Aladura doctrine, ritual and gender practices. All websites were visited both before and shortly after the Hirschluch conference 11–15 September 2003, and with the exception of the CLA, gender-related information varied minimally.

Christ Apostolic Church websites

Consulted CAC websites, available in English only, represent CAC-WOSEM (World Soul Winning Evangelistic Ministry), which began as a ministry within CAC in Nigeria.[37] With minimal reference to WOSEM's African origins, Prophet T. O. Obadare is listed as founder of 'CAC in America'. Under 'Ministry in America', 18 branches are listed in the US and Canada.[38] The international scope of the ministry is reflected at a link about Prophet Obadare visiting assemblies in Britain, Germany, Austria, Italy and the United Kingdom.[39] Listed online tenets include belief in the divine inspiration of the Bible, the Trinity, baptism by emersion and divine healing.[40] Few graphic images were discovered online, none of women.[41] In sum, CAC is represented as a transcultural expression of evangelical Christianity with minimal references to explicitly African or Aladura rituals or practices, e.g. holy water or anti-witchcraft activities. Furthermore, there are no references to CAC gender practices, such as the prohibition against women's ordination or exclusion from the chancel area. Still, focusing on women's reproductive roles, 'Special Prayers' lists weekly 'Prayers for the Barren' and 'Prayers for Pregnant Mothers for Safe Delivery' asserting that, 'God is delivering his people and giving them children'.[42]

Church of the Lord (Aladura) website

As the 3,367th visitor on 11 July 2003 to the CLA website, available in English, French, German and Spanish, the author met the self-definition of CLA as 'Pentecostal in power, Biblical in pattern, evangelical in ministry and ecumenical in outlook'.[43] Recurrent themes were evangelism, ecumenism and the missiological role of AICs in the twenty-first century. This was elaborated upon in an online article by His Eminence Primate Dr. Rufus Ositelu, who has authored a book on African Instituted Churches and holds doctorates in both Computer Science and Religion.[44] In the article, he argues that despite the negative association of the word 'mission' with western political expansionism and 'cultural transfer', a newly revitalized worldwide mission is underway in which African Christianity contributes, among other things, a spiritually enlivened liturgy.[45]

The 'organizational profile' link listed international sub-headquarters on three continents, and the homepage, with a link to the World Council of Churches (WCC), listed CLA's many ecumenical activities and memberships beginning with its 1975 admission to the WCC. The 'Faith Statement' link addressed CLA doctrines: divine inspiration of the Bible, the Trinity, gift of tongues, baptism by immersion, the millennium and divine healing. Uniquely CLA practices were communicated on specialized pages such as the 'Info' link, which lists the 'Love Feast . . . every first Sunday of the month after worship', comparable to the 'Lord's Supper' in mainline churches.[46] As with CAC, few graphic images were discovered; none were of women, one was of Primate Rufus Ositelu, and the other was of the youth camp mass choir.[47] The name of 'Spr. Mother Barbara Ositelu', however, was listed along with her contact cell phone number on the 'Info' link. Conspicuously absent were references to CLA gender practices.[48]

That was the state of the website before the Hirschluch conference. As visitor 4,713 on 7 April 2004, the author found two new links: the annual 'Tabieorar' pilgrimage link and another entitled 'Women', which describes female ordination policy as divinely revealed to the founder Josiah Ositelu and provides examples of female membership on governing bodies throughout gender-symmetrical church offices. Because web-pages are data fields in flux, change is to be expected, but why then?

The Primate added this link shortly after the September 2003 Hirschluch conference, when he attended a session at which an earlier version of this article was presented. That paper pointed out that the CLA website had missed an excellent opportunity to celebrate its female inclusive policies in cyberspace. The Primate's enlightening response made the point that female ordination was so normative in CLA that it had not commanded special attention; but, while such inclusivity is normative in CLA, in other AICs, women's roles have been limited to ceremonial rather than political arenas of power.[49]

Celestial Church websites

As visitor 44,489 to the (CCC) homepage, available in English and French, the author encountered a church with strong African historical and cultural origins.[50] At the 'Parishes Worldwide' link there were detailed listings of parishes in America, Europe and Africa. Other links provided the CCC origin history, a brief biography and photo of the founder Oshoffa, dressed in traditional Yoruba garb. Roles of Celestial women were delineated in the 'Code of Conduct' and 'Important Days', which referenced menstrual taboos and weekly 'Wednesday Service for the Needy, Barren Women', respectively.[51] The online Celestial constitution, also accessible from the homepage, referenced practices of worshipping barefoot in white garb, ritual bathing, holy water, triumphing over 'witches and other powers of darkness', visions and prophecies. As in the printed version three of the twelve 'tenets' were gender-related prohibitions.[52] 'Role of Female Members' stated further that while women may preach outside the sanctuary, 'in accordance with St Paul's injunction (1 Cor. 14.34–35; Gen. 3.16)' they 'are not allowed to perform any spiritual functions connected with conducting of services in the Church other than saying the prayers when asked and reading portions of the Bible quoted by the preacher'. Similarly, a biblical basis for 'mandatory purification for women after menstrual period' is provided under the 'Biblical Justification' link.[53]

Several parishes maintain their own websites, such as the North Atlanta parish in Georgia[54] and the North London Parish in the UK.[55] Their religious content, including gender practices, are consistent but positions on CCC succession varied. The Celestial Church in Los Angeles parish, for example, 'inspired through numerous visions and revelations', decided it would stay neutral.[56] www.Celestialchurch.com graciously lists this neutral website as well as an opposing pro Jesse-Maforikan website.[57] It took a strong position, however, in support of Emmanuel Oshoffa, son of the founder.

Accessible from its homepage link, under 'Who is Rev. Emmanuel Oshoffa?', one finds an article that not only documents the succession debate but the role of female church leaders in the controversy. 'Lace Superior Senior Elder Sister' Mrs. Sodeinde, discussed above, was interviewed as a Celestial 'stalwart' and 'member of the pastor-in-council'. Of the three council members interviewed, the first cited is Mrs. Sodeinde.[58] The pastor-in-council, which directs 'the over all machinery' of church governance, is composed of the pastor, diocesan head, board of trustee members and 'such non-permanent members as the Pastor may from time to time ask to be co-opted'. That Mrs. Sodeinde is a member of this powerful council and was interviewed about the succession crises adds an important dimension to female leadership in CCC.

Unlike CAC and CLA websites, this Celestial website has graphics through-out, including a 'Photo Studio' of a properly appointed Celestial altar and a chart of hierarchical 'Celestial Ranks', organized by gender and prophetic or non-prophetic lines.[59] On the homepage, there is a photo of a Celestial man and women at worship in white garb, a single male in the foreground.[60] Because the vast majority of website photos are of clergy, they were necessarily most of males as Celestial women are not ordained.[61]

Conclusion

Cyberspace is instructive. For example, gender rules cited on the CCC website demonstrate a connection between ritual, power, and the female body, for women are excluded both from holy space and from holy office; yet, citing Mrs. Sodeinde's opinion on CCC succession suggests that, within ascribed roles, Celestial women can directly affect church policy. Cyberspace is also in flux, ephemeral and interactive, mapping institutional change and its underlying symbolic content as well. Thus, since first consulted, gendered content of CAC-WOSEM and CCC websites may have changed little but in time should provide a window on changing gender rules in the cultural mélange of the Aladura Diaspora. The CLA website, now, with its "Women" link, reflects the primate's participation in both academic dialogue and ecumenical discourse on gender parity.

The CAC WOSEM website represents a transcultural and transnational church with little connection to Africa. It is a "gender-neutral" website omit-ting CAC gender practices such as prohibiting female ordination and women's exclusion from the chancel. Relatedly, ritual practices regarding barrenness and fertility appear on deeper levels of website links. Thus, minimizing such cultural differences reinforces WOSEM's self-definition as a worldwide ministry transcending cultural particularity with global appeal.

Regarding implications for future study of AICs in Diaspora, findings rein-force the point that Aladura gender rules defy sweeping generalizations about compliance of AICs with, or resistance to, gender models of colonial mission churches. These websites communicate, both explicitly and implicitly, varied gender practices ranging from biblically based female exclusion from ordina-tion (CAC), to ritually elaborated and divinely revealed female exclusion from holy office and holy space (CCC), to biblically based and divinely revealed ordi-nation of women (CLA). These findings also expand the notion of 'African churches in the Diaspora' to include transnational virtual realities where cyber visitors may access AIC websites via their computers anytime and anywhere.

While all sites reviewed for this study welcome non-members into their fold with contact information, CCC seems primarily directed to members, providing reminders of ritual and doctrinal orthodoxy against which believers may test their faith. All three sites have kept the faithful abreast of local church events such as weekly CAC prayers for barren women, the Celestial succession crisis, and the revival tours of Prophet Obadare. While the CLA also provides these kinds of local data, it also locates CLA within global contexts, highlighting ecumenical affiliations and its missiological role.

As in African American Instituted Churches (AAICs), patriarchy has not been toppled in AICs. On both sides of the Atlantic, second wave churches reject religious hegemony and affirm cultural heritage, but their gender practices are often far from entirely equitable. Still, nothing remains the same forever, so it will be useful to note how the Aladura in this study respond to their deepening roots within religious landscapes abroad. In future, as more non-Africans visit Aladura churches and their websites, there will be a need for dialogue about the cosmological significance of African menstrual rituals. The parameters of this dialogue, may interest and genuinely concern academic-outsiders; however, it is for church members to discern the place of these valued cultural legacies in the future of their church.

Notes

[1] Kwame Nkrumah, 'Speech at Conference of Independent Africa States, Accra', 15 April 1958; quoted in John S. Pobee, *Toward an African Theology* (Nashville: Abington Press 1979), 15.

[2] Holloway, Joseph, 'Origins of African America Culture', in Joseph Holloway, (ed) *Africanisms in American Culture*, (Bloomington: Indiana University Press, 1991), 1–18, here p. 14; Opala, Joseph, *The Gullah: Rice, Slavery, and the Sierra Leone-American Connection* (Freetown: United States Information Service, 1987), 4–7.

[3] This thesis is argued at greater length in 'On Both Sides of the Atlantic: A Transatlantic Assessment of Afro-Christian Independent Church Movements – Nigeria and the United States Compared', in Afe Adogame (eds), *Mapping Nigerian Religious Landscapes: Festschrift in Honor of Prof. Jacob K. Olupona*. (forthcoming).

[4] George, Carol, *Segregated Sabbaths – Richard Allen and the Emergence of Independent Black Churches 1760–1840* (New York: Oxford University Press, 1973), 34, 51–59, 74; Washington, Joseph R., *Black Sects and Cults* (Garden City: University Press of America, 1984), 36–82; Scherer, Lester B., *Slavery and the Churches in Early America 1619–1819* (Grand Rapids: Wm. B. Eerdmans Publishing Company, 1975), 147; Frazier, Franklin E. and Lincoln, Eric, *The Negro Church in America: The Black Church Since America* (New York: Schocken Books, 1974), 32–34; Baer, Hans A. and Singer, Merrill, *African American Religion in the Twentieth Century: Varieties of Protest and Accommodation* (Knoxville: University of Tennessee Press, 1992), 19; Walls, William J, *The African Methodist Episcopal Zion Church: Reality of the Black*

Church (Charlotte: A. M. E. Zion Publishing House, 1974), 48, 111; Lincoln, C. Eric and Mamiya, Lawrence H., *The Black Church in the African American Experience* (Durham: Duke University Press, 1990), 50–60.

5 Sanneh, Lamin, *West African Christianity: The Religious Impact* (London: C. Hurst. 1990), 176–98; Kalu, Ogbu U., 'The United Native African Church in Nigeria', in Ogbu Kalu, (ed.), *Christianity in West Africa: The Nigerian Story* (Ibadan: Daystar Press, 1978), 333–36: 333; Ola, C. S., 'Foundations of the African Church in Nigeria', in Ogbu Kalu, (ed.), *Christianity in West Africa: The Nigerian Story*, (Ibadan: Daystar Press, 1978), 337–42.

6 Washington 1984: 58–59; Sanders, Cheryl, *Saints in Exile: The Holiness-Pentecostal Experience in African American Religion and Culture* (New York: Oxford University Press, 1996), 3–5, 9, 16, 70; Gilkes, Cheryl Townsend, 'Some Mother's Son and Some Father's Daughter: Gender and Biblical Language in Afro-Christian Worship Tradition', in Clarissa W. Atkinson, Constance H. Buchanan, and Margaret R. Miles, (eds), *Shaping New Vision: Gender and Values in American Culture* (Ann Arbor, MI: UMI Research Press, 1987), 73–95, here p. 8; Gilkes, Cheryl Townsend, 'The Role of Women in the Sanctified Church', *The Journal of Religious Thought, 43*(1) (1986): 24–41, here pp. 33, 25–28; Best, Felton O., 'Breaking the Gender Barrier: African-American Women and Leadership in Black Holiness-Pentecostal Churches 1890–Present', in , Best Felton O. (ed.), *Flames of Fire: Black Religious Leadership From the Slave Community to the Million-Man March* (Lewiston: The Edwin Mellen Press, 1998), 153–68, here p. 153; Carpenter, Delores C., 'Black Women in Religious Institutions: A Historical Summary from Slavery to the 1960s', *Journal of Religious Thought, 46* (1989–1990): 7–27, here pp. 9–10; Payne, Daniel A., *History of the African Episcopal Methodist Church* (New York: Johnson Reprint Corporation, 1891/1968), 457.

7 Kalu 1978: 333; Ola 1978: 337–42; Sanneh 1990: 176.

8 Raboteau, Albert, 'Introduction', in Johnson, Clifton (ed.), *God Struck Me Dead: Voices of Ex Slaves* (Cleveland: Pilgrim Press, 1993), xxiii; Grant, Jacquelyn, 'Black Women and the Church', in Cole, Johnnetta B. (ed.), *All American Women: Lines That Divide, Ties That Bind* (New York: The Free Press, 1986), 359–69, here p. 368; Sanders 1996: 17, 32–33; Best 1998: 153–58, 161–65; Gilkes 1987: 81.

9 Hollenweger, Walter, *The Pentecostals*, (London: SCM Press. Ltd. 1972), 22–24, 43; Sanders 1996: 4, 19–20, 29–32; Tinney, James, 'Black Origins of the Pentecostal Movement', *Christianity Today, 15*(4–6) (1971): 4; Lincoln and Mamiya 1990: 78–81.

10 Crumbley, Deidre H., 'Impurity and Power: Women in Aladura Churches', *Africa, 62*(1) (1992): 505–22, here p. 514–19.

11 Gilkes, Cheryl Townsend, 'The Politics of "Silence": Dual-Sex Political Systems and Women's Traditions of Conflict in African-American Religion', in Paul Johnson, (ed.), *African-American Christianity* (Berkeley: University of California Press, 1994), 80–109, here pp. 90–94.

12 Sanders 1996: 4, 19–20, 29–32; Tinney 1971: 4; Lincoln and Mamiya 1990: 78–81.

13 Best 1998: 158–61, 168.

14 Crumbley 1992: 505–21.

[15] Peel, J. D. Y., *Aladura: A Religious Movement Among the Yoruba* (London: Oxford University Press, 1968), 148; Oshun, C. O., 'The Pentecostal Perspective of the Christ Apostolic Church', *Orita, 17* (1983): 105–14.

[16] Ositelu, Rufus O., *African Instituted Churches* (New Brunswick: Transaction Publishers, 2002), 91–93.

[17] Crumbley 1992: 510.

[18] During her 2000–2001 tenure as a fellow at Harvard University's Women Studies in Religion program, Dr Oyeronke Olajubu reported this about Mrs Odeleke and CAC. Dr Olajubu has attended CAC in Nigeria where she is also teaches on the faculty of the Department of Religion at the University of Ilorin.

[19] Christ Apostolic Church Theological Seminary (CACTS) Ibadan Campus, 2003 Souvenir Program of the 5th Graduation Ceremony, 5 July 2003 (Ibadan: God's Will Printing Press, n.d.), 11–12.

[20] Ositelu 2002: 130.

[21] Turner, Harold W., *History of an African Independent Church: The Church of the Lord (Aladura)*, Vol. 1&2 (London: Oxford University Press, 1967), 2, 7–8; Ositelu 2002: 29–30.

[22] Sorinmade, E. S., *Lecture Delivered to Mark the 10th Anniversary of the Death of Dr J. O. Oshitelu* (Ake: Abeokuta, n.d., 1976), 8–10; Turner 1967: 135–41.

[23] Ositelu 2002: 176; Church of the Lord (CLA) Constitution, Year 2000 Revised Constitution of the Church of the Lord Aladura (World Wide) (Ibadan: Grace Enterprises 2001).

[24] Douglas, Mary, *Purity and Danger* (London: Routledge and Kegan Paul, 1966), 3–4, 35, 113.

[25] Buckley, Thomas and Alma Gottlieb, 'A Critical Appraisal of Theories of Menstrual Symbolism', in Thomas Buckley and Alma Gottlieb (eds), *Blood Magic: The Anthropology of Menstruation* (Berkeley: University of California Press, 1988), 1–50, here pp. 4–33; Gottlieb, Alma, 'Menstrual Cosmology among the Beng of Ivory Coast', in *Blood Magic* (Berkeley: University of California Press, 1988), 55–74.

[26] Olabiyi Yai: Personal interview by the author, 24 April 1989.

[27] Abraham Akrong: Personal interview by the author, 13 September 2005.

[28] CLA Constitution 2000: 62, 18.

[29] Adejobi, E. O. A., *The Observances and Practices of the Church of the Lord (Aladura) in the Light of Old Testament and New Testament* (Nigeria, Enterprise Du Chez, 1976), Preface.

[30] Celestial Church of Christ Diocese of Nigeria. 1980. *Celestial Church of Christ: Constitution*, Board of Trustees for the Pastor-In-Council: 7.

[31] CCC Constitution 1980: 35.

[32] CCC Constitution 1980: 29.

[33] Obafemi, O., *Life and Times of Papa Oshoffa*, Vol. 1 (Nigeria: CCC Lagos, 1985), 6.

[34] Adogame, Afe, *Celestial Church of Christ: The Politics of Cultural Identity in a West African Prophetic-Charismatic Movement* (Frankfurt am Main: Peter Lang, 1999), 94.

[35] Gerloff, Roswith, 'Africa as the Laboratory of the World: The Africa Christian Diaspora in Europe as Challenge to Mission and Ecumenical Relations', in

Gerloff, Roswith Mazibuko, (ed.), *Mission is Crossing Frontiers: Essay in Honor of Bongani A.* (Pietermaritzburg: Cluster Publications, 2003), 343–81.

[36] U.S. Department of Homeland Security, Yearbook of Immigration Statistics, 2002 (Washington DC: US Government Printing Office, 2003), 12–14, 17–18.

[37] Accessed 5 April 2004, available at <cacamerica.org>, <wosem.com>, and <christapostolicchurch.org>

[38] Accessed 5 April 2004, available at http://www.wosem.com/products.htm

[39] Accessed 5 April 2004, available at http://www.cacamerica.org/news2.htm; accessed April 10, 2004, available at http://www.christapostolicchurch.org/tape%20ministry.htm

[40] Accessed 5 April 2004, available at http://www.cacamerica.org/about.htm

[41] Accessed 5 April 2004, available at http://www.christapostolicchurch.org/pastor.htm; http://www.christapostolicchurch.org/founder.htm

[42] Accessed 5 April 2004, available at http://www.christapostolicchurch.org/weekly.htm; http://www.christapostolicchurch.org/special%20prayers.htm

[43] Accessed July 11, 2003 http://www.aladura.de/index.htm

[44] The current primate 'holds a doctor of Philosophy in Computer Science and Doctor of Philosophy in Religion' Ositelu 2002: 200.

[45] Accessed 11 July 2003, available at http://www.aladura.de/artikel.htm

[46] Accessed 11 July 2003, available at http://www.aladura.de/news.htm

[47] Accessed 5 April 2004, available at http://www.aladura.de/ymcl.htm

[48] Accessed 11 July 2003, available at http://www.aladura.de/news.htm

[49] Jules-Rosette, Bennetta, 'Privileges Without Power: Women in African Cults and Churches', in Rosalyne Terburg and Andrea Benton Rushing (eds), *Women in Africa and the African Diaspora* (Washington DC: Howard University Press, 1987), 99–119; Idem, 'Women in Indigenous African Cults and Churches', in Steady, Chioma (ed.), *The Black Woman Cross-Culturally* (Cambridge: Schenkman Publishing Co., 1981), 185–207; Idem, 'Women as Ceremonial Leaders in an African Church: The Apostles of John Maranke', in Jules-Rosette, B.(ed.), The New Religions of Africa, (Norwood: Ablex, 1979), 127–44.

[50] Accessed 8 April 2004, available at http://www.celestialchurch.com

[51] Accessed 9 April 2004, available at http://www.celestialchurch.com/aboutus/reference/code.htm;   http://www.celestialchurch.com/aboutus/reference/importan.htm

[52] Accessed 8 April 2004, available at http://www.celestialchurch.com/aboutus/reference/constitu.htm

[53] Accessed 9 April 2004, available at http://www.celestialchurch.com/aboutus/reference/bib_just.htm

[54] Accessed 8 April 2004, available at http://www.celestialministry.org

[55] Accessed 8 April 2004, available at http://www.celestialchurch.mcmail.com/nlp.html

[56] Accessed 8 April 2004, available at http://www.celestialchurch-la.com

[57] Accessed 8 April 2004, available at http://www.celestialchurch.com/cele/00000098.htm

[58] Accessed 8 April 2004, available at celestialchurch.com/news/newsroom/ccc_meets_in_ny.htm

59 Accessed 8 April 2004, available at http://www.celestialchurch.com/aboutus/ reference/gallery/default.htm

60 Accessed 8 April 2004, available at http://www.celestialchurch.com/news/ newsroom/news_2004.htm#Dingdong%20over%20noise

61 As Celestial women are not ordained clergy, it is not surprising that these photos are all of males; however, two photos of women were discovered. One is photo of Rachael Olorunisola, with a link to her ministry, although she is not dressed in white sutana and cap worn by worshipping Celestial women during worship (accessed 8 April 2004, available at http://www.celestialchurch.com/aboutus/ gospel/default.htm). Accessible from the homepage 'Music Library' link, there is a photo of gospel singer Fumi Fowobaje, also not wearing sutana and white cap (accessed 8 April 2004, available at http://www.celestialchurch.com/ musiclibrary/fowobaje/Fowobaje.htm).

Chapter 11

Petticoat Partition or Faith-full Friendship? Motives and Outcomes of British Women's Immigration to Africa from the Scramble to the Present

Deborah Gaitskell

Introduction: Women, Immigration and the Partition of Africa

There were no states*women* present in Berlin in 1884–1885 when 'Africa was sliced up like a cake' between five European powers with the Belgian King Leopold at their centre,[1] nor were they *female* European soldiers, traders, politicians and administrators who suddenly had possession – on paper – of virtually a whole continent, comprising 30 new colonies and protectorates and 110 million subjects. (Of course, there was a queen in London on whose behalf a greater empire was being acquired.) Apart from South Africa, where there had been Dutch settlers from 1652, joined by the conquering British from1806, European women did not generally come to the continent until the scramble was well under way. But how far did they see themselves as sharing in that male enterprise of a division of spoils, of partitioning Africa, only in petticoats? Or was theirs a softer, more caring face of colonialism, more genuinely concerned with Africa's conversion, health, education and welfare, rather than its subjugation, exploitation and control? Or will such simplistic dichotomies not take us very far? Is it rather (to use the subtitle of an important book from over a decade ago), a case of both 'complicity and resistance', sometimes even within the same individual or institution?[2]

The Late-Nineteenth-Century: Compliant vs. Dissident Settler Women

The emigration of single women to the British empire in the nineteenth century did not prioritize South Africa, but there was nevertheless, both through formal female emigration societies and informally, a steady stream of British women entering the country, though never enough to swamp (as some hoped) the Afrikaner majority among the white population. While missionary, humanitarian and professional motives could be important, for most women 'the main motive for emigration was the need to escape from conditions or circumstances in the home country which they found personally frustrating or economically intolerable'. Middle-class women especially feared downward mobility, but saw employment in the colonies as less likely to threaten their standing as 'ladies' (who were not meant to work). Lower-class women hoped to move on from the invariable job in domestic service (especially once they saw that such work was mostly done by blacks) to make an 'advantageous marriage in a country with an excess of males'.[3]

Structurally, the settler wife in British South Africa was just as likely as her Afrikaans-speaking counterpart to identify with the concern of her menfolk for their own physical and economic survival in what they perceived as a hostile environment, and hence to distance herself from the indigenous African population. She had a vested interest in and generally an unquestioning loyalty to the success of the colonial project. For its (and her own) survival, she often had to work extremely hard herself, not necessarily with masses of servants on hand, in perhaps teaching or midwifery and shop-keeping in town, like two of the 1820 settlers brought out to strengthen the Eastern Cape frontier: Mary Anne Webb, spouse of a struggling wagon-driver, or Hannah Dennison, who left an abusive husband.[4]

In Natal, the other nineteenth-century British colony in South Africa, the unceasing domestic labour of one of the 1850 Byrne settlers, Ellen McLeod, along with her five children, was pivotal to the family's survival and farming efforts; by producing goods like butter for sale, she compensated for bad times in agriculture and contributed to the cost of children's schooling.[5] Settler women also helped to uphold class and national identity, trying to safeguard their social standing and their Englishness, and recreating a domestic sense of belonging in home and garden with familiar flowers and refinements of crockery and cutlery.[6] Though such references were often crowded out by family concerns and personal afflictions,[7] where local Africans did feature in women's letters home, it was as labourers and domestic servants in more settled areas or, where the frontier had not yet been pacified, as negative stereotypes of a 'scourge' of hostile, predatory, threatening savages.[8] Indeed, perhaps the very unstructured intimacy of inter-racial interactions around domestic chores required of settler women a certain 'suppression of perception' in order the create the 'social distance' necessary to the colonial setting,[9] and there could be ugly 'black peril' scares when it was felt that not only black men but white women too had perhaps overstepped the mark in terms of gender propriety.[10] British settler women, it has been said, had to go 'through a process of becoming used to, learning to control and, finally, learning not to notice their black servants'.[11]

Nineteenth-century missionary wives, by contrast, might well have adopted a more outgoing, perhaps maternalistic, even at times motherly attitude towards African charges.[12] But it is a vivid trio of independent-minded missionary daughters from very different parts of South Africa whom I wish to conjure up briefly here, Bessie Price (1839–1919), Olive Schreiner (1855–1920) and Harriette Colenso (1847–1932). All moved beyond – sometimes well beyond – their father's model of how the Christian European behaved in Africa. All showed lasting commitment to the people and continent of their upbringing alongside ongoing interactions – religious, literary, political – with the British metropolis.

Bessie, the daughter of Robert Moffat and herself married to a missionary among the Tswana, at first saw her duty as keeping up the spirits and civilized living standards of her husband, the 'real' missionary (though invariably referred to as 'poor Roger'), and her home. It was on grounds of this busyness with domesticity and conjugality that she at first rebuffed the importunate Bantsang, chief Sechele's daughter, who was eager to learn English. Bessie, however, came in later life to a much warmer appreciation of the people's strengths and deeper understanding of Tswana culture than her parents achieved, calling herself an African and running a group for the royal ladies reading the 'Pilgrim's Progress' in Tswana. Bantsang, still devoted to book-learning, helped as leader and expositor. Bessie's relationship with Bantsang's sister Ope, struggling with an unconverted husband, was also close, while the third sister, Kuanteng, made yet another choice, in finally rejecting Christianity.[13] Bessie, argues Wendy Urban-Mead, 'in time, came to recognize missionaries' apparent complicity in the colonizing process, which accelerated in her later years'[14] as the Scramble got more fully under way.

Another powerful critique of imperialism came from Olive Schreiner. Growing up in the Cape, she abandoned the formal Christianity of her parents but retained a restless, idealistic spirituality and expressed in her novels and political writings a passion for justice for oppressed and exploited peoples – whether her own female sex, the Ndebele slaughtered to build Rhodes's colony, the Boers on whom the might of the British army was focused in 1899, or the black majority on whose labour rested the wealth of the coming South African Union of 1910 and who deserved equal rights.[15]

Harriette Colenso, dubbed her father's 'walking stick' or staff and guide for her supportive devotion to him during his lifetime as the controversial heretic Bishop of Natal, took on after his death a dogged lifelong commitment to justice for the Zulu royal house, a much-wronged victim, in her eyes, of the local imperial Scramble. One of Jeff Guy's major objectives in his recent book is to 'demonstrate by means of historical reconstruction that Harriette Colenso was, in her interaction with those around her in Africa and in Europe, knowledgeable and informed, practical and sensible, and in possession of genuine insight into African and imperial affairs'. As he observes, 'it remains very difficult for historians of women in Empire, particularly at a more popular level, to avoid stereotyping and trivializing their subjects as, for example, the devoted female missionary, the friend of the natives, the dedicated crusader for justice, or the intrepid lady traveller in the tropics'.[16]

Another notable Cape Victorian woman who might be so stereotyped, Jane Waterston (1843–1932), went out in 1867 as a Scottish missionary to found Lovedale Girls' Institution, then trained as a doctor among the 1870s UK female pioneers. She was bitterly disillusioned to find that, whereas she 'was judged fit to teach Anatomy in London', male chauvinist mission colleagues in Nyasaland thought her fit only to teach the alphabet to rather idle girls.[17] So she resigned from the mission but, nevertheless, returned to South Africa to set up as Cape Town's first woman doctor, founding the Ladies' Branch of the Free Dispensary in 1888 and working among the city's poor women and children for 30 years. Unlike the aforementioned three missionary daughters, she *was* swept up in the expansionist imperial enthusiasms of the late 1880s and 1890s, while continuing to be a valuable public defender of African education and pressuring government about harsh treatment of women convicts, lepers and prostitutes.[18] All four of these women settled permanently in South Africa but defied conventional expectations of female settler behaviour. Armed by family, faith and often formidable intelligence, they were friends rather than foes of Africa and Africans.

1900–1960: British Women Immigrants Negotiate Segregated Southern Africa

Especially after the World War I, this was the era of high colonialism. It began with the most concentrated interest in single British women immigrants for the newly conquered Transvaal as part of Milner's broader Anglicization scheme.[19] Furthermore, women also helped build white settler life in the Rhodesias and Kenya in these years, though the formal focus in the 1920s was more on male immigrants via ex-servicemen schemes.[20] Post-World-War II, especially, numbers in the Rhodesias shot up with the Central African Federation in view. The white population of Northern Rhodesia, for instance, more than trebled between 1946 and 1962, to 77,000, many of them (40% in 1956) born in South Africa. Despite mining's predominance, the gender ratio was not too extremely skewed, with 83 settler women per 100 men. Rather than white women there straightforwardly creating racial tension by widening the gap between colonizer and colonized, suggests Hansen, late colonial tensions owed much to British class-bound practices – though women's hidden and later increasingly public work contributed to family status production, while their 'insistence on decorum [especially the sexual decorum of husbands] helped keep colonialism going'.[21] Kennedy, by contrast, stresses how their 'tenuously held position of predominance in the colonial order', the 'mixed dangers and benefits' of their circumstances, built settler solidarity and cross-class community. It made whites in Southern Rhodesia and Kenya avoid 'contact and interchange with the indigenous population' and try above all 'to isolate and institutionalize white settlement within a rigid set of physical, linguistic, social, economic and political boundaries'. Its 'insular, defensive, conservative pattern of behaviour'[22] was seen in times of solidarity provoked by (and almost needing?) racial fears of rebellion and rape.[23]

It was Southern Rhodesia that produced the remarkable Ethel Tawse Jollie, a writer and thinker with 'the propaganda skills necessary for a simultaneous confrontation with the imperial and South African governments, local capitalists and the ruling British South Africa Company [in her central role in the achievement of responsible government in 1923]'. As the first woman parliamentarian in the British overseas empire, she particularly 'sought to promote European settlement and improve the educational, health and communications infrastructure of Southern Rhodesia', while also fostering white solidarity and empire loyalty.[24]

These were also the years of intensified African labour migration from throughout the region to South Africa, particularly to the mines – though such incomers were definitely viewed as short-term migrants only. 'In the past only whites could be [true] immigrants',[25] as researchers now point out. Yet not even all whites were equally desirable: 1913 regulations, originally intended to keep more Indians out, were amended in the 1930s in an expressly anti-Semitic move to discourage excessive, 'unsuitable' Jewish immigration.[26]

But among those who queried the automatic primacy of white interests, single women missionaries were again important. In fact, urban missionary wives living in segregated white suburbs may have found it harder than did their more isolated rural predecessors, to sustain the intimacy with African converts facilitated by joint mission households (however hierarchical) or shared residence on an institutional campus. Women like Ellen Cox and Esther Burnet in South Africa, British wives of Methodist ministers working among Africans, for example, were vital link-persons between the divided worlds of white and black churchwomen in the Transvaal in the second decade of the twentieth century. Likewise, Clara Bridgman of the American Board mission not only spent a very active widowhood in the 1920s and 1930s stirring up the Zulu women of her own mission church to temperance activism but also built on white philanthropic goodwill to raise money for both the Helping Hand Club, a domestic servants' hostel and the Bridgman Memorial Hospital, the first African maternity provision in the province.

The fact that some single women missionaries could and did live among urban Africans even as Johannesburg was increasingly enforcing segregation, marked them out as different from conventional immigrants. Two who returned to the UK eventually perhaps thereby did not qualify as permanent incomers

but made their mark nevertheless. Dora Earthy (1874–1960), in the Doornfon-
tein slumyards from 1911, was described as 'charming, gentle, steady,
persevering, daunted by nothing, acquiring the languages with great rapidity,
loving her work, and a missionary out and out'. The African churchwomen
of Potchefstroom lamented her 1917 departure for southern Mozambique,
'showering little farewell gifts upon' her and praising the way she had come
'from a far land to make herself one with us, we black people'.[27] During the
final dozen years of her mission career, she proved to be a real scholar, observ-
ing rural religion, culture and customs among Valenge women, mastering the
languages, doing field work in 1928 and writing a monograph which was published by the International African Institute in 1933, 3 years after she was retired
back to England.[28] Yet even then her commitment to Africa persisted – she
undertook a fact-finding trip to West Africa for Save the Children and was active
in their London circles through the 1930s.

A later Johannesburg missionary successor, Dorothy Maud (1894–1977),
established what she called a 'settlement house' in the vibrant, racially mixed
suburb of Sophiatown in 1929, intending it to be The House of Peace or 'Eku-
tuleni', to make peace, through Christ, between the races (not between the
classes, as in the East End London settlements). Living on the spot gave urgency
to social activism (in fruitful partnership with monks from the Community of
the Resurrection) to cajole the municipality into building more schools and
putting up streetlights. She and female colleagues ran clubs, leadership training and spiritual outreach among the children and teenagers not only of
Sophiatown but, in due course, in Soweto itself, while her mission model was
replicated in townships in Pretoria and Rhodesia's Salisbury.

From the 1930s and then more prominently in the 1950s, there was a handful
of white female immigrants more overtly activist in the black cause, especially
regarding political rights. They were often neither British nor Christian, but
Jewish women whose families came from the Baltic republics (especially Lithua-
nia) and who were linked to the Communist Party – trade union organizers like
Ray Alexander or journalists Ruth First and Hilda Bernstein. In 1954, they
joined African women activists and a few Coloured and Indian women in setting up the Federation of South African Women.[29] The FSAW particularly
campaigned against the extension to African women of passes (the hated documents controlling mobility which had long blighted the lives of African men).
Its national secretary was Helen Joseph, a British divorcee who later became a
keen Anglican, and endured spells in detention (initially as a Treason Trial-
accused), under banning orders and later house arrest for her opposition to
apartheid.

In 1960, in the government clampdown after the Sharpeville shootings and
the banning of the liberation movements, Helen Joseph ended up in the same
prison cell as Hannah Stanton (1913–1993), the Anglican missionary warden of
Tumelong, the Pretoria offshoot of Dorothy Maud's Sophiatown settlement.

This experience not only provided vital emotional support but also remedied Stanton's political ignorance regarding the African National Congress,[30] to which the FSAW was committed, and she wished the church had taken a stronger stand against apartheid. Compelled to leave South Africa, Stanton published a book about her experiences, *Go Well, Stay Well*, which has echoes of Trevor Huddleston's *Naught for your Comfort.*

Her subsequent 8 years as Warden of the women's hall of residence at Makerere University in Uganda was a profound learning experience about independent Africa, but sent her back to England when her time was up – unlike Helen Joseph, she did not stay on in Africa. Yet she, like Earthy or Maud a generation earlier, had an advocacy role to play back in the UK – active in the Anti-Apartheid Movement and sustaining personal and church links with Africa through years of hospitality and skilled party-giving.[31] It was at one such Stanton party that a former Makerere colleague, Dr Louise Pirouet, met Desmond Tutu. After completing her formal church stint in East Africa, Pirouet, like her Kenyan mission contemporary Jocelyn Murray, did doctoral research in mission history – another important contribution to African Christianity from such 'temporary immigrants' – and has recently worked a good deal, partly in the African cause, in the field of refugees and asylum-seekers.[32]

1960 to the Present: Women of British Descent under Apartheid and After

While the Nationalist government of 1948 was initially hostile to diluting Afrikaner power by encouraging British newcomers (as Smuts had done in a 1946 drive which netted 60,000), they more actively promoted white immigration by the early 1960s, increasing it by 300%. The Afrikaner government did not welcome all whites equally warmly: those leaving newly independent Africa were wanted, but not the unskilled, Catholic or Southern European.[33] In the last long years of apartheid, by contrast with the two earlier periods already explored, dissident local English-speaking women (usually descendants of immigrants) and the organizations they built had more significance than the stance taken by (a drastically dwindling supply of) incoming British missionaries. I can only touch on four examples very briefly, across succeeding decades.[34]

My first comes from the 1950s, when Coloureds were going to lose their voting rights and a small group of middle-class white women set up an organization to mourn the demise of the constitution by wearing distinctive black sashes in silent protest. Black Sash started out with very explicit trust in God and some of its notable leaders in the 1980s – Sheena Duncan, Mary Burton and Di Weaver – were also prominent Anglicans. While the movement's religious language waned as more politically radical young professional women joined,

Sash became an impressive human rights body running invaluable advice offices and monitoring injustice more widely.[35]

Second, in the 1970s Methodist Shirley Turner established Church Women Concerned to bring white, African and Coloured women together, on a religious basis, for pioneering and mutually enlightening weekends of political and social sharing. These led to joint speaking engagements that aimed at changing perceptions and building reconciliation. Sindiwe Magona enthused about the movement's potential and the emotionally charged togetherness it fostered, but also conceded how great and exhausting was the inter-racial cultural challenge.[36]

Third, in the 1980s and 1990s, the three racially divided Methodist church-women's groups (the African Manyano, the white Women's Auxiliary and the Coloured Women's Association) were repeatedly urged to form one united organization, but struggled to find the right constitutional formula that could satisfy their diverse traditions and historical priorities. Partly with the help of ministers' wives, links across the racial divide had been sustained, albeit in flawed and hierarchical ways. A key Women's Auxiliary link person was the late Peggy Attwell, one such clergy wife, who co-ordinated a group effort at writing the history of the white movement. This book, *Take Our Hands*, also hints at some of the rewards and heartaches of the movement's 80-year support of African Biblewomen, which was terminated in 1996 as outmoded in the new South Africa.[37]

While the Methodist Manyano has some 100,000 members, the almost entirely African equivalent and largest Anglican women's church group in South Africa is the Mothers' Union, with nearly 55,000 members in 2001, a branch, of course, of an international movement founded in Victorian Britain. But the Anglicans' more recent, much smaller local body, begun in 1965, the Anglican Women's Fellowship (AWF), now numbering close to 10,000 members, provides a final heartening current example of cross-racial female solidarity – not least because of the pivotal bridging role of Coloured women serving on the Executive and as President in recent years. The movement, originally led by white women, has been expanding its African membership, such that 55 of the 80 or so attending the 2002 national council were African. Depressingly, seeming to confirm the slowness of suburban white parish transformation, only four white women attended. Though many local white Anglican groups meet regularly in the suburbs, they appear to hold back from fuller national, inter-racial involvement.

But at the Council, two of these four white women displayed an openness, personal warmth and commitment to their fellow members and the work of the AWF that keep alive the hope of female Christian solidarity. One enthused about her pioneering trip with three other non-African leaders to meet the young women from the remote former eastern Transkei (now the new diocese of Umzimvubu) eager to link up with the AWF, as a result of which Natal women had helped pay for their attendance at the Cape Town Council meeting.[38] The other went to Australia in 2003 with the Coloured AWF President, a good friend from the same town, to attend an Anglican women's gathering, and was full of plans to build inter-racial church links between women locally near Port Elizabeth, while also heading up a Wellness training programme to help church-women deal with HIV/AIDS.[39]

A former AWF president and clergy wife, Jenny Frye, acknowledged in 2002 the great potential offered by the quarter of a million members in the women's movements of the leading Protestant churches (Anglican, Methodist and Congregational/Presbyterian) represented in the Women's Church Unity Committee. As chair, she had recently rekindled its goal of greater reconciliation within the women's organizations of each denomination and the desire to 'speak with one voice on matters of common concern and . . . aim to work together on projects', with AIDS action again a priority, as well as special prayers for women as part of the annual National Day of Prayer in South Africa.[40] In this way, we can see how some female settler descendants have been helping build a truer, more inclusive church there than their forebears ever wanted or attempted.

Conclusion

It is sobering to learn how the pressing immigration issue in South Africa today concerns not so much the British settlers of the past who might have reinforced racial division and economic inequality, but rather the perceived xenophobia about immigrants from elsewhere in Africa – the French-speakers, especially from the Congo; migrants from Lesotho and Mozambique; or the Nigerian entrepreneurs.[41] As for the privileged settlers, instead we have studies explaining why whites are leaving South Africa[42] or British newspapers printing tales of white pensioners in Zimbabwe reduced to penury or suicide as the value of their government pension evaporates.[43]

Our rapid overview has highlighted a range of motives for British female immigration to Africa: hopes of economic, professional or social advancement; accompanying a husband or father to new opportunities and work abroad; seeking adventure; evangelistic and missionary impulses. Some of the outcomes discernible might include: the bolstering of British family life in the colonies, including the strengthening and tighter monitoring of sexual and social boundaries between the races; yet also the challenge by some Christian (and other) women to discrimination and division, through their critiques of imperialism and racism, their building of (often faith-based) friendships and alliances with the indigenous population, and the lifelong labour of some, operating with varying degrees of egalitarianism and local appreciation, in religious, educational, health and welfare, or political ventures. I would want to echo Shula Marks's argument that the fact that women of different races came together in such ways not only helped keep alive some idea of a single society through all the years of oppressive separateness and brutality under apartheid, but helps explain the relatively peaceful transition to democracy in South Africa in the 1990s.[44] This was not a society with separate female worlds only (as the subtitle of her 1987 book suggested),[45] but also cherishing some shared values, beliefs and relationships, however imperfect, among women, especially women of faith. This is likewise what gives hope for the future.

Notes

[1] Pakenham, Thomas, *The Scramble for Africa 1876–1912* (London: Weidenfeld and Nicholson, 1991), xv.

[2] Chaudhuri, Nupur and Strobel, Margaret (eds), *Western Women and Imperialism: Complicity and Resistance* (Bloomington & Indianapolis: Indiana University Press, 1992).

[3] Swaisland, Cecillie, *Servants and Gentlewomen to the Golden Land: The Emigration of Single Women from Britain to Southern Africa, 1820–1939* (Oxford & Providence: Berg; Pietermaritzburg: University of Natal Press, 1993), 159.

[4] Erlank, Natasha, ' "Thinking it Wrong to Remain Unemployed in the Pressing Times": The Experiences of Two English Settler Wives', *South African Historical Journal*, 33 (1995): 62–82.

[5] Parle, Julie, 'History, She Wrote: A Reappraisal of *Dear Louisa* in the 1990s', *South African Historical Journal*, 33 (1995): 33–61, here pp. 36–38, 43.

[6] Ibid.: 49–52.

[7] For 'the deep waters of Affliction' for Mary Anne Webb after her husband's death, see Erlank 1995: 66–67.

[8] Erlank 1995: 71–72, 80; Parle 1995: 53 and 56, for friendlier celebrations'.

[9] So argues Dagut, Simon, 'Gender, Colonial "Women's History" and the Construction of Social Distance: Middle-Class British Women in Later Nineteenth-Century South Africa', *Journal of Southern African Studies*, 26 (3) (2000): 555–72, here pp. 562–67.

[10] See Martens, Jeremy, 'Settler Homes, Manhood and "Houseboys": An Analysis of Natal's Rape Scare of 1886', *Journal of Southern African Studies*, 28 (2) (2002): 379–400, here pp. 392–98.

[11] Dagut 2000: 569.

[12] Ibid.: 567, however, suggests that, in domestic matters, Annie Wilkinson, wife of the bishop of Zululand, 'differed little from other middle-class colonial wives'.

[13] Urban-Mead, Wendy, 'Dynastic Daughters: Three Royal Kwena Women and E. L. Price of the London Missionary Society, 1853–1881', in: Allman, Jean, Geiger, Susan and Musiki, Nakanyike (eds), *Women in African Colonial Histories* (Bloomington & Indianapolis: Indiana University Press, 2002), 48–70, here p. 49.

[14] Ibid.: 59.

[15] See Stanley, Liz, *Imperialism, Labour and the New Woman: Olive Schreiner's Social Theory* (Durham: sociology press, 2002) for a powerful and lucid portrayal of Schreiner as a notable 'woman of ideas' (p. 160) and social theorist.

[16] Guy, Jeff, *The View across the River: Harriette Colenso and the Zulu Struggle against Imperialism* (Charlottesville: University Press of Virginia; Oxford: James Currey; Cape Town: David Philip, 2002), x.

17 Bean, Lucy and van Heyningen, Elizabeth (eds), *The Letters of Jane Elizabeth Waterston 1866-1905* (Cape Town: Van Riebeeck Society, Second Series No. 14, 1983), 168.

18 Ibid.: 213, 193, 224, 232.

19 See Swaisland 1993: 168, Appendix 1.

20 Kennedy, Dane, *Islands of White: Settler Society and Culture in Kenya and Southern Rhodesia, 1890–1939* (Durham: Duke University Press, 1987), chapter 3.

21 Hansen, Karen, 'White Women in a Changing World: Employment, Voluntary Work, and Sex in Post-World War II Northern Rhodesia', in: Chaudhuri and Strobel (eds) 1992: 247–68, here pp. 247 and 249 ff. For in-depth analysis of white relations with domestic servants there, especially sensitive to the sexual complexities of female settler aversion to African women servants, see Idem, *Distant Companions: Servants and Employers in Zambia, 1900–1985* (Ithaca and London: Cornell University Press, 1989), Part I.

22 Kennedy 1987: 189, 192, 191.

23 Ibid.: 146–47 of chapter 7, 'Black Perils'.

24 Lowry, Donal, ' "White Woman's Country': Ethel Tawse Jollie and the Making of White Rhodesia', *Journal of Southern African Studies*, 23 (2) (1997): 259–81, here p. 259.

25 Peberdy, S. and Crush, Jonathan, 'Rooted in Racism: The Origins of the Aliens Control Act', in: Crush, Jonathan (ed.), *Beyond Control: Immigration and Human Rights in a Democratic South Africa* (South African Migration Project (SAMP), Cape Town: Idasa and Queen's University, 1998), 19.

26 See discussion in Peberdy and Crush 1998: 22–29.

27 Quoted in Gaitskell, Deborah, 'Female Faith and the Politics of the Personal: Five Mission Encounters in Twentieth-Century South Africa', *Feminist Review*, 65 (2000), 68–91, here pp. 74, 69. This paragraph and the two following draw on this article.

28 Earthy, Dora, *Valenge Women: The Social and Economic Life of the Valenge Women of Portuguese East Africa. An Ethnographic Study* (London: Oxford University Press for the International Institute of African Languages & Cultures, 1933).

29 See Walker, Cherryl, *Women and Resistance in South Africa* (London: Onyx Press, 1982), Part Three.

30 Gaitskell 2000: 85, based on Stanton, Hannah, *Go Well. Stay Well* (London: Hodder & Stoughton, 1961), 187–225.

31 For a fuller evaluation, see Gaitskell, Deborah, 'Apartheid, Mission, and Independent Africa: From Pretoria to Kampala with Hannah Stanton', in: Stanley, Brian (ed.), *Missions, Nationalism, and the End of Empire* (Grand Rapids, Michigan, and Cambridge, UK: Eerdmans, 2003), 237–49.

32 Pirouet, M. Louise, *Whatever Happened to Asylum in Britain? A Tale of Two Walls* (New York and Oxford: Berghahn Books, 2001). Chronologically, these later comments apply more to my final period, post-1960.

33 Peberdy and Crush 1998: 31.

34 The next four paragraphs draw on Gaitskell, Deborah, 'Whose Heartland and Which Periphery? Christian Women Crossing South Africa's Racial Divide in the Twentieth Century', *Women's History Review*, 11 (3) (2002): 375–94, here pp. 381–89.

[35] See Spink, Kathryn, *Black Sash: The Beginning of a Bridge in South Africa* (London: Methuen, 1991).

[36] See Magona, Sindiwe, *Forced to Grow* (London: The Women's Press, 1992), 125–35.

[37] Attwell, Peggy (ed.), *Take Our Hands: The Methodist Women's Auxiliary of Southern Africa 1916–1996* (Cape Town: The Methodist Church of Southern Africa Women's Auxiliary, 1997), chapter 6. But see also Gerloff, Roswith, 'Mission and Empowerment in the Women's Manyano Movement in Southern Africa', in: Gerloff, Roswith (ed.), *Mission is Crossing Frontiers* (Pietermaritzburg: Cluster Publications, 2003), 117–34 and Theilen, Uta, *Gender, Race, Power and Religion: Women in the MCSA in Post-Apartheid Society* (Frankfurt am Main: Peter Lang, 2005) for a slightly different perspective on the relations between the white (WA) and black (Manyano) movements.

[38] See Uys, Joan, 'Trip to Diocese of Umzimvubu', typescript report to AWF Provincial Council (2002).

[39] See further Gaitskell, Deborah, 'Crossing Boundaries and Building Bridges: The Anglican Women's Fellowship in Post-Apartheid South Africa', *Journal of Religion in Africa*, 34 (3) (2004): 266–97, here 277–28, 284, 288.

[40] See Frye, Jenny, 'Church Unity Commission: report from the Women's Committee', typescript report to AWF Provincial Council (2002).

[41] See Crush, Jonathan and McDonald, David A. (eds), *Transnationalism and New African Immigration to South Africa* (Cape Town and Toronto: SAMP and Canadian Journal of African Studies, 2002). See also Crush (ed.) 1998; Crush, Jonathan and Williams, V. (eds), *The New South Africans: Immigration Amnesties and their Aftermaths for Migrant Workers* (Cape Town: SAMP, 1999). Bouillon, Antoine, *New African Immigration to South Africa* (Cape Town: Centre for Advanced Studies of African Society, Occasional Paper No. 3, 1998); Idem, (ed.), *Immigration Africaine en Afrique du Sud: Les Migrants Francophones des Annees 90* (Johannesburg and Paris: IFAS and Editions Karthala, 1999); Mattes, R., Taylor, D. M., McDonald, David A., Poore, A. and Richmond, W., *Still Waiting for the Barbarians: South African Attitudes to Immigrants and Immigration* (SAMP Migration Policies Series No. 14, Cape Town: Idasa and Queen's University, 1999).

[42] Van Rooyen, Johan, *The New Great Trek: The Story of South Africa's White Exodus* (Pretoria: Unisa Press, 2000).

[43] 'Pensioners Who Built Zimbabwe Have 40p a Month', *The Times* (30 August 2003): 22.

[44] Marks, Shula, 'Changing History, Changing Histories: Separations and Connections in the Lives of South African Women', *Journal of African Cultural Studies*, 13 (2000): 94–106, here p. 99.

[45] Marks, Shula (ed.), *'Not Either an Experimental Doll': The Separate Worlds of Three South African Women* (Durban: Killie Campbell Africana Library; Pietermaritzburg: University of Natal Press, 1987).

Chapter 12

HIV/AIDS Discourse and the Quest for a Rebirth in Africa: A Theological Perspective

Nico Botha

Statement of Problem

The purpose of this article is to introduce some discourses on HIV/AIDS with particular reference to theological discourses on the disease. The different discourses will be looked at in the context of the ongoing quest for an African renaissance. Are the diverse manners in which we talk about HIV/AIDS helpful in enhancing the search of a rebirth in Africa or are they self-fulfilling prophecies?

Discourses on HIV/AIDS

More often than not the estimates on the spread of the disease in Africa are of a highly speculative nature and so is the question on whether condomization would minimize the problem and the rather technical debate on whether the HIV virus causes AIDS. What is, however, not speculative is that real people of flesh and blood are suffering from the disease and are bearing the brunt of its devastation. An example of the deconstruction of HIV/AIDS discourses is found with Ruether[1] who writes on how internationally mediated stances on HIV/AIDS were challenged at the AIDS in context conference. In reference to South Africa she contends that one of the fundamental issues in the debates on HIV/AIDS ever since high state intervention started in 1996 is who commands the undiluted power to define disease, AIDS and the political responses to it.

At the conference, Ruether goes on to show how competing regimes of knowledge were unveiled and how a combination of these was used to challenge dominant discourses on AIDS. In the present study the deconstruction happens perhaps more implicitly than explicitly if the reconstruction of fragmented voices, which will be undertaken below, could be viewed as such. Let us now turn to the five discourses to be brought into play here.

Language Discourse

To begin with, in very broad terms, language discourse on HIV/AIDS refers to the hegemonic notion that the disease is irresistibly and irrefutably upon us. To describe something in this manner is to say that there is very little or virtually nothing one can do about it. More often than not language on HIV/AIDS seems to be having a paralyzing rather than an energizing effect on people. A few random examples must suffice. The examples pressed into service are about instances where the spread and effects of AIDS are described in dramatic terms, using words like 'pandemic', 'devastating', 'agony' as well as suggestions in almost apocalyptic fashion of a 'radical break' and of Africa 'changed forever'.

In most texts on HIV/AIDS one is struck by the ease and the consistency with which the term 'pandemic' is used. Sometimes, the issue is compounded by using words like 'rapidity' in conjunction with 'pandemic'. The formulation in the journal of the 'Reformed Ecumenical Council, REC Focus'[2] that AIDS 'is the worst pandemic disease to hit the world in 500 years', is almost apocalyptic in nature. Other words used for a description of AIDS in dramatic terms are words like 'frightening'[3] and 'scare'.[4] Typical of the language used to create awareness of the disease is the heading of a billboard from Malawi, reading 'AIDS is killing Africa'.[5] The description of HIV/AIDS in these terms has become part of the ideology on AIDS. Katongole sees AIDS as the new icon for Africa that is entrenching the notion of Africa as the underdeveloped, dark and dying continent, widening the suspicion of the West on Africa.[6]

Numbers Discourse

The most dominant of discourses on HIV/AIDS is the numbers discourse. Sources consulted for writing this article, reveal that statistics come into play, one way or another. Diagrams, graphs and tables are used and most of the time a sophisticated grid is pressed into service. It has become virtually impossible to keep track of the number of sites on the internet that deal with numbers. In the context of this article the estimates for Africa in general and South Africa in particular are quite startling. Sub-Saharan Africa with just over 10 per cent of the world's population, hosts 60 per cent of all people living with HIV, numbering 25.8 million. The number of those newly infected was estimated at 3.2 million in 2005 and 2.4 million adults and children died of the disease. The prevalence of HIV in women attending antenatal clinics has increased from 7.6 per cent in 1994 to 27.9 per cent in 2003. Approximately 12.9 per cent of the South African population of 45 million is infected with the disease. Scary stuff, not necessarily because the statistics are correct, but more in terms of the point made elsewhere in this article that the more we try to get a statistical grip on AIDS, the more overwhelming it becomes. To avoid an entirely lopsided view on the situation in South Africa, attention should be drawn to the advances made since 1994 when democratic rule dawned upon the country. There is a good government policy in place. In 2004 what is known as the 'Comprehensive HIV/AIDS Care, Management and Treatment Plan' was implemented. One of the key features of the plan is the administration of antiretrovirals to thousands of South Africans living with HIV/AIDS. The 2004–2005 budget has committed close to 1.5 billion rand for programs and services related to HIV/AIDS.

The usefulness of statistics for strategic planning purposes cannot be denied. However, in this article I will argue that statistics around HIV/AIDS are highly speculative and more often than not they reinforce the feeling of helplessness. In a television interview, the President of South Africa, Thabo Mbeki[7] raised the issue of how we arrive at our AIDS statistics. He pointed out that for the period 1996–2002, two million deaths were recorded at the Department of Home Affairs. He went on to say that unless a thorough breakdown is given on the causes of death, he would find it difficult to see any numbers on HIV/AIDS as credible. Much as the South African government's AIDS policy[8] might have been criticized in the past, specifically as far as the stance on the administration of antiretrovirals is concerned, the thrust of Mbeki's argument cannot be avoided. How do we arrive at credible statistics on HIV/AIDS?

Technocratic Discourse

The term 'technocratic' is used here for the very sophisticated debate on whether the HIV virus causes AIDS or not. The issue here is simply that the debate is almost a luxury and of such a technical nature that its contribution to the onslaught we face, is highly questionable. The essence of the debate is captured in a very simple, but not simplistic manner by the General Secretary of the Treatment Action Campaign (TAC), Sipho Mthathi, in her little editorial on 'Science and Human Rights' (2006). On the one hand the issue that AIDS is caused by a virus, is scientifically so clear that a three dimensional image of HIV can be constructed from photos of the virus. What is equally clear is that antiretrovirals save lives. On the other hand this is questioned by none other than the South African President, Mr Thabo Mbeki. He is, however, not alone, but finds himself in the company of dissidents who question the 'single germ theory'.

Moralistic Discourse

Moralistic discourse refers to the attempts at stemming the tide by introducing the ABC which stands for 'Abstain, Be faithful, Condomise'. The South African government in general, the Department of Health in particular, a number of non-governmental organizations and religious bodies are firmly committed to the ABC. The focus of the discussion here will be on the 'C' in ABC, namely condomization, by using the insightful arguments raised by Katongole[9] as an illustration. He argues that the question whether the use of a condom in sexual intercourse is halting the spread of AIDS or not, is not the actual question, but whether condomization is not disclosing and promoting a particular culture.

In exposing one of the pitfalls of post-modern culture, Katongole contends that the disposability of the condom can quite easily be understood to mean that not only consumer goods, but also relationships and attachments are disposable. In line with the post-modern culture of endless 'progress' without any stable or permanent base, condomization, says Katongole, is not merely about the convenience of disposable condoms, but about the popularization of a kind of sexual behaviour which assumes that one's sex partners are equally disposable. This brief illustration à la Katongole shows that particular forms of moralistic discourse, however well-meaning, can quite easily create moral problems of a very serious nature. The argument is not about the promotion of promiscuity or not, but on a much deeper level it is about relationship and attachment.

Theological Discourse

A diversity of theological discourses on HIV/AIDS has emerged the past few years. It is simply no longer true that theology is silent on the disease. The responses go into different directions and what will be presented here is nothing more than illustrations on how theology attempts at engaging the disease. I shall, however, relate each of the responses to the African renaissance.

Bible and HIV/AIDS

How do we read the Bible in HIV/AIDS times? This seems to be the fundamental question theologians try to answer in engaging HIV/AIDS from the perspective of reading and interpreting the Bible. Interesting examples of looking at HIV/AIDS from the perspective of the creation story are found with Dube[10] in her argument on why HIV/AIDS should be part of the Biblical Studies curriculum. She contends that since Biblical Studies is a discipline that centres on the divine creation of life and the search for the divine will for all life and relationships, it cannot ignore HIV/AIDS' attack on life and how it affects particularly socially disadvantaged populations, who face poverty, gender inequality, violence, international injustice, racism ethnic conflict, denial of children's rights, discrimination on the basis of sexual orientation and ethnicity.

Further examples on locating the HIV/AIDS debate in the creation story are found with Rubingh[11] who connects with African cosmology and how God walked with the people in perfect harmony. Rubingh goes on to say that this is exactly the truth taught by the Bible. However, like in the African story so in the Bible something terrible happened. In Africa, so the story goes, a woman pounding manioc or yams or guinea corn with her pestle hit God as he was passing by. God, in not taking this lightly, left the Africans and now dwells in the far distance. The parallel with the creation story of the Bible is that a being that was evil came into God's good creation. In reflecting on these stories from an African perspective (examining the catastrophe with African eyes), Rubingh alludes to the African understanding of life as life in community and death as alienation and the cutting away from family and community life. There are other devastating consequences still. AIDS is mentioned as one of the devastating consequences which have reached global proportions.

A very intriguing and I suppose, controversial perspective on HIV/AIDS in the light of the creation story is found with Benn.[12] His basic argument is that the presence of a disease like HIV/AIDS in the world should be understood in terms of the notion of the free will. Just as humans have been created with a free will and can therefore choose what they want to do, so has nature been endowed with a free will to develop in whatever way. The presence of natural disasters in the world and the devastation caused by a disease like AIDS can only be understood on the basis of the free will, not only of human beings, but also of nature.

A diversity of perspectives on the Bible and HIV/AIDS emerges in the August 2001 edition of the Journal *Missionalia*.[13] In answering the question whether the Hebrew Bible has anything to tell us about HIV/AIDS, Siebert[14] develops interesting ideas on God as the one who inflicts illness as well as removes it. In addressing herself to the pertinent question of HIV/AIDS in the Bible, Siebert states categorically that there is no mention of the disease in the Bible. There is, however, a skin disease mentioned in the Bible which in her understanding offers some parallel with AIDS. What emerges from the Bible is that such disease was seen in some instances as a form of retribution from God for disobedience like in the cases of Miriam and Uzziah. In most cases, however, the disease was seen as uncleanness without taking the moral disposition of the one who has contracted the illness into consideration. Siebert raises the important point that there is no logic in the distribution of the disease. In terms of the Bible the 'good' and the 'wicked' are struck. Siebert's finding is that the purpose of disease in the Bible is not always clear. Sometimes there seems to be a theological purpose and sometimes there does not seem to be a discernable purpose. Informed by this finding, Siebert then concludes that it is not possible to regard an illness like AIDS as a divine punishment for wrongdoing.

In her contribution to the above-named edition of *Missionalia*, Masenya[15] offers an insightful contextual reading of the story of Job. She contends that engaging AIDS with the story of Job, opens up important therapeutic moments for the innocent who suffer unjustly. There are also responses on the reading of the Bible in HIV/AIDS times which are located in the New Testament. By and large these responses are on how the Christian community reacts to AIDS sufferers. Benn,[16] for example, arrives at an intriguing interpretation of the body of Christ in the context of HIV/AIDS. His contention is that the church can only be truly the body of Christ if it suffers like Christ and if it displays the type of solidarity that would allow for AIDS sufferers to be fully taken up in the body. Another example is the manner in which Percy[17] interprets healing stories from the New Testament in the light of AIDS. With specific reference to the story of the haemorrhaging woman in Lk. 8.40–56, he asserts that Jesus takes on the suffering and affliction of those he cures in a way that it becomes part of him. A last illustration here on reading the Bible in HIV/AIDS times is the manner in which the commandment of love could be interpreted creatively and in a refreshingly new way in the context of AIDS sufferers.

Theological learning and HIV/AIDS

Two proposals on the integration of HIV/AIDS in theological learning will be looked at. Dube's[18] proposal deals with the incorporation of HIV/AIDS in the discipline of Biblical Studies, and Maluleke's proposal is about developing an HIV/AIDS sensitive curriculum. In telling the story on how the teaching of the synoptic gospels in an HIV/AIDS context has forced her to rethink the purpose of the academy, Dube formulates a number of pertinent questions to be answered by African scholars and teachers of Biblical Studies. In the main the question is about the re-reading of the Bible in the light of HIV/AIDS. In responding to the question on how HIV/AIDS can have a bearing on university work, Dube shows how particular methods can be used for the mainstreaming of HIV/AIDS in Biblical Studies. In elaborating on historical criticism, literary methods, social scientific methods and cultural anthropology, she creatively and convincingly works out how these methods could mediate the integration of HIV/AIDS in Biblical Studies. Turning to what she understands to be African methods of reading, she shows how inculturation and liberation hermeneutics could be pressed into service to assist in re-reading the Bible in the light of HIV/AIDS.

The interesting part of Dube's proposal is not so much that she is introducing brand new methods, but that she creatively indicates how existing methods of reading or interpreting the Bible could be used to shed light on HIV/AIDS. Maluleke's[19] proposal is on how the theological impotence in the face of HIV/AIDS could be overcome by drawing from African theologies as theologies that have 'not developed outside of or in disconnection from the lives of African Christian communities and African churches'. In mapping an agenda for what Maluleke sees as a theology of AIDS, he arrives at the following points. First, there is a need for both theological learners and educators to be critically engaged on issues of theological and cultural assumptions. Second, a theology of AIDS will have to deal with the dichotomy between knowledge about AIDS and the things people do or in Maluleke's terms, between said things and done things. Third, a certain level of information is needed in an attempt to combat untenable and dangerous beliefs about HIV/AIDS. Fourth, the building of individual and community character should form part of a theology of HIV/ AIDS. Fifth, the production of more theological material on HIV/AIDS than is currently available is needed. Sixth, the development of a curriculum on HIV/ AIDS that is practical and measurable with identifiable ends. Seventh, developing an understanding of AIDS which grasps the total condition of the disease and not only the individual human body under attack. In Maluleke's interpretation it is about understanding the 'spiritual, ideological, material and religious chaos into which Africa has been thrown as a result of HIV/AIDS'.

An almost indispensable aspect of Maluleke's proposal is his insistence upon allowing flows of African theology to inform the quest for a theology of AIDS and its integration in theological learning. Indeed, a theology of AIDS that is not informed by the real life stories of AIDS sufferers and all those affected by the disease will remain impotent.

Pastoral care and the dying process

The illustration that will be pressed into service here is to argue that in counselling AIDS patients it is not always necessary to reinvent the wheel, but that existing research results could be used in new ways. Kgosikwena[20] draws from Kübler-Ross in showing the stages which people dying of AIDS go through. Not only they themselves, but also their family members and even the whole of society proceed through the stages of denial, anger, isolation, bargaining, depression and finally acceptance. In describing what AIDS patients experience as emotional turmoil, Kgosikwena arrives at an holistic understanding of pastoral care to include meeting the needs of those dying of AIDS in three areas: spiritually, emotionally and physically. He identifies compassion and encouragement as indispensable dimensions of such pastoral care.

Spiritual care of persons living with HIV/AIDS

Smith[21] defines spiritual care as the care given to individuals suffering from AIDS and their families by trained and certified chaplains, pastoral counsellors and spiritual directors. He sees the challenge facing these spiritual care professionals as follows: 'to discern ways in which we may help individuals and families to cope with a prevalent life-threatening virus for which there are increasingly effective treatments, but still no cure'. Informed by the insights and experiences of people living with HIV/AIDS, Smith takes a narrative approach in arriving at his understanding of spiritual care. By selecting an individual named Bob to be the human voice and by entering into an extensive conversation with him, a speculative discussion on spiritual care was avoided.

The story of Bob is that he is in his thirties, Roman Catholic, a successful executive in a Fortune 500 company and at the time that he was selected to tell his story, he has been living with AIDS for 4 years. The temptation here is to quote Bob quite profusely in relating his own story or in Smith's interpretation his spiritual journey as someone living with HIV/AIDS. Space does not allow for that. In essence, Bob's spiritual journey reveals the following elements. First, the disease has forced him to take stock of his life and in so doing he has arrived at a deeper spirituality. Second, in using the metaphor of a wide-angled lens, he has developed a broader perspective on life. Third, in adjusting to the news that he has AIDS, God has come to him in a more powerful way. Fourth, for Bob living with HIV/AIDS has not always been filled with the light of God's comforting presence. He refers to dry periods during which the 'last thing I wanted to see is a cross, or to be reminded of the sufferings of Christ'.

African Renaissance and HIV/AIDS

Is the manner in which we speak about HIV/AIDS enhancing the quest for an African renaissance or does it serve as an impediment? My speculation is that unintentionally the most well-meaning discourses on HIV/AIDS have the potential of retarding the renaissance rather than expediting it. What is the African renaissance? Or should the question rather be what does the *auctor intellectualis* of the notion, the South African President, Mr Thabo Mbeki, understand by an African renaissance? Literature[22] on the issue indicates essentially two elements. First, there is the element of what is seen to be Mbeki's dream, his political philosophy on a rebirth in Africa. Mbeki's understanding of an African renaissance is strongly informed by what he sees as a context of war and destruction.

Boesak[23] in picking up on how Mbeki analyses the African context, points to the different areas of armed conflict in the continent. He alludes to how Mbeki speaks of Africa as an abyss of violent conflict where the silence of peace has died and war has usurped the place of reason; a continent where children continue to be consumed by death, whose limbs are too weak to run away from the rage of the adults. Mbeki also speaks of the random violence in some areas, including Kwazulu-Natal in South Africa and of the 'criminals who would acquire political power by slaughtering the innocents'. Two other issues which distinctly form part of Mbeki's analysis are corruption and poverty. He sees poverty as an enemy that needs to be struggled against.

Turning to the intellectual heritage of Africa and in reference to Sadi of Timbuktu, an intellectual from the Middle Ages, mastering Law, Logic, Dialectics and Rhetoric, he poses the question – where are Africa's intellectuals today? Having stated briefly Mbeki's understanding of context, what then is his dream? What is his understanding of the African renaissance? The rediscovery of the soul of Africans is for Mbeki the starting point of a renaissance. For him the only way of escaping from the abyss is through rebellion. The call for an African renaissance is therefore, in his interpretation, a call for rebellion against tyrants and dictators who steal the wealth of the people and against ordinary criminals who murder, rape and rob. It is a rebellion against poverty. In essence, according to Mbeki, this is the definition of an African: participation in rebellion, participation in the African renaissance.

In the context of this article it is of great significance to note that Mbeki remains silent on the issue of HIV/AIDS in his analysis of the African context. In an address to the United Nations University on 'The African Renaissance, South Africa and the World', he does make a brief allusion to HIV/AIDS (in the context of the African renaissance), when he says:

> We must take decisive steps to challenge the spread of HIV/AIDS, of which Africa accounts for two-thirds of the world total of those infected. Our government has taken the necessary decisions directed at launching and sustaining a big campaign to confront this scourge.[24]

The importance of locating HIV/AIDS squarely within the debate on the African renaissance can hardly be overstated. If this will not be interpreted as a cynical remark, any notion of a renaissance is unthinkable if HIV/AIDS that is ravaging the continent remains unchecked. In a context where bodies and relationships and families are falling apart, what sense would it make to embark upon rediscovering the soul of Africa? Second, in terms of strategic planning five areas have been identified: the emancipation of women, mobilization of the youth, broadening, deepening and sustenance of democracy, cultural exchange and sustainable economic development.[25]

The focus on women and the youth in the framework of this article is of significance. If statistics are anything to go by, they indicate that these are the categories affected most adversely by HIV/AIDS. To seek the emancipation of women from patriarchy in Africa and the mobilization of the potential amongst the youth, without simultaneously struggling against AIDS, will undoubtedly render the African renaissance unachievable.

HIV/AIDS and the African Diaspora

In the context of the conference where this paper was initially read, is there anything to be said in relation to HIV/AIDS and the African diaspora? A very brief note must suffice. An interesting connection between HIV/AIDS and the diaspora is found with Njoroge in her article entitled 'Come now, let us reason together'.[26] It represents almost an intellectual plea to her fellow Africans to reflect rationally, theologically and ethically on HIV/AIDS. Yet, it is a different kind of reflection where the values and the customs of the continent are not excluded, but a source of reasoning on the disease. In seeing herself as a Kenyan in the diaspora, Njoroge describes how the disease developed when she was away from home. In moving fashion she goes on to reflect on her deepest emotions in noticing how people very close to her have succumbed to AIDS. She writes:

> I have increasingly felt helpless in this situation but, worse still, I have become angry about the whole loss of life in Africa in general and Kenya in particular. Anger and disillusionment have become part of my journey. I have found myself asking: 'Is God angry too?'

Njoroge's response, however, is not paralysis, but a rational, theological–ethical and holistic community-based approach to the eradication of HIV/AIDS. In using Njoroge's response as an illustration, the African diaspora across the globe can contribute immensely to the fight against HIV/AIDS in terms of their intellectual capacity, bringing diverse academic disciplines into play. Here and there they might also have access to other resources which are lacking in the continent.

Theology, HIV/AIDS and the Quest for a Rebirth in Africa

Hopefully the study has shown thus far that theology, HIV/AIDS and the African renaissance are inextricably linked to one another. Put negatively, any attempt at creating dichotomies between the three, will greatly jeopardize the ongoing search for something radically new in the continent. In terms of a number of very broad strokes I shall conclude to make the following theological proposal.

First, Maluleke's[27] strong suggestion that the prevalence of HIV/AIDS in Africa constitutes a 'kairos', should form part of our theological analysis of HIV/AIDS. As a potent theological category 'kairos' speaks not only of danger, but also of opportunity. With HIV/AIDS there is an opportunity of developing new forms of human solidarity, family life and indeed a moral renewal. Second, there is a need to revisit a 'struggle' hermeneutic. Or to speak with the South African President, a rebellion hermeneutic is paramount. Third, I concur with Dube[28] in her understanding that a liberation hermeneutic is still very necessary pertaining to HIV/AIDS. There is a need to develop an understanding that in Africa HIV/AIDS is an unliberated zone. Fourth, in the area of healing there is a need to overcome the dichotomies and to return to an integration between spiritual, emotional, psychological, physical and social wellbeing. This is what the African notion of holistic healing is made of. I concur with Boesak[29] that no manner of economic development alone will restore the African soul. There is a need for a moral re-awakening and for a spiritual quality to our politics in Africa.

Fifth, the centrality of life in some theological responses to HIV/AIDS, should be regarded as highly significant in any debate on HIV/AIDS and the African renaissance. Fundamentally HIV/AIDS threatens the very life of the continent and fundamentally the African renaissance is about creating new life. The Biblical story of Jesus who came to regenerate and to bring life in abundance constitutes an indispensable moment in the hermeneutic cycle between HIV/AIDS and theology. Sixth, theology needs an African approach in responding to HIV/AIDS. The term African approach is used loosely here to allow for the expansion of rationality in terms of including stories, rituals, metaphors and myths.[30]

Notes

[1] Ruether, Kirsten, 'Stirring the Spirits in a Baffled Struggle for Constructive AIDS Politics'. A report on the AIDS in Context Conference, Johannesburg, 4–7 April 2001, *Missionalia, 29*(2) (August 2001): 321–41; Also cf, to Katongole, Kealotswe, Maluleke, Masenya, Njoroge, Ruether, and Stiebert as cited throughout the chapter!

[2] Van Houten, Richard, 'HIV/AIDS: An Overview', *REC Focus* 2(1) (2002): 2–43, here p. 2.

[3] Stiebert, Johanna, 'Does the Hebrew Bible have Anything to Tell us about HIV/AIDS?' *Missionalia, 29*(2) (August 2001): 174–85.

[4] Kealotswe, Obed N. 'Healing in the African Independent Churches in the Era of AIDS in Botswana' *Missionalia, 29*(2) (August 2001): 220–31.

[5] Granted, the billboard is not communicating anything else, but to draw attention to the serious nature of AIDS. Yet a slogan like this can quite easily exacerbate the notion of Africa as a dark, dying continent. Afro-pessimists will surely feed into this.

[6] Katongole, Emmanuel M. 'Christian ethics and AIDS in Africa today: Exploring the Limits of a Culture of Suspicion and Despair' *Missionalia* 29(2) (August 2001): 144–60.

[7] Mbeki, in an interview with SABCTV, June 2004.

[8] Before the 2004 General Elections in South Africa, the government policy on HIV/AIDS came under scrutiny from especially the Treatment Action Campaign (TAC), but was updated significantly with reference to the administration of antiretrovirals to AIDS patients. The government policy/plan is known as the Comprehensive HIV/AIDS Care Management and Treatment Plan.

[9] Katongole 2001: 144–60.

[10] Dube, Musa, (ed.). 'Biblical Studies and HIV/AIDS. Methods of integrating HIV/AIDS in Biblical Studies' in *HIV/AIDS and the Curriculum: Methods of Integrating HIV/AIDS in Theological Programmes* (Geneva: World Council of Churches, 2003), available at: http://www.wcc_coe.org/wcc/what/mission/hiv-curriculum-index.html.

[11] Rubingh, Eugene, 'Theological and Ethical Reflections on HIV/AIDS in Africa' *REC Focus, 2*(1) (March 2002): 44–64.

[12] Benn, Christopher, 'Solidariteit en Gemeenschap: Een Theologische Beschouwing over HIV/AIDS' *Wereld en Zending, 29 ste jaargang* (2) (2000): 63–70.

13 See for the AIDS/HIV debate *Missionalia 29*(2) (August 2001) the entire issue.

14 Stiebert 2001.

15 Masenya, Madipoane, 'Between Unjust Suffering and the 'Silent' God: Job and HIV/AIDS Sufferers in South Africa' *Missionalia, 29*(2) (August 2001): 186–99.

16 Benn 2000.

17 M. Percy, 'Christ the Healer: Modern Healing Movements and the Imperative of Praxis for the Poor', in *Studies in World Christianity 1/2*(1995): 122–24.

18 Musa Dube, available at: http://www.wcc_coe.org/wcc/what/mission/hiv-curriculum-index.html.

19 Maluleke Tinyiko S. 'The Challenge of HIV/AIDS for Theological Education in Africa: Towards an HIV/AIDS Sensitive Curriculum', *Missionalia, 29*(2) (August 2001): 125–43.

20 Kgosikwena, Kagiso B. 'Pastoral Care and the Dying Process of People Living with HIV/AIDS: Speaking of God in a Crisis', *Missionalia, 29*(2) (August 2001): 200–19.

21 Smith, Walter J., *Spiritual Care of Persons Living with HIV/AIDS in Handbook of Spirituality for Ministers*. (New York: Paulist Press, 1995), 447–68.

22 There is a growing body of literature on the African renaissance. A search of the catalogue of the University of South Africa library, shows 46 titles and a search of the internet more than 99,000 sites where pieces of information, speeches and articles could be found. The literature consulted for this paper is:
available at: http://www.anc.org.za/ancdocs/history/mbeki/1998/tm0928.htm; http://www.anc.org.za/ancdocs/history/mbeki/1998/tm0813.htm; and http://www.unv.edu/unupress/mbeki.html.
Boesak, Allan A., *The Tenderness Of Conscience: African Renaissance and the Spirituality of Politics* (Stellenbosch: African Sun Media, 2005); Mathebe, Lucky, *Bound by Tradition: the World of Thabo Mbeki* (Pretoria: University of South Africa, 2001); Shell, Robert, *HIV/AIDS: a Threat to the African Renaissance?* (Johannesburg: Konrad-Adenauer-Stiftung, 2000); Mbeki, Thabo, Statement by Deputy President Mbeki at the African Renaissance Conference Johannesburg, 28 September 1998 (undated), available at: http://www.anc.org.za/ancdocs/history/mbeki/1998/tm0928.htm; Mbeki, Thabo, The African Renaissance Statement of Deputy President, Thabo Mbeki, SABC Gallagher Estate, 13 August 1998 (undated), available at: http://www.anc.org.za/ancdocs/history/mbeki/1998/tm0813.htm; Vale, Peter C. J. and Maseko, Sipho, 'South Africa and the African Renaissance', *International Affairs 74*(2) (1998): 271–87.

23 Boesak 2005.

24 Mbeki, Thabo, The African Renaissance, South Africa and the World. South African Deputy President Thabo Mbeki speaks at the United Nations University, 9 April 1998 (undated) http://www.unu.edu/unupress/mbeki.html.

25 Boesak 2005.

26 Njoroge, Njambura J. 'Come Now, Let Us Reason Together', *Missionalia 29*(2) (2001): 232-257.

27 Maluleke 2001: 125, 129–30.

28 Musa Dube, available at: http://www.wcc-coe.org/wcc/what/mission/hiv-curriculum-index.html.

29 Boesak 2005.

[30] Scholars like Alvermann, Donna E., *Narrative Approaches* (undated), available at: http://www.readingonline.org/articles/handbook/alvermann/idex.html; Denis, Philippe, 'Sharing Family Stories in a Time of AIDS', *Missionalia*, *29*(2) (August 2001): 258–81, and Müller, Julian, 'HIV/AIDS, Narrative Practical Theology, and Postfoundationalism. The emergence of a new story', available at: http://www.julianmuller.co.za/emergence_story.pdf, have shown the fruitfulness of a narrative approach to research on HIV/AIDS.

Part Three

Charismatic/Pentecostal Perspectives

Chapter 13

Transnational Religious Networks and Indigenous Pentecostal Missionary Enterprises in the West African Coastal Region

Matthews A. Ojo

Introduction

This chapter,[1] from historical and contextual perspectives, discusses transnational religious networks and their interrelationship with the missionary enterprises initiated and promoted by Nigeria-based independent pentecostal and charismatic movements[2] within West Africa. Among other things, the study highlights the nature and dynamics of these networks as parts of the African initiatives in Christian missions, and lastly relates them to the globalization of African Christianity. Religious networking has become an important strategy for charismatic movements in Africa in their transborder expansion and in their attempts to operate within a global dimension. While not all transnational networks had missionary concerns, nevertheless on a global level they have bearing on missionary enterprises. Essentially, transnational networks have continued to provide structural visibility to transnational civil society in the West African sub-region.[3] Consequently, the missionary enterprises clearly depict the generative capacity of the charismatic movements, and they have become a way of furthering the contextualization of African Christianity.

Previous studies on the independent pentecostal and charismatic movements have not paid much attention to the significance of networking. Ojo[4] examined the growth of charismatic movements in Western Nigeria, while Ruth Marshall[5] focused on their socio-political involvement in the public sphere. Gifford[6] from various perspectives presented the growth of charismatic movements in many countries within one edited volume. Moreover, Gifford later[7] noted the influence of Nigerian pentecostalism on the growth and activities of some Ghanaian charismatic organizations, but failed to pursue the dimension of regional networking. Hackett[8] examined linkages in the appropriation of media technology by pentecostal and charismatic movements in Nigeria and Ghana. Ojo[9] examined in details cross-cultural missionary activities of Nigerian pentecostal and charismatic movements in Africa. Marshall-Fratani and A. Corten[10] largely examined pentecostal movements in Africa within the context of transnationalism and globalization. This chapter therefore advances our knowledge on the symbiotic relationship that exists in religious networking and indigenous missionary enterprises within the Anglophone and Francophone West African countries.

The rapid spread of the pentecostal and charismatic movements in Africa since the 1970s constitutes a major development within contemporary African Christianity. The movements were the fastest growing endeavour in West Africa in the 1980s and 1990s. From about 10 independent charismatic organizations in the mid-1970s largely restricted to Nigeria, the number has grown to over 10,000 groups across the continent. The membership is substantial with about 10 per cent of the 48 million Christians in Nigeria, about 6 per cent of the Christian population in Ghana, and not less than 2 per cent for the French-speaking countries. By the 1980s, this religious awakening had assumed social prominence due partly to increased media attention, and also to the proliferation of a large number of new churches advertising themselves seriously in the print and electronic media.

Charismatic movements in Nigeria were the first to be articulated after its small beginning as an evangelical revival among existing inter-denominational Christian student organizations in Nigerian universities and colleges. Contacts with pentecostal churches and freelance evangelists transformed the revival and it eventually became pentecostal in its doctrinal emphases and practices. By 1975, the renewal had stabilized with the appearance of charismatic organizations established by graduates who had participated in the revival on the campuses. By the 1980s, these organizations have become independent pentecostal churches. Through contacts in international conferences hosted by evangelical groups and through evangelistic campaigns, by the late 1970s, the Nigerian movements had planted branches in other African countries and have stimulated the growth of the charismatic renewal in these other countries. Particularly, the activities of Nigerian charismatics were more noticeable in the West African Francophone countries from the early 1980s. By the 1990s, the Nigerian movements had become the largest and the most active in the continent, and they have fostered the emergence of similar movements in other countries. Independent pentecostal and charismatic movements continue to spread because they are pragmatic in their approach to social and religious issues, and are also responding to the existential needs of Africans within the contemporary situations of socio-political disequilibrium.

Majority of the membership and leadership are youths, mostly college students and recent graduates. Pentecostal religion as a purveyor of modernity and its emphasis on personal empowerment seem to offer greater openings to the global world, hence its attraction to the young mobile educated people seeking self-realization amidst the deteriorating socio-economic and political situations in the continent. Moreover, the quest of the movements for modernity has continued to be demonstrated in the use of English as a medium of communication, in the use of electronic musical equipments, and in their appropriation of media technologies such as video, satellite broadcasting, and the Internet. Indeed, global communication has greatly aided the transmission of charismatic renewal all over the world.

The Dynamics of Transnational Religious Networks in West Africa

The phenomenal growth of pentecostal and charismatic movements in Africa since the 1970s is partly linked to the movements' mode of transmission as a transnational phenomenon. Marshall-Fratani and Corten have suggested that pentecostalism 'seems to be at the heart of processes of transnationalism and globalization'.[11] Hence, in their transfrontier expansion from Nigeria into other African countries, a web of networks was created with similar pentecostal churches in other African countries. Trans-national religious networks in West Africa are diverse and have been promoted for various motives. Improvement in road and telecommunication networks and the subsequent promotion of economic integration, following the establishment of Economic Community of West African States (ECOWAS) in 1975, have opened new possibilities for transborder expansion for religious movements.

Different modalities have enabled pentecostal and charismatic churches to become a transnational and transcultural phenomenon. Among these is the creation of mega-churches with multi-ethnic congregations, which often afterwards expand and create branches in other countries. Second, there exists a corporate self-presentation of their image as international based on the fact that they have branches in other countries, or have extended their missionary activities beyond Nigeria. This global outlook has become a prominent feature, and has enabled them enter other cultural contexts in and outside Africa. Third, there are linkages with Africans in the Diaspora, and with similar movements in the Western world. Fourth, Rosalind Hackett and Ruth Marshall-Fratani in 1998 have noted the appropriation of the media and media technologies as part of the globalizing options available to Ghanaian and Nigerian charismatic movements. Last, the churches' entrepreneurial organization, sophisticated marketing techniques, and modernizing tendencies have facilitated large-scale networks across political borders. This has further been enhanced by the gospel of prosperity, which is being promoted using a transnational register. Certainly, African pentecostal and charismatic churches have shown that they can transcend their restricted local origins and enter into new cultural milieus. Among the ways these informal networks have been promoted are the following.

First, there are churches in other West African countries planted by Nigerians either as branches of existing Nigerian churches or new churches altogether. The most noticeable among these is the Deeper Life Bible Church, which was established in April 1973 in Lagos by William F. Kumuyi, then a mathematics lecturer in the College of Education, University of Lagos. From being a small Bible study group, Deeper Life had a steady and rapid growth among young people throughout the 1970s. This was achieved through the use of literature and vigorous evangelistic activities. From the late 1970s Deeper Life embarked on expansion into other African countries.[12] In 1978, Kumuyi was invited to Kumasi, Ghana where he addressed an assembly of pentecostal leaders. Thereafter, a camp meeting held in 1979 resulted in a regular Bible study group, which in 1982 was transformed into an independent pentecostal church. The expulsion of Ghanaians from Nigeria in 1983 aided the growth of the church as some returnees who had become charismatics in Nigeria joined this branch.[13]

Likewise, Deeper Life was the first Nigerian church in the post-independence era to get to Cameroon. In 1982, a Bible study group was established in the coastal town, Limbe, but unable to secure a resident permit, a pastor posted from Nigeria left within a year. Another pastor sent in 1987 stayed till 2001, and fully established Deeper Life in the country.[14] Likewise, in Lomé, Togo, some Nigerians established a branch of Deeper Life there about 1982. In Benin Republic, a Deeper Life Bible Church that was established in Cotonou in the mid-1980s later expanded to Porto Novo in 1991. By 2001, the number of Deeper Life churches had increased to four in Port-Novo and its environs.

From the mid-1990s, many more Nigerian evangelists and charismatic churches established their presence in West African countries. The most important is the Living Faith Church (Winners' Chapel), a church that places much emphasis on success and prosperity, and accordingly has appealed to the young mobile educated people seeking self-expression within a modernizing milieu. In January 1995, Winners' Chapel was established in Monrovia Liberia and Freetown, Sierra Leone, when two pastors sent from Nigeria began Bible training on faith and prosperity theology.[15] In early 1996, additional branches were established in other West African countries, including a branch each in Accra, Ghana; Lomé, Togo; Niamey, Niger Republic; and Douala, Cameroon. By the end of the 1990s, Winners' Chapel has established at least a branch in the capital cities of about 30 African countries.[16] The Redeemed Christian Church of God expanded from Nigeria to Benin Republic, Cameroon and Ghana in the late 1990s. As the Nigeria-based churches expanded in the 1990s, they created more networks with their foreign counterparts.

Second, there are several West Africans who had gone for Bible training, religious conferences or for educational pursuits in Nigeria and then returned to their respective countries already inspired by their Nigerian experience.

Some of these have established independent charismatic churches in their countries and have continued to maintain regular contacts with their Nigerian benefactors, some of whom are leaders of pentecostal organizations. Undeniably, it was Benson Idahosa, who was the leading figure in creating educational and ministerial opportunities for other West African nationals, and who eventually had a lasting impact as he facilitated significant networks in the West African sub-region. Benson A. Idahosa established the Church of God Mission International in Benin City, Nigeria in 1970. Claiming a divine mandate to preach the gospel all over the world, he inaugurated the 'Idahosa World Outreach' in the mid-1970s as an organ to prosecute his evangelistic campaigns. He was the first African evangelist to promote the prosperity gospel, and he demonstrated this with his flamboyant lifestyle and by his emphasis on faith, miracles and prosperity. By the mid-1980s, Idahosa had traveled to about 76 countries, and in the course of these evangelistic campaigns he initiated networking with other African pentecostals.[17]

For example, in 1978, Idahosa conducted evangelistic campaigns in regional capitals, such as Accra, Kumasi, and Takoradi – all in Ghana. Delighted with the success of this campaign, Idahosa offered some scholarships to Ghanaians for Bible training in Nigeria. During the next five years, between 20 and 30 Ghanaians were trained each year under the Idahosa scholarship at the All Nations for Christ Bible Institute (ANCBI), Benin City, which Idahosa had established in 1975.[18] The 9-month Bible and theological training brought together many Africans, with Ghanaians being the largest group. For example, among the 1988 graduates there were 15 from Ghana, 7 from Chad, 2 from Zimbabwe, 3 from Kenya, 2 from Cameroon, 4 from Cote d'Ivoire, and 1 each from Sierra Leone and Togo.[19]

The Idahosa's scholarship scheme became an effective means of exporting the Nigerian pentecostal model and concepts across West Africa as most of Idahosa's disciples returned to their countries with strong pentecostal convictions. In addition, Idahosa in the early 1980s commenced a television programme, 'the Redemption Hour', on Ghana Television, and this broadcast was used largely for networking between Ghana and Nigeria. Benson Idahosa exerted a lasting influence on those trained in All Nations for Christ Bible Institute. Among these was Duncan Williams who in 1979, upon his graduation and return to Ghana established the Christian Action Faith Ministries International (CAFM) as Ghana's first indigenous charismatic Church. Besides, the Associate Bishop of the CAFM, Bishop James Saah also trained at ANCBI and for about a decade was the editor of the 'Redemption Faith magazine' while working with Idahosa in Nigeria. There is also Bishop Charles Agyem-Asare who trained in Nigeria in 1986 and later established the World Miracle Bible Church, as one of the largest charismatic churches in Ghana.[20] There are many other Ghanaians influenced by Idahosa who contributed in strengthening his networking with Ghana. Likewise, Pastor Suleiman Umar, who also trained at ANCBI upon his return to Niamey, Niger Republic, established 'Eglise Vie Abondante', in 1990 as the first independent charismatic church in the country.[21] Indeed, it was largely Idahosa's influence that brought independency to charismatic Christianity in some West African countries, because Idahosa instilled in those he trained that each of them could become a 'a giant', and truly some of them did become giants. Idahosa's style of preaching boldly and the ethic of hard work were reflected in many of his disciples.

Third, there are independent and itinerant Nigerian evangelists and missionaries who are living in other West African cities and are operating as pastors or evangelists, and have subsequently established churches. Among these is Bishop Raymond Ngwu who established the Living Word Fellowship in Yaoundé in 1992.[22] It is the second largest charismatic organizations in Yaoundé, the country's capital. Another one is Segun Adekoya, a Nigerian who had participated in the 1970 charismatic renewal in Nigeria and later relocated to Abidjan, Cote d'Ivoire, where he established the 'Eglise Du Plein Evangile' in December 1989.[23] This church is one of the earliest independent charismatic churches in the country. The influx of Nigerian pentecostal and charismatic churches also stimulated more indigenous initiatives, and later resulted in the proliferation of local pentecostal churches and organizations.

Furthermore, there is a burgeoning trade in and exchanges of pentecostal products such as recorded audio and video cassettes, home video films on religious themes, religious songs on cassettes and CDs, devotional literature, etc. mostly produced in Nigeria and distributed widely in the West African sub-region. These products, found in homes, offices and bookstores, provide a continuous flow of Nigerian pentecostal culture into other West African countries; hence they have become tangible resources for strengthening the networks. The popularity of Nigerian religious products can be explained in terms of their contextual relevance to the African situation and the fact that they also provide a richer variety of sources for spiritual nourishment more than similar products from other countries. Indirectly, a dependence on Nigeria was created for the sourcing of these products.

By the late 1990s, Nigeria's media power exhibited principally in the home video films either of Christian or secular themes, which have flooded markets in the West African coastal region, consequently projected Nigerian cultural values. By the beginning of the twenty-first century, Nigeria-based charismatic churches were already purchasing airtime on the radio and television stations of other countries. A prominent example on Ghana's Metro TV every Sunday afternoon is a religious program on relationships for young people, and is hosted by Bimbo Odukoya's the Fountain of Life Church, based in Lagos.[24] Likewise, Nigerian evangelists were purchasing airtime on 'Radio Bonne Nouvelle' in Yaoundé, and in other countries to broadcast their messages. More important is the fact that financial buoyancy of Nigerian charismatic churches in comparison with those of other West African countries have enabled

Nigerians to influence the pace and nature of religious networking on the West African coast.

Religious networking between Nigeria and other West African countries increased substantially in the 1990s through constant and free movement of people along the West African transnational highways. Personal friendship and entrepreneurial considerations were the catalysts for these transnational networks, which became more vigorous amidst the competition fostered by contemporary pentecostalism. Although, religious networks emanating from Nigeria are prominent and wider in scope than others, there are indeed cross-currents of networking from other West African countries into Nigeria. For example, by the mid-1980s Dr Zacharias Fomum, a Cameroonian and lecturer in the University of Yaoundé, had established an independent charismatic church, 'Communauté Missionanaire Chrétienne Internationale'. With a small discipleship group, and aided by a vigorous publishing outlet, a new phase of expansion began for pentecostalism.[25] For the first time in Cameroon, Fomum brought pentecostalism to a new limelight as a religion, not only for the deprived and the poor but also the educated elite. Through evangelistic activities and an effective literature ministry, Fomum created a large followership and numerous networks in other African countries. For instance, as far back as the late 1980s, Fomum's books have been sent freely from Cameroon to other charismatic churches and Christian students organizations in Nigeria, and in 1992 Dr. Zacharias Fomum was a guest speaker at a well-advertised religious gathering at the University of Ibadan, Nigeria.[26]

Other avenues for initiating and strengthening networking were the various conferences hosted in Nigeria by various pentecostal and charismatic churches, to which other Africans were invited. These include the 'International Consultation on Missions' held in Jos in August 1985,[27] the GoFest conferences in 1988 and 1998, and the much-advertised August 1992 'International Church Growth Conference', hosted in Lagos by Deeper Life. In 2002, Winners' Chapel initiated the 'Maximum Impact Summit' in some branches in other African countries. Through these conferences, new networks were initiated with some Africans pentecostal churches and their founders.

Indigenous Pentecostal and Charismatic Missionary Enterprises

The vitality of charismatic movements since the early 1970 was derived partly from its emphasis on evangelism, which eventually, provided the vehicle to disseminate the spirituality of the movements. In the early 1980s, healing was incorporated into evangelistic activities, and since then healing has grown to occupy a pivotal role among the doctrinal distinctives and religious practices held by charismatic movements in Nigeria. Charismatics have articulated the emphasis on evangelism in biblical and contextual contexts. In its biblical context, evangelism is directed towards conversion of people. In its cultural dimension, healing constitutes a metaphor of power and transformation freeing and rescuing humans from the grip of evil spirits, witches, forces of darkness, principalities, enemies, bad luck, repeated failures, which are ever present and prevalent in the African worldview. This new emphasis has recently been termed 'deliverance'. Indeed, Gifford[28] has recently highlighted those theological components of pentecostalism such as deliverance, faith gospel, and Christian Zionism that have both local and global dimensions.

Additionally, in its contemporary context, evangelism has become the antidote bringing positive change to the deteriorating socio-economic and political situations in Africa. charismatics and pentecostals hope that the economic, social and political situations of Africa will be transformed into a better one when the gospel has saturated the continent. 'Social reform therefore must always start with the individual by seeking to bring him into a saving relationship to Christ'[29] says a leader of a charismatic organization. 'Africa's deliverance', as a charismatic said, 'does not lie in shrewd politicians, renowned economists or learned educationists . . . but in using the strategy of evangelism'.[30] Therefore, to charismatics, evangelism constitutes a causality of change first in the individual and later in the society as a whole. This expansive perspective depicts how the local functions within the global transmission of pentecostalism.

The initial effort at becoming transnational was inspired by a missionary commitment, which arose from an ideological belief that Nigerian pentecostals have global responsibilities. It was the Christian Student Social Movements of Nigeria (CSSM), a charismatic organization among college and university students in the late 1970s and 1980s, which in its doctrinal emphases first linked evangelism to the global responsibilities of Nigerian charismatics. Thereafter, this orientation supplied the ideological impetus for the transcultural and the transborder activities of the Nigerian movements.[31] A constant stream of prophecies published in the CSSM's monthly bulletin and in the publications of other charismatic organizations kept on this transnational agenda. CSSM believes that there is a link between the political arena and the spiritual realm; hence, Christians must pray and uphold the political realm for the benefit of the society. One of the publications of CSSM stated that 'God intends that Nigeria should be the beacon of the gospel in Africa. The mantle of leadership in AFRICA . . . falls on the CHURCH in Nigeria. It is for this reason we are a little bit prosperous . . . This is for no other purpose that to enable the CHURCH champion God's ultimate will for Africa'.[32]

Another publication from another charismatic organization similarly stated that 'we must realize that the present revival and move of the Holy Spirit all over Nigeria is not only for Nigeria, but God has chosen Nigeria as the base from which He is going to invade other West African countries with the gospel of liberation and deliverance'.[33] At the May 1982 launching ceremony of the Christian Missionary Foundation, Emeka Nwankpa, one of the leading charismatics at that time said, 'God expressly intends that Nigeria should be the base for the gospel for West Africa and indeed the whole of Africa'.[34] The CSSM publication earlier quoted expatiated this responsibility thus, '. . . looking through the West African belt, Nigeria is surrounded by poverty-stricken and grossly under-developed nations. It is an act of Divine Providence that Nigeria stands out differently as the richest nation in terms of human and material resources in this belt. This is for no other purpose than to enable the Church champion God's ultimate will for Africa'.[35]

The linking of evangelism to a global responsibility was aided by the country's buoyant economy of the 1970s, which came from the oil boom following the October 1973 Arab-Israeli War and the consequent Arab oil embargo to the West. The oil boom enabled Nigeria to project its foreign relations to help the liberation struggles in southern Africa and give significant political leadership in Africa. It was in this era that Nigeria hosted the Second World Festival of Black Arts and Culture (FESTAC), a cultural festival that projected Nigeria image to the world. Moreover, the buoyant economy attracted millions of other Africans into the country for educational pursuits and greener pastures. The presence of these Africans within the same space as charismatics further broadened their outlook, and subsequently evangelistic campaigns were directed to these foreigners.

In response to these prophecies claims, some charismatic organizations adopted a missional emphasis, and soon initiated cross-cultural and transnational missionary enterprises within the West African sub-region. The earliest of such organizations was the Calvary Ministries (CAPRO), which was established in April 1975 in Zaria by some young Christian graduates undergoing their compulsory National Youth Service in Northern Nigeria. After an earlier unsuccessful evangelistic campaign to the Muslims in the Zaria old city, by 1976 CAPRO has firmly taken off as an evangelistic association targeting Muslims in Northern Nigeria and in the neighbouring Sahelian countries.

In 1980, following a visit of a member of CAPRO to Gambia, it established a network with a foreign-based mission group working in the country, and in that year sent out its first foreign missionary. In 1982, an additional missionary was added. By 1987, CAPRO foreign missions have been extended to Senegal, Niger Republic and Guinea Conakry. As it expanded into other African countries in the late 1980s and early 1990s, it created numerous networks with indigenous evangelicals and pentecostals in these countries to sustain its mission work.

Another Nigeria-based organization that has created regional networking through its missionary activities is the Christian Missionary Foundation (CMF), which was established as the evangelistic and missionary arm of CSSM. CSSM sought to incorporate socio-political concerns with evangelistic outreaches based on the ideological conviction that Nigeria and the whole continent of Africa will become more comfortable to live in when the Christian faith and its ideals completely penetrate and permeate the fabric of the national life. As part of CSSM's plans to reach out to the rural areas with its social gospel, Idere, a village in the Ibarapa division of Oyo State was chosen for its outreach following reports of widespread guinea worm infection. Subsequently, in May 1981, rural and medical missions were organized to Idere with some Christian doctors, medical and nursing students from the University College Hospital, Ibadan.[36] After an initial success, these efforts became more co-ordinated with the formation of the CMF on 13 September 1981. CMF was established with the aim of carrying on the work in Idere with medical, agricultural and industrial work, and to prepare Nigerian Christians for missionary work within Nigeria and abroad.[37] Students and young graduates were recruited as volunteer evangelists and missionaries to sustain the various emphasis of CMF work in Idere, and later outside Nigeria.

Equally significant for regional networking are CMF's foreign missions. The beginning of these can be traced back to student initiatives. After its public launching in May 1982, it took over all the exiting networks and contacts that CSSM's student volunteers have made with Christians in other West African countries. In October 1982 it began missionary work in Benin Republic, and in the same month it sent out its first missionary to Cote d'Ivoire; a country that became strategic for its networking with the Francophone countries. By the late 1990s, CMF was working in eight West and Central African countries.

In 1980, Deeper Life established the 'International Bible Training Centre' in Lagos for the training of Africans all over the continent. By 1981, there were about 600 students from about 20 countries in the institution.[38] Indeed, through such training facilities, charismatic movements spread rapidly across frontiers.

From 1989, a new era of religious networking for Nigeria-based charismatic organizations began when their missionary enterprises received international recognition and Nigerians were appointed into the leadership of international missionary organizations such as the Third World Missions Association, which was established in May 1989. The internationalizing of charismatic missions indirectly aided the growth of African immigrant religious communities in Europe and USA from the early 1990s as pentecostal literature from Africa strengthened the cultural base of these new communities, and provided a constant linkage with Africa. Economic decline, which intensified the migrations of Africans to the developed economies of the Western world in the late twentieth century, swelled the ranks of Nigerian migrants and 'African churches' in the Western countries. Besides, historic memory of the past and constant reference to the religious effervescence of pentecostal churches in Nigeria further provided additional linkages to the home countries. Moreover, confronted with secularization of the Western society, these immigrant Christians soon came to the belief that there was a divine task in their migration, which is to execute a God-given mandate to evangelize and re-invigorate the churches of their host communities. Kingsway International Christian Centre, founded in 1992 by Matthew Ashimolowo, is one of such churches with a missionary purpose. Regularly he broadcasts his success in the West on Nigerian television stations, thus further fueling the belief that Nigerians have a mission mandate to the entire world.

Conclusion

This chapter has outlined the growth, nature and significance of religious networking and missionary enterprises promoted by Nigeria-based independent pentecostal and charismatic organizations from the mid-1970s to the beginning of the twenty-first century. The missionary activities gave impetus to the movements to become transcultural and transnational. As the movements spread across the West African sub-region, they benefited from the institutional structures of the Economic Community of West African States (communications, highway networks, transportation, free movement of people, etc.) and from the support of Nigerian immigrant communities in other African countries for the consolidation of their growth. The growth of religious networking from the 1990s, as already noted, was due to a new orientation of entrepreneurship as competition sets in amongst the organizations. These networks are remarkable because they stimulate other social changes in the West African sub-region: they encourage cultural interchanges, provide theological and ideological support for doctrinal emphases and practices, and promote trade.

Equally important to the structures are the doctrinal emphases on healing, deliverance and prosperity that were transported from the local environment to become global through the Nigerian home video films and other media products widely distributed in Africa and in the Western world. That the local can transform and become global has become evident in the rapid growth of pentecostalism across Africa and beyond since the 1970s.

Notes

[1] This chapter has benefited from two research projects: a 1995–1997 research with funding provided by the Research Enablement Program, a grant program for mission scholarship supported by the Pew Charitable Trusts, Philadelphia, PA, USA, and administered by the Overseas Ministries Study Centre, New Haven, CT, USA; and a 2002–2003 project funded by the French Institute for Research in Africa (IFRA) under its program 'Transnational Networks and New Agents of Religion in West Africa'.

[2] The term 'independent charismatic movements', is used to distinguish these contemporary indigenous phenomenon from the classical pentecostal churches

such as the Assemblies of God, Foursquare Gospel Church, etc. which were introduced to Africa as a result of Western missionary work in the 1930s and 1940s.

3   Rudolph, Hoeber S. and Piscatori, James, (ed.), *Transnational Religion and Fading States* (Boulder, CO: Westview Press, 1997).

4   Ojo, Matthews A., 'Deeper Christian Life Ministry: A Case Study of the Charismatic Movements in Western Nigeria', *Journal of Religion in Africa*, *17*(2) (1988): 141–62; Idem, 'The Contextual Significance of the Charismatic Movements in Independent Nigeria', *Africa: Journal of the International African Institute*, *58*(2) (1988a): 175–92.

5   Marshall, Ruth 'Pentecostalism in Southern Nigeria: An Overview', in: Gifford, Paul, (ed.), *New Dimensions in African Christianity* (Nairobi: All African Conference of Churches, 1992), 8–39.

6   Gifford, Paul (ed.), *New Dimensions in African Christianity* (Nairobi: All African Conference of Churches, 1992).

7   Gifford, Paul, 'Ghana's charismatic Churches', *Journal of Religion in Africa*, *24*(3) (1994): 241–65.

8   Hackett, Rosalind J., 'Charismatic/Pentecostal Appropriation of Media Technologies in Nigeria and Ghana', *Journal of Religion in Africa*, *28*(3) (1998): 258–77.

9   Ojo, Matthews A., 'The Dynamics of Indigenous Charismatic Missionary Enterprises in West Africa', *Missionalia*, *25*(4) (1997): 37–561. Internet edition in Ojo, Matthews A., 'The Place of Evangelism in the Conception of Work among Charismatics in Nigeria', *Asia Journal of Theology*, *10*(1) (1996): 49–62.

10 Corten, André and Marshall-Fratani, Ruth, (eds), *Between Babel and Pentecost: Transnational Pentecostalism in Africa and Latin America* (Bloomington: Indiana University Press, 2001).

11 Ibid.: 10.

12 Ojo, Matthews A., 'Deeper Life Bible Church in Nigeria', in: Gifford, Paul, (ed.), 1992: 135–56.

13 Adubofor, Samuel B. 'Evangelical Parachurch Movements in Ghanaian Christianity c. 1950–early 1990s' (University of Edinburgh: Unpublished PhD thesis, 1994), 325–26, and interviews with some Deeper Life pastors and others in Accra, May 1996 and 1997.

14 Interview with various people in Douala and Yaounde, Cameroon in September 2002.

15 Living Faith Church, *Wonders of the Age* (Lagos: Dominion Publishing House, 1996), 283.

16 See http://www.winners-chapel.com/TheMinistry/AboutUs/INDEX.HTM

17 *Redemption Faith magazine*, (official voice of Idahosa World Outreach), Vol. 3 (Nov. 1985): 8–9.

18 Interviews with a number of Ghanaian Charismatics in Accra and Kumasi in February 2003.

19 Redemption Faith Magazine, Vol. 4(23) (March–April 1988): 8.

20 Gifford 1994.

21 Interview with Pastor Suleiman Umar, Niamey, Niger Republic, March 1997.

22 Interview with Bishop Christian Raymond Ngwu, Yaounde, 19 September 2002.

23 Interview with Dr Segun Adekoya, Abidjan, Cote d'Ivoire, 24 August 1996.

24 Personal observation while in Ghana in February 2003.

25 Interviews with Dr R. Ondoa, L. Naida and others in Douala and Yaounde, Cameroon in September 2002.
26 Personal experience as a leader of a Nigerian group who had distributed Fomum's book in the late 1980s.
27 Gbade, Niyi (ed.), *The Final Harvest: Mobilizing Indigenous Missions* (Jos: Nigeria Evangelical Missions Association, 1988), 1–4.
28 Gifford 2001.
29 Christian Social Responsibility, *Christian Students' Social Movement*, Working Manual No. 2 (Ile-Ife: CSSM, 1980), 7.
30 *Christian Missionary Foundation (Ibadan, Nigeria) Newsletter*, Vol. 6, combined nos. 4–6 (July–November 1987): 8.
31 CSSM was established by certain Christian students in the Universities of Ibadan and Ife in November 1977.
32 Christian Students' Social Movement of Nigeria, The Way out of Our Present Predicament: A Clarion Call on the Church (Advert issued in December 1983): 6.
33 *Herald of the Last Days*, No. 32, p. 9.
34 Nwankpa, Emeka, 'Missionary Challenges Facing Nigeria Christians Today', address read at launching ceremony of Christian Missionary Foundation on 15 May 1982 (Typescript, CMF archives, Ibadan, Nigeria, 1982): 3.
35 Christian Students' Social Movement of Nigeria 1983: 6.
36 Mission Focus: A Bulletin of the Christian Missionary Foundation (Nigeria), Maiden issue, (1982): 7.
37 Christian Missionary Foundation (Ibadan, Nigeria), 'Report of the Inaugural Meeting held at Idere (Ibarapa Division), 12 and 13 September 1981, pp. 1–4, CMF archives; see also the Constitution of the Christian Missionary Foundation' (Nigeria), typescript, 1.
38 Deeper Life Newsletter (Lagos, Nigeria) (September and October 1983): 12–13.

Chapter 14

The Role of Charismatic Christianity in Reshaping the Religious Scene in Africa: The Case of Kenya

Philomena Njeri Mwaura

Introduction

The last three decades of the twentieth century witnessed the most remarkable and significant development within African Christianity. This is the emergence of the pentecostal or charismatic movement. As Ruth Marshall observes, 'literally thousands of new churches and evangelical groups have cropped up in cities and towns, forming a broad-based religious movement which is rapidly becoming a powerful new and religious force'.[1] This type of Christianity has been lauded as 'the new dimension of Christianity in Africa which is drastically reshaping the face of Christianity'.[2] This is manifest all over Africa where the churches have gained prominence due to their aggressive evangelistic campaigns through the mass media, involvement in personal, social and political transformation and emphasis on a pietistic deliverance theology. Ogbu Kalu sees Pentecostalism as a:

> third response by Africans to the gospel message propagated by missionaries following the initial response by black cultural nationalists of the nineteenth century and the pneumatic response at the turn of the twentieth century by the so called 'Bantu Prophets' or 'praying people', . . . 'Aladura.' Pentecostalism became another kind of pneumatic response characterizing the modern period of African Church history.[3]

Allan Anderson views this type of African Pentecostal Christianity as not fundamentally different from the Holy Spirit movements and the so called 'prophet – healing' and 'spiritual churches' that preceded it in the African Instituted Churches (AICs).[4] Despite the various interpretations of the phenomena by scholars and the labels given to it, what is noteworthy is that all these manifestations of the pneumatic experience are a response of the Africans to their encounter with God through the power of the Holy Spirit. The responses form a continuation of movements within African Christian history and are all a response to the existential needs of Africans within their different contexts. The pentecostal movement is heterogeneous and cannot be grouped into one category. It comprises various churches, parachurch organizations and ministries. There are varying doctrinal emphasis, denominational affiliation as well as strategies in mission and engaging in social economic and political issues. All over Africa, the movement is said to have its roots in the parachurch evangelical associations which gained much prominence in the 1990s.[5]

Scholars of Pentecostalism in Africa identify two major phases of revival within African Christianity which have led to the evolvement of two distinct strands of churches. Matthew Ojo[6] writing about Nigeria distinguishes between pentecostal and charismatic groups while Ruth Marshall[7] distinguishes between the holiness movement and the pentecostals. The latter terms are confusing but seem to be based more on the historical foundations of these movements and their doctrinal emphasis. Ruth Marshall prefers to refer to the whole revival movement regardless of periodization as 'born-again'. To her, the common denominator in the movement is the conversion experience of being 'born again' through an individual act of repentance and submission.

The holiness/pentecostal churches have their roots in the student movement and fervent missionary activity of the 1960s and 1970s. In structure and organization they are close to their mother churches, that is, the classical pentecostal churches that were introduced by American and British missionaries in various parts of Africa between the 1920s and 1950s. Their doctrinal stress is on perfection, strict personal ethics, biblical inerrancy and a disdain for the world, interpreted as materialism and carnal pleasure which are viewed as sinful. They also emphasize personal salvation, baptism in the Holy Spirit and speaking in tongues. In different parts of Africa the onset of this type of Christianity was also influenced by various factors within each particular context.

The charismatics or pentecostals (as Ruth Marshall designates them) have their roots in the revival within the holiness churches in the 1970s, 1980s and 1990s. This revival gave birth to transdenominational charismatic groups with a base in universities and student groups. This was fuelled by an influx of American pentecostals through their literature, radio and television broadcasts and personal visits to Nigeria, Kenya, South Africa and elsewhere. Unlike the holiness churches which were characterized by a retreatist attitude from the world, the charismatics adopted a faith gospel, focussed on a this-worldly blessing and a deliverance theology. They have a doctrine of prosperity 'in which the spiritual and material fortunes of a believer are dependent on how much he gives spiritually and materially to God who will reward him by prospering him'.[8]

This revival has also been associated with the rise of the Faith Movement all over Africa influenced by American Evangelism. Several African founders of charismatic churches have been trained or mentored by proponents of the Faith and Prosperity Gospel like Kenneth Hagin Snr. and John Avanzini. Such renowned African church founders and leaders like Benson Idahosa of the Church of God Mission, David Oyedepo of the Winners' Chapel International and Enoch A. Adeboye, overseer of the Redeemed Christian Church of God (all Nigerian), Margaret Wanjiru of the Jesus Is Alive Ministries, Arthur Kitonga of the Redeemed Gospel Church and Gerry Kibarabara of the Church of the First Borns (all Kenyan) have been influenced by their encounter with the writings of and people like Kenneth Hagin Sr, John Avanzini, Oral Roberts, Billy Graham, T. L. Osborne, Derek Prince, Joyce Meyer and Myles Monroe.

The charismatics have incorporated a much higher percentage of educated, upwardly mobile youth and a more charismatic doctrine which stresses experiential faith, the centrality of the Holy Spirit and the spiritual gifts of speaking in tongues, faith-healing, miracles and evangelism. Marshall observes that in Nigeria these churches are designated as pentecostal.

In Ghana, these churches speak of themselves as 'charismatic churches' or 'charismatic ministries'.[9] In Kenya, the churches perceive themselves as pentecostal. Nevertheless scholars of the phenomenon prefer to label them African pentecostal churches or Neo-Pentecostal churches (NPCs), to distinguish them from the classical pentecostal churches that were established at the beginning of the twentieth century like the Pentecostal Assemblies of Canada and the Apostolic Faith Mission of Iowa. Allan Anderson applies the term 'Newer Pentecostals'[10] to refer to this variety of pentecostal churches and movements to distinguish them from classical pentecostals which originated from western pentecostal missions and the spiritual African Instituted Churches (AICs) and movements of renewal that arose independently of Anglo-American Pentecostalism, particularly within the African mainline churches.

Anderson rightly observes that the entrance and pervading influence of many different kinds of Neo- or Newer Pentecostal churches on the African scene now makes it even more difficult to develop a typology of the phenomenon. He further argues, 'it is becoming increasingly difficult to define 'pentecostal' precisely and if we persist in narrow perceptions of the term, we will escape reality'.[11] 'Charismatic movement' is a term solely used to refer to the renewal within mainstream Christianity, both Protestant and Catholic. Nevertheless, in order to avoid confusion, this chapter will restrict itself to using the term charismatic to describe the newer form of pentecostal Christianity which emerged in the 1970s and gained momentum in the 1990s.

The Origin of Charismatic Christianity in Kenya

When Charismatic Christianity emerged in Kenya, it found a ground that had already been prepared by classical pentecostal missionaries from the United

States of America and Canada and by the East African Revival movement. As early as 1912, revival had already occurred in the Anglican Church in Kenya and manifested itself in a popular charismatic (Roho) movement among young people. Its main leaders were Ibrahim Osodo and Alfayo Odongo Mango. Besides experiences of spirit baptism, zealous evangelism and other experiences of the Holy Spirit, the movement exhibited anti-colonial sentiments.[12] Later in 1926, revival occurred in the Friends African Mission (Quakers) in Kaimosi, the Apostolic Faith Mission of Iowa (AFMI, later Pentecostal Assemblies of Canada) at Nyang'ori, Western Kenya and in the Africa Inland Mission at Kijabe in Central Kenya.

Most of the protestant missions in Kenya[13] at the beginning of the twentieth century were evangelical and used the evangelistic strategy of open-air meetings. Evangelism by these churches entails verbal proclamation of the Gospel to the masses, appeal to salvation, conversion or spiritual rebirth and change of heart. Some African Instituted Churches and charismatic preachers that originated from these mission churches retained an evangelistic character and a focus on spiritual renewal through the charismatic gifts of speaking in tongues and mediation of healing.

The revival during this period stressed personal salvation and the experience of the Holy Spirit as a sign of sanctification. Confession of sins and speaking in tongues was later stressed by the African converts as evidence of receiving the Holy Spirit. The emergence of the revival was an African reaction to a Christianity that did not adequately address their religious experiences. This pentecostal experience resulted in the emergence of AICs of the Spiritual/Zionist/Roho variety.[14]

During the same decade in 1927, the East African Revival started in Rwanda and spread to Uganda, Tanzania and Kenya. The revival commonly referred to as the 'Balokole' (saved ones in Luganda) or 'Ahonoki' (saved ones in Gikuyu) evolved within missionary churches. Winters defines the movement as a 'revival in which nominal or "backslidden" Christians are "revived" in their commitment to the faith; it is not primarily a movement of charismatization affecting non-Christians'.[15] The movement was interdenominational, interracial, and interethnic and had a preponderance of women and the youth. It evolved as a response to the perceived lethargy of missionary Christianity and its being compromised by worldliness. It was an informal and spontaneous mass movement initiated and sustained mainly by both African laity and clergy but predominantly lay. Doctrinally, it reinforced the need for salvation as a personal encounter with Jesus, need for public confession of sins to attain forgiveness, personal holiness, asceticism, moral rectitude among its members, cleansing and power for believers through the death and resurrection of Jesus Christ.[16]

The revival was enhanced by the visit of international evangelists and the enthusiasm of the youth in schools and colleges. In the 1960s and 1970s, American Evangelists like Billy Graham and T. L. Osborne visited Kenya.

Between 26 February and 1 March 1960, Billy Graham, Joe Blinco and Grady Wilson held 'crusades' in Kisumu and Nairobi. The 'Kisumu crusade' is estimated to have attracted 22,300 people and 3,406 enquirers.[17] In 1966, the Billy Graham Evangelistic Association (BGEA) held another campaign in Nairobi and in December, 1976, they were amongst the key sponsors of the Pan-African Christian Leaders Assembly (PACLA) held in Nairobi. T. L. Osborne and his wife Daisy held 'crusades' in Mombasa in 1957 and 1986. Oral Roberts of Tulsa Oklahoma and Morris Cerullo are other evangelists who contributed to enhancing revival in Kenya in 1968 and 1973, respectively, through their faith-healing and prosperity message as well as training and equipping Christian leaders and laity for leadership and evangelism. The visits of international evangelists enabled Kenyan revivalists to discover that revival was a worldwide phenomenon and entailed more than revival preaching. It encompasses other charismatic gifts like healing. In schools, colleges and universities revival work was carried out by a section of the pentecostals who particularly targeted the youth perceived as the future of the church.

There also developed Christian ministries which focused on the youth and educational institutions such as the Kenya Students Christian Fellowship (KSCF), Campus Ministry, Trinity Fellowship, Life Ministry, the Fellowship of Christian Unions (FOCUS), and Youth for Christ and Ambassadors for Christ. The KSCF is significant for it is still an active youth ministry today. It was officially inaugurated in 1958 and registered with the Registrar of Societies in 1959. It consisted initially of Christian students from different districts in Kenya. It encouraged formation of evangelistic outreach teams within educational institutions. The teams challenged students to have an evangelistic obligation to their rural home areas and churches. KSCF still holds youth rallies and camps which have an evangelistic emphasis. FOCUS on the other hand was initially part of the Pan-African Fellowship of Evangelical Students (PAFES). It gained autonomy from PAFES to become a Kenyan movement in 1974. Both KSCF and FOCUS have been important bedrocks of the evangelistic activities operating in liaison but with independent church supervision. They work with Christian Unions which comprise Christian students and staff, especially in primary and secondary schools, colleges and universities. They train students in evangelism strategies and leadership skills.

Many people who were involved in the revival whether as adults or students later became prominent personalities and even founded churches and Para church organizations for example Joe Kayo, founder of the Deliverance Church, David Kimani, founder of the Bethel Mission, and Rt. Rev. Margaret Wangare, presiding Bishop of the Church of the Lord. The churches they founded are dotted all over the country. The revival therefore and the Pentecostal churches it gave birth to are the precursors of modern day charismatic leaders and churches.

From the 1980s to the present, pentecostal/charismatic fellowships, ministries and churches have proliferated, some founded by indigenous Kenyans and others founded by international evangelists from Asia, North America and the rest of Africa. Itinerant evangelists like Reinhardt Bonnke, Benny Hinn, Morris Cerullo, Joyce Meyer, Cecil Stewart, Emmanuel Eni and Simon Iheancho of Nigeria have marked Kenya's capital, Nairobi and other major towns. As Mugambi observes, these personalities preside 'over personal enterprises not directly related to any specific denominations . . . they claim to have spiritual gifts and charismatic powers of preaching and faith-healing'.[18] Emphases in these campaigns have been a 'spiritual renewal' and numerical expansion of Christianity. Though the East African Revival formed the foundation and background to the revival and charismatic Christianity in Kenya, other factors non-religious are also responsible for their emergence and have contributed towards the shape that this Christianity has adopted.

The Development of Charismatic Churches in Kenya

We have traced the evolvement of Pentecostal Christianity from its foundations in the classical Pentecostal missions and the East African Revival whose impact was felt between 1937 and 1965. The revival operated within the churches but with time Pentecostal churches emerged, particularly when revivalists were expelled from the mainline churches or fellowships grew and evolved into churches. Nevertheless, these types of Pentecostal churches have a different character from the charismatic/Pentecostal churches that emerged after the 1970s. It is nevertheless noteworthy that even these 1970s Pentecostal church leaders have had exposure to new teachings and doctrines of the Faith Movement and Prosperity Gospel and have therefore been transformed into Neo-Pentecostal churches. An example of such a church is the Redeemed Gospel Church of Bishop Arthur Kitonga.

Allan Anderson observes that all over Africa in the 1970s, new independent Pentecostal and charismatic churches began to emerge. Many of these churches were influenced by the 'pentecostal and charismatic movement in Europe and North America and by established Pentecostal churches in Africa',[19] but were already seen as independent of foreign control with an African foundation. As also noted, many arose in the context of interdenominational and evangelical campus and 'school organizations from which young charismatic leaders emerged with significant followings, and often the charismatic churches eventually replaced the former interdenominational movements'.[20]

In leadership structures, theology and liturgy, these churches differ quite markedly from the classical AICs, former mission churches and classical Pentecostal churches. As Anderson further observes, the following are the characteristics of the charismatic churches:

Their services are usually emotional and enthusiastic and many NPCs use electronic musical instruments, publish their own literature, and run their own Bible training centers for preachers, both men and women, to further propagate their message. These movements encourage the planting of new independent churches and make use of schoolrooms, cinemas, community halls, and even hotel conference rooms for their revival meetings. Church leaders sometimes travel the continent and other continents; and some produce glossy booklets and broadcast radio and television programs. They are often linked to wider international networks of independent charismatic preachers, some of which, by no means all, are dominated by North Americans. [21]

The charismatic churches have changed the face of Christianity in Africa particularly due to their emphasis on the pneumatic factor and providing space for women and youth. Scholars have viewed this pneumatic factor as the link between the spiritual AICs and the charismatics. According to Kalu, 'both lie on the same side of the typology of Christian forms. Both draw from the same issues raised in primal religion'.[22] They operate from the same map of the universe though colouring it differently. The charismatics also appropriate the American Prosperity Gospel, 'riveting to holiness and intercessory traditions'.

Factors behind the Upsurge of Charismatic Churches

What are the reasons for the emergence and appeal of charismatic churches in Kenya and elsewhere in Africa? Factors behind the emergence of charismatic churches can be located in social, economic, theological, cultural, religious and political spheres. Various scholars have given various postulations all of which make valid claims. Modern charismatic churches and new religious movements generally, can be linked to current economic, theological, cultural and political trends. Gifford for example attributes the upsurge of NPCs to the ailing economic situation in Africa since the 1980s.[23] The argument is that economic deprivation occasioned by poverty, bad governance and abuse of human rights in the Africa of the 1980s led to people seeking solace and welfare in the churches for they provided material, spiritual and social support. Sociologists also argue that new religious movements of any sort 'have their sources in crises in traditional social and religious institutions, brought on by modern life'.[24] This crisis of modernity has been the result of the undermining of traditional structures by physical, social and economic changes. Peter Berger avers:

> While modernization brings promises and tangible benefits it also produces tensions and discontent both institutionally and psychologically. In addition to the external institutional dislocations resulting from changes in the economic and political structures, there is massive alienation as a result of

the loss of community and the turbulent upheavals caused by social mobility, urbanization and technological transformations of everyday life.[25]

One result of modernization is secularism. This is a state in which according to Shorter, 'religion looses its hold both at the level of social institutions and at the level of human consciousness'.[26] It is a worldview that denies the immanence of God. Although by any standards, Kenya has a thriving Christianity, there is no doubt that secularism is creeping in. A survey of church attendance in Nairobi in 1989 and 1996 shows that although 80 per cent of Nairobians profess to be Christian, only 20 per cent attend church.[27] This is a serious indication that the forces of urbanization and other aspects of modernity have affected the religious consciousness of Kenyans. This theory is plausible because new religious movements do arise as a response to the problems of secularism and destruction of social structures.

Other scholars view the growth of charismatic churches as linked to the current globalizing trends in other spheres of life. Most noteworthy is the inherent tendency of Pentecostalism to align itself with modernity. This increases the force of externality in African Christianity. Indeed, Adrian Hastings postulated that pentecostals are an extension of the American electronic church. This does, however, not mean that African Pentecostal Christianity is totally foreign. There have indeed been local initiatives and as Gifford rightly observes, 'Africa's Christianity is both localized and part of the world religion'.[28] He further observes that 'the growth of Christianity in Africa was never unrelated to its relation with the wider world; externality has always been a factor in African Christianity'.[29] Yet this view seems to disregard African imprints on Christianity. They have indeed appropriated it as their own religion, and in many respects Pentecostal Christianity resonates with the African world view. To scholars of African Christianity like Ogbu Kalu, this is the single most factor that has led to the numerical growth of Christianity in Africa in the recent past. Though the issue of globalizing forces is significant, the former is much more prominent.

To Kalu, it is the pneumatic factor in Christianity that resonates with the vibrancy of primal African spirituality.[30] He further argues that 'the quest by Pentecostals to root their message into the African maps of the universe is buttressed by the efforts of African Christians of various hues. . . to interpret the Gospel from their meaning systems'.[31] To him too, African spatial conception of the world and their local conceptions and discourses of evil forces, witchcraft, possession and aetiology of disease and misfortunes resonate very well with Pentecostal ideology. This is the realm of African religiosity that was undermined by western missionary denigration of African spirituality and healing systems, having themselves come out of the enlightenment. Thus 'local discourse on emotions, and conceptions concerning witchcraft, misfortune, illness and possession became muted and downgraded but never really disappeared as they were part of the basic structures of society'.[32]

The fact that charismatic churches have highly developed ministries of deliverance where illness and lack of well-being is interpreted as emanating from witchcraft, sorcery, magic and a host of other evil forces emanating from the African worldview, bears out the validity of this theory. The concern with prosperity is also viewed as not a totally foreign view, as Africans, too, are primarily concerned with the pursuit of well-being which in some respects is understood in material terms. Nevertheless, preoccupation with prosperity has resulted in dangers of materialism and a diminishing of the central Gospel message of love, mercy, justice and humility.

To Van Djik, the growth of charismatic churches is catalysed by the born-again ideology with its attendant gifts of speaking in tongues and an ideology of leading a purified born-again social order. It empowers the young to challenge authority of the elders who had dominated religious leadership in the mainline churches and in government up to 1991. He argues,

> What the young preachers propound is a 'born again' identity that lies outside the control of gerontocratic authority exerted in tradition, church and party. Instead of utilizing a mnemonic scheme that keeps alive rituals and symbols related to the position of the elderly, the young preachers utilize elements that serve a mimetic scheme.[33]

Durkheim has observed the integrative value of religion. He underlines the instrumentality of shared societal values and moral beliefs as a basis for collective 'consciousness'.[34] Besides this sociological explanation which may tend to be reductionist and ignore other salient factors, there is what Kalu calls a providential model or theory. This model sees Pentecostalism and charismatic Christianity as a 'spontaneous global outpouring of the Holy Spirit'.[35] This is particularly evidenced by the rise of young itinerant preachers for example in Malawi, and the work of the student movements in Kenya, Nigeria, Uganda and elsewhere. The catalyst behind this propensity to proliferation is attributed to the 'fatigue of mainline churches and their collusion with years of corruption and power monotony. This thus 'elicited a pneumatic challenge perceived by some as God's judgment and reclamation of God's people'.[36] All these factors are therefore crucial to the emergence of charismatic churches but each context favours particular issues over others.

The Challenges of Charismatic Christianity in Reshaping the Christian Landscape in Kenya

The charismatic churches have challenged mainline Christianity in a variety of ways and particularly, to be more concerned with the spiritual yearnings of Africans derived from their worldview. The challenges are to be found in theology, teachings, and involvement in social and political concerns. These issues will be discussed in the following. It has already been mentioned that the charismatic churches are Pentecostal and therefore share basic teachings that are common to Pentecostalism. According to the Ghanaian Larbi the significant characteristics of Pentecostalism include,

> A strong Christology especially the name and blood of Jesus, biblical literalism, mission consciousness and spirit power concepts with special reference to 1 Corinthians 12, of which tongue speaking has an utmost significance. Other emphases are believer's baptism, baptism of the Holy Spirit (believed to be subsequent to salvation), strong evangelistic ethos, and the gift of the Holy Spirit.[37]

Some pentecostal denominations emphasize power-evangelism characterized by 'signs and wonders'. The major ones also place a strong emphasis on salvation from the guilt and power of sin through Christ's atonement. Anderson notes that, 'theologically, NPCs are christocentric but share an emphasis on the power of the Holy Spirit with other Pentecostals'.[38] There is also a particular focus on personal encounter with Christ (being born-again), long periods of individual and communal prayer, prayer for healing and for such problems as unemployment and poverty, deliverance from demons and the use of spiritual gifts such as speaking in tongues and prophecy.

One particular constitutive element of charismatic Christianity is the offer of a direct and particularly intense encounter with God which makes possible a profound change in the life of the person who experiences it. The reference to the Holy Spirit – which from the doctrinal point of view is characteristic of Pentecostalism – has to do fundamentally with the direct character of this encounter. Through the Holy Spirit, God makes Himself directly accessible to the believer who seeks Him, thus destroying the necessity of any kind of priestly mediation. The Holy Spirit takes possession of the believer and fills his/her life with new meaning. This encounter experienced as speaking in tongues and in other ecstatic experiences, makes possible the change in the life of the person who experiences it. It is not necessary for an immediate change in the objective conditions of the life of the person concerned, but rather in his/her subjectivity. That is in the way one sees him/herself and the way one perceives life. This is what is called healing. It leads to the acquisition of a new identity, security in belonging to a community that cares, and affirmation of oneself as a child of God who has worth. This leads to the re-orientation of a person's way of thinking, particularly when one's bondage to perceived traditional covenants with 'familial spirits,' are broken and one experiences liberation.

We agree with Anderson that Pentecostalism which has now become a predominantly third-world-phenomenon, privileges experience and practice. These are more important than formal ideology or even theology. Though there are yet no available statistics showing the growth trends of charismatic Christianity, scholars seem to agree that the Pentecostal fire has spread so rapidly that classical AICs and mainline churches have been losing members to the NPCs. The AICs and mainline churches have therefore been challenged to incorporate charismatic elements in their liturgy and theology in order to respond to the experiential dimensions of African spirituality. By strategically opening themselves to charismatic influences, the mainline churches have not yet only stemmed numerical loss, but have experienced real growth. As Kalu further observes, the 'broad character of African Pentecostalism is very ecumenical, against ethnicity or tribalism while effecting a new unity in Christ among Christians of various hues'.[39] Evangelism is a major focus of charismatic churches. It is seen as the central mission of the church. The goal of evangelism is primarily conversion. The mission initiative is cross-cultural but it is not mainly directed to non-Christians but to Christians already in other denominations. The purpose is to create awareness of salvation by exposing people to Gospel values and realities. However, the conventional meaning of mission as an outward-bound, cross-cultural and cross-religious drive is not totally absent. As Ojo observes,

> Evangelism is seen as a work of redemption to loosen and free human beings from the grips of evil spirits, witches, forces of darkness, principalities, enemies, bad luck and repeated failures, all of which are prevalent in the African worldview.[40]

A variety of strategies are employed for evangelism, which include 'crusades', door-to-door, bus- and street-evangelism, use of mass media and media technologies, bill boards, hand bills and tracts. Personal testimonies are also important features of evangelism. One great service that the charismatic/Pentecostals could offer to revitalize mission is the re-evaluation of personalized testimony, communicated in the very language of the people's experience of life.

Modern day charismatics have now developed a social and political ethic. Not only are they involved in welfare ministries to the needy but are joining other churches (ecumenicals and evangelicals) to comment on pertinent social and political issues in the country. This was particularly evident in Kenya between 1997 and 2004 in the struggle for democratization and the review of the Kenyan Constitution. This is a radical departure from previous stances of these churches that were seen as otherworldly. The charismatic churches have truly contributed to the development of an authentic African Christianity.

Conclusion

This chapter has argued that charismatic Christianity has reshaped the religious scene in Africa, and is moving towards being the characteristic form of

Christianity on the continent. Though it only gained prominence towards the last two decades of the twentieth century, it has contributed to church growth and evolvement of a theology more consonant with the spiritual needs of the African Christian. This contribution is evident in a theology of deliverance that takes the Africa's cosmology seriously, emphasis on evangelism, self-help discourses that enables Christians to surmount life problems, and holiness ethic that stresses individual transformation. Though charismatics have started engaging in social-political and economic concerns, they however, need to go beyond a focus on personal transformation to critiquing social, political and economic structural evil. They still face the danger of over-spiritualizing evil.

Notes

[1] Marshall, Ruth, 'Pentecostalism, in Southern Nigeria: An Overview' in: Gifford, Paul (ed.), *New Dimensions in African Christianity* (Nairobi: All Africa Conference of Churches, 1992), 7–32, here p. 7.

[2] Kalu, Ogbu, U. *Power, Poverty and Prayer. The Challenge of Poverty and Pluralism in African Christianity 1960–1996* (Frankfurt: Peter Lang, 2000), 103.

[3] Kalu, Ogbu, U. 'Preserving a World View: Pentecostalism in the African Map of the Universe', *Pneuma 24*(2) (2002): 110.

[4] Anderson, Allan, H. 'The Newer Pentecostal and Charismatic Churches: The Shape of Future Christianity in Africa', *Pneuma 24*(2) (2002): 167–83, here p. 167.

[5] Marshall 1992: 19.

[6] Ojo, Matthew, 'Deeper Life Bible Church of Nigeria', in: Gifford, Paul (ed.) 1992: 135–56, here pp. 135–37.

[7] Marshall 1992: 15.

[8] Ibid.

[9] Asamoah-Gyadu, Kwabena, J. '"Fireballs in our midst," West Africa's Burgeoning Charismatic Churches and the Pastoral Roles of Women', *Mission Studies, XV–1*(29) (1998): 15–31, here p. 15.

[10] Anderson 1992: 168.

[11] Ibid.

[12] Hoehler-Fatton, Cynthia, *Women of Fire and Spirit: Faith and Gender in Roho Religion in Western Kenya* (Oxford: Oxford University Press, 1996), 74–75.

[13] These missions included the Anglican Church (Church Missionary Society), United Methodist Mission, Church of Scotland Mission, Salvation Army, Evangelical Lutheran Church and Africa Inland Mission.

[14] Anderson, William, B. *The Church in East Africa 1840–1974* (Nairobi: Uzima Press, 1977), 118–20.

[15] Winter, Mark, 'The Balokole and the Protestant Ethic: A Critique', *Journal of Religion in Africa, XIV*(1) (1983): 58–73, here p. 69.

[16] Mambo, George, K. 'The Revival Fellowship (Brethren) in Kenya', in: Mambo, George K., McLaughlin, Janice, and McVeigh, Malcom J. (eds), *Kenya Churches Handbook: The Development of Kenyan Christianity 1498–1973* (Kisumu: Evangel Press, 1974), 110.

17 Samita, Zachariah, W. 'Development of Crusades in Kenya' (Unpublished PhD Thesis, Kenyatta University, 2004) 42.

18 Mugambi, Jesse, N.K. 'Evangelistic and Charismatic initiatives in Post Colonial Africa', in: Vahakangas Mika and Kyomo, Andrew, (eds), *Charismatic Renewal in Africa: A Challenge for African Christianity* (Nairobi: Acton Publishers, 2002), 111–44, here p. 127.

19 Anderson 2002: 169.

20 Asamoah-Gyadu, Kwabena, J. 'Traditional Missionary Christianity and New Religious Movements in Ghana', (MTh Thesis, University of Ghana, 1986), cited in Anderson, 2002: 170.

21 Ibid.

22 Kalu 2000: 105.

23 Gifford, Paul, *African Christianity: Its Public Role* (London: Hurst & Co., 1998), 324.

24 Hoover, Stewart, M., *Mass Media Religion: The Social Sources of the Electronic Church* (London: Sage Publications, 1988), 24.

25 Berger, cited in Hoover 1988: 24.

26 Shorter, Aylward and Njiru, Joseph, *Secularism in Africa: A Case Study of Nairobi City* (Nairobi: Paulines, 1997), 14.

27 Daystar University, Summary of Nairobi Church Survey (Nairobi: Daystar University College, 1985), 89–95.

28 Gifford 1998: 47.

29 Gifford 1998: 318.

30 Kalu 2002: 115.

31 Ibid.

32 Van Djik, Richard, 'Young Born Again Preachers in Post Independence Malawi: The Significance of an Extraneous Identity', in: Gifford, Paul (ed.) 1992: 57.

33 Ibid.: 77.

34 Durkheim, Emile, *Elementary Forms of the Religious Life* (New York: Collier Books, 1965), 402.

35 Kalu 2002: 125.

36 Ibid.

37 Larbi, Emmanuel, K. *Pentecostalism: The Eddies of Ghanaian Christianity* (Accra: Center for Pentecostal and Charismatic Studies, 2001), 32.

38 Anderson 2002: 171.

39 Kalu 2002: 129.

40 Ojo, Matthew, 'The Charismatic Movement in Nigeria Today', *International Bulletin of Missionary Research, 19*(3) (1995): 114–18, here p. 116.

Chapter 15

'I Will Put My Breath in You, and You Will Come to Life': Charismatic Renewal in Ghanaian Mainline Churches and its Implications for African 'Diasporean' Christianity

J. Kwabena Asamoah-Gyadu

Introduction

The explosion and growth of the Pentecostal movement is the single most important development that has occurred within Christianity in sub-Saharan Africa since the turn of the twentieth century. Exact statistics are difficult to come by, but the sheer numbers of pentecostal churches encountered in Africa's sprawling towns and cities, and the increasing numbers of publications dedicated to the study of African Pentecostalism, attest to the growing significance of Pentecostalism on the continent. The 'pentecostalization' of African Christianity began with the rise of independent indigenous pentecostal churches many of whom walked out of existing historic mission churches in order to give active expression to their new-found experiential religions. These older independent churches have been the most intensely studied form of African Christianity. From the middle of the twentieth century, but particularly within the last three decades, new forms of pentecostal movements have emerged in Africa. The neo-pentecostals, as I prefer to call these newer churches, have manifested in three main categories. These are: first, independent indigenous charismatic churches, second, transdenominational fellowships, and third, renewal groups within historic Western mission denominations. This chapter examines the history, mission, and theological orientations of the last of the three. Charismatic renewal movements have sustained a direct 'pentecostalizing' impact on the mother churches within which they operate.

Cephas N. Omenyo's recent study titled 'Pentecost outside Pentecostalism' has drawn attention to the growing significance of charismatic renewal movements within Ghanaian non-pentecostal denominations. The impact of renewal groups extends beyond their home countries into African Diasporas. Another important development in African Christianity as recent studies have shown is the rise of African churches in the Western European and North American diasporas. Many of these 'diasporean' congregations include several that trace their roots to historic mission denominations headquartered in Africa. On the one hand, the African historic mission denominations in the West are keen to preserve their traditional identities as Methodists, Roman Catholics, or Presbyterians. On the other hand however, the challenge from their independent pentecostal compatriots and the attraction that their informal, exuberant, and expressive charismatic worship hold for Africans, often forces the 'exiled' traditional denominations, in keeping with trends at home, to incorporate elements of Pentecostalism into their own liturgies.

These developments often raise tensions, because for many Africans in the Western diaspora, maintaining the Methodist or Presbyterian 'traditional' forms of worship, helps them connect with a certain identity that they find difficult to do away with. Using Ghana as a case study, this essay explores the antecedent factors leading to the popularity of charismatic renewal groups within historic mission churches, and the long shadows that activities at home often cast on branches operating abroad. The aim is to establish that branches of historic mission denominations abroad do not operate independently, and that their activities are virtually 'remote-controlled' by developments in their home countries.

Streams of Renewal within Ghanaian Christianity

This chapter, as we have noted, examines the phenomenon of 'pentecostalization' or 'charismaticization' of Ghanaian historic church Christianity. It pays particular attention to the response of church authority to the phenomenon of charismatic renewal within non-pentecostal churches. The central thesis here is that the push for the integration of a charismatic agenda into non-pentecostal liturgies is facilitated by charismatic renewal prayer groups operating within historic mission denominations. In his publication referred to earlier, Cephas Omenyo points out that 'whilst these groups have become catalysts for renewal in some denominations, they have also been the cause of conflict and misunderstanding in others'.[1] Using specific examples from Ghana, I will discuss some of the tensions that arise out of the desire to integrate charismatic Christianity into otherwise very formal historic mission church liturgical structures. Ghanaian historic Western mission denominations have followed the lead of their pentecostal/charismatic compatriots in establishing branches in Western countries. In keeping with the theme of the Berlin Conference as a forum for engagement between academics and practitioners on African diasporic Christianity, references are made to that context, too. The examples are drawn both from Roman Catholic and Protestant sources in order to give a broader picture of the phenomenon of charismatic renewal within historic mission Christianity in Ghana and its effects on similar churches in the Diaspora.

Pentecostalism is a religion that values, affirms, and 'actively' promotes the experiential presence of the Holy Spirit as part of 'normal' Christian life. As an enthusiastic form of religion, Pentecostalism generally promotes radical conversions, baptism of the Spirit with speaking in tongues, and other pneumatic phenomena including healing, prophecy, and miracles in general. The coterminous expression 'charismatic' comes from 'charismata', meaning 'gifts of grace'. 'Charismatic' is thus used to refer to 'renewal prayer groups' and movements operating within historic mission churches with the aim of revitalizing the life of the church through the restoration of the 'charismata pneumatika', 'spiritual gifts' to its worship life (I Cor. 12–14). 'The charismatic experience finds expression in a variety of spiritual gifts which are granted by the Holy Spirit for the benefit of the entire community'.[2] Pentecostal/charismatic Christians believe that 'pentecost', wherever it occurs, does so in fulfillment of the prophecy of Joel (2:28 f.), and that signs and wonders must accompany the ministry of today's church as they did in the ministry of the Apostles in Acts. Pentecostals and charismatics 'like to feel that they are alert to God's signs and wonders of whatever kind, wherever they have occurred, are occurring now, and will occur in the future'.[3]

In July 2003, one of the congregations of the Evangelical Presbyterian Church of Ghana (Global Evangelical Church since August 2003) advertised a revival program under the theme 'Breaking Family Curses'. Within the 'healing and deliverance' worldview of African pentecostal/charismatic Christianity, the source of problems in people's present may be traceable to acts of commission or omission located within their past. In that case a people's present, it is believed, may be influenced negatively until through prayer and deliverance rituals, they are freed from such supernatural encumbrances. The advertisement in question appeared on a street overhead banner that hung for several weeks across the busy Accra-Legon-Adenta road in the capital of Ghana. This mode of advertising Christian programs, inspired by the growing influence of Pentecostalism in Africa, would have been considered out of character for a historic mission denomination only a few years ago. With the gradual integration of charismatic renewal phenomena into historic mission church life, a 'charismaticization' of Christianity is currently underway in Africa. This is evident not only in the adoption of pentecostal/charismatic media cultures, but also in the programs and liturgical reforms occurring in historic mission Christianity. In the words of Omenyo, 'members of the various charismatic renewal groups are determined to remain in their "impoverished" churches and to revitalize them with the introduction of charismatic/pentecostal spirituality'.[4]

Historic mission Christianity established under the auspices of Western mission bodies from the nineteenth century have always been associated with

Enlightenment-oriented ordered liturgical forms and rationalist theologies. In Africa, the pressure from independent indigenous pentecostal churches appearing from the early years of the twentieth century has generated reforms within historic mission Christianity. The reforms started with the incorporation of locally composed choruses, drumming, dancing, and prayer vigils into historic mission church life. With the challenge coming from the presence of the newer independent pentecostal churches, these reforms have almost come full circle. The charismaticization of historic mission Christianity, now includes the insertion of informal 'praise and worship' segments into church liturgy, the use of holy expletives like shouts of Amen and hallelujahs in response to preaching, hand-lifting, kneeling, and spontaneous applauses during corporate worship. In Ghana today, historic mission churches now organize prayer pilgrimages for members. They hold national evangelistic/healing crusades, anointing services, and other renewal-oriented programs meant to empower people in the Spirit. The developments in question, I contend, constitute historic mission responses to the forceful challenge of pentecostal/charismatic Christianity in Africa.

In Ghana these pneumatic reforms have taken almost a century to take root in historic mission Christianity. Adherents of charismatic renewal groups who approve the Holy Spirit inspired experiences described above, would refer to is as 'refreshment', 'renewal', 'revival', 'the movement of the Spirit', or 'restoration of the church'. On the other hand those who dislike it call it 'emotionalism', 'enthusiasm', or even 'occult'.[5] The reference to charismatic renewal phenomena as belonging to the occult by its critics, recalls how the Musama Disco Christo Church (MDCC) started in Ghana. The MDCC is one of the biggest and oldest African instituted churches (AICs) in Ghana. Its name means 'Church of the Army of the Cross of Christ'. Around 1923, when Ghanaian Methodist catechist, William Egyanka Appiah, started speaking in tongues, seeing visions, prophesying, and healing the sick through prayer, he and his sympathizers were 'firmly ordered' by the Methodist Church authority to stop all their 'occult activities' because 'the Methodists were not like that'.[6] Almost a century later, historic mission churches accommodate charismatic renewal groups and phenomena within their ranks because their very survival has come to depend on how open they are to a pentecostalist culture.

Historic Mission Church Reactions to Charismatic Renewal

The success of independent churches like Egyanka Appiah's MDCC is based on the fact that historic mission churches in Ghana were pressured into renewal as a result of the drift of their members into Spiritual churches. In the words of the Presbyterian Church of Ghana Synod, 'it must be of interest to us that the

Presbyterian Church is proportionally best represented [in the Spiritual churches] including even some Church agents'.[7] Ironically, the Methodist Church Ghana, studying the same Spiritual church phenomenon, had also concluded in a 1968 Conference report that the Methodists 'had become the principal patrons' of these independent churches. Whether they were patronized mainly by Methodists or by Presbyterians, the bottom line was that, considerable numbers of the membership of historic mission denominations maintained allegiance to their mother churches for Sundays. In the rest of the week, however, the same members went in search of Christian spirituality that made sense in a precarious African environment with its belief in malevolent forces that impede human health and progress. The panic that followed the success of Ghana's Spiritual churches is evident in the Synod Proceedings and the Conference Reports of the Presbyterian and the Methodist churches on what to do about their own Christianity.

A Presbyterian response

The Presbyterian Church of Ghana (PCG) Synod was quite honest in her assessment of the situation and responded by setting up a committee in 1965 to study the phenomenon of charismatic renewal and advise the Church on what steps to take. The PCG Synod Committee clarified its mandate as 'an expression of the concern of the Church about the large numbers of people who leave the Presbyterian Church in order to join a Spiritual Church or to attend meetings of healers and prophets, and second, about groups forming themselves within the Church which often adopt similar practices usually unfamiliar to Presbyterian Church life'.[8] In the PCG, 'practices unfamiliar to our church' referred basically to speaking in tongues, healing and deliverance sessions, holding of all-night vigils characterized by loud mass extemporaneous prayers, the use of choruses (instead of hymns), prophecies, visions, revelations and other pneumatic phenomena associated with pentecostal/charismatic worship services. People joined the Spiritual churches because these churches provided the indigenous ecclesial contexts where the pneumatic phenomena facing resistance within the PCG enjoyed freer expression. One of the conclusions of the PCG Synod Committee is thus very instructive for our purposes:

> A large number of Christians join them because they are disappointed with their former churches. They complain that the worship there is dull and that there is no 'spiritual power', and that there is not sufficient prayer in the old churches. They therefore seek a younger, more zealous and more 'spiritual' fellowship.[9]

A number of people in the mainline churches, we have noted above, consequently adopted a system of plural belonging by maintaining membership of

their mother churches but worshipped with one of the many Spiritual churches
around at the time.

A Methodist response

At the 1969 Annual Conference of the Methodist Church Ghana (MCG) meeting in Sekondi (Western Region of Ghana), similar concerns regarding plural
belonging of Church members were expressed. In a report on 'The State of the
Work of God', it was suggested that it was necessary to study the phenomenon
of African Christian independency, 'and find out what is lacking in our Church
which members think is available in the so called Spiritual churches'.[10] The
MCG Conference subsequently agreed that 'everything possible should be
done rightly to guide the prayer groups and to retain them within the Church,
to the 'enrichment' of our prayer meetings . . . and the life of the Church as
whole'.[11] The Methodists suddenly revived their camp-meeting tradition in
which various circuits spent selected periods gathered in prayer in order to
experience the blessing of the Holy Spirit and bring revivals to their congregations. The MCG revisited the issue of renewal groups 10 years ago, when the
thirty-second Annual Conference constituted an Ad Hoc Committee to restudy
the charismatic movements and make recommendations on how they should
be handled. So in both the PCG and MCG communions, charismatic renewal
groups started as grassroots lay initiatives, 'groups forming themselves within
our Church'. Church authority only attempted to accommodate the movements on realizing that they could help to stem the tide of the loss of members
into existing independent indigenous pentecostal groups.

A Roman Catholic response

The response of the Roman Catholics towards the charismatic challenge has
been relatively smooth because of the official recognition that the Vatican has
for the movement. However at the local levels, things have not been that
straightforward. The case of the Charismatic Evangelistic Ministry (CEM)
formerly based at the University of Ghana, Legon, typifies the tensions caused
by attempts to accommodate movements that cherish spontaneity and direct
religious experience within one that remains highly formal and hierarchical
in Christian expression and liturgy. The leadership and initial core of the
membership of CEM were originally part of the University of Ghana Catholic
Charismatic Renewal movement.

   Steve Mensah and his twin brother Stanley were then two of its prominent
leaders. Steve is a preacher who exercised the gift of a pastor, and Stanley is a
gifted singer who was in charge of music and worship. Through the charismatic
leadership of Steve and Stanley, the Legon Catholic Charismatic group became
one of the most prominent in Ghana. The Movement's meetings attracted

many non-Catholics. This ecumenical spirit and the reluctance of Catholic charismatics to recognize certain cherished traditions of the Church led to tensions with the RCC authority. After protracted attempts to deal with the matter failed, Steve and Stanley announced their independence of the RCC in 1990. A considerable number of the original group followed the seceding brothers and continued meeting as an independent charismatic fellowship. Three years later, the fellowship was inaugurated as an independent charismatic church, the Charismatic Evangelistic Ministry, which adopted as its motto 'No Oil no Flame'. On the reason why they decided to sever links with their mother Church, Steve told me in an interview that 'the Catholic Church structures were too stiff and we had to move out to do what God wants us to do'.

Tradition and Change

Charismatic movements are oriented towards direct access to the sacred, so the hierarchical and mediatorial nature of Catholic priesthood and liturgy became a problem. Recounting the experiences of one Nigerian community, S. U. Erivwo points to how members of Catholic Charismatic Renewal movements seceded to join the late Nigerian charismatic Archbishop Benson Idahosa. Many of the members had gone through religious experiences that they described as being 'born again'. Subsequently, they rejected such traditional Catholic doctrines as: regular and auricular confession of sins to the priest, prayers offered through departed saints and the Virgin Mary, the habit of eating meat on Good Friday, the use of the rosary and the devotional habit of kissing the cross.[12] Some conclusions arise out of the responses of Ghana's historic mission churches to the phenomenon of charismatic renewal that are revealing for our discussion.

1. The acknowledgement by the Synod Committee of the PCG of the veracity of the complaint that Presbyterian worship is 'dull and lacked vitality', and that as a result, members were filling the vacuum in their liturgical lives elsewhere.
2. The reference to groups 'forming themselves within our Church' which shows that the groups concerned were grassroots movements through which ordinary lay people had taken their spiritual destiny into their own hands. This development has deeper implications for lay involvement and ecumenism.
3. The PCG Synod Committee and the MCG Conference both submitted that their churches should recognize the internal renewal groups in order to curb the loss of members to independent Spiritual churches.

The result of these observations is that from the 1970s, charismatic renewal prayer groups started enjoying more tolerant responses from historic mission churches in which they operated. A former moderator of the Presbyterian Church of Ghana, the Rt. Rev. Anthony A. Beeko, gives the following account of how he himself, following an initial attitude of hostility and skepticism, later came to accept the Bible Study and Prayer Group (BSPG) as a vital part of PCG church life. He was responding to a query from me on his perceived tolerance of the BSPG. 'I used to be skeptical of the BSPG myself, but an experience I had has changed that completely'. According to him,

> whilst serving as the Chairman of the Akim Kibi Presbytery of the Presbyte-rian Church of Ghana, I was in the office one morning preparing a conference paper. Suddenly I heard loud noises from a crowd that had gathered at the office premises. When I went out to enquire what was happening, I was confronted with a traditional priestess followed by a sizeable crowd. The priestess claimed she had been told by a certain 'voice' to come to see me, and that I would deliver her from her fetish. She had become ecstatic and a member of the crowd told me that the woman was a priestess of the river deity 'Bootwiri' of Kibi. I was confused because I had no knowledge of how to undertake deliverance, yet the woman wanted to be free from the deity to become a Christian. I dismissed the crowd, and with a few of my elders, we sang some hymns, I prayed and then read Psalm 23. At the end of these prayers, the priestess had become sober. I then invited the leaders of the BSPG who I knew were conversant with the ministry of deliverance to deal with the situation. They did exorcise the spirit of *Bootwiri* from the priestess. The former priestess was subsequently baptized and she enlisted as a member of the Presbyterian Church at Akim Kibi.

The Rt. Rev. Beeko was unambiguous in his conclusion: 'The experience taught me that the BSPG had more to offer than I knew; above all they taught me that I must move away from my book theology'. In 'Pentecost outside Pentecostalism' referred to earlier, Omenyo has articulated for us the histories, presence, nature, and theology of charismatic groups functioning within historic mission denominations in Ghana. Members of charismatic groups, as he notes, tend to be very active members of the respective churches with some even holding leadership positions. Historic mission denominations are thus 'compelled to take a stance towards the charismatic groups'.[13] There are at least three main areas in which tensions may arise between traditional churches and charismatic renewal movements, and these I identify to be: first tensions relating to whether the exercise of charismata should be treated as a valid option for the church or as essential gifts; second, tensions arising out of lay involvement in charismatic renewal; and third the struggle to retain identity in the face of change instigated by charismatic renewal. In the rest of this presentation, I will examine each of these tensions briefly and relate them to historic mission Christianity in the diaspora.

Valid Option or Essential Gift?

Peter Hocken has discussed the nature of the tension between charismatic renewal and historic mission churches in an article relating to the RCC.[14] He explains that RCC authority initially categorized the charismatic movement as a 'spirituality' by accepting it as a valid expression of Christian faith, but essentially making it one valid option among many. In the example of the PCG to which we referred earlier, one of the recommendations of the Synod Committee was to treat the BSPG as an 'organization that could be constituted and recognized as a Church movement like the Singing Bands [and others]'.[15] In the case of the RCC, members of the Charismatic Movement, Hocken explains, found this attitude unacceptable because for them, 'the renewal is for the whole Church'. This creates a tension with non-members who with some reluctance treat the movement as one option among several spiritualities or organizations in the church, and participants who see the movement as directed towards the renewal of the whole church.[16]

What Hocken describes in relation to the Catholic Church, is a common tension associated with the relationship between church authority and members of renewal movements. For participants in the charismatic renewal movements, the entire historic mission church needs the spirit of renewal. They are 'dry bones' that need the invasion of the Spirit of the Lord to experience new life. In Pauline thought, the church of the New Testament was thoroughly charismatic, that is, a fellowship in which the Spirit of God was experienced as his 'empowering presence'. Charismatic renewal prayer groups, and the endowments of the Holy Spirit, if the historic mission churches were to be true to the spirit of the NT, must therefore be treated as 'essential gifts' and not optional extras that the church could do without.

Lay Involvement

In the events surrounding the Legon charismatic fellowship I narrated above, the participation of non-Catholics in a Catholic movement, and the expression by lay persons of ministries normally reserved for priests, are two of the issues that made the existence of the movement untenable from the RCC viewpoint. I share the opinion of Sepúlveda that the constitutive act of the pentecostal movement is an 'offer of a direct and particularly intense encounter with God which makes possible a profound change in the life of the person who experiences it'. Through the Holy Spirit, as he explains, 'God makes himself directly accessible to the believer who seeks him, thus destroying the necessity of every kind of external priestly mediation'.[17] The key expression here is 'direct accessibility' to the Spirit. When that happens, the legitimacy of priesthood comes to be based on experience rather than theological training and ordination.

It is instructive that in the story narrated above, the former moderator of the Presbyterian Church had to rely on the un-ordained members of his Church to deal with a case of spirit possession. In African contexts, once people realize that profound religious experiences enable ordinary people to minister to their needs, trained clergy may be ignored in favour of pastoral care from the new people of the Spirit. The attempt by renewal movements, based on the principle of direct accessibility to God, to recapture for the life of the church some spiritual vitality, tends, as Gordon Fee observes, to make institutionalized Christianity nervous in both positive and negative ways.[18] The positive response has been that historic churches created the needed space for renewal movements to operate. Patrick J. Ryan, a Jesuit priest and former professor of religion at the University of Cape Coast in Ghana, was candid in his opinion on how renewal has helped the Roman Catholic Church in Ghana, and cautions ordained clergy against adopting a negative attitude towards them:

> In his providence, twenty years ago God provided Ghanaian Catholicism with a partial answer to the problems posed by neo-Protestant Pentecostalism. Too few priests have recognized the importance of that answer and have tried to ignore or even relegate that answer to an insignificant corner. Catholic Charismatic Renewal fully Catholic and fully Charismatic can and does offer Catholics all that might otherwise attract them away from humdrum masses and devotional exercises to the religiously attractive realm of neo-Protestant Pentecostalism. When priests ignore charismatic prayer groups in the pastoral bailiwicks, the prayer groups sometimes go astray, as many of us have learned from sad experience.[19]

A direct access to the Spirit radicalizes the Protestant principle of the priesthood of all believers, introducing a more NT pattern of ecclesiology into churches in which priesthood may have hitherto been defined only in terms of the ordained ministry. The rise of this new form of 'lay spirit-filled pastor' makes the trained clergy uncomfortable often leading to resistance that is overstretched to cover charismatic renewal groups. Allan Anderson has pointed to the import of the involvement of the laity in Pentecostalism as a major strength of the movement, noting that, once people had a direct access to God through their Holy Spirit experiences, they felt, 'there was no need for a theologically articulate clergy, because cerebral and clerical Christianity had, in the minds of many people, already failed them'. What was needed, according to Anderson, 'was a demonstration of power by indigenous people to whom ordinary people could easily relate'. This, in his words, 'was the democratization of Christianity, for henceforth the mystery of the gospel would no longer be reserved for a select privileged and educated few, but would be revealed to whoever was willing to receive it and pass it on'.[20]

The discomfiture of the historic mission churches with the rise of movements over which they do not have much control is evident in a document circulated by Catholic Bishops in Ghana among parishes operating charismatic renewal groups. The document states in part that in order not to lose the Catholic identity of the Charismatic Movement, 'leaders must be practicing Catholics, capable of sharing in the full sacramental life of the Church; leaders must be people with a mature grasp of the Catholic Faith; they must avoid introducing into prayer meetings non-Catholic ways, and modes of teaching incongruous with Catholic doctrine'.

The Identity Question

We have noted that to stem the tide of their members drifting into independent churches in search of renewal, historic mission churches started tolerating renewal movements that they had hitherto fiercely resisted as non-conformist to their inherited Western Christian traditions. The attitude of tolerance instead of full acceptance and integration contributes to the tensions between agitators of renewal and pushers for the maintenance of inherited ecclesial traditions. Charismatic renewal movements have changed the nature of worship in historic mission churches, and tensions continue to exist between those stressing the maintenance of tradition in order to retain their identity as Methodists, Anglicans, Catholics, and Presbyterians, and those pressing for change because the rigid liturgies do not minister to the needs of church members.

Forms of worship operating within historic mission churches today tend to be an amalgam of the informal charismatic style and the received orders of service from their Western missionary traditions. In the case of the MCG for example, some of the collects and designated prayers that are read during services, and the singing of Canticles and Psalms have been dropped, or in some cases, shortened in favour of the charismatic styled informal 'praise and worship' segment. In the 'praise' part, pentecostal choruses are sung accompanied by handclapping and dancing. The 'worship' segment is where the singing of songs slows down considerably and with gestures such as hand-lifting, kneeling, interspersed with personal words of exultation, people pray to acknowledge who God is and what he means to his people.

For Church authority and members who are traditionally or denominationally minded, the 'charismaticization' of historic mission churches by renewal groups threatens their identity as Methodists, Presbyterians, and Roman Catholics. In one case discussed by Birgit Meyer, these tensions led to a session within the Ghana's Evangelical Presbyterian Church in 1992.[21] The tensions exist because the choice for charismatic renewal results from conflicts between a Christianity centred on what has been described as the 'subjectivity' of dogma in which faith consists of formal conscious and rational acceptance of determined beliefs or doctrines, and one that gives primacy to the subjective experience of God in which faith is a response to a kind of possession of one's being by the divine. Charismatic renewal expresses a kind of popular

Christianity 'which reacts against changes, which, in their process of institution-alization, have become very distant from the people, in their language, or theology, in their practices, as well as in their religious or social aspects'.[22]

Charismatic Renewal and Mission Churches in the Diaspora

Emmanuel Akyeampong has discussed how the 'diaspora' has become an important economic and political resource-base for Africans as well as a stage for redefining one's social identity.[23] He observes: 'in this century, Africa and its diaspora exist in a closer physical union than in any previous period'.[24] Gerrie ter Haar has affirmed that Ghanaians constitute 'the largest African population in Europe' and has discussed some of the religious collectives emerging out of the large group of African immigrants.[25] Much of the discussion on African Christianity in the diaspora has however, centred on the pentecostal/charismatic churches. In the last decade or so, a number of historic mission congregations have also emerged in the diaspora. For example, there are Ghanaian Methodist Churches in Toronto, New York, New Jersey, Washington, Hamburg, Düsseldorf and Parma. These churches were not initiated by the mother churches, but rather by ordinary church members who have come together in order to maintain a certain historic mission church identity. So for these churches, the maintenance of liturgical identity is perhaps the single most important factor that keeps them together as a religious union. The members had previously worshipped in the independent pentecostal/ charismatic churches in the diaspora, but had quickly moved out so that they could worship in a more 'Methodist', 'Presbyterian', 'Anglican' or 'Roman Catholic' way.

Being Methodist or Presbyterian in such contexts, often means following the liturgical formula in use by those traditions back home in Ghana. Yet there may be members who had been part of renewal movements back home and who try to push that agenda. In the process, similar tensions arise against the backdrop of the attempt to be Methodists and at the same time remain open to the phe-nomenon of renewal that has come to characterize the mother churches at home. The general complaint of those unhappy with the 'charismaticization' of their Methodist or Presbyterian churches abroad is that, the charismatic inno-vations erode the distinctions between them and the many pentecostal and charismatic churches that have proliferated in the diaspora within the last dec-ade. Many of these 'hustlers' as Ghanaians in the diaspora are generally called, have obviously been away for long periods, sometimes for decades, and so have nostalgic memories of historic mission church worship as it pertains at home. In other words, the 'closer physical union' that Akyeampong talks about between Africans at home and in the diaspora, is applicable to the Christian religious context too, especially in the case of the historic mission churches whose aim is to replicate what they have always known as the Methodist or Presbyterian way of doing things.

The 'Valley of Dry Bones'

Theologically, the phenomenon of charismatic renewal within Ghanaian historic mission church Christianity as I have approached it, could be interpreted in terms of the imagery of 'life for dry bones' found in Ezekiel. In a World Council of Church publication, Arnold Bittlinger explains the theological significance of charismatic renewal movements as representing longings for:[26]

1. A truly spiritual life, in reaction against an over-cerebral Christianity.
2. Real fellowship (one in which the gifts of the individual are taken seriously), in reaction against a Christianity that reduced church members to minor supernumeraries.
3. Strength, in reaction against a Christianity which denied or explained away the miracles and mighty works attested in the New Testament.'

In this view, Christianities that are 'over-cerebral', tend to reduce members to minor supernumeraries and deny the miraculous elements of the gospel, are references to the attitudes of the established historic denominations to the phenomenon of charismatic renewal. In the attempt to integrate charismatic experiences into historic mission church life, tensions arise particularly between church authority and adherents of renewal movements. These tensions have much to do with the nature of 'charisma' itself. Charisma is spontaneous, unpredictable and aggressive, and so has difficulty in being integrated into traditional institutional arrangements. Renewal movements, through their informal expressive modes of worship, stand as critiques of mainstream religion for being preoccupied with outward forms and ordinances. Through charismatic renewal, authentic Christianity gets restored as an affair of the heart through the activity of the Spirit.[27] To quote the words of Middlemiss, 'the desire to restore the primitive spirituality of the early church permeates the charismatic movement. Its aim is to be like the church of the NT in its simplicity, commitment, radicalism, and power'.[28]

Edith Blumhofer has also written that the modern pentecostal movement emerged at the turn of the century 'as a protest against dry denominationalism'. In her words:

> [Pentecostals] sought to reverse the overwhelming trend toward 'carnality' in the churches and among church members. Everything from church-sponsored socials to the pervasiveness among Christians of stylish clothing

and secular amusements, as well as declining attendance at prayer meetings, verified their conviction that the church had lost spiritual power. 'Formal, cold, dead denominational churches' seemed to contrast sharply with the noisy fervour that marked early Pentecostal gatherings. Their faith centred on a series of defining encounters between the individual and God that they regarded as the hallmark of true Christianity.[29]

This aim of charismatic renewal groups to revitalize the staid, silent, and over-formalized liturgical practices of historic mission denominations, recalls the image of the dry bones in the prophecy of Ezek. 37. In that passage, we encounter the symbols of 'wind' and 'breath' in the restoration of life and vitality to dead bones in the 'valley' symbolizing death and hopelessness. In contemporary charismatic hermeneutic, the 'valley of dry bones', images the religious life of historic denominations without the activity of the Holy Spirit who alone, as the breath of God, restores life and vitality to a lifeless and despondent church as he did for Israel under the prophetic mandate of the prophet, Ezekiel. There are some who believe in tradition because it sustains identity. The result is that the desire to integrate charismatic renewal phenomena into traditional churches, whether at home or in the Diaspora, has often given rise to tensions, the nature of which I have attempted to explain in this chapter.

Notes

[1] Omenyo, Cephas N., *Pentecost Outside Pentecostalism: A Study of the Development of Charismatic Renewal in the Mainline Churches in Ghana* (Amsterdam: Boekencentrum, 2002), 7.

[2] Gelpi, Donald L., *Pentecostalism: A Theological Viewpoint* (NY: Paulist Press, 1971), 83.

[3] Barrett, David B., 'Signs, Wonders, and Statistics in the World of Today', in: Jan A. B. Jongeneel (ed.), *Pentecost, Mission, and Ecumenism: Essays in Intercultural Theology* (Frankfurt am Main: Peter Lang, 1992), 188.

[4] Omenyo 2002: 7.

[5] Middlemiss, David, *Interpreting Charismatic Experience* (London: SCM, 1996), 1.

[6] Baëta, Christian G., *Prophetism in Ghana* (London: SCM, 1962), 35.

[7] Presbyterian Church of Ghana, Minutes of 37th Synod Report (29–31 August, 1966), 44.

[8] Presbyterian Church of Ghana 1966: 41.

[9] Presbyterian Church of Ghana 1966: 42.

[10] Methodist Church Ghana, 'Report of the Committee on the Life of the Church to the Annual Conference', *Representative Session Agenda* (Sekondi, 1969), 34.

[11] Methodist Church Ghana 1969: 35.

[12] Erivwo, S. U., A Consideration of the Charismatic Movement among the Urhobo and Isoko Speakers: 1929 to Date', *Orita, 15* (1983): 26.

13 Omenyo 2002: 7.
14 Hocken, Peter, 'Charismatic Renewal in the Roman Catholic Church: Reception and Challenge', in: Jan A. B. Jongeneel, a.o. (ed.), Pentecost, Mission and Ecumenism: Essays on Intercultural Theology (Frankfurt am Main: Peter Lang, 1992), 301–9.
15 Presbyterian Church of Ghana 1966: 52.
16 Hocken 1992: 302.
17 Sepúlveda, Juan, Reflections on the Pentecostal Contribution to the Mission of the Church in Latin America, *Journal of Pentecostal Theology, 1* (1992): 100.
18 Fee, Gordon D., *Paul, the Spirit, and the People of God* (London: Hodder and Stoughton, 1996), 185.
19 Ryan, Patrick J., 'The Phenomenon of Independent Religious Movements in Ghana', *Catholic Standard (March 15-21)* (1992): 6.
20 Anderson, Allan H. and Walter J. Hollenweger (ed.), *Pentecostals after a Century: Global Perspectives on a Movement in Transition* (Sheffield: Sheffield Academic Press, 1999), 222.
21 Meyer, Birgit, *Translating the Devil: Religion and Modernity among the Ewe of Ghana* (Edinburgh: Edinburgh University Press, 1999).
22 Sepúlveda 1992: 95.
23 Akyeampong, Emmanuel, 'Africans in the diaspora: the diaspora and Africa', *African Affairs, 99*(395) (April 2000): 183–215.
24 Akyeampong 2000: 188.
25 Haar, Gerrie ter, *Halfway to Paradise: African Christians in Europe* (Cardiff: Cardiff Academic Press, 1998).
26 Bittlinger, Arnold, 'Charismatic Renewal: an Opportunity for the Church?', in: Arnold Bittlinger (ed.), *The Church is Charismatic* (Geneva: WCC, 1981), 9.
27 Middlemiss 1996: 7.
28 Middlemiss 1996: 9.
29 Blumhofer, Edith L., 'Introduction', in: Edith L. Blumhofer, Russel P. Spittler and Grant A. Wacker, *Pentecostal Currents in American Protestantism* (Urbana and Chicago: University of Illinois Press, 1999), ix–x.

Chapter 16

Churches of the Spirit: The Pentecostal/ Charismatic Movement and Africa's Contribution to the Renewal of Christianity[1]

Roswith Gerloff

Worldwide Transformation of Religion

In the twentieth century, the centre of gravity of Christianity has shifted from north to south where, different from the northern–western hemisphere, it encounters rapid growth. Henry Van Dusen of Union Theological Seminary in New York[2] prophesied after a visit to the Caribbean in the 1950s a 'new reformation' and a 'third mighty arm in Christendom' after the Eastern Orthodox and Western both Catholic and Protestant missions, regarding the latter as essentially springing from the same roots. In the twenty-first century, the dynamic development of Christian churches in Africa, Asia and Latin America is largely due to the growth of pentecostal/charismatic movements or (with the WCE 2001) the 'Churches of the Spirit'.[3] This development of a 'transcultural, transnational and polycentric' pattern of Christianity[4] poses a challenge to the traditional, often ethnocentric and monocultural, ways of doing theology and of being church. Hence some scholars in religious studies and the history of religions regard the movement not only as an equivalent to the renewal in Islam,[5] but also as a mirror of the global change of religion as such – a message which in the successful blending of diverse traditions transcends barriers, grants hope to frustrated and fragmented people in post-modern times, and introduces a cultural and religious renewal from below. Humans, suffering from poverty, chaos and turbulence, become aware of themselves and search for images and symbols which give meaning to their lives, create order, and promise destiny in the transition from death to life.

Historical Roots of Pentecostalism

The *New Dictionary of Pentecostal and Charismatic Movements*[6] describes the pentecostal/charismatic movements as two large renewals of the twentieth century, the first with roots in the Azusa Street Revival in Los Angeles 1906–1908, the latter in the charismatic renewal within the historic denominations from 1960. Such a definition overlooks that there were similar uprisings with 'signs and miracles' (Acts 2.11) as in the New Testament not only in the history of Eastern and Western churches, but also in Asia, Africa, Latin America and the Caribbean long before Azusa, such as in the 'Jamaica Revival' 1860–1861 – a first symbiosis of African and Christian elements in the Caribbean with large-scale religious, social and political consequences; in Tirunelveli 1860–65, Travancore 1873–1881, and the Mukti Mission 1905–1907 in India;[7] among the Bataks in Indonesia, the Karans in Myanmar and indigenous groups in China; in the Korean renewal movement from 1903 (Pyongyang 1907),[8] or in the early beginnings of the African Indigenous churches (AICs) at the turn from the nineteenth to the twentieth centuries.[9]

From here arises the critical question where to find the 'historical roots of Pentecostalism', and this in two directions – the search for the black (or African) and white roots and their mutual encounter within the early American movement; and the issue of a far-reaching more phenomenological interpretation, that is, the blending of Christian with indigenous elements in the 'laboratory' of the two-thirds world[10] – counter-image to Western institutionalisation and a mere rational way of theologizing. Both interpretations run counter to an exclusively Eurocentric model, and to only one fixed historic pattern of the outpouring of the Holy Spirit. This means they derive from the discovery of a 'series of sparks' in Los Angeles, Wales, South Africa, Ghana, Chile, Brazil, Armenia, China or elsewhere. Bergunder calls pentecostalism therefore a construct which combines a 'diachronous' with a 'synchronous network of global dimensions'.[11]

Searching for the origins, we must distinguish between several 'parallel streams':

- the 'self-interpretation' of the early 'classical' pentecostals;
- the unquestionable interaction and continuity with the 'Azusa Street' revival, that is, the rise of the early movement from the mutual encounter of African American elements with Western-Christian traditions in North America;
- a 'providential' explanation which traces the Holy Spirit's operations worldwide: their vast expansion on other continents from 1970 to 1980, especially through neo-pentecostal groups in Africa, the Pacific-Asian realm, and a 'popular Protestantism' in Latin America;
- a 'functional' understanding of what Asian, African and the world views of Indios have to offer about the 'spirit world', human empowerment, healing, and a wholesome concept of the cosmos over against progressing misery of people; and
- consequently, the challenge this all creates for a 'new interpretation' of theology and church, exegetical, systematic and practical.

This very complex spectrum or phenomena springs from several sources, includes all continents, initiates ever new contextual patterns of church life, and contributes as partners in transnational networking to the creation of a global human culture.

A Common Ground

Walter Hollenweger,[12] referring to the early classical movement, analyses 'five theological roots' which have contributed to its global impact and dispersion: the 'oral culture and religion of the African slaves' exiled to America; 'Catholic, Methodist and evangelical' concepts of Christian faith and life; liturgical, socio-political and theological 'protests' in remembering suffering and injustice; and the 'ecumenical intercultural movement' of the twentieth century (Poewe adds a sixth 'Asian' root, the reception of the Jesuit and Pietist mission through Asian, especially Chinese Christians).[13] In such an interpretation, the black elements in the Azusa revival are perceived as a 'preludium' and as Africa's 'gift' to Western theological traditions to initiate a worldwide renewal: source or spring-board, not byproduct. In contrast, some white American scholars emphasise more the theological heritage of the Holiness movement and Wesley's teaching of 'Christian perfection',[14] to avoid 'romanticising' the African contribution.

This controversy between white and black scholars in pentecostalism compels us to ask what the 'essence of biblical theology' is in present times: the propositional interpretation, sometimes antagonistic, through denominational dogmas inherited from the past, or rather the 'empowerment' of people in different cultural and political milieus by doing theology from their own. Summing up, the common ground of the pentecostal/charismatic movement and its origins does not lie so much in doctrine and rational propositions, but in an 'experiential and practical spirituality', or (in the language of faith) in the operations of the Holy Spirit in most diverse cultural and socio-economic contexts. The pentecostal awakening in 1906 among the marginalized in North America repeated itself and multiplied among the poor, women and children on other continents. The rise of the movement, for example, in India, Korea and South Africa before 1906 was followed by revivals inspired by Azusa, for example, in: Mexico from 1906 (Assemblies of God, Church of God), China and Korea from 1907, India from 1908, South Africa from 1908 (Apostolic Faith Mission) and 1910 (Zion Christian Church), Chile from 1909 (Iglesia Metodista Pentecostal), Brazil and Argentina from 1910, Japan from 1913, Ghana and Nigeria (Christ Apostolic Church) from 1914, and Congo from 1921 (Kimbanguists).

Definition and Statistics

The issue how to 'define' the movement is difficult in view of the rather confusing variety of denominations (e.g. the controversy between Trinitarian and

'Oneness' pentecostals), informal groups, charismatic awakenings outside and inside the established churches, healing evangelists, mega-churches, global networks and ever new developments leading to quite heterogeneous ethical and creedal positions. Generally, we recognize today 'three waves' worldwide: The 'classical' pentecostal churches; the 'charismatic renewal' within the former mission churches; and the so-called 'third wave': autochthon movements, post-denominational and neo-charismatic. The WCE 2001[15] defines the latter, in distinction to white pentecostals, as 'spirit-led' groupings in twenty-six variations of 'indigenous, independent, apostolic churches'. It includes under this category such different groups as the AICs, the Spiritual Baptists (Caribbean), Yi chan and Miao (China), and neo-charismatic movements.

Such an inclusive interpretation, however, is controversial, not only among Western scholars, but also among many pentecostal/charismatic churches. They guard themselves against accusations of being 'syncretistic' and displaying aspects drawn from traditional religion, and postulate that they have entirely broken with the religious past. This we find illustrated by the debate about shamanistic elements in Korean pentecostal groups.[16] Against Barrett's WCE, we also note that the systematic classification into three waves contradicts the 'chronological' fact that the AICs and comparable groups on other continents came into being much earlier than the neo-pentecostals; and that in Latin America the charismatic renewal among Catholics happened earlier and was more accentuated than elsewhere. Campos[17] therefore distinguishes between pentecostality as the essence of the movement and Pentecostalism as ever new expressions and concepts in a pluriformity of churches.

Statistics[18] at the start of the twenty-first century confirm the largely African, Asian and Latin American face of the movement, that is, 28 per cent of all Christians which comprise 95 per cent of the earth's population and are present in 9000 ethnolinguistic cultures, 8000 languages and more than 80 per cent of urban areas. In 2001, 71 per cent of all pentecostal/charismatic Christians were 'non-white', poor (87%), family- and community-oriented and settled in urban areas. In this, the rapid development of 'mega-cities' outside the western–northern hemisphere play a decisive role, as does charismatic networking, for example, between Nigeria, South Korea, India, Brazil and America. In 2002, 543 million, with overlappings but increased tendency, belonged to one of the spirit-type groupings, the majority in Latin America (141 million), followed by Asia (135 million) and Africa (126 million), that is, three-quarters of all pentecostals and mostly 'third wavers'.

Next to the expansion of religious movements through mission, 'migration' is the most important factor of religious dissemination.[19] This we see illustrated in the steady flow of migrants from other continents to the core-countries of Western Christianity. The emerging 'diaspora churches', with partly traumatic experiences, a deep-rooted faith in their religious (not always Christian) traditions, and the determination to survive in dignity, form kind of an antithesis to European rationality and human and social fragmentation. In our specific context, this means that not white pentecostals, but Korean, Ghanaian, Nigerian, Congolese or Caribbean Christians are representing the movement in Europe. The established Christian bodies of the region, Catholic or Evangelical/Protestant are challenged by a 'reverse mission' – the 'tip of an iceberg' or better, the vibrations from other parts of the world.[20]

Yet, German and French churches have only lately begun to recognize the presence of African or Asian congregations in their midst, although many have rented halls for worship. Contacts are often only of a technical nature, at best of some social care and legal advice for immigrants and refugees.[21] Intercultural and inter-religious dialogue hardly takes place, and theological issues such as what constitutes church and mission, what is worship, what brings about healing, or what signifies the operations of the Holy Spirit among us, are rarely tackled – compared with the program developed from 1978 by the Centre for Black and White Christian Partnership (CBWCP) at the University of Birmingham.[22]

Yet, European institutions will not remain untouched by this global development, in view of the south-north tension, increased international cooperation within the movement itself, and a growing influence of charismatic theology on the former mission churches.[23] First beginnings take place on local, national and international levels, such as the formation of the Council of Christian Communities of an African Approach in Europe; a similar organization by Korean Christians; educational projects at the Academy of Mission in Hamburg (ATTIG) and the United Evangelical Mission in Wuppertal; the emphasis put on research during the African Diaspora conferences in Leeds, Cambridge and Berlin from 1997; and studies promoted by anthropological, sociological and theological faculties.[24] The WCC fosters since Canberra 1991 the ecumenical dialogue either through national councils of churches or through special consultations.[25]

Anthropological and Sociological Interpretations

Anthropological and sociological studies of pentecostalism interpret the development from 1980 onwards as a 'post-modern transnational' movement which paradoxically combines the pre-modern with the modern, creates valid alternatives to Western logic, political and clerical power, and serves as an antidote to the manifold alienating processes in urbanization, industrialization, migration, poverty and the HIV/AIDS pandemic. As such it constitutes a *walk-out* from the status quo of political corruption and powerlessness in favour of a new orientation, a sphere of freedom, participation and hope for the coming of the Kingdom of God. For Latin America, Martin[26] relates the movement to the 'essence of secularism', because it fosters the process of social differentiation, breaks up monopolies and leads to a pluralism in which competition on the religious field goes hand in hand with commitment, community and a sense of belonging. Pentecostal spirituality knows 'that the Jesus of the Gospels is no abstract', and that a global human theology is possible precisely because of its rootedness in very specific local encounters. Tensions occur where pentecostal churches convert the lower classes in Latin America and the voiceless in Africa and Asia to a new life, but also charismatic elites develop which through better opportunities, the emphasis placed on education, work ethics and 'prosperity' tend to forsake the dialogue with the poor masses.[27]

In Africa, according to Ogbu Kalu,[28] neither the former mission churches nor African traditional religions have the capacity to cope with raging poverty and brutal violence. He therefore interprets the pentecostal/charismatic development from 1970 in its numerical strength not only as a spiritual renewal but also as a possible vehicle for a new political praxis and theory. Paul Freston[29] makes a similar claim for the increasingly powerful evangelical movement in the two-thirds world. However, the claim of an active political role of the pentecostal faith in the process of democratization of civil societies, is controversial, partly for lack of a theology of social responsibility, partly for some ambiguous participation in politics in Latin America from 1950.[30] Yet, the growing involvement of pentecostal/charismatic churches in social activities from the perspective of the 'victimized' bears a potential for a new socio-political awareness.

Comparisons

Some comparisons throw light on the foregoing: First, as early pentecostalism drew its inspiration from the discovery and mutual encounter of African elements with white American Christian traditions, we distinguish between 'white' and 'black' Pentecostals, not only because of the ensuing apartheid history of pentecostalism in the United States, but also because of the considerable cultural and social differences between the two components in the early movement.[31] In Azusa white members soon withdrew from their black sisters and brothers and later tried to isolate and silence William J. Seymour, the spiritual father of the movement. Western pentecostal churches and also the charismatic renewal within the historic denominations grapple with this racist legacy. Only by acknowledging their origins among the poor, black and marginalized of society, and by beginning to appreciate the operations of the Holy Spirit in those amazing happenings, will they *be* the Gospel they are called to proclaim.

Second, the Latin American scene differs from other regions by a kind of 'hybridity' between popular religiosity and Catholic influenced Christendom, resulting in pentecostal churches becoming the instruments for mobilizing the lower classes.[32] Meanwhile two thirds of all Protestants on this continent belong to the charismatic stream. On the other hand, Asian and African pentecostals are natural partners,[33] facing similar issues, not least the one-sided American/ European interpretation of the movement which continues to sideline them. They therefore call upon a 'shared vision' and the necessity 'to speak for themselves', freed from Western-only concepts and categories.

Third, still, there are enormous 'differences between the continents' and their post-colonial history. Asia, after liberation from Japanese hegemony and with inexhaustible resources, has experienced a process of rapid modernization, industrialization and 'enlightenment'. In contrast, Africa is continuously tormented and endangered by poverty, fragmentation, political conflicts, epidemics, emigration and instability of governments. In all this, the pentecostal/charismatic movement must be perceived as a 'powerhouse'. Other than in the northern hemisphere, 'conversion' to Christianity in Africa is not to Pentecostalism as a denominational entity, but to a non-denominational 'all-embracing faith': from the old to a culturally and religiously new order.[34]

In future, no doubt, the charismatic mobilization of the masses in the two-thirds world will be a driving force in Christian mission – with all promises and risks. The religious renewal (comparable with the development in music) allows people to be themselves in today's social fabric, express themselves in their own languages, cultural symbols and communal patterns, and at the same time practice non-violence and offer peace to the wider human family. Misrepresentations and distortions within the movement do not undo the positive potential.

Search for Meaning and Human Dignity

The movement cannot be explained from political and economic factors only but must be understood and analyzed as emerging from a deeply 'religious' worldview and the longing of people for meaning in life and human dignity. Gustavo Gonzalez,[35] a Cuban, speaks of the overdue search for one's own identity or a *una nueva cultura*; Harvey Cox,[36] an American, of a 'primal spirituality' beyond creeds and rituals – or the global undercurrents of emotional and ecstatic traditions which link us with the energy of life itself; Amos Yong[37] of the 'pneumatological imagination', or the Holy Spirit as the symbol of divine presence 'par excellence' and the vision of a renewed earth. At stake is the recovery of religion and the gospel for the basic re-interpretation of human life in the breakdown of traditional paradigms and the failure of socio-political mechanisms. This poses a tremendous challenge to Western theology which so far has paid much attention to liberation theologies and the renewal in Islam, but not enough to these Christian movements.

Concluding, I summarize issues at stake – traditional themes and also radically new perspectives – which may induce the overdue dialogue between the 'churches of the spirit' and the 'churches of the book'.[38]

1. A theology of 'spiritual experience and renewal of society': the Holy Spirit as both personal and cosmic power, penetrating, filling, directing and controlling: This pneumatology is not yet sufficiently developed in the literary output of the movement,[39] but it is relevant for the interpretation of mission history and present global developments. God was present before the arrival of white missionaries, and is present in people's deprivation and migration today. It embraces the whole of creation, fertility, welfare, healing, freedom, victory over evil, reconciliation and redemption of past injustices. Thus it challenges the classical distinction between immanence and transcendence, material and spiritual, sacred and profane, and functions, with Daneel,[40] as 'healer of the land'.

2. The issue of 'power' – 'vital force in participation' – confirming biblical concepts where evil spirits are confronted by the much stronger power of the 'Spirit of Christ'; hence the idea of 'spiritual warfare' with 'principalities and powers' such as in the Pauline letters (Eph. 6, 12): Perceived not only in individualistic but communal terms,[41] it stirs the conflict between those who merely rely on 'miracles', and those who utilize spiritual power also for socio-political analysis and action.[42]

3. The Bible as 'fundamental directive as well as corrective for life' here and now, a narrative model beyond the confines of both sacred and abstract propositions – like art and poetry, a symbolic language for the transparency of daily life, enabling communication between diverse cultural expressions: Fundamentalism is not an invention of pentecostal-charismatic piety but a rational import by missionaries in past and present,[43] who began to use the new converts' un-reflected access to Scripture for establishing doctrinal and denominational systems. In contrast, many black pentecostals are in search of biblical, critical training on the relation between text, context and congregational life.[44]

From here some further essentials are briefly mentioned:

4. 'Worship, prayer, rhythms and ecstatic utterances' as instruments or vessels of unmediated divine encounter and celebration of life: Prayer as the direct dynamic relationship with God; worship as the process by which the person 'is elevated to a state where the spirit finds a new plane of existence';[45] glossolalia as a liberating experience turning inhibited people into witnesses and instruments of God's grace.

5. 'Deliverance' as liberation from evil forces, present in the Spirituals and at Azusa, but further developed in teaching and praxis by the newer charismatic churches: Interdenominational teams and healing camps call young and old to be delivered from nightmares, desires, quarrels, infertility, illnesses, depressions or social paralysis.[46]

6. 'Healing' in the widest sense, personal and communal, as God's central promise of a redeemed world, based on an understanding of the 'body–mind relationship' in healing, dreams and visions as intuitive, interpersonal powers,[47] responding to the physical as well as social needs of the whole person.

7. A 'prosperity gospel' understood as God's promise of 'abundant blessings' and sustenance, necessary for survival and development under poverty and misery, and the protest against missionaries who preached that 'poverty promotes humility': Young Africans seek solutions for society's instability, unemployment, exclusion, shortage of finance and housing, epidemics, violence and wars.[48] Kalu insists that the rapid growth of neo-charismatic movements in Africa can also lead to a political theory and praxis by which faith tackles unjust systems and challenges the misuse of power at the very roots.[49]

8. The development of a 'demonology' which corresponds to African, Asian, Latin American and Caribbean worldviews and claims the power of Christ as stronger than the forces of evil: Calling upon Jesus' intensive relationship with demons, it is here where the decisive struggle between good and evil is taking place in human existence.[50] This, undoubtedly, produces dualistic tendencies.

9. The issue of a theologically responsible 'syncretism' that allows for similarities between indigenous worldviews and hence recognizes both the 'continuity' in the cultural blending between traditional and Christian elements, and also the 'discontinuity' in the radical re-interpretation or 'conversion' to a new religious significance: Christian faith needs 'discernment of spirits', but it also adapts to diverse religious, cultural and socio-political contexts.[51]

10. The development of a 'theology of religions', such as suggested by Yong,[52] based on the 'pneumatological imagination', the liberation by Christ's Spirit to dialogue with other religions: Asian Pentecostals are in the process of developing a pentecostal theology which is evangelical but adaptable to non-Christian contexts, christocentric but capable of encountering the spirit world.[53] Comparable developments are under way among Afro-pentecostals. But still, there is hostility to Islam and failure to develop inter-religious bridges.

11. Finally, a re-interpretation of 'salvation' not as otherworldly but as saving people in the 'here and now', the radical re-thinking, not 'ex cathedra', but from the perspectives of the grassroots in their struggle for survival in dignity. Confronted with this kind of spiritual protest from the two-thirds-world, we face a decisive leap in post-modern human experience. With Ogbu Kalu:

> It is the claim of Pentecostal faith and the warrant of Pentecostal ministry to insist that the Bible provides the materials out of which an alternately

construed world can be properly imagined. Pentecostalism is, therefore, a child of the demise of modernism, a product of the great shift in interpretive practice which asserts that in the post-Cartesian situation, knowing consists not in settled certitudes but in the actual work of imagination.[54]

Notes

1 A longer German version of this text was published under the title 'Vorreiter und Anfänge der Pfingstkirchen und Charismatischen Bewegungen in Afrika, Asien und Lateinamerika', in Holger Stoecker und Ulrich van der Heyden (eds), *Mission und Macht im Wandel politischer Orientierungen* (Wiesbaden: Franz Steiner Verlag, 2005), 525–45.

2 Van Dusen, Henry P. 'Caribbean Holiday', in *The Christian Century 72* (August 17, 1955), 946–48; Idem, 'The Third Force in Christendom' *Life 44* (June 9, 1958): 113–24.

3 See WCE, 'Terminology of the World Christian Encyclopedia' in D. B. Barrett, G. T. Kurian and T. M. Johnsson (eds), *World Christian Encyclopedia* (Oxford: Oxford: Oxford University Press, 2001).

4 Poewe, Karla (ed.), *Charismatic Christianity as a Global Culture* (Columbia: University of South Carolina, 1994), 1–2; Cox, Harvey, 'Foreword', in Allan H. Anderson and Walter J. Hollenweger (eds), *Pentecostals after a Century* (Sheffield: Sheffield Academic Press, 1999), 12; César, Waldo, 'From Babel to Pentecost', in André Corten and Ruth Marshall-Fratani (eds), *Between Babel and Pentecost: Transnational Pentecostalism in Africa and Latin America* (London: Hurst & Co, 2001), 36–40; Droogers, André, 'Globalisation and Pentecostal Studies', in Corten and Marshall-Fratani (eds) 2001, 41–59; Martin, David, *Pentecostalism: The World Their Parish* (Oxford: Blackwell, 2002), 1, 167; cf. Paul Gifford, *African Christianity: Its Public Role* (London: Hurst & Co, 1998); E. Kingsley Larbi, *Pentecostalism: The Eddies of Ghanaian Christianity*, Accra: Centre for Pentecostal and Charismatic Studies (SAPC Series 1), 2001.

5 Martin 2002: 167, 173.

6 Burgess, S. M., McGee, G. M., and Alexander, P. H. (eds), *New Dictionary of Pentecostalism and Charismatic Movements* (Grand Rapids: Zondervan, 2001 [Fifth edn]).

7 See for India: Hoerschelmann, Walter, *Christliche Gurus* (Frankfurt a. M.: Peter Lang 1977); Bergunder, Michael, *Die südindische Pfingstbewegung im 20. Jahrhundert* (Frankfurt am.Main: Peter Lang, 1999); Satyavrata, Ivan M. 'Contextual Perspectives on Pentecostalism as a Global Culture: A South Indian View', in Murray W. Dempster, Byron D. Klaus and Douglas Petersen (eds), *The Globalization of Pentecostalism* (Oxford: Regnum, 1999), 203–21; Burgess, S. M., 'Pentecostalism in India', *Asian Journal of Pentecostal Studies 4*(1) (2001): 85–98; George, A. C., 'Pentecostal Beginnings in Travancore, South India', in *Asian Journal of Pentecostal Studies 4*(1) (2001): 215–37.

8 See for Asia: Yoo, Boo-Wong, *Korean Pentecostalism* (Frankfurt am.Main: Peter Lang, 1987); Allan H. Anderson and Edmond Tang (eds), *Asian and Pentecostals* (Oxford: Regnum, 2003).

9   See for AICs: Anderson, Allan H. *Zion and Pentecost: The Spirituality and Experience of Pentecostal and Zionist/Apostolic Churches in South Africa* (Pretoria: UNISA Press, 2000); Kalu, Ogbu U. *Power, Poverty and Prayer* (Frankfurt am. Main: Peter Lang, 2000); Ndlazi, Thulani, 'Bridging the Gap between Christianity and African Culture', in Gerloff (ed.), *Mission is Crossing Frontiers, Festschrift in Honour of B.A. Mazibuko* (Pietermaritzburg: Cluster, 2003), 103–16; Oosthuizen, G. C. 'Relevance of the African Indigenous Churches for New Approaches to the Study of Christianity', in Gerloff (ed.) 2003: 314–327.

10 Gerloff, Roswith, '"Africa as the Laboratory of the World": The African Christian Diaspora in Europe as Challenge to Mission and Ecumenical Relations', in Gerloff (ed.) 2003: 343–81.

11 Bergunder, Michael, 'Constructing Indian Pentecostalism: On Issues of Methodology and Representation', in Anderson and Tang (eds) 2003: 141–44 (453).

12 Hollenweger, Walter J. *Pentecostalism: Origins and Developments Worldwide* (Peabody, MA: Hendrickson, 1998), 2.

13 Poewe 1994: 7.

14 Cerillo, A. Jr. and Wacker, G., 'Bibliography and Historiography' in Stanley Burgess and Eduard van der Mass (eds.), *New International Dictionary of Pentecostal and Charismatic Movements*, (Grand Rapids: Zondervan, 2002), 403.

15 Barrett, D. B., Kurian, G. T. and Johnsson, T. M. (eds), *World Christian Encyclopedia*, Vol. 2 (Oxford: Oxford University Press, 2001), 19; cf. P. Johnstone and J. Mandryk (eds), *Operation World: 21st Century* (Carlyle, 2001).

16 On the Shamanism debate: see Hollenweger, Walter J. 'The Contribution of Asian Pentecostalism to Ecumenical Christianity', in Anderson and Tang (eds) 2003: 11–19; Young-Hoon 2003: 396–97; Hee, Jeong Chong, 'The Korean Charismatic Movement as Indigenous Pentecostalism', in Anderson and Tang (eds) 2003: 431–32; Cox, Harvey, *Fire from Heaven* (London: Cassell, 1996), 218–19, 224–28.

17 Campos, Bernardo L. 'In the Power of the Spirit: Pentecostalism, Theology, and Social Ethics', in Benjamin F. Gutiérrez and Dennis A. Smith (Mexico: AIPRAL, 1996), 49; cf. Idem, *De la Reforma Protestante a la Pentecostalidad de la Iglesia: Debate sobre el Pentecostalismo en América Latina* (Mexico: Ediciones CLAI, 1997).

18 WCE: vol. 1 (mega cities), 537, 543–44; vol. 2, 19–21: Tables for all countries.

19 Gerloff 2003: 343.

20 Ibid.

21 Introduction to Dahling-Sander, Christoph, Funkschmidt, K. M. and Mielke, V. (eds), *Pfingstkirchen und Ökumene in Bewegung* (Frankfurt am. Main: Otto Lembeck, 2001), 11; cf. Gerloff, Roswith, 'Afrikanische Gemeinden als Herausforderung an die Volkskirche', in *Weg und Gestalt* (Berlin: WDL-Verlag, 1998), 199–223.

22 Gerloff, Roswith, and Simmonds, Martin, *Learning in Partnership* (London BCC, 1980). Content, praxis and methodology of the CBWCP 1978–1985 are described in detail in Gerloff 2003.

23 The author, visiting Ghana in 2003, observed how charismatic renewal revitalizes the former mission churches.

24 Gerloff, Roswith, 'The Significance of the African Christian Diaspora in Europe', *Journal of Religion in Africa XIX*(1) (1999): 115–120. Cf. Third African Christian

Diaspora Conference, 11–15 September 2003, Hirschluch, and the Festival of Korean Churches Together in Europe, 28–31 May 2003, Kassel.

25 WCC consultations with Pentecostal Churches, Lima, Peru, 14–19 November 1994; AICs, Ogere, Nigeria, 9–14 January 1996; African and African-Caribbean Church Leaders in Britain, Leeds, 30 November–2 December 1995, see Van Beek, Huibert and Gerloff, Roswith (eds), *African and African-Caribbean Church Leaders in Britain, Leeds, 1995* (Geneva: WCC, 1996); International Consultation on 'Faith, Health, Healing and Mission', Achimota, Ghana, 4–8 December 02.

26 Martin, David, *Tongues of Fire* (Oxford: Blackwell, 1991), 277, 286; Martin 2002: 71–82.

27 Gaxiola, Manuel J., 'The Pentecostal Ministry' in *IRM*, 66, 1977: 60–63; Hollenweger, Walter J., 'The Pentecostal Elites and the Pentecostal Poor: A Missed Dialogue', in Poewe (ed) 1994: 200–14; Freston, Paul, *Evangelicals and Politics in Asia, Africa and Latin America* (Cambridge: Cambridge University Press/ Oxford: Blackwell, 2001), 310.

28 Kalu 2000: 103–10.

29 Freston 2001: 315–19.

30 Freston 2001: 1–2, 212–26, 263–80.

31 Cf. Gerloff 2003: 358–360 (early Pentecostalism).

32 Westmeier, Karl W. *Protestant Pentecostalism in Latin America* (London: Associated University Press, 1999), 119–24.

33 Clark, Mathew, 'Asian Pentecostal Theology: A Perspective from Africa', *Asian Journal of Pentecostal Studies 4*(2) (2001): 181–99.

34 Ibid.: 189.

35 González, Gustavo L., 'Mission in the Land of Manãna' *Encounter 29* (1972): 278–79.

36 Cox 1996: 81–82, 101.

37 Yong, Amos, *Discerning the Spirit(s): A Pentecostal-Charismatic Contribution to Christian Theology of Religions* (Sheffield: Sheffield Academic Press, 2000), 29–31.

38 Oosthuizen 2003: 317.

39 Exceptions are Sepúlveda, Yong and Gaxiola.

40 Daneel, Marthinus L. *African Earthkeepers: Wholistic Interfaith Mission* (Maryknoll: Orbis, 2001), 164–65, 231–36.

41 Kalu 2000: 103–10, 193.

42 Interview with Mensah Otabil, International Central Gospel Church, Accra, 14 April 2001; cf. Gifford, Paul, *African Christianity: Its Public Role* (London: Hurst & Co, 1998), 78–88.

43 Hollenweger, Walter J., 'The Significance of the New Churches for the Future of Mission, Theology, Ecumenism and the Renewal of Christianity' in Gerloff (ed), 2003, 328–42, here p. 332.

44 Botha, Nico, 'Metaphors and Portrayals of Jesus in the New South Africa and their Implications for the Creation of Missiological Knowledge', in Gerloff (ed), 2003, 78–102, here p. 81; Mazibuko, Bongani A., 'Mission in Context', in Gerloff (ed), 2003, 208–10; cf. CBWCP.

45 Simmonds, Martin H., 'Is Worship Cultural?', *Christian Action Journal, London* (autumn 1982): 28.

[46] See healing camps in Ghana as encouragement and liberation for women, children, the ill and marginalized.

[47] Hollenweger, Walter J., 'Priorities in Pentecostal Research', in J. B. A. Jongeneel (ed), *Experiences of the Spirit* (Frankfurt am.Main: Peter Lang, 1991), 7–22, here pp. 9–10.

[48] Gifford 1998: 73, 336.

[49] Kalu 2000: 103, 110–11, 116.

[50] Yong, Amos, 'The Demonic in Pentecostal/Charismatic Christianity and in the Religious Consciousness of Asia' in Anderson and Tang (ed) 2003: 68–95, pleads for an 'exegetical and ethical approach to a cross-cultural and interreligious theology of the demonic' (p. 90); cf. Suurmond, Jean Jacques, *Word and Spirit at Play* (Grand Rapids: W.B. Eerdmans, 1994), 201.

[51] Cox, Harvey, 'Pentecostalism and Global Market Culture' in Dempster, Murray W., Klaus Byron D., and Petersen, Douglas (eds), *The Globalisation of Pentecostalism* (Oxford: Regnum, 1999), 386–95 describes how shamanistic elements, Christian faith and the spirit of enterprise blend in urban regions.

[52] Yong 2000.

[53] Hollenweger 2003: 13–14; Anderson and Tang 2003: 453–56.

[54] Kalu 2000: 108.

Chapter 17

Elements of African Religious Spiritual Practices in African American Worship: Resounding Practical Theological Implications

Antipas L. Harris

Introduction

Churches that belong to the pentecostal genre have marked a moment in history and are effecting a global change in the world. While pentecostalism has become a cross-cultural growing trend, each culture brings to bear it own influence on the expression of the experience. In the summer of 2003, I was part of a 32-date ministry tour, performing music and preaching at churches in the USA. and Canada. Most of these North American churches to which we ministered were African American pentecostal-type[1] churches. Given this experience the thesis of this chapter stems from my personal, historical and theological perspectives. I will draw from observations within the contemporary African American church experience and interpret them theologically by utilizing biblical theology with focus on Luke's 'Acts of the Apostles'. Much of what I have to present is the product of reflections on my observations both as a second-generation African American pentecostal participant, and as an academic researcher on African American pentecostal-type churches. The goal of this chapter is to move towards a pentecostal practical theology.

Thesis Statement

Theologically, I argue that the Holy Spirit has a dual purpose: the Holy Spirit reveals and expresses itself through a plethora of expressions, magnifying the God of diversity. That is to say, the Holy Spirit affirms the sacred worth of peoples' diverse ethnic cultural identities, and simultaneously the Holy Spirit penetrates and critiques culture. My focus is the African American church, but the theology developed here is also applicable to churches among other cultures as well. I will build on Roswith Gerloff's description of common African religious elements among pentecostals as a springboard for this theology, towards proving my thesis. The outcome of this chapter will be to offer an apologia[2] on the blurring of distinction that once was clearer between the African American pentecostal worship service and the one of other African American denominations. In conclusion, I will outline a theological analysis that I grasped from Scripture and observed as relevant before my eyes by the Spirit's move among African American churches. This theology may also be relevant to other cultures around the world. The reader will notice that this chapter briefly makes mention of the fact that while the Spirit affirms culture, the Spirit also critiques culture.

Disclaimers

Before I proceed to elaborate on my thesis, I must set forth the parameters of this chapter. First, the tone of this chapter is not intended to be reductionist. The premises set forth are in response to particular events of history as pertains to Africa American people. I do not intend to suggest that all cultures descendent from Africa can be lumped together, but instead I suggest that each has its own particularities. Second, I do not intend to suggest that culture is identical with the Holy Spirit nor that cultural tendencies have pre-eminence over the Holy Spirit. Rather, I argue that cultural expressions may aid expressions related to the work of the Spirit in praise and worship. Third, I do not intend to make a sweeping conclusion that all dynamics of culture are worthy for Christian affirmation or adaptability. I limit my claims on culture (in this chapter) to the expressions that I mention.

Fourth, I do not intend to suggest that there are clear bifurcations before what constitutes African-ness or blackness. My approach is not a philosophical one; rather, I make my claims from the perspective of socio-cultural observations, combined with biblical theology rendering a practical theology. Fifth, I do not suggest a clear ontological definition of what it means to be black or African, as some may suppose. I am suggesting a view that incorporates the sacred worth of cultural expressions with the work of God in the world. I hope to offer an 'apologia' for expressions that once were marginalized by the mainstream of American Christianity but are now becoming more and more part of the worship experience. Particularly, this is the case among the African American Christian churches; yet this is not limited to these.

Sixth, I do not intend to imply limitations on African expressions by suggesting that an African American, who is not as ecstatic as another, would be less African. Seventh, I do not suggest that all African Americans who are open to freedom of expression in worship are intentionally Afro-conscious. Rather, I intend to submit that the appreciation for expressions that many white

Americans and some African Americans alike once marginalized and misunderstood as unacceptable in worship, are precisely the means through which the Holy Spirit is able to have free course among a people who practice the culture from which their expressions are born. Finally, intentionally I do not submit glossolalia as an expression of spirituality that is born out of African Religion. I believe that glossolalia (in a Christian context) is of a different nature than any other record of ecstatic utterances or forensic speech. However, this point is not argued in this project. I state these eight points with the intent to crystallize my focus and to help guide the reader in the following pages.

African Religious Elements as Expressions of the Spirit among African American Christians

In a 'Plea for British Black Theologies', Roswith Gerloff observes what she calls consistent African religious elements found also in African Diaspora Christianity:

- God is a living reality able to enter the depth of human lives . . . God is life-giving Spirit, one with people, earth and cosmos, creating, sustaining and reviving life . . . God is power befalling, touching, and healing. God is history in the lives of people . . . God is – love, and the very same love with which we love. And just as love cannot be discussed but must be experienced, so the life-giving Spirit can only be acknowledged, invited, accepted, encountered and exalted.
- Black expressions, symbols, songs and patterns of worship are part and parcel of oral culture. Their way of communicating is not literary or 'ocular', not just fixed on books, but from face to face, heart to heart, body to body, person to person, community to community and generation to generation.
- African religion in many of its forms, whether in Lagos, Accra, Kingston, Port-of-Spain, New York or London, embraces the spirit world and reckons with superhuman forces. . . . They believe in Spiritual forces, but more so in the supreme power of the Holy Spirit.
- African worship is an all-embracing experience, giving God the glory from the brokenness of human existence and receiving God's graces against the disruptive forces of humanity. . . . Worship is empowerment. . . . Black worship at its best dramatizes the gospel, and in so doing speaks its own word and creates a new liturgy. Music and rhythms are the heartbeat of this worship, the instrument and motor by which the Spirit can descend.[3]

Here, Gerloff is in agreement with scholars such as Sanders, Kossie and Anderson that the inculturating nature of Christianity since its earliest form in Acts 2 allows for unique African originated expressions to be included in the Christian experience beyond the traditional euro-centric, euro-originated or euro-approved expressions of Western Christianity. I have observed that the similarities between African religion and African American Christianity seem strongest in spiritual expressions in music, dance sing-song and call and responsive homiletical styles.

Allan Anderson describes the rise of the African Indigenous churches (AICs), which in many ways seem consistent with the pattern of spiritual expressions among African American churches. Based on his description of the AICs, their expressions of spirituality[4] are similar to what I see perpetuated among many African American churches. Pentecostals can no longer claim the expressions of extreme emotions (jerking, falling in the Spirit, screaming, preaching with extreme emotion, shaking and rolling) as their denominational trademark.

In the early days of what may be seen as the outbreaking of the Holy Spirit in America, traces of what appeared to be parallels to African religious practices occurred among the people. In his 1978 edition of 'Slave Religion', historian Albert J. Raboteau indicates that white Americans frowned upon some of the slave Christian expressions of worship and praise of God and accused them of being 'heathenistic' and 'sinful'.[5] According to Raboteau:

> In the ring shout and allied patterns of ecstatic behaviour, the African heritage of dance found expression in the evangelical religion of the American slaves.... For the situation of the camp-meeting revival, where enthusiastic and ecstatic religious behaviour was encouraged, presented a congenial setting for slaves to merge African patterns of response with Christian interpretations of the experience of spirit possession, an experience shared by both blacks and whites.... While the North American slaves danced under the impulse of the Spirit of a 'new' God (Holy Spirit), they danced in ways that their fathers in Africa would have recognized.[6]

Felton O. Best quotes Richard Allen, the African American co-Founder of the African Methodist Episcopal Church, teaching his congregation that 'most of ecstatic worship such as dancing and excessive clapping were motivated by 'satanic' influences and rendered one to appear ignorant'.[7] This means that some black Christians, post-slavery, looked to whites as the models of civilization. They unwittingly adopted ideas that there was no sacred value in their indigenous religious expressions; and that these should be shunned because they were incompatible for adaptation with the Christian worship and praise experience. As the black theologian Major J. Jones notes, though slavery was abolished in 1863, the African Americans seemed to have been stripped of their culture and left with a demeaning heritage: they saw themselves as lowly black people in a white man's world.[8] Many African American Christians were blindfolded to the sacred worth of their African heritage because they were convinced that Christianity is less 'heathenistic' than their African-ness.

Consequently, extreme emotion and ecstatic expressions of praise and worship became offensive and inferior expressions for many African American mainline denominations, such as Baptists, Methodists, Episcopals, etc.

Robert Anderson reports in his 'Vision of the Disinherited' that when the white founder of classical Pentecostalism, Charles Fox Parham, visited the integrated Azusa Street Revival in Los Angeles in 1906, he rejected what he considered to be 'unintelligent, crude negroisms' and 'animalisms' being practiced there. Even in early American Pentecostalism, Parham scolded whites who adopted the same motorial behaviour as blacks: shaking, jerking, dancing, falling down 'under the power' of the Holy Spirit.[9] Roswith Gerloff references Zora Neale Hurston and Melville Herskovits as suggesting that 'the jerking, rolling, and shouting' associated with the early movement in America (and now extended among other African American churches) may have been the contribution of influences from African slave religion.[10] I think that it is better to say that these are patterns that are translated as expressions of Christian spirituality among African Americans rather than simply an extension of African religion.

As an illustration, two African American Baptist ministers who experienced the baptism of the Spirit at Azusa Street, Charles P. Jones and Charles H. Mason, were resistant to the acquisitions from white mainline denominations in favour of African expressions in Christian praise and worship. They, taking Ps. 150 seriously, and being 'ridiculed by outsiders as "holy rollers" because of the emotional expressiveness of their services, introduced the use of secular musical instruments such as guitars, pianos and drums into their religious services that made a major contribution to the development of black gospel music'.[11] They were convinced that this music stirred the praise and worship, inviting the presence of the Spirit that would eventually overtake the service, and people would express themselves in response to the power and presence of the Holy Spirit.

The African American Pentecostal church historian, David Daniels, suggests that the 'sanctified church' adapted those African expressions such as the ring dance and other practices of Spirit release and manifestations of the Spirit.[12] This was the evidence in the services for 'letting the Spirit have its way in the Service' or 'letting the Spirit have free course'. Partially because of this, Jones and Mason were expelled from their denomination, forcing them to establish a different church, the Church of God in Christ (CoGiC), 'where meaningful worship traditions could be preserved, practiced and produced unencumbered by charges of heathenism or heresy'.[13]

Furthermore, it is my observation that the once unacceptable expressions of African-ness emerging in worship have become as a whole more acceptable among African American Christian denominations that once distinguished themselves as more proper in worship from more ecstatic, charismatic Pentecostalism. This obvious change has brought reform to African American Christianity. Herein lies the point of entry into the present blurring of African American denominations.

Scholars such as Cheryl Sanders and Karen Lynell Kossie, the latter in her 1998 dissertation at Rice University, provide support for my argument in that what we see in these churches is a heightened appreciation for African expressions of spirituality that are extended as part of expressing our Christian faith. Concerning the pentecostal churches, Kossie argues that they have been unabashed preserves of African worship modalities. Thus, Bishop C. H. Mason, the founder of the largest African American Pentecostal Church (CoGiC), was ahead of his time in his attempt to recapture the African expressions of spirituality, reserving the ring dance of the plantation praise houses. Thus he transplanted sites of African religious expressions into African American Christian spiritual experience.[14] In her introduction to 'Saints in Exile', Cheryl Sanders describes the 'Sanctified church' of America as one that is interconnected with its African roots and the 'black experience' of African Americans. Sanders states:

> The label 'sanctified church' emerged within the black community to distinguish congregations of 'the saints' from those of other black Christians, especially the black Baptists and Methodists who assimilated and imitated the cultural and organizational models of European-American patriarchy.[15]

In short, the 'Sanctified church' or early twentieth century black Pentecostal movement resisted European stipulations on how to 'have church', while other black denominations, together with many white churches, frowned upon the 'Sanctified church' because of its assumed negative 'negroistic' or 'heathenistic' nature of worship which, however, the African American Pentecostals valued as sacred.

Currently, African American churches, regardless of denominational affiliation, are breaking free of the biases against pentecostal forms of worship. They are migrating to free-style praise, making room in their services for the moving of the Spirit and expressions of charismata. This now makes it hard to distinguish an African American pentecostal church from other denominations.

Practical Illustrations

In 1990, my singing group, the A-Boyz, was the first to bring drums into New Hope Baptist Church in my hometown, Manchester, Georgia. This Southern Baptist church does not represent all African American Southern Baptist churches in America neither in the south nor in Georgia. However, New Hope does represent the crumbling sentiment of many non-pentecostal African American churches that once drew blacks of an elevated socio-economical status, who often conformed to the mistaken ideal that to be 'educated' required one to imitate much of the white Christians' form of worship. At one time, the officials at New Hope were resistant to accepting drums because they represented the lower class worship of the pentecostals across town, particularly Bridge Street Church of God in Christ and the House of the Living God Church of Jesus Christ, my home church.

However, in the late 1980s and early 1990s, the return to African roots (ethnic dressing, music etc) became the quest of most African American Christians. A hunger for more than merely 'religion' but for genuine spirituality was the desire of more and more African American people of all denominations, and so it reached also many black churches of the Deep South. Perhaps this explains the surprising occasion when the A-Boyz were invited to sing for a special event at New Hope Baptist Church. The usher hesitantly asked the matriarch and the head-deacon of the church if it were acceptable that the A-Boyz play drums as a part of their presentation; they consented. Since then, the church has opened up to what was known until then as mere pentecostal form of worship. Of course in the North and in places other than New Hope Baptist Church, this opening up occurred much sooner than 1990.

Beverly Lawrence's in her 1996 edition of 'Reviving the Spirit: A Generation of African Americans Goes home to Church', argues similarly that the Black church provides avenue for African Americans in the African cultural return.[16] John Bryant, a 1988-elected bishop of the African Methodist Episcopal Church (AME), was concerned with the coldness or spiritlessness in his denomination, concluding that it needed to return to its African heritage and recapture the sacred worth of ecstatic expressions. According to Lawrence, Bishop Bryant became 'the spirit of the neo-pentecostal movement . . . in the larger theological community'.[17] Bryant's contribution to Bethel AME Church and the denomination at large was to make it 'a filling station for the soul',[18] exceeding mere worship services. However, its charismatic pattern of worship, by design, was an important part in his search to return to the sacred worthiness of the African spiritual expressions.

A renowned pastor of a Baptist denomination, a musician and recording artist, the late Rev. James Cleveland, commented on the African American pentecostal church:

> I love to go down to the 'sanctified church', where they don't mind praising the Lord; they don't mind clapping their hands; they don't mind stomping their feet; they don't mind dancing.[19]

It is my judgment that we (the African American people), whether consciously or unconsciously, are in touch with a particular part of our African selves when we invite the movement of the Spirit through dance, drums, exciting music and other ecstatic expressions into our lives. Therefore, my proposition is deeply rooted in my pneumatology. The opening up to the sacred value of these particular cultural expressions has made room for the Spirit to have free course among the once exiled in ways that was once unconceivable.[20] Therefore. I argue for more than a spirituality ingrained in our ethnic and cultural roots. I argue for practical theological implications of this recovery, as it relates to the biblical account of Pentecost, for today's Christian church, mission and evangelism.

When Culture Meets the Spirit in Acts 2

In Christianity, no culture or ethnic group has the right to make an exclusive claim of the faith. The event of the Spirit at the birth of the first church supports this point. At Pentecost in Acts 2 the Spirit used cultural dynamics as a partner with the Spirit to bring about the *missio Dei* in and among all people, extending the family of God beyond the limits of the Hebrew people. Luke's purpose is to defend God's activity in the world, as believers from various cultures encounter God. The New Testament Scholar, Luke Johnson, calls this God–human encounter of Acts a theodicy 'in the broadest sense'.[21] That is to say, Luke intends to help believers to see the picture of the encounter between God and human beings so that they identify themselves culturally with the story of God whether their ethnic identity is Jew or non-Jew.

Note, in Luke's account, non-Jews were not asked to become Jewish in order to be accepted as part of the family of God! Rather, by their faith in Jesus, the Spirit, fulfilling the promises of God to Israel that Gentiles would join with them at the end time, invites them in,[22] accepting them as Gentiles from various ethnic, cultural identities. Thus, the new thing is not the salvation of the Gentiles, but that they are saved simply as people and become part of the family of God without adopting Jewish cultural customs.[23] The Gentile Christians were allowed to be God's people without conforming to the Jews' approval. According to the account of Pentecost in Acts 2,

> When the multitude came together . . . every person heard them (those baptized in the Holy Spirit) speak in one's own language.[24]

Few New Testament scholars have noted that the unique activity of the Holy Spirit in Acts 2 is that it affirms the variety of indigenous cultures that are present. It appears that no one who witnessed the outpouring of the Spirit was accustomed to religious experiences different from their own and expressed in diverse cultures. This we can read from two important questions asked in the text:

> Look! Are not all of these, which speak Galileans? Nevertheless, how do we hear everyone in our own language, wherein we were born?[25]

From Acts 2, one may gather that the initial uniqueness concerning the birth of the church in Acts 2 is the bridging of culture with the new experience of Spirit baptism. Certainly, the Holy Spirit of Acts 2 works miracles among people and affirms 'everyone' in their birth language so that they may see that there is no exclusively sacred culture in Christianity when it comes to 'magnifying God'.[26]

Conclusion

In conclusion, African American Pentecostal-type worship is emerging in America as a 'mainline' expression of Christian worship. This might in part explain why it is now sometimes hard to distinguish pentecostals from other African American churches. From a practical theological perspective, this reality suggests to me that God is revealing that the Holy Spirit expresses itself through a plethora of expressions, magnifying the God of diversity and affirming the spiritual roots of peoples' diverse, ethnic, cultural identities. Of course, I have focused on African American culture, as illustration of this point, but this relates also to Africa and other parts of the world.

Framed in the words of Lamin Sanneh at Yale University in his book 'Translating the Message', the fundamental assertion is that any culture is the 'authentic destination of God's salvific promise, and as a consequence, has an honoured place under the kindness of God with the attendant safeguards against cultural absolutism'.[27] The comfort to be able to express one's Christian self in terms of the meaningful elements of one's own culture, grants affirmation to one's cultural identity, which all human beings need in order to feel at home in the Christian faith. I believe that the increasing acceptance of African-influenced cultural expressions in worship and praise among African American Christians, combined with biblical theology deriving from Acts 2 and the earliest Church, suggest a practical theology that speaks affirmation to the cultural and/or ethnic self, while the Gospel transcends culture.

Relating my argument to the African continent with all of its cultural diversity as well as the broader rise of a global movement in Christianity, Acts 2, with its awareness and stamp of approval towards cultural diversity in worship expressed in diverse languages, leads to a theology of Christian inculturation (a Christianity where people are not only welcomed by other Christians but even more so empowered by the Holy Spirit to 'glorify God' in their own [language] cultural expression unapologetically).

In addition, this same biblical passage exposes that while Christianity is adaptable to culture, it also critiques culture as it is bigger than culture. It becomes clear by the end of the chapter that cultural divides are not approved by the move of the Spirit and the birth of the church. Rather, there is a certain transcendent character of the gospel that empowers diverse cultures to maintain uniqueness while they coexist with cultures that are diverse (unity in diversity exemplified in the term, koinonia). In short, the Holy Spirit makes it possible that what became known as Christianity is both adaptable and transcendent to culture. These two characters of cultural adaptability and gospel transcendence, as relating to the rise of the global movement, must remain in close tension in today's Christianity, as they did in the earliest form of biblical Christianity.

Notes

[1] Throughout this chapter, I will use 'pentecostal-type' churches based on the wide-spread ambiguity among Spirit-filled churches in the USA. Increasingly, churches that might have pentecostal characteristics resist being called 'pentecostal' in order to distinguish their doctrinal differences beyond the shared emphasis on the 'charismata' as viable part of their worship. Therefore, with due respect, I allude to such churches as 'pentecostal 1-type churches'.

[2] An 'apologia', as used in this chapter, is a statement of defense.

[3] Gerloff, Roswith, *A Plea for British Black Theologies: The Black Church Movement in Britain in its Transatlantic Cultural and Theological Interaction* (2 volumes) (Frankfurt am Main, Bern, New York, Paris: Peter Lang, 1992), 61–64.

[4] See Anderson, Allen, *Zion and Pentecost: The Spirituality and Experience of Pentecostal and Zionist/Apostolic Churches in South Africa* (Pretoria: University of South Africa Press, 2000).

[5] Raboteau, Albert J. *Slave Religion* (New York: Oxford University Press, 1978), 72.

[6] Ibid.

[7] Best, Felton O. 'Black Religious Leadership from the Slave Community to the Million Man March: Flames of Fire, "Breaking the Gender Barrier: African-American Women and Leadership" ', in *Black Holiness-Pentecostal Churches 1890-Present* (Lewiston, Queenston, Lampeter: Edwin Mellen Press, 1998), 153 (Best does not indicate a primary source for this quotation from Bishop Richard Allen).

[8] Jones, Major J. *Black Awareness: A Theology of Hope* (Nashville and New York: Abingdon Press, 1971), 19.

[9] Anderson, Robert, *Vision of the disinherited: the making of American Pentecostalism* (Peabody, MA: Hendrickson Publishers, 1992), 190.

[10] Gerloff 1992: 64.

[11] Raboteau, Alberto J. *African American Religion* (New York: Oxford University Press, 1999), 98.

[12] Daniels, David D. III, 'The Cultural Renewal of Slave Religion: Charles P. Jones and the Emergence of the Holiness Movement in Mississippi', PhD Dissertation, Union Theological Seminary (1992), 185.

[13] Sanders, Cheryl, *Saints in Exile* (New York, Oxford, Oxford University Press, 1996), 16.

[14] See Kossie, Karen Lynell, *The Move Is On: African American Pentecostals/Charismatics in the Southwest* (Dissertation Project: Rice University, 1998).

[15] Sanders 1998: 4.

[16] See Lawrence, Beverly Hall, *Reviving the Spirit: A Generation of African Americans Goes Home to Church* (New York: Grove Press, 1996).

[17] Ibid.: 128.

[18] Ibid.

19 'Oh Happy Day', the Reverend J. Cleveland comments before he leads the song, 'Cant No Body Do Me like Jesus' (Published Video 1987).
20 'Quench not the Spirit', I Thess. 5.22 (RSV).
21 Johnson, Luke Timothy, *The Acts of the Apostles: Sacra Pagina Series V5* (Collegeville, MN, Liturgical Press, 1992), 7.
22 Jervell, Jacob, *Luke and the People of God: A New Look at Luke – Acts* (Minneapolis, MN: Augsburg Publishing House, 1972), 15.
23 Ibid.: 66
24 Acts 2.6.
25 Acts 2.7–8.
26 Acts 2.11.
27 Sanneh, Lamin, *Translating the Message: The Missionary Impact on Culture* (Maryknoll, NY: Orbis Books, 2001), 53.

Part Four

Diasporic Perspectives

Chapter 18

Religion on the Move: Transcultural Perspectives. Discourses on Diaspora Religion between Category Formation and the Quest for Religious Identity

Klaus Hock

Apart from the intentional expansion of religions by mission, migration is one of the most important factors effecting religious dissemination. This is especially the case for African individuals and communities. Africa, a continent perpetually on the move, has gone through various phases of internal and external migration, thereby experiencing the trauma of the transatlantic slave trade as an unprecedented mode of forced migration, as well as undergoing the new quality of intercontinental migration in the context of accelerated globalization in the second half of the twentieth century. This has also brought about the presence of smaller or larger migrant groups of Africans in Europe – and, in fact, the presence of religious traditions alien to the traditionally quite homogeneous religious set-up in Europe.

Against this background, it is amazing that, traditionally, for a long time migration research has not taken into account the significance of religion both for specifically, migrant communities, and generally, for migration as a global phenomenon – not even in view of the transatlantic African migration. On the other hand, the phenomenon of 'religion on the move' has only recently attracted the attention of scholars of Religious Studies who have finally started to acknowledge the significance of migrant religions for Religious Studies and the History of Religions.[1]

For some time now, Migration Studies have started to focus on 'diaspora' as a specific mode of migration, whereas 'diaspora religion(s)' as a specific mode of religion on the move have drawn the interest of scholars of Religious Studies. But the very notion 'diaspora' poses some problems which only recently came under closer scrutiny. On the one hand, the term has been broadly used in the humanities as some kind of descriptive category, referring to situations of migrant communities living abroad in a minority situation. On the other hand, the notion 'diaspora' bears a strong religious connotation which was coined by

Jewish and early Christian religious history, and even if applied to contemporary phenomena, the term is employed with a certain theological connotation re-interpreting selected dimensions of the older religious usage. Consequently, the notion 'diaspora' poses quite a challenge as it is at the very heart of at least two discourses: one putting emphasis on the religious associations deriving from the term, another one aiming at conceptualizing 'diaspora' as an analytical category. Let us give a short outline of these discourses, elaborating on incompatibilities as well as on points of contact or even intersections.

Diaspora Discourses: Emancipation and Analysis

Theological traditions

The term diaspora, deriving from the Greek verb 'diaspeírein', is normally translated as 'dispersion', 'diffusion', 'scattering', 'dissemination' etc. Originally, the verb was mostly associated with negative, calamitous connotations, focussing on the aspect of dissolution or even disintegration of elements which are supposed to be disconnected, heading towards their destruction.[2] The noun 'diaspora' has developed later and was – apart from some exceptions – mainly restricted to the biblical usage. What is important here is that a semantic transformation of the notion took place in the third century AD when the Hebrew Holy Scriptures were translated into Greek, known as the Septuagint. Here 'diaspora' was transformed into a category with geographic as well as sociological connotations, now referring to three aspects: the land where the Jews were dispersed, the situation of being dispersed, and the people being dispersed. At the same time, the notion was embedded into a soteriological concept describing a process: 'diaspora' was considered to be a punishment for disobedience against the Law with the prospect of repentance, renewed obedience and subsequent gathering and return to the Promised Land. This soteriological orientation was still kept in the New Testament and in early Christianity, in modern times making the way for the usage of 'diaspora' with a focus on its geographic and sociological connotation, and since the reformation referring to confessional minorities ('Catholic' or 'Protestant' diaspora) or more recently to the situation of faithful Christians in secularized societies. Evidently, this understanding of 'diaspora' has still kept its theological dimension, apart from its geographical and sociological implications. Due to this religious background, the notion 'diaspora' has been re-discovered in its theological dimension in the course of the twentieth century. Since then, it was mainly (but not exclusively) used in this sense by members of diaspora groups as self-description, emphasizing aspects of (violent) dispersion, distress and degradation as well as of self-esteem and confidence in an emerging emancipation and salvation.

In search of diaspora as an analytical category

Apart from these theological discourses, a different usage of the term 'diaspora' has developed in various disciplines of the humanities. Since the 1960s and more expressly since the 1970s, particularly in Social and Political Sciences, we can observe a growing popularity of the term, followed by a boost to 'Diaspora Studies' as a peculiar field of research which became evident in the launching of a specific academic Journal called 'Diaspora' in 1991. In the first issue of this Journal, its editor shared his observation that the term diaspora 'now shares meanings with a larger semantic domain that includes words like immigrant, expatriate, refugee, guest worker, exile community, overseas community, ethnic community',[3] thereby addressing one of the crucial problems of dealing with the notion 'diaspora': its semantic pluralism and lack of theoretical identification, or, as has been pointed out by another scholar: the notion 'diaspora' is both 'over-used' and 'under-theorized'.[4] If we take a look back to the origins of this development, we come across a short article by the American Political Scientist John Armstrong on 'Mobilized and Proletarian Diasporas'.[5] In this study, 'diaspora' was very loosely more or less defined as a migrant group in a minority situation. At about the same time, other scholars in Social Studies started to apply the notion of 'diaspora' to the situation of Africans living outside of Africa, thereby highlighting the aspect of enforced migration which was seen as an analogy to the dispersion of Jews in Early Judaism. Interestingly enough, though, and as far as we can trace it back, in academic discourses the notion 'African diaspora' was coined already in the mid-1960s,[6] indicating the start of Diaspora Studies as a subfield within African Studies. Consequently, in the 1970s and 1980s, the category was broadly used in African Studies, thereby boosting its usage in Social and Political Studies as well as in Cultural Anthropology, especially since the 1990s. Building on these discourses, scholars like Robert Hettlage, Theodor Ikonomu, Robin Cohen, James Clifford, Chantal Saint-Blancat, and others[7] tried to further systematize and theorize the phenomenon of 'diaspora'. These efforts were complemented by additional studies and enquiries, analyses and definitions, descriptions and synoptic documentations[8] – all of them being part of an academic discourse aiming at establishing 'diaspora' as an analytical category.

A 'third party perspective': diaspora in Religious Studies

It is amazing that both discourses (or better: both 'clusters' of discourses) have developed in quite an isolated way: scholars of Jewish Studies and Christian theologians have mainly been concerned with Jewish and Christian (confessional) diasporas, respectively, whereas scholars of Cultural Anthropology, Social, Political or Literary Studies and other disciplines have primarily been dealing with phenomena like migrant groups in minority situations, transnational networks, concepts of ethnicity, models of assimilation vs. segregation, etc., mainly in a contemporary set-up. This resulted in rather serious consequences: On the one hand, 'theological' discourses run danger of presenting 'diaspora' as an analytical category despite the fact that in these discourses, 'diaspora' represents a set of implicit religious postulations derived from the strong religious connotation of the term.

On the other hand, academic discourses in the context of the other disciplines are not at all concerned with religion, thereby simply ignoring a factor which is in many cases of major importance to the analysis of diaspora. Here, a 'third party perspective' may be of help: the perspective of Religious Studies (as distinguished from Theology). In Religious Studies, we find enough expertise required to fulfil a difficult twofold task: first to de-contextualize the category 'diaspora' from its religious connotation in order to establish it as an analytical category; and second to recognize religion as a salient factor in many a diaspora situation in order to open new perspectives in the field of Diaspora Studies which, so far, have turned a blind eye to religion. But this is more easily said than done: whereas Diaspora Studies have not been interested in religion, Religious Studies have been quite disinclined to do any serious in-depth research into diaspora. It was Ninian Smart who had turned his attention towards 'The Importance of Diasporas'[9] in the late 1980s. However, only in the mid-1990s, the discussion was seriously taken up and pursued by scholars like John Hinnells, Kim Knott and Martin Baumann[10] It was Baumann who continuously took pains to work towards the conceptualization of 'diaspora' in order to use it as an analytical category in Religious Studies. Baumann suggests to switch our attention from the noun 'diaspora' to the adjective 'diasporic' – a neologism instrumental in moving the focus from the problem of giving a 'definition' of diaspora to the prospect of researching into particular empirically given and concretely tangible phenomena.

Diaspora is no longer referred to as an essentialistically perceived substance, as an inherent quality. Rather, phenomena become 'diasporic', if a diasporic quality is attributed to them. Accordingly, his working definition does not refer to 'diaspora' as such but to what is taken as diaspora-constitutive, namely: 'the relational facts of a perpetual recollecting identification with a fictitious or far away existent geographic territory and its cultural-religious traditions'.[11] As the process of ascribing a 'diasporic' quality to particular phenomena takes place in the frame of specific interpretations of reality, the issue of what is considered to be diasporic may differ. Accordingly, an outsider's perspective may be different from – and independent of – an insider's perspective. This, however, opens on the one hand the prospect of distinguishing between the above mentioned discourses, and bringing both of them into close relationship. On the other hand, discourses focus here on generalizing perspectives, stressing the quality of 'diaspora' as an analytical category; and discourses there expound the religious tradition of diasporic concepts, highlighting the theological dimension of diaspora and its impact on the (religious) proliferation of diasporic communities. We do not suggest a separation, but a clear distinction between these two discourses and the different usages and implications of the term 'diaspora' – both on behalf of sound research and for the sake of the migrant communities' integrity.

Discourses on the African Dimension: Africanicity and 'Unfinished Identities'

Another aspect we would like to raise is the significance of the 'African experience' in terms of African self-awareness, on the one hand, and in terms of historiography, on the other. Again, we are faced with two discourses: One draws its inspiration from the idea of the 'African-ness' of African migrants as constitutive both for their diaspora community and for their diaspora religion, thereby stressing the implications of a definitely African diasporic consciousness; the other highlights the specific character of the 'African experience' for African diaspora communities and their diaspora religion as compared to the experience of other migrant communities, thereby focussing on peculiar features of African historiography.

African-ness as an essential feature

By transferring the notion of diaspora to the situation of Africans outside their homeland – simultaneously with reference to the Jewish situation –, the seed was sowed for an interpretation of 'African diaspora' emphasizing aspects of cultural self-reassertion and political emancipation.[12] But there are older discourses dating back to the late-nineteenth-century and having developed ever since on both sides of the Atlantic, creating an early black diaspora consciousness, thereby pre-configurating more recent emancipatory discourses on 'African Diaspora'.[13] One of the roots of those discourses was established by Edward Wilmot Blyden who draws a close connection between Africans and Jews: 'Africa is distinguished as having served and suffered. In this, her lot is not unlike that of God's ancient people, the Hebrews, who were known among the Egyptians as the servants of all . . .'[14] Due to their 'African personality', characterized by a specific 'esprit de corps' and a particular kind of spirituality, Africans are commissioned to act for the spiritual deliverance and renewal of humankind.

Some years later, William Du Bois developed the concept of 'double consciousness', a vision of merging African roots and American experiences in order 'to make it possible for a man to be both Negro and American'[15] which materialized in the Pan-African movement. In the early-twentieth-century, again, black diaspora consciousness found expression in the movement initiated by Marcus Garvey, to be later adopted by the Rastafarian movement as some kind of millennial mode of Garveyism. Once again, a link between Africa and Jewish experiences was established: Africans living in America were referred to as Israel's lost tribes looking forward to a new exodus taking them back to Ethiopia, that is: Africa. More recent discourses along this line brought about a merger of research and political emancipation in the so-called 'African American Studies' or 'Black Studies', focussing on the (re-)construction of Black identity and aiming at establishing a tradition of Afro-centric research.[16] Many of these discourses are designed for validating African-ness as some kind of genetically coded ethnic identity marker, rooted in the idea of an African 'substance' or 'essence' being intrinsically inherent in people of African origin.

Diasporic identities

Another string of discourses, also starting from the perception of the African Diaspora as a peculiar phenomenon, takes a different direction, though. Here, the peculiarity of African Diaspora is seen against the background of the transatlantic slave trade as a unique event in the history of humankind which cannot simply be equated with any other major migration movement. Without any precedent, this traumatic experience has moulded the collective memory of Africans where it finds its repercussion up until today. Unlike discourses focussing on an essentialistically perceived African-ness, discourses taking their starting point from here generally focus on the aspect of diaspora identities as 'constantly producing and reproducing themselves anew, through transforma-tion and difference'.[17] Thereby, emphasis is put on the 'diasporic' character of African diaspora, not on its alleged 'African' essence. This is not to say that discourses along this line are unrelated to the aim of political emancipation and cultural reassertion. The emphasis, however, is on different aspects. Paul Gilroy, for instance, has introduced the notion of 'Black Atlantic', thereby providing a new category which may serve black identity politics in a similar way as approaches focussing on 'Africanicity' as essentials intrinsic to 'the' African diaspora. Nevertheless, he talks about 'unfinished identities' generating 'new configurations'.[18]

Identity, emancipation and category formation

A nuance in emphasis may be the reason for a major difference in the perce-ption of the intention of African migrant groups in Europe: In her study on African Christians in the Netherlands, Gerrie ter Haar tried to show that African migrants prefer not to label themselves in categories of ethnicity, there-fore playing down identity markers which may underline their African-ness.[19]

Instead, in ritual practice they favour a type of symbolic communication with other Christians which is supposed to effect not cultural, ethnic, or social demarcation, but to engender religious communion. From a divergent perspective and with a different emphasis, Roswith Gerloff puts emphasis on the significance of the 'African factor' for African migrants: their African-ness is fundamental both to their identity and to their religion. Consequently, Africanicity and religion are closely inter-related, representing two sides of the same coin, so-to-speak.[20] This view is indeed supported by African theologians who hold that religion is forming 'the foundation and the all-governing principles of life for Africans'.[21] Furthermore, they highlight 'the significance of the African dimension in the present global transformation of Christianity'.[22]

It is not our intention at this point to discuss whether the appraisal of religion as constituting the foundation of life for Africans here echoes the popular sentiment that Africans are 'notoriously' religious;[23] neither do we want to reflect on possible analogies between discourses on ethnicity fostering Black identity politics and discourses on Africanicity and religion promoting theological self-awareness of African Christians. For asserting the theological relevance of the African diaspora, however, we would opt for a different approach which we shall mention in a moment and which should diligently be distinguished – though not separated – from explicitly non-theological approaches. Meanwhile, we would suggest, again, to distinguish between discourses which are heading towards different objectives, even if this may mainly be a difference in emphasis: here, the pursuit of emancipation and the quest for religious identity; there, the endeavour for analysis and the effort for category formation.

Diaspora and Transculturation

We have tried to distinguish various discourses dealing with diaspora religion: one taking its departure from the religious connotations of the term diaspora, the other aiming at establishing diaspora as an analytical category; furthermore, one focussing on the significance of Africanicity for the sake of political emancipation and religious self-awareness, and yet another one emphasizing the aspect of 'unfinished identities' (re)producing 'new configurations' against the background of traumatic historical experiences, thereby requiring ongoing analysis and striving for category formation. We could disentangle this confusion of discourses by subsuming the notion 'diaspora' as a sub-category with religious connotations under the generic category of 'transnational communities', as recently suggested.[24] However, we have our doubts about the practicability of such an arrangement. Rather, we would suggest to link up with the present academic discourse on diaspora from the perspective of Religious Studies: Here, Martin Baumann has established 'diaspora' as a generic term, de-contextualized from its religious connotation and therefore, in his view, adaptable as an analytical category not only to Religious Studies but to all disciplines involved in the study of diaspora. Furthermore, he drew attention to religion as a salient factor in a diaspora situation. Therefore, he presented 'diaspora' as a 'transcultural tool' of analysis,[25] providing a major heuristic potential in Religious Studies and beyond, and suggested to use it as a starting point for further developing our discussion on the question of how we can, methodologically and theoretically, grasp the multifaceted phenomena involved in a whole world of changes among 'religions on the move'.[26]

Although we may agree with the general perspective of Baumann's approach, we must raise a caveat. While Baumann's model – like many other theories on diaspora and religion – is trying to transform traditionally essentialistic categories into flexible tools appropriate for research into a field which is characterized by extremely fluid changes, his approach in its general set-up may still bear some reminiscences of static predicaments. The frame of reference, it seems, is a multi-cultural model of interaction between 'diasporic' groups and the recipient society. In this respect, we may raise the question whether the conceptualization of 'diaspora' as a social form does not put too much emphasis on diaspora as an identifiable group, thereby consequently emphasizing structural conditions in the interaction between migrant groups and recipient society.[27] Furthermore, in this model, 'religion' seems to be referred to just as an institutionally solid system of symbols.[28] Consequently, Baumann's approach in dealing with religion, diaspora and culture may be implicitly based on a 'generic model'[29] still too static to cope with the transitory quality of migration and 'religion on the move'.

Beyond Static Entities

The transcultural dimension of the category 'diaspora' is of specific significance to the study of a subject which is characterized by an emphatic transitory quality: Generally, 'transculturation' refers to dynamic, reciprocal and multi-dimensional processes of exchange between cultures and religions. It 'sets its own framework by referring to synthesizing or concurring as well as pluralizing or contradicting, even mutually neutralizing processes of translation, adaptation, redefinition and appropriation engendered by the encounter between people coming from different cultural and religious backgrounds'.[30] Accordingly, by applying the transcultural tool of diaspora as a research category, 'religion on the move' is analyzed as a non-static, variable phenomenon which is part of a 'poly-contextual' world.[31] In consequence, essentialistically conceived static 'entities' like culture, ethnicity, African-ness, etc., are fundamentally challenged by the adjectival application of 'diaspora' – diasporic – as a transcultural category, vividly showing the dynamic, non-static, perpetually changing aspects of these entities.

By applying this approach to the study of 'religion(s) on the move', we shall have to refrain from referring to any static meaning of the concepts involved. So when we talk about the African Christian diaspora, we should take care not to read a compact or even substantialistic quality into the notions involved. Neither an alleged 'African-ness' nor a supposed religious (Christian) essence, and likewise not a combination of both dimensions, crystallized in some kind of a 'Christian Africanicity' is at the very heart of those phenomena. Furthermore, not 'diaspora', and not even the 'diasporic' dimension, should be regarded as the fundamental entity upon which the distinctive character of African Christianity in Europe and elsewhere outside Africa is based. Rather, it is the discursive character of these fluid dimensions – African, Christian, diasporic – which makes up the specific features of the African Christian diaspora.

'Religion on the Move' as Transcultural Phenomenon

What is true of alleged static entities like 'African', 'Christian', 'diaspora', is also true of 'religion(s)', generally: both the migrant group's religion and the recipient society's religion are considered transcultural phenomena whose assumed 'substance' results from processes of transcultural communication. While we can observe phenomena of 'compartmentalization', that is, the diversification of originally synthesized cultural-religious complexes into different 'compartments',[32] these processes can again be thoroughly analyzed by tracing its '(re)constructive discourses', that is, by inquiring into processes of '(re-)inventing' religious identities. In this context, the category of diaspora/diasporic may be of help, in a way, though not primarily, as an analytical tool, as Baumann and others have hoped. Rather, examining the 'diasporic' character of a (religious) group can become a crucial heuristic tool of research into processes by which this group establishes its (religious) identity. Consequently, identity discourses move into the focus of our interest.

As for the African Christian diaspora, these identity discourses tap various sources for providing identity markers of different kind – be it religious, ethnic, cultural, or political, etc. So 'Africanicity' may be used as an identity marker in order to put stress on a distinctive feature that helps to differentiate one's group from the recipient society, on the one hand, and to establish a retrospect identity emphasizing the group's 'African roots', on the other. Conversely, religion as a primary identity marker may be instrumental in bridging the gap between one's own group and the recipient society – or, at least, some sections of it. Due to its dynamic and flexible character, the pentecostal type of Christianity serves this purpose better than other established forms of Christianity, by facilitating identity discourses to oscillate between its affiliation to (a) local and global Christian community/communities.[33]

We must be cautious, though, not to over-emphasize the aspect of deliberate strategic features in the emergence of discourses on Africanicity, diaspora, or religion. If we did so, we would run risk of subsuming the rationale of these discourses under a general functionalism or some kind of rational choice theory.[34] Therefore, we must also take into account non-conscious factors as constituent features in the development of these discourses. Lastly, we should be aware of one aspect which lies at the very heart of the 'transculturation' paradigm, namely that due to the reciprocal entanglement of Religion and Religious Studies,[35] we have to bear in mind that as researchers, we are part and parcel of the processes into which we are researching. This does *not* imply, however, that our research itself becomes 'religious'. Rather, we must distinguish between religious and non-religious discourses. To maintain this differentiation is in line with the 'ethos' of Religious Studies and reflects the widespread acknowledged consensus of scholars in this field.

Open Space beyond All Boundaries: The Theological Dimension of the Periphery

Finally, we would once again like to pick up the question of the theological relevance of the African diaspora. Based on our findings about the discursive and (re-)constructive character of the constituent features – 'African Christian diaspora' – we can conclude that this relevance is neither due to the alleged significance of an 'African' dimension in the present transformation of Christianity, based on some kind of African-ness as a congenital feature of the African Christian diaspora. Nor is it due to religion as some kind of a genetic code inherent in 'the Africans'. Rather, the theological relevance of the African diaspora derives from its boundary situation which is considered to effect a challenge to all boundaries,[36] from its liminality that is supposed to transcend all limits and limitations.

   The question of crossing boundaries is one of the major themes, if not 'the' main motif of the Christian faith. It is at the very heart of the Christian under-standing of God's revelation – a God who, as God incarnate in Jesus Christ, has transgressed the borderline between God and humans and, as manifest in the manifold expressions of the Holy Spirit, is transcending any frontier what-soever. Conventionally, Christian theology has conceptualized this assertion in terms of a '*missio Dei*' – a fundamental 'theologoumenon' lying at the very heart of missiological reflection, too. This concept has not lost its relevance in view of the African diaspora, and its boundary situation specifically, and in view of the Christian congregation as God's people, which are called 'in' the world thought not being 'of' the world, generally. Theologically speaking, God is calling His people to move beyond all boundaries, and if necessary even beyond the boundaries of traditional churches. There, at the very periphery, he has prepared an open space[37] for sharing the experience of Christ's pres-ence in a joint struggle towards justice and liberation on the road to the fulfilment of the human destination.

Notes

[1] For further details see Hock, Klaus, 'Catching the Wind: Some Remarks on the Growing Interface of Migration Studies and Studies on African Religions', in Ludwig, Frieder and Adogame, Afe (eds), *European Traditions in the Study of Religion in Africa* (Wiesbaden: Harrassowitz Verlag, 2004), 329–39.

[2] Van Unnik, Willem Cornelis, '"Diaspora" and "Church" in the First Centuries of Christian History', in Idem, *Sparsa Collecta. The Collected Essays of W. C. Van Unnik, Part III: Patristica. Gnostica. Liturgica* (Leiden: Brill, 1983), 95–105, here 86 f, cf. also Idem, in van der Horst, Pieter W. (ed.), *Das Selbstverständnis der jüdischen Diaspora der hellenistisch-römischen Zeit* (Leiden: Brill, 1993).

[3] Tölölyan, Khachig, 'The Nation-State and Its Others: In Lieu of a Preface', *Diaspora. A Journal of Transnational Studies 1*(1) (1991): 3–7, here p. 4; cf. Idem, 'Rethinking Diaspora(s): Stateless Power in the Transnational Movement', *Diaspora. A Journal of Transnational Studies 5*(1) (1996): 3–36.

[4] Anthias, Floya, 'Evaluating "Diaspora": Beyond Ethnicity?', *Sociology 32*(3) (1998): 557–80, here p. 557; cf. the same observation made by Cohen, Robin, 'The Diaspora of a Diaspora: The Case of the Caribbean', *Social Science Information 31*(1) (1992): 159–69, here p. 159.

[5] Armstrong, John, 'Mobilized and Proletarian Diasporas', *American Political Science Review 70*(2) (1976): 393–408.

[6] Shepperson, George, 'The African Abroad or the African Diaspora', in Ranger, Terence O. (ed.), *Emerging Themes of African History* (London: Heinemann, 1986), 152–76 (first published in African Forum: *A Quarterly Journal of Contemporary Affairs 2* (1966): 76–93).

[7] Hettlage, Robert, 'Diaspora: Umrisse einer soziologischen Theorie', *Österreichische Zeitschrift für Soziologie 16*(3) (1991): 4–24; Ikonomu, Theodor, 'Europas griechische Diaspora: Dimensionen einer interdisziplinären Bestandsaufnahme', *Österreichische Zeitschrift für Soziologie 16*(3) (1991): 94–113; Cohen, Robin, *Global Diasporas: An Introduction* (London: UCL Press, 1997); Clifford, James, 'Diasporas', *Cultural Anthropology 9*(3) (1994): 302–38; Saint-Blancat, *Chantal, L'Islam de la diaspora* (Paris: Bayard, 1997); Vertovec, Steven and Cohen, Robin (eds), *Migration, Diasporas and Transnationalism* (Cheltenham etc.: Elgar, 1999).

[8] See, for example, Cohen 1992; Segal, Aaron, *An Atlas of International Migration* (London: Zell Publ., 1993); Chaliand, Gérard and Rageau, Jean-Pierre, *The Penguin Atlas of Diasporas* (London: Viking, 1995) and others.

[9] Smart, Ninian, 'The Importance of Diasporas', in Shaked, Shaul, Shulman, David, G. G. Stroumsa, and Guy G. (eds.) *Gilgul* (Leiden: Brill, 1987), 288-297.

[10] Hinnells, John (ed.), *A New Handbook of Living Religions* (Oxford/Cambridge, Mass.: Blackwell, 1997); Knott, Kim, 'Hinduism in Britain', in Coward, Harold G., Hinnells, John R., Williams, Raymond Brady (eds.), *The South Asian Diaspora in Britain, Canada, and the United States* (New York: State University of New York Press, 2000), 89–107; Baumann, Martin, 'Diaspora: Genealogies of Semantics and Transcultural Comparison', *Numen 47*(3) (2000): 313–37; Idem, *Alte Götter in neuer Heimat. Religionswissenschaftliche Analyse zu Diaspora am Beispiel von Hindus auf Trinidad* (Marburg: Diagonal-Verlag, 2003); Idem, 'Religion und ihre Bedeutung für Migranten', *Zeitschrift für Missionswissenschaft und Religionswissenschaft 88*(3) (2004): 250–63, here further references.

[11] Baumann 2000: 327. For further discussions on the relationship between dia-spora and religion, cf. the contributions in Kokot, Waltraud, Tölölyan, Khachig, Alfonso, Carolin (eds), *Diaspora, Identity, and Religion: New Directions in Theory and Research* (London: New York: Routledge, 2004), 131–204, reflecting different approaches while stressing the aspect of non-essentialistic categories in the study of the inter-relationship between religion and migration; also Vertovec, Steven, 'Three Meanings of "Diaspora," Exemplified Among South Asian Religions', *Diaspora 6*(3) (1997): 277–99, and others.

[12] This conflicts with Shepperson's intention who had introduced the term 'African Diaspora', hoping to keep it clear of subliminal political or ideological undertones.

[13] Dorsch, Hauke, *Afrikanische Diaspora und Black Atlantic. Einführung in Geschichte und aktuelle Diskussion* (Münster: Lit-Verlag, 2000), 83–118.

[14] Blyden, Edward Wilmot, *Christianity, Islam and the Negro Race* (Edinburgh: Edin-burgh University Press, 1967, repr. 1887), 120.

[15] Du Bois, William Edward Burghardt, *The Souls of Black Folks* (Greenwich: Fawcett, 1964 [1901]), 17.

[16] Goyal, Yogita, 'Theorizing Africa in Black Diaspora Studies: Caryl Phillips' Cross-ing the River', *Diaspora 12*(1) (2003): 5–38.

[17] Hall, Stuart, 'Cultural Identity and Diaspora', in Rutherford, Jonathan (ed.), *Identity. Community, Culture, Difference* (London: Lawrence & Wishart, 1990), 222–37, here p. 235.

[18] Gilroy, Paul, *The Black Atlantic: Double Consciousness and Modernity* (Cambridge: Harvard University Press, 1993), 1. For a discussion of Gilroy see, among many articles, for example, Chivallon, Christine, 'Beyond Gilroy's Black Atlantic: The Experience of the African Diaspora', *Diaspora 11*(3) (2002): 359–82.

[19] Ter Haar, Gerrie, *Halfway to Paradise: African Christians in Europe* (Cardiff: Cardiff Acad. Press, 1998); Idem (ed.), *Strangers and Sojourners, Religious Communities in the Diaspora* (Leuven: Peeters, 1998).

[20] Gerloff, Roswith (ed.), 'Open Space: The African Diaspora in Europe and the Quest for Human Community', *International Review of Mission 89* (2000): 273–510.

[21] Abiola, O. U., *The Work of Aladura in Britain, London,* n.d., quoted from: Gerloff 2000: 275.

[22] Bediako, Kwame, *Christianity in Africa* (Edinburgh: Edinburgh University Press, 1995), 252.

[23] Platvoet, Jan and Rinsum, Henk van, 'Is Africa Incurably Religious? Okot p'Bitek versus John Samuel Mbiti', *Saga Bulletin 2* (2001): 1–2, there further references, cf. Rinsum, Henk van, ' "They became slaves of their definitions." Okot p'Bitek (1931–1982) and the European Traditions in the Study of African Religions', in Ludwig, Frieder and Adogame, Afe (eds) 2004: 23–38.

[24] Krings, Matthias, 'Diaspora: historische Erfahrung oder wissenschaftliches Konz-ept? Zur Konjunktur eines Begriffs in den Sozialwissenschaften', *Paideuma 49* (2003): 137–56, here p. 151.

[25] Saler, Benson, *Conceptualizing Religion: Immanent Anthropologists, Transcendent Natives, and Unbounded Categories* (Leiden: Brill, 1993), here p. 263.

[26] Baumann 2003: 292 and passim.

[27] Vertovec 1997.

[28] Bergunder, Michael, 'Pfingstbewegung, Globalisierung und Migration: Einige vorläufige Überlegungen', *Zeitschrift für Mission 1-2* (2005): 79–91.

[29] Ibid.: 89.

[30] Hock, Klaus, 'Beyond the Multireligious – Transculturation and Religious Differentiation: In Search of a New Paradigm in the Academic Study of Religious Change and Interreligious Encounter', in Mortensen, Viggo (ed.), *Theology and the Religions: A Dialogue* (Grand Rapids/Cambridge: Eerdmans, 2003), 52–63, here p. 61.

[31] See Idem, 'Catching the Wind: Some Remarks on the Growing Interface of Migration Studies and Studies on African Religions', in Ludwig, Frieder/ Adogame, Afe (eds.), 2004: 329–39, here p. 336 for further references.

[32] In view of the Hindu diaspora in the Netherlands, Van Dijk, Alphonse, 'Hinduismus in Surinam und den Niederlanden', *Zeitschrift für Missionswissenschaft und Religionswissenschaft 80*(3) (1996): 179–97, here p. 193 was even talking about the phenomenon of 'religionization' of Hindu traditions.

[33] Bergunder 2005: 89–91.

[34] Cf. further details of this criticism in Vertovec 1997.

[35] Tenbruck, Friedrich H., 'Die Religion im Maelstrom der Reflexion', in Tenbruck, Friedrich H., Hahn, Alois, and Luckmann, Thomas (eds), *Religion und Kultur. Sonderheft der Kölner Zeitschrift für Soziologie und Sozialpsychologie 33* (1993): 31–67.

[36] Kevin Ward, quoted from Gerloff 2000: 278; cf. Idem (ed.), ' "Africa as Laboratory of the World": The African Christian Diaspora in Europe as Challenge to Mission and Ecumenical Relations', in *Mission is Crossing Frontiers* (Pietermaritzburg: Cluster, 2003), 343–81, here p. 354.

[37] Gerloff 2000: 54.

Chapter 19

Who do they think they are?
Mental Images and the Unfolding
of an African Diaspora in Germany

Afe Adogame

Introduction

The transcultural encounter and exchange between Europe and Africa has a long history that predates the fifteenth century and the era of the obnoxious human trafficking. Generally, European presence and interest in Africa from this era onwards was largely split between commerce, politics and religion. The socio-cultural, political milieu under which Africans emerged and lived in Germany during the pre- and post-European War years precipitated a largely undocumented history. This paper takes a historical excursion into the various circumstances that led to the emergence and growth of an African Diaspora in Germany prior to and after the Berlin 1884 Conference. It examines whether, how and to what extent this historic event has served to shape the status and identity of Africans in Germany; as well as the mental images about Africa, from the late nineteenth century to the contemporary era.

From 15 November 1884 to 26 January 1885, the erstwhile European powers convened at the famous Berlin Congress (a.k.a. Congo Conference) in order to organize the imperialistic division of Africa. Germany joined the inner caucus of European imperial rulers only from 1884 and exited in 1918 when her defeat following the First European (World) War stripped her of colonial strongholds.[1] This historic event of 1884 prompts the weaving together of various aspects of the pre- and the short-lived colonial history of Germany with a view to unearthing the obscured and untold stories of Africans in Germany. It also helps to illuminate how and to what extent the milieu in which they lived has come to shape an African diasporic identity. The label 'African Diaspora' is understood here as one of the theoretical constructs used to refer to the global dispersal of indigenous African populations throughout the world. By employing 'Black Atlantic', Gilroy[2] contextualizes the voluntary and involuntary migration of Africans to Europe, Latin America and North America since the

Age of Discovery. The breadth of African Diaspora even transcends the popular geographical fixation to Europe and the New World and includes the Mediterranean and Arab world as well as cross-migration within the African shores.[3]

Prior to the apogee of World War I (1918), Africans in Europe were almost always few in numbers. The distension of Europe created several situations that brought Africans to Germany. Public records and local history narratives document the physical presence of Africans in many German states almost continuously since the eighteenth century. What is the importance of the presence, experience and prestige of Africans in Germany (Europe) before 1918? In which way did they influence the development in Africa? What impact did Africans living in Europe during the centuries make on European culture? How did they bring an 'African heritage' to the European culture? Their contribution to German and European culture may not be obvious, and it often has been of the indirect kind – Africans present in Europe directing European minds to reconsider their attitude towards Africa and Africans. As Debrunner[4] aptly remarked:

> But the Africans in themselves are interesting and important by their very presence and by the prestige they enjoyed or suffered. Their story is often a story of adaptation and survival of individuals trying to find their own identity between Africa and Europe; their experiences belong to the great subject of inter-cultural relations – the history of Africans in Europe is important even if neither Europeans nor Africans did 'vastly gain from one another' and although the Africans present in Europe before 1918 were always relatively few.

He continued: 'what counts in reality should not be the 'image of Africa', but the willingness to accept, understand and appreciate individuals and groups on their own values, from their own premises – and to be able to live together or at least alongside them'.

To fully comprehend the mental pictures of Africans in Germany prior to 1884, it is expedient to understand the reasons why Africans were brought into Europe in the first instance. The treatment accorded them before and beyond this era ties neatly with how Africa and Africans were generally perceived in the eyes of Europe.[5] Thus, the experiences and images of Africans in Germany largely mirror the relationship between Germany and its erstwhile colonies in Africa. Debrunner's 'six reasons for bringing Africans to Europe'[6] from the fifteenth century is quite illustrative here because they remain cogent in explaining the cause which brought Africans into Europe in subsequent centuries.

The first reason adduced was curiosity, as evident in Henry the Navigator, and the will to adventure. Africans remained in the eyes of the Europeans a strange continent of marvels and exotic surprises. Even the increased number of Africans coming to Europe did not at first change this attitude. These

Africans were often dressed up exotically so as to conform to preconceived ideas. A second primary motive was commerce. The need for increased trade in order to feed the expanding economy of Europe at the end of the Middle Ages is even more obvious as the motive of adventure and the beginnings of scientific interest. European colonialism probably began when Henry looked especially for the Gold of the Sudan. In the beginning, the gold trade appeared for a long time to be far more important than the plantation produce and the slave trade, which had begun rather as a side-line. But it was the slave trade above all which brought Africans to Europe. The first captives (Berbers and Negroes) were shipped to Portugal in 1436 on the command of Prince Henry as informants about trading possibilities, to be trained as interpreters and also for political and missionary reasons.[7]

Henry's third reason was military. As Grand Master of the Order of Christ (Portugal's semi-religious military organization), there was quest for information, in order to know the full extent of the 'Infidels' power. The crusading motive remained the publicly avowed principal aim of all Iberian exploration and conquest in Africa, Asia and even in America. The sixteenth century was also the period of the contest between Iberians and Turks. Both sides fought under the pretext of religion. The first African slaves reaching Europe directly in this way were considered prisoners in the Holy War against Islam. Closely related were religious reasons which included the search for 'Christian allies' to aid Henry in war with the Moors (Portugal's quest for Prester John as a potential ally), and his so-called great desire to increase the 'holy faith in our Lord Jesus Christ, and to lead to this faith all souls desirous of being saved'. He was indeed trying to instruct captives, slaves and sons of chiefs in Christianity. He preferred a profitable gold and pepper trade with converted Africans to a large influx of captives as slaves to Portugal. The Portuguese saw no contradiction in the fact that military and above all commercial interests were closely allied to these missionary endeavours. The sixth reason for his endeavours was linked to 'the constellation of the stars'.

While these explanations may be understood in one sense as specific and peculiar to Prince Henry and his Portugal, it nevertheless casts a panoramic view of the situation in most of imperial Europe. In fact, one import of his exploratory endeavours is that through them he established a pattern in the relationship of Europe towards Africa which persists until contemporary times. Exploration, slave trade, colonialism, poverty, cultural exchange and ecological disasters all contributed to an African Diaspora that has scattered Africans to Europe and elsewhere. Chronologically, I have outlined the historical trajectory of an African Diaspora in Germany and the changing public perceptions in four phases. This does not in any way suggest that events described in one phase is exclusive to it, nor does it treat Germany as an exception. In fact, except for some contextual peculiarities, there seem to be some common underlying currents flowing across Europe in terms of imperial policies and public images of Africa and Africans; and most importantly of the peculiar situation and experiences in the unfolding of African Diaspora communities in Europe.

First Phase: Africans as Essential Commodities and Prestige Goods (Early Sixteenth to Early Nineteenth Century)

It is well documented that contacts between Europe and Africa were constant throughout Europe's Antiquity, Middle Ages and the so-called Modern Age.[8] Africans lived in what is now Germany as early as the first half of the sixteenth century at a time when the trading houses of Wesler and Ehinger became involved in the Atlantic slave trade.[9] In 1528 Charles V, the Roman emperor, authorized the trading houses of Wesler and Ehinger in Konstanz to transport four thousand Africans as slaves to Santo Domingo.[10] The German nobility and wealthy merchants, like their counterparts in other parts of Europe, took Africans as serfs, domestic servants and soldiers. Documents such as the 1696 'Memorandum on the Delivery of Slaves by Ships' from Brandenburg to St Thomas, provides further information about German participation in the slave trade. The life and works of Anton Wilhelm Amo on the one hand, and the 'Mohrenstraße' (Moors' Street) in the Berlin-Mitte district makes us aware of this part of the history of people of African descent in Berlin.[11] African slaves as essential commodities were very much required in Germany and other parts of Europe as well as in America. All sorts of Europeans both at home and abroad became used to the service of Africans. When white men returned to Europe from all over Africa, they brought the 'odd' African along with them, often leaving these in seaports. Thus, Africans at the initial stage tended to be found in smaller or bigger groups in ports like Hamburg.[12]

Africans became prestige goods – 'a spoiled plaything' and symbols.[13] The light-hearted, almost joking attitude – alternating with admiration and even fear – towards Africans expressed itself most in the image of African women.[14] Ludolf reports an Ethiopian sailor arriving towards the end of the seventeenth century at Hamburg seaport, where he was made fun of by other sailors. It was, however, only towards the end of the eighteenth century that African sailors were accepted here and there on ships – the bright boys who had been serving captains, becoming seamen and even midshipmen and captains. While the main function of Africans during this period remained the performance of domestic duties,[15] other aspects of African service struck the eye of contemporaries and were perpetuated on numerous portraits. Thus, Africans were not only a commodity but also an adornment, 'Negro servants were a fashion and a fad'.[16] The fashion was furthered by the presence of African servants in the ports, soon, however, spreading to the nobility and the upper middle classes.[17]

One of the pages delivered to Berlin by the Dutch West Indian Company was the African Anton Wilhelm Amo, who became perhaps the most outstanding African in Europe in the eighteenth century. The Ghanaian-born who arrived in Germany in 1707 was first attached to a German prince,[18] and by dint of hard work he pursued university degrees in Helmstedt, Halle (Prussia), Wittenberg (Saxony) and Jena. In 1734, he obtained a doctorate with a dissertation on the theme *De humanae mentis apatheia* and later became a distinguished lecturer in philosophy at the German universities in Halle and Jena, respectively.[19] In matters of religion, Amo was a partisan of rationalism. His story exemplifies how Africans were directly involved in spiritual controversies of the day. As an exponent of the Enlightenment, he fought against Pietism. This celebrated intellectual success was however short-lived. First, he underwent financial embarrassment and had to struggle hard after losing the support of the Dukes of Wolfenbüttel. Although he earned the respect of many of his contemporaries, others thought him dangerous enough so as to fight his opinion and to slight him in public.[20] His disillusionment with Germany and Europe led to his abrupt return home to Ghana in about 1743. Amo no doubt remained a model and standing figure of admiration and encouragement for next generations of Africans in Germany, his life and works also influenced modern Afro-American writers and German historians.[21] Amo, who in his later life became a renowned African professor and philosopher, exemplifies the continuation of the practice of adorning the Renaissance courts with exotic plants, animals and people.[22]

Second Phase: Africans as Adornments and Exotic Exhibits 1807–1883

The second era is located after the successful War of Independence in North America (1775–1783). Coming on the heels of the official abolition of the obnoxious slavery and slave trade by 'institutional traffickers', was the development of ideologies that were just as restrictive and humanly debasing as slavery itself. Pioneer anthropologists of the eighteenth century, such as Johann Friedrich Blumenbach (1752–1840), were advocates of the essential humanity of the African. But even they advanced taxonomy of racial characteristics in which the European was the norm and all others were 'degenerations' of that original racial grouping. In 1798, the philosopher Christoph Meiners (1745–1810) from Göttingen wrote a book in which he sorted human beings into the categories of 'beautiful' and 'ugly'. Those who did not – like the Europeans – look 'light-skinned' were sentenced to being 'ugly' and 'half-civilized'.[23] Reed-Anderson aptly suggests that, 'The "scientific" racial theory that emanated during this period formed the basis and essential justification for the injustice, exclusion and genocide that has taken place since the nineteenth century'.[24]

The fashion of the eighteenth century brought a demand for African children in Europe as a minor branch of the slave trade.[25] Advertisements for such children on sale were printed in the newspapers, or exhibited in public auctions. This crazy fashion of keeping African children as an adornment lingered on into the nineteenth century and even took a more explosive, degrading dimension as human beings (Africans) overtook 'art objects' for public exhibitions. The Hamburg great game hunter Carl Hagenbeck introduced the 'Völkerschauen' (Exhibition of Exotic Peoples) as a form of entertainment, in particular, in the late nineteenth century. Africans and many other non-Europeans were exhibited in zoos and other similar places between 1874 and 1885.[26] All major German cities as well as other European cities such as London, Paris, Glasgow, Vienna, Basle or Geneva, Sweden and Norway became destinations where tour programmes were held. In 1877, the 'Völkerschauen: "Nubier" from Egypt and Sudan (the Exhibitions of "Exotic Peoples": Nubians) were held in Berlin, Hamburg, Frankfurt, Dresden. By the following year 1878, it had become a booming business and an entertainment event with the exhibition of "exotic peoples" (Nubians in Berlin) staged during the "Oktoberfest" (October Festival) in Munich'.[27]

As captains and traders brought back young Africans to Europe ostensibly for selfish reasons, so did the missionaries. As it were, these young Africans were to be educated in Christianity. The Moravian settlements in Marienborn, Herrnhut and other locations in Germany had quite a number of Africans from the West Indies, too. The presence of African converts and children in the continental Moravian settlements was part of the endeavour to gather from all over the world the 'first-fruits of the pagans'.[28] Missionary work also took Germans to Africa but the main impulse was usually trade. To a large extent, the European brand of Christianity that was introduced to Africa was that which embraced slavery, racism, segregation, discrimination, inequality and injustice. As these vices were perpetrated against Africans, the missionaries either acted as collaborators while others not physically engaged in these atrocities, shut their ears and eyes to them, or in fact legitimized such inhuman actions as divinely sanctioned or prescribed.

Third Phase: The Scramble and Partition of Africa till the Inter-war Years 1884–1945

The third phase stretches from the scrambling for colonies to the actual official partition of Africa at the Berlin Conference of 1884/85, and ends with the inter-war years. Physical contact between Germans and Africans increased in frequency in the nineteenth century. Decades-long agitation for overseas colonies as settlement areas, sources of raw materials, and markets for the manufactured goods preceded the colonial politics of the 1880s and subsequent bisecting of Africa into spheres of influences for European degradation and exploitation. Hamburg trading houses such as C. Woermann, Jantzen & Thormälen, Gaiser, and Godeffroy and Sohn pressured officials of the 'Reich' to begin a vigorous programme of colonial expansion and protect the interests of their overseas enterprises. As Hopkins aptly remarked:

> The Berlin Conference of 1884/5 was the vehicle for German colonial aspi-
> rations and, as was the case in the Cameroons, commercial interest was just a
> prelude to an albeit reluctant decision by Bismarck and the monarchy to
> protect German interests by securing colonies in Togo, Southwest, Duala
> (Cameroon), and East Africa. From 1884 almost to the beginning of World
> War I, Germany needed its military might to retain control over these African
> territories and the bloody Herero War and the war against the Nama in South
> West between 1904/7 demonstrated that Imperial Germany was ready to
> annihilate native populations to protect its acquired rights.[29]

In February 1885, the Conference ended with the assembled powers (Belgium, Denmark, France, Britain, Italy, The Netherlands, Spain, Russia, USA and the host Germany) agreeing on the framework for new policies. Consequently, the African continent was partitioned into artificial geographical zones of European influence, exploitation and expropriation.[30] Most colonies became established through the brutal military might (force) of the impe-rialists,[31] sometimes also in collaboration with corrupt African sovereigns. Notable African kings and chiefs often sent their sons to Germany ostensibly to be educated and later to assume some position in the colonial apparatus. Many such Africans who came to Europe encountered tremendous difficulties, faced horrendous humiliations, harassments and castigations because of their race.[32] The celebrated story of Mpundo Akwa, son of King Akwa of Duala, who had been sent to Germany to be educated for a role in the German colonial admi-nistration is a case in point here. He resided in Northern Germany between 1884 and 1911. As an interpreter for the German governor of Duala (Jesko von Puttkamer), Mpundo witnessed firsthand the inequities and corruption of German rule.[33] Ernst Anumu, a Togolese educated in Germany tried unsuccess-fully to survive as an entrepreneur in Hamburg from 1913–1937. His application for citizenship in 1917 was rebuffed on purely racist grounds. As Hopkins noted:

> Anumu belonged to a small but determined group of displaced Africans who
> lived in Weimar, Germany without the possibility or even the desire to return
> to their homelands which were under French or English rule. The framers of
> the Versailles Treaty had pointedly denied self-determination to the colonial-
> ized peoples, and individuals such as Anumu or Peter Makemba, both
> residents of Hamburg, were left without a recognized nationality.[34]

The exhibition of exotic peoples in post-1885 Germany presumed an institutional dimension and further heightened the public perception of an African as commodity and adornment. In 1896, the *Erste deutsche Kolonialaustellung* (First Colonial Exhibition) took place in the Treptower Park with one hundred African contract-workers assembled from all German colonies. In the same year, there were exhibitions of the Tunisian Harem at the 'Passagenpanoptikum' in Berlin, as well as '33 wild women from Dahomey' at the Hamburg Cathedral.[35] Reed-Anderson best encapsulates the impact of this barbaric, uncivilized practice on Africa and Africans when she remarked:

> The 'Exhibitions of Exotic People' as a form of employment was exploitative and degrading for the Africans and the others. The relationship between the audience and the people of African descent, as was the case for other groups, was characterised by a lack of communication and distance. The amazement and the acceptance of these exhibitions of other peoples as a form of 'cultural exchange' meant that foreign people were not viewed as equals. These exhibitions continued to attract audiences in Europe into the late 1920s . . . The first meetings and the attitudes of the population had a continuing influence on the initial and future circumstances for the people in the developing African Diaspora in Berlin.[36]

Generally, the prestige of Africans in Europe is interwoven into the history of art, literature and folklore. Aspects like 'Africans in European art, in European literature, in European folklore' are important. Africans became active in German show business of the time, though mainly in the capacity of embellished objects.[37] African participation in German colonial films was popular in the 1930s and 1940s but was not restricted to this period.[38] A major distinction between Germany and other erstwhile colonial powers like France and Britain is based on the fact that Germany provides fewer professional role models for Africans, thus making acculturation more difficult.[39]

We should perhaps capture a vivid picture of how European painters and writers see Africans in Europe between 1850 and 1890. These illustrative works will help provide a clearer view of the presence and prestige of those Africans present in Europe without being connected with institutions. Painters on their artistic voyages were delighted to draw the odd African they met. Thus, the German painter Karl Brechen (1798–1840) painted two Africans in southern Italy in 1829.[40] Quite a number of ceramic figures of Africans were made in the eighteenth and nineteenth centuries. While a few of these were relatively realistic, most of these paintings on canvas or figurines were ideal ized or even fancy-exotic imaginations of Africans. These imaginations served to symbolize playfully Africans as representatives of a strange continent of wonders and horrors.[41] The German artist Ludwig Kraus returned from Paris and was based in Düsseldorf and Berlin where he became famous with his paintings especially within the circles of the bourgeoisie of the time.[42] In 1872, the German artist Wilhelm Trüber met an African whom he employed for three paintings.[43]

Typical of the flippant attitude towards Africans are cartoons of Africans. There were numerous cartoons depicting Africans in the 'Fliegende Blätter', a humorous periodical published in Munich around 1885 by the well-known cartoonist Oberländer.[44] Wilhelm Busch, the German cartoonist and publisher of world-famous comics occasionally shows Africans, mostly 'as funnily-cruel and somewhat silly semi-savages'.[45] A nineteenth century classical author of picture-books, Dr Heinrich Hoffmann (1809–1894), propagated through his books the type of bourgeois morality dear to the age: obedience, cleanliness, kindness to girls and respect for others. His *Struwwelpeter* appeared first in 1845. Generations of European children have ever since pitied the African, parading with an umbrella and being mocked by nasty white boys, till these, rightly, were put by 'the great Nicolas' into a huge inkstand, so that they became black as well.[46]

The German church cannot be exonerated from this dubious and malicious portrayal of Africans. A feature which is even more gravely contentious in the formation of a popular image of the African in Central Europe was the 'Negerli' ('little African') on Mission collection boxes, who thankfully bowed his head every time a coin was inserted into the box. This little African was the fascination of generations of children in Sunday schools and at children's services in German speaking countries. The mental image formed was that of Africans as 'thankful, polite, a little bit stupid, but . . . so poor species'.[47]

In a resumé, the Berlin conference of 1884–1885 and its aftermath partly helped to legitimize the hitherto untoward attitude towards Africans as well as stamped a dented image of Africa and Africans. The institutional dimension as exemplified in the degrading exhibitions of 'exotic peoples' is indeed a public show of shame to Europe. The role of scholars, writers, painters, artists and others in shaping the moral conscience and public view of their societies is very significant. It is these perceptions that have continued to make enduring impressions on the psyche and thinking of many Germans about Africans and Africa. This elite group largely influenced and shaped public opinion, image and perception of Africans, a legacy that has been carried on until today.

It should, however, not be assumed or mistaken that Africans who encountered these inhuman ordeals were docile or even liked the enterprise. Of course, many Africans were not content to be treated as cheap servants or as mere prestige goods. They sought to assert their personality; many tried and fought hard to win their freedom. Africans in royal or courtly circles often won their freedom through faithful service or achieving distinction in service.[48] There were exceptional cases of Africans who rose to high, enviable positions in German society and thus used their privileged statuses to cry foul of the prevailing dehumanizing situation. Amo's most notable contribution at the University of Halle was his first disputation, 'De iure Maurorum in Europe' (1729), in which he argued that Africans should not be treated as slaves and bondsmen in Europe because they had a tradition of civilization at least as old as Europe's.[49]

Africans also came to the assistance of one another in trouble. Africans hauled into prison were usually visited by their fellow Africans (freed slaves), and in some cases offered financial and material assistance.[50] An attempt to further ameliorate the tensile situation of Africans, led a group of similarly displaced Africans to inaugurate the 'Afrikanischer Hilfsverein' in Hamburg in May 1918 with membership drawn from Africans residing in all corners of the 'Reich'.[51] Although isolated in Germany from their homelands, these Africans were not isolated from each other. Also important to note is that during these life phases, Africans – servants and free men and women – liked to associate together, thus developing a social life of their own. This was how an African Diaspora started to unfold in Germany and elsewhere. Baptisms for example were great occasions celebrated together, even though there were no African churches or congregations in existence at the time.

The racial policies of the Third Reich (Nazi Germany) and the fate of Africans or bi-racial Germans deserves to be given special attention in order to fully understand the historical trajectory and the extraordinary circumstances surrounding an indeterminate number of Africans and African Germans residing in Germany during the Third Reich.[52] The phenomenon of *Besatzungskinder* (illegitimate coloured occupation children or 'brown' babies) drew public gaze and carried with it significant social, political and cultural consequences. Thus, the experiences of bi-cultural, bi-racial families lucidly exemplify what is known today about everyday life of the Africans living in Germany between 1920 and 1950.[53] In 1937, children born of liaisons between German women and black Africans, Afro-Americans, or the bi-racial Rhineland French (French colonial occupation troops stationed in the Rhineland during the early 1920s – after the World War I) were forcibly sterilized by the Nazi government in order to neutralize the perceived internal threat to racial hygiene.[54] An even darker side of everyday life for Africans in Nazi Germany 'appears in the account of Doris' attempt to visit her cousin in the Bromberg concentration camp and her narrow escape from sterilization in 1937/38 when German health officials sterilized most of the bi-racial children born during the occupation of the Rhineland'.[55]

Bi-racial individuals growing up in the Federal Republic of Germany had to cope with a culture whose language was rife with expressions and terms that portrayed them as something or someone of lesser value.[56] Perhaps most devastating is the linguistic battery 'Nigger' in German on bi-racial children entering puberty. The psychological, physical and emotional damage of racism and discrimination is even better appreciated when placed in particular in the racially conscious context where miscegenation was perceived as a grave threat that will undermine racial purity, the presumed Aryan superiority. Samples remarks that, 'Unlike the Jews, the African Germans and other black foreign nationals and colonials were automatically set apart from the Aryan Germans by their usually darker complexions'.[57] As she argues, the resilience of the Africans in the Third Reich, where racism was a state policy, is linked 'to their very blackness'. Anthropological and scientific propaganda was employed to confirm the inherent racial differences and hence inequalities.[58] The strident racial propaganda did make the daily existence of 'non-Aryan' foreign nationals uncomfortable. While racism became a state policy during the Third Reich, it was already extremely prevalent in the Weimar Republic. In terms of racial ideology and racial hygiene, a definite continuity existed between the Weimar Republic and the Third Reich.[59]

Racism and discrimination took an embarrassing leap, a dimension that woke up the Nazi government from their slumber. Policies towards ameliorating the situation of Africans by providing financial support and procuring employment made some belated but decisive efforts. As Hopkins[60] remarked, 'Although Germany denied the Africans citizenship, some segments of the National Socialist bureaucracy assumed the role of an ombudsman in the hope that fair treatment of Africans in Germany might translate into favourable treatment of German commercial interests in Africa'.

Fourth Phase: Post-war Germany

This phase runs up to contemporary era and began immediately after the end of the European (World) War II. This time is characterized in its early stages by anti-colonial nationalist sentiments and struggles that coalesced in independent African nation-states. Other features of this phase includes the Cold War and its aftermath, the impact of racial theories in all their manifold manifestations as well as racially motivated violence, exclusion, economic exploitation and resistance to these, and the continual enlargement of the African Diaspora in the metropoles of the former European colonial powers.[61] The post-World-War II era was the period when the German 'economic miracle' attracted workers and students from Southern Europe, North Africa, the Middle East and the developing countries. Consequently, the fate of Africans in Germany underwent a radical overhaul. As Hopkins noted:

Not only did the number of people of colour living there increase dramatically, but the concept of race collided with evolving new perceptions of self and nationality. The political and economic upheavals of the 1940s and 1950s had a profound impact on Germans' sense of their national identity especially after the physical and spiritual devastation of the lost war. Perceptions of race continued unchanged by the experience of war and the confrontation with the question of collective guilt for the Holocaust.[62]

He opined further that 'The OPEC boycott following the Munich Olympics and a concomitant downturn in the world economy helped unleash latent xenophobic and racist tendencies that, especially after reunification, precipitated violent outbursts against Africans and other people of colour residing in the Federal Republic and the former GDR (German Democratic Republic)'.[63] A remarkable shift took place from the image of the black man as a friend and helper, to that of the 'ugly African'. Although the nuances in the image of the black (African) may be said to oscillate between negative to the positive depending on the theme or influenced by events, yet there have been persisting negative stereotypes that fed largely on earlier perceptions of blacks (Africans).[64] The myth of blackness tended to view blacks as exotic inferiors. The representation of the Black G. I as an importunate child incapable of controlling his emotions recalls earlier portrayals of the colonized Africans.[65] In the 1950s and 1960s, the German government had to cope with the controversial issue of *Besatzungskinder* (occupation children), and official reaction contrasted markedly with that of its predecessors in 1937/38. The presence of over 3,035 children (according to 1951 official estimates) triggered off public responses and reactions laced with ignorance, racism and good intentions tinged with pity.[66] Equivocally, the government in 1951 recommended a 'family reunion' with their fathers because of the 'unsuitability' of Germany's climate.

Conclusion

The paper has attempted to show the social, cultural and political milieu in Germany within which an African Diaspora has been unfolding across many centuries. It has demonstrated that the mental images of Africans and Africa which have been drawn, painted and transmitted in time-space must be located not only within developments in the local context but transcend Germany to Europe and other parts of the globe. The perceptions of Africa and Africans on the one hand; and the experiences of Africans in Germany on the other hand, have persisted, though with levels of refinement. Present-day Europe is still relatively slow and reluctant in discovering the vital importance of African culture – art, music, literary traditions, social structures and worldview. Debrunner largely underscored this fact when he said:

We Europeans have not much to be proud about in our past treatment of Africans in our midst. There has been too much manipulating people, sending Africans here and there against their will; making it difficult for those Africans who came willingly to profit from their stay in Europe; too much ridicule of the supposed 'savage', too much patronising of the 'converted' African, too much general indifference towards African aspirations; false standards were applied in judging African achievements. Not only the general public, but also the educated elites of Europe, did not have enough information about the Afro-Europeans in their midst.[67]

In the same vein, Hopkins aptly remarked that 'the growth of non-German populations in the post-war era, especially in the Federal Republic, not only challenges the traditional perception of what is "German," but also transformed Germany's "nolens volens" into a multicultural society that finds itself confronted with the gargantuan task of integrating disparate racial and ethnic groups despite official and public resistance into a harmonious and prosperous society'.[68]

The question we need to contend with is simply this: As a society that is increasingly assuming a multicultural posture, what implications are these mental pictures likely to perpetuate for Africans who live in Germany? If we agree that in the past false images and perceptions have been maliciously stamped on a people, and are still being continued in refined forms, how and to what extent can we revamp such already dented images and pictures in an environment where media images are still unscrupulously biased and misleading?[69] Is it not timely that certain aspects of the educational system should undergo a radical overhauling in a setting where the darker skin colour of the African generally remains a theme in the most popular children's books for all ages? When will this image of a dark, handicapped continent known for no other than crisis, wars, genocide, HIV/AIDS, corruption and a host of other woes be 'whitewashed' at least? Most importantly, if we consider the grave impact of the partition for African Christianity, especially when faced with a 'reverse mission flow', the question that remains in limbo is whether Germans and other Europeans will really 'listen' and 'accept' the 'good news' from Africans instead of lingering on in their mindset? This is one gargantuan hurdle that needs to be surmounted for African churches to be able to make a profound and far-reaching impact on the German religious and secular landscape.

Notes

1   The disbandment of the German colonial empire only temporarily interrupted German economic strings to Africa but it stranded an unspecified number of Africans in Germany. For a concise documentation of Africans who were left without a nationality, see Oguntoye, Katharina, *Eine afro-deutsche Geschichte: Zur Lebensituation von Afrikanern und Afro-Deutschen von 1884 bis 1950* (Berlin: Hoho Verlag Christine Hoffmann, 1997).

2   Gilroy, Paul, *The Black Atlantic: Modernity and Double Consciousness* (Boston: Harvard University Press, 1993).

3   Our scope here is limited to African Diaspora in Europe, with particular reference to the German context.

4   Debrunner, Hans W., *Presence and Prestige: Africans in Europe. A History of Africans in Europe before 1918* (Basel: Basler Afrika Bibliographien, 1997), 7.

5   Cf. Mark , Peter A., *Africans in European Eyes* (Syracuse, NY: Syracuse University Facs. Publications, 1975).

[6] Debrunner 1997: 33–63. This was based on the reasons for Prince Henry of Portugal's exploration in 'Chronicle of Azurara'. See Almeida, Virginia de Castro e (ed.), *Conquests and Discoveries of Henry the Navigator, being the Chronicles of Azurara* (transl. by B. Miall) (London: Allen and Unwin, 1936).

[7] Debrunner 1997: 34.

[8] Debrunner 1997.

[9] Some excellent surveys that chronicle the presence of Africans in Germany from the Middles Ages to mid-nineteenth century include Martin, Peter, Schwarze Teufel, Edle Mohren (Hamburg: Junius, 1993); Oguntoye 1997; Reed-Anderson, Paulette, *Eine Geschichte von mehr als 100 Jahren. Die Anfänge der Afrikanischen Diaspora in Berlin* (Berlin: Die Ausländerbeauftragte des Senats, 1995).

[10] The 'Germans' delivered in excess of the number stipulated, and the surplus of about 800 was sold. See Leroy Hopkins, 'Inventing Self: Parallels in the African-German and African-American Experience', in: Blackshire-Belay and Carol Aisha, (ed.), *The African-German Experience – Critical Essays* (Westport, CT: Praeger, 1996), 37.

[11] Reed-Anderson, Paulette, *Rewriting the footnotes: Berlin and the African Diaspora*, (Berlin: Die Aüslanderbeauftragte des Senats, 2000).

[12] Hamburg was strategically located and had strong links via the Woermann Line to Africa. As Germany's most important port and the home of very vocal supporters of the colonial mission, it was well positioned to benefit from German imperialism.

[13] Debrunner 1997: 59–60.

[14] Debrunner 2000: 60.

[15] See Debrunner 1997: 94.

[16] Debrunner 1997: 92.

[17] See Debrunner 1997: 96–97.

[18] As a child Amo was brought to Amsterdam by the West India Company and 'presented to the Duke of Wolfenbüttel'. At Wolfenbüttel he was baptised on 29 June 1707 by the name of Anton Wilhelm after the reigning Duke Anton Ulrich and the Duke's son Wilhelm August. See Debrunner 1997: 107.

[19] Debrunner 1997: 107. Amo was a disciple of the German philosopher Wolf, the main representative of the Enlightenment in Germany at the time.

[20] Debrunner 1997: 107.

[21] Debrunner 1997: 108. Burchard Brentjes wrote a doctoral dissertation on Amo with the title: Antonius Guilemus Ame Afer aus Axim in Ghana (Martin-Luther-Universität, Halle 1968). For a shorter account on Amo, including a German translation of Amo's thesis, see Brentjes, Burchard and Anton Wilhelm Amo, *Der schwarze Philosoph in Halle* (Leipzig: Koehler and Amelang, 1976).

[22] Leroy T. Hopkins, Jr, 'Race, Nationality and Culture: The African Diaspora in Germany', in: Hopkins, Jr Leroy T., *Who is a German? Historical and Modern Perspectives on Africans in Germany* (Washington, DC: The Johns Hopkins University, American Institute for Contemporary German Studies, 1999). 2. In addition to Hofmohren, Africans also arrived as Moravian converts and as trainees for the colonial economy in the Danish West Indies. Perhaps the most interesting aspect of the African presence in eighteenth century Germany was the African

American loyalists who travelled with the 'Hessian' troops returning from America in 1783–1784 and their impact on the emerging scientific discourse on race.

23 Reed-Anderson 2000: 12. Cf. the philosopher Carl Gustav Carus' (1789–1869) thesis on the skin-colour discourse, and the English natural scientist Charles Robert Darwin's (1809–1882) racial theories about nature, see also Reed-Anderson 2000: 12 and 14. These writings portray the fact that similar thoughts and perceptions about discrimination on the basis of race and skin colour pervaded the entire Europe from that time.

24 Reed-Anderson 2000: 14.

25 Hopkins has argued that 'the tradition of bringing young Africans to Europe is a century old practice probably grounded in attempts to determine whether or not the African was indeed human; that is, capable of becoming literate in the European sense. Many European intellectuals felt, as did Hegel, that Africa was a land without history, that is devoid of culture, and Europeanizing the Africans might just spark some latent humanity in their otherwise primitive souls', Hopkins, Jr 1999: 3.

26 Reed-Anderson 2000: 22.

27 Reed-Anderson 2000: 16.

28 Debrunner 1997: 110.

29 Hopkins, Jr 1999: 3.

30 Although German overseas colonial expansion and acquisition was short-lived, yet it has tremendous historical significance. As Carol Aisha Blackshire-Belay noted: 'The German colonial expansion of the 1880s helped to set off the partition of Africa among the European powers, an event of obvious significance for African and European history'; see Carol Aisha Blackshire-Belay, 'Historical Revelations: The International Scope of African Germans Today and Beyond', in: Blackshire-Belay (ed.), 1996: 100.

31 Administrative structures were set up without voting or participation rights, and in total defiance and disregard of the cultural, socio-political structures they met on ground. The restriction of democratic civil rights, professional and educational opportunities were also tolerated or legalized in the African Diaspora in Europe and America. Along with colonialism, the internal ization of the endeavours of persons of African descent to achieving civil rights characterizes this third period (1884–1945). The first victories of national liberation movements were only reported in Africa more than half a century later. Reed-Anderson 2000: 14.

32 Katharina Oguntoye has documented a list of Africans who went through these ordeals while living in Germany between 1884–1950. See Oguntoye 1997.

33 Hopkins, Jr 1999: 4.

34 Hopkins, Jr 1999: 5.

35 Reed-Anderson 2000: 18.

36 Reed-Anderson 2000: 22.

37 See a vivid description of how some Africans were organized and featured in travelling shows similar to those popular ized in Europe by P. T. Barnum, Buffalo Bill and Hamburg's Carl Hagenbeck in Forgey, Elisa, 'Die große Negertrommel der kolonialen Werbung: Die Deutsche Afrika-Schau 1935–1943' *Werkstatt Geschichte, Heft 3*(9) (Dezember 1994): 25–33.

38 See Oguntoye 1997: 142; Reed-Anderson 1995: 29.

39 Hopkins Jr 1999: vi.

40 Debrunner 1997: 283–4.

41 Debrunner 1997: 285.

42 For further details about his work and activities, see Debrunner 1997: 288.

43 Ibid.

44 Debrunner 1999: 288. Among his catalogue of obnoxious representation of Africans was a cartoon of an African actually in Europe 'Signs of civilization'.

45 Debrunner 1997: 289.

46 Ibid. Hoffmann was professor of anatomy and later director of a mental hospital at Frankfurt.

47 Ibid.

48 Debrunner 1999: 104. However, the freed Africans were considered by slave-traders and masters as an idle and even dangerous lot; the spirit of independence in all Africans is noted as 'preparing a revolution' (Debrunner 1997: 102).

49 Susann Samples 'African Germans in the Third Reich', in: Blackshire-Belay 1996: 39. As Samples further noted: 'This sense of self and identity was fully developed in Amo as is apparent in his registering himself at the university as 'Antonius Guilelmus Amo, Guinea-Afer'; 'Afer' means 'African'.

50 Debrunner 1997: 102–3.

51 Hopkins, Jr 1999: 5.

52 See accounts of the persecution and forced sterilization of African Germans during the Third Reich, as well as the public and political reactions in Pommerin, Reiner, *Sterilisierung der Rheinlandbastarde. Das Schicksal einer farbigen deutschen Minderheit 1918–1937* (Düsseldorf: Droste Verlag, 1979); Burleigh, Michael and Wippermann, Wolfgang, *The Racial State: Germany 1933–1945* (Cambridge: Cambridge University Press, 1991); Susann Samples, 'African Germans in the Third Reich', in: Blackshire-Belay (ed.), 1996: 53–69.

53 Hopkins, Jr 1999: 6. A significant example is the case of Madenga Diek (1971–1943) who came from Duala in 1891 to be educated in Hamburg. He fathered Doris and Erika under unstable marital circumstances.

54 A conservative estimate puts the total number of African Germans living in Germany during the Third Reich to about a thousand. See Pommerin 1979: 59 and 72.

55 Hopkins, Jr 1999: 7.

56 Hopkins, Jr 1999: 10. There has been a recent emergence of a racial minority referring to itself as Afro-Germans or 'Black Germans'. This largely invisible German minority which is by no means a homogenous bi-racial group identifies culturally both with Germany and with a global black (African) culture.

57 Samples 1996: 54.

58 Ibid. Bi-racialism was an abomination that was reinforced by slogans taught in the schools: 'Alle Weißen und Schwarzen hat Gott gemacht, die Mischlinge stammen vom Teufel. Die Mischlinge können nur die schlechten Eigenschaften von beiden Rassen erben' ('God made all whites, and blacks, half-breeds originate from the Devil. The half-breeds can only inherit the bad characteristics from both races').

59 Samples 1996: 57.

60 Hopkins, Jr 1999: 6.

61 Reed-Anderson 2000: 14.

[62] Hopkins, Jr 1999: 8.

[63] Hopkins, Jr 1999: 2.

[64] See Lester, Rosemarie K., *'Trivialneger': Das Bild des Schwarzen im westdeutschen Illustriertenroman* (Stuttgart: Akademischer Verlag Heinz, 1982); Sadji, Amadou B., *Das Bild des Negro-Afrikaners in der Deutschen Kolonialliteratur (1884–1945): Ein Beitrag zur literarischen Imagologie Schwarzafrikas* (Berlin: Dietrich Reimer, 1985).

[65] Hopkins, Jr 1999: 8.

[66] Lester 1982: 93 & 287.

[67] Debrunner 1997: 8.

[68] Hopkins, Jr 1999: v.

[69] Hopkins has shown that the representation of blacks as caricatures – simple-minded, jovial and mischievously devious – certainly links the colonial films of the Nazi Germany with popular films such as 'Tante Wanda aus Uganda' or 'Zehn kleine Negerlein' of the 1950s. See Hopkins, Jr 1999: 10.

Chapter 20

'… the land which the LORD your God giveth you': Two Churches Founded by African Migrants in Oststadt, Germany

Evangelos Karagiannis and Nina Glick Schiller

Introduction

On this particular Sunday, Pastor Joshua's[1] sermon focused on the importance of testimony. He stood before the congregation on the stage of the main audi-torium at the Theological School of the university. Dressed in a dark suit, his voice came through the amplification system clearly, in Nigerian accented English using an Ibo saying or a German phrase as emphasis. After more than 6 years in Germany, marriage to a German wife, and several years spent working in a German factory in western Germany, he is comfortable in German as well as English. But the pastor uses English to reach the several hundred English-speaking Africans, primarily Nigerian, who make up the base of the congregation. On any Sunday there are also a handful of German women, most of who attend because of their connection to African men with whom they have had children and/or they have married. Over the past 3 years the congregation has changed, growing from Sunday services with less than 30 people to well over 100.

The pastor seemed disturbed that although during the week people had come to him with their ailments, he had prayed with them, and 'God had healed them', they did not come before the congregation on Sunday and testify to the power of God. His sermon moved across time and space to prove examples of the importance of testifying about the work of what, in one song, the congrega-tion declares as 'the ever-living God'. The ancient land of Israel and Oststadt, a small city in eastern Germany, where the congregation is located, were the same terrain, a place where Jesus walked and could heal the sick and bring prosperity to the righteous. Nonetheless, in this sermon and almost weekly in the pastor's Sunday sermons, particularities of locality were important. Oststadt and Germany was of central concern because it was the mission of the congregation and Pastor Joshua to win this city and country for God.

Let us now consider another site in the same city. About 25 people had assembled in the top floor of the Meeting Centre for Foreigners and Germans in the old industrial area of Oststadt to attend the Sunday services. The tables of the room that is mainly used as cafeteria or ballroom had been pushed aside to make space for the chairs, which are arranged in rows with a centre aisle. Almost all congregants are French-speaking Africans. On that day, the women had brought a meal to the church. After the services, a dinner took place. The church bore the expenses. As customary, the congregants wore their casual clothing. Only the Congolese pastor, Pastor Mpenza wore as always a suit. Of impressive stature: tall, broad, his demeanour was serious as usual. He could look back on two decades of pastoral and missionary activity, first in Africa and then Germany, where he came to as asylum seeker 8 years earlier. Before moving to Oststadt 4 years ago, when his wife and child, also asylum seekers, were sent to live here, he had founded a congregation in a big city in West Germany. His Congolese wife, who had two brothers serving as pastors in another European country, was a member of the choir of the church. Pastor Mpenza chose to address the congregation in French rather than in Lingala, the two languages that he shares with the vast majority of the congregants.

The congregants were listening carefully to the pastor. That day he tried to explain the importance of patience. He quoted the story of the golden calf and referred to it as the story of impatience. 'Impatience leads people to look for other solutions', he said. 'If we don't get something immediately, we often doubt about God. However, nobody can do anything against God. God designates a certain time for the resolution of your problems. You must hold on to God; then he will give you what he has promised you'. He went on referring to Joseph: 'He had been left without family, without brothers – his brothers maltreated him – and he went abroad, to a foreign country. But he has never lost his trust in God. And the day came, when they knelt before him. The people will kneel before you. It will take one or ten years. But it will be reality. . . . There have been times I had lost my courage. I went to my pastor and told him that the blessing has not come yet. He asked me not to loose the faith. And as the time arrived, I started counting the blessings. Many friends of mine have died or gone mad. But I am still here'. Exultant acclamations: Hallelujah, Amen!

The previous year pastor was given political asylum after a long time of waiting. There are few other members of the congregation who have also been granted the right to stay in Germany, however no one can understand, why some people obtain a residence permit while others do not. Is it a matter of blessing? Some congregants are sure about it, as well as about the various forms of God's blessing. Behind the pastor, in a small alcove, one could see the property of the congregation: keyboards, drums and other percussion instruments, microphones, boxes, lights. A former congregant who won 4,000,000 DM at the national lottery donated all this equipment to the church before leaving for West Germany.

There is much that can be said about these pastors, these churches, and the concept of testimony and evidence in contemporary pentecostal Christianity. In this paper, we wish to focus on the particular way both the English- and French-speaking congregations in Oststadt in their ideology and practices challenge existing migration theory and policy.[2] The data for this paper comes from a comparative study examining simultaneous incorporation of immigrants living in two small cities that are experiencing a new migration, one in eastern Germany and another in the New England region of the USA. In this particular paper we will focus on Germany, although Africans are also becoming active in the pentecostal churches and networks in the city we are studying in the USA.

The Discourse on Migrant Integration in Germany

The Federal Republic's migration policy has been shaped, on the one hand, by the insistence on the formula 'Germany is not an immigration country' and, on the other hand, the actual incorporation of migrants into the welfare system of the country.[3] Germany's self-description as a 'non-immigration country' has not, however, hindered the development of an integration discourse. This discussion was conducted mainly by the churches, the welfare organizations and some officials in the administration (in particular the Commissioners for Foreigners at federal, state and municipal levels). As Anette Treibel pointed out, the German policy makers were not willing to talk about immigration, but nonetheless expected the guest-workers to behave as immigrants,[4] that is, to integrate into the German society. Integration in the political-normative sense has always meant in Germany an adaptation performance of the migrants, a performance that at its heart was to signal their full assimilation into the receiving society. The success of this performance has been regarded as dependent on the migrants' willingness and capabilities to adapt.[5] This point of view on the one hand implied a particular differentiation of the immigrants as more or less 'alien',[6] and on the other hand, contained a particular judgment concerning the locus of responsibility for migrant incorporation: 'The failure of incorporation goes back to the immigrants themselves; they just cannot or do not want to become incorporated'.

Integration and assimilation also became the core issues of German-language migration research from the very beginning.[7] Despite considerable differences, the political-normative incorporation semantics and that of the migration research share some common features. We want to point out three of them that are particularly important for the issue of the present article. At first, in both cases integration is conceived of as a unilateral adaptation of the immigrants to the majority society.[8] Albeit with different emphasis, both views focus, among other things, on the increased interaction of the immigrants with the indigenous population through their participation in associations, organizations and networks of the latter, and the acquisition of culture patterns of the host society by the immigrants. Organizations founded by immigrants and migrant in-group interaction in general are met with distrust and mostly viewed as impediments to incorporation.[9]

Second, the frame of reference of the political-normative term of integration, as well as the incorporation semantics of mainstream migration research, has always been the nation-state. Consequently, both the role of transnational connections and the possibility of multiple forms of migrant identification were overlooked in incorporation discourse in Germany. Yet there is increasing evidence that transnational connections may allow for and often facilitate certain types of incorporation within the new land of settlement. Migration discourses often constructed the migrants' dilemma as a choice: identify with either the host nation-state or the nation-state of origin. Even if dual identification was found acceptable by some, the emphasis on identification in terms of nation-state remained as an 'idée fixe'. The result of the methodological nationalism[10] in these views was that the national background of immigrants was portrayed as a primary feature of migrant settlement. The possibility that nationality may not necessarily represent the cardinal orientation of individuals (either migrants or Germans) was consistently overlooked.

Finally, both the political and sociological incorporation discourses in Germany generally refer to either labour migrants ('guest-workers') and their descendants or ethnic Germans mainly from the countries of the former Soviet Union (*Aussiedler*), thereby ignoring the large number of refugees and asylum seekers, most of whom have no residence permit but nonetheless have lived in the country for many years.[11] As Bade and Bommes pointed out, German politics towards refugees and asylum seekers has been about neither integration nor even immigration.[12] The political treatment of this category of migrants has been more or less reflected in the migration and integration research in Germany. Refugees and asylum seekers can by no means be regarded as a favourite subject of German migration research. Moreover, in the few cases, in which researchers turn their attention to them, they focus on those who have been granted asylum, that is, a very small part of those who came to Germany. This silence about the incorporation strategies of refugees and asylum seekers in German migration research may be, to some extent, a result of the difficulties of empirical research on these particular migrants. However, we suggest that the main reason for this silence is that these people and their strategies of incorporation do not fit into the dominant conceptualization of adaptation as a long-term unilateral process of increasing similarity to the majority population.

Our concept of incorporation breaks with the dominant migration discourses in German politics and social science. Incorporation can take multiple forms that can hardly be reduced to a common denominator. Migrants, irrespective of their particular legal status, develop their own incorporation strategies that do not necessarily fit into the prevalent expectations of politics and migration sociology. To differentiate our view from the dominant ones we prefer to speak of 'pathways of incorporation'. These pathways can be simultaneous in that they connect people both within and beyond Germany. The pentecostal churches we are referring to in this paper provide an example of such a pathway.

German Policy towards Refugees and Asylum Seekers

In order to understand the pathway of incorporation of the churches we must review German immigration policy and particularly the policy towards asylum seekers that set the frame of the living conditions of majority of the congregants in our study. In the 1980s, at the same time that the German Federal State was offering the guest workers repatriation incentives (*Rückkehrhilfen*), it reacted to the increasing number of people seeking asylum in Germany with the so-called 'reduction of migration incentives' (*Verminderung der Zuwanderungsanreize*). With these measures, the German policy makers wanted to anticipate the 'misuse of the right of asylum' by 'economic refugees' (*Wirtschaftsflüchtlinge*). This issue shaped the discourse on migration in Germany for many years and led, finally, to the revision of the particular law.[13] In essence, the 'reduction of migration incentives' meant the adoption of a policy of deterrence, a policy that consisted and still consists in the systematic 'abnormalization' of the refugees' everyday life.[14]

Since 1980, when this policy was first introduced in the State of Baden-Württemberg, German policy is organized to restrict the chances of the asylum seekers to conduct an independent and self-sufficient life. The state is interested in defining the scope of individual action, setting considerable limits to individual incorporation strategies. Furthermore, an essential part of this policy is to make the refugees suffer in Germany and to complicate their lives as much as possible. They are often housed in special asylum homes under very bad conditions that among a host of consequences cause conflicts among them (particularly where only men are housed). They have no opportunity to learn German or acquire other relevant qualifications for the German labour market. They are, in effect, not allowed to work.[15] They are not allowed to cross the borders of the municipality, in which they live without special permission. As a migrant from Sudan said, 'we are only allowed to eat and to sleep'. These measures that denied asylum seekers self-sufficiency in conjunction with the refugees' incorporation into the welfare system (social welfare benefits and medical care etc.) presented them as illegitimate benefit recipients. After all, the social welfare was originally conceived of as a means to self-sufficiency (*Hilfe zur Selbsthilfe*), whereas the asylum seekers remained dependents. Needless to say, that this image caused resentments among the German population.

With the adoption of the Asylum Seekers Benefits Law (*Asylbewerberleistungsgesetz*) in 1993, the policy of the abnormalization of the refugees' everyday life reached a culmination point. The refugees were excluded from all benefits of the standard welfare system that allegedly exceed those absolutely required for survival. According to the Asylum Seekers Benefits Law, asylum seekers are to receive considerably less money than the social welfare payment, which is considered to be the minimum necessary for a dignified life. In addition, the restrictions on living circumstances and movement mentioned above continue to exist.

A Pathway of Incorporation

The migrant churches challenge this policy, offering activities that allow migrants to see themselves as part of the new locality, and to, thereby, maintain their sense of self-respect. Both congregations, despite their separate structures, serve to incorporate their members into Oststadt, Germany and transnationally, providing support for individuals and linking individuals through the institutional connections of the church. Both pastors help congregants meet the contingencies and pressures of daily life created, to a large extent, by the German policy towards them. The churches represent an important network of social support for their congregants. Francois, a member of the French-speaking congregation, without housing or money found both through the church. He also utilized connections of the pastor to the German Protestant Church to obtain more social benefits.

One church organizes various offerings to support congregants who are in difficult situations; the other uses its collections to provide financial support for members in need. At the same time, through regular and special events, the churches organize everyday life. They hold Sunday services, Bible classes, days of abstinence, all-night prayers, programs of intense praying and studying the Bible (called 'seminars' which last several days), deliverance sessions, regular and extraordinary meetings of various committees to discuss ongoing and special concerns, rehearsals of the choir, and visits to churches in near-by locations. In addition, they organize 'glamorous' occasions such as celebrations, memorial services, and even concerts enjoyed by the churches' members as opportunities of sartorial elegance and elaborate hair-styles. These activities fill the congregants' days, and structure their lives, challenging the irrationality of German immigration policy, that is, the policy of 'eating and sleeping'. Both churches create sociability and provide the congregants with the opportunity of enjoying normality. In short: within the scope of their potential, they try to establish exactly what the German state policy intends to circumvent.

At the same time, the churches can hardly be regarded as isolated ethnic enclaves. They are open to integrative initiatives, but, as we shall see later, in particular ways. They attach great importance to the translation of the services into German, even if there is only one German among the visitors in a service. Furthermore, both pastors call upon the congregants to learn German and support them in doing this. Pastor Joshua, making use of humour, has repeatedly referred to the unpleasant consequences that the lack of appropriate linguistic knowledge can have. For example, if one, answering questions of the police, can only say 'ja', one runs the risk of being deported by one's own approval.

Through their participation in an ecumenical service, within the framework of the 'Africa Week' (a festival dedicated to Africa and celebrated in Oststadt annually), to which the citizens of Oststadt were invited, the two churches have provided further evidence of their openness to the city. In 2003 this service concluded the official program of the festival. Rather than indicating involvement of other Christian churches in the organization of the service or even a sermon bridging confessional lines, the use of the term 'ecumenical' appears to refer to the multireligious and multiconfessional composition of the audience of this particular event. Furthermore, among the visitors of the services were prominent members of the city, such as members of the city council, pastors/ priests of several churches, officials of political organizations, and well-known people working with immigrants. Pastor Mpenza also accepted with pride the invitation of the organizers of the Africa Week 2003 to be the guest speaker of the festival's core event, the wreath laying in honour and remembrance of Anton Wilhelm Amo, an African philosopher who had graduated and taught at the University of Oststadt during the age of Enlightenment. Furthermore, he participated in the founding of a 'Network Integration' of the city of Oststadt, an initiative targeted at the coordination of various measures and projects dealing with immigrant incorporation in the city.

Both pastors meet frequently with German pastors in other cities, particularly in a large city close to Oststadt, invite them to render a sermon, and attend pentecostal conferences. The congregations have been formally registered in Germany, as is legally necessary, for more than 5 years. They both are working with a German pentecostal church that is based in the capital of the state (*Bundesland*), to which Oststadt belongs, to become formal members of a German pentecostal umbrella organization (*Bund freikirchlicher Pfingstge-meinden*). The pastors and the members of the church committees, which lead the churches, desire this level of official recognition, even though it means changing some of their internal organization procedures.

Both churches are connected not only within Germany but also transnationally. Among the visiting preachers of the English-speaking church are pastors who are part of a global pentecostal network of pastors. An Indian pastor has visited more than once and has convinced the English-speaking church to support his missionizing work in India by sending funds on a regular basis. Through another global Christian ministry located in the United States, the church sends funds to Christianize Israel. Several members of the church attended a pan-European pentecostal conference in Berlin in June 2003 that was called to organize a European-wide organization of pentecostal churches. During his sermon, Pastor Joshua claimed to continuously receive calls from The Netherlands, USA, Austria, Italy, England, Cameroon and many states (Bundesländer) of the Federal Republic. He continually refers to other churches and miraculous healings abroad that provide evidence of his world-wide networking and frame of reference. His description of miracles is global, ranging from Mongolia through Germany to Nigeria and USA. Referring to a church in a Ukrainian city, Pastor Joshua stressed that their pastor succeeded in attracting a considerable part of the city population including its political elites. Although considerably smaller and with less resources at their disposal, the French-speaking congregation has similar transnational connections with churches and pastors abroad, that is, Belgium, France, Sweden, Congo-Kinshasa, Congo-Brazaville and even Chad.

Christian Identity and Mission

In 2003, the pastor and leadership of the English-speaking church were all Nigerians with the exception of a German woman. In the French-speaking church they are predominantly Congolese and Angolans. However both pub-licly identify their congregations as neither Nigerian/Congolese nor African. When we asked the Congolese pastor whether he regards his congregation as a Congolese one, he answered: 'No, no. It is not a Congolese church. . . . This is not the origin of the Word of God. I have told you about my origin. I have come from Congo where I met my Lord, where I worked for the Lord. And now I am here, in Germany, where I had the feeling that the inhabitants were in need of the same message. So, I have clearly said that this church is not a Congolese church. I have clearly said it is a church of Jesus'.

Instead of claiming particular national affiliations, church members see themselves as representing true Christians whose mission is to bring God back to Oststadt, Germany and Europe. One of the core members of the English-speaking church returned from the Berlin conference saying that the presence of people from all over the world at the conference was for her evidence of the power of God and the rightness of her beliefs. This question of evidence can be said to reflect part of the ideology of Christianity as the 'true modernism'.[16] The modern world is one of scientific evidence. God's presence in the world today is proved by God's constant miracles. In Pastor Joshua's words: 'What is God's loud speaker? Action; miracles; the miracle is his loud speaker. . . . If you do not believe me, believe the voice of the miraculous. He is not dead; he is alive; he is in the miracle business'.

Because of this power of evidence, the English-speaking church emphasizes healing, but the purpose of God performing this healing is not just to respond to individual faith but also to provide testimony of the power of God to Oststadt and to the world. In Pastor Joshua's eyes the testimony to the healing power of God is an obligation of those having been blessed and God's will as well. 'The secret of power is the testimony', he said. 'God wants and expects you to testify. You have to use your testimony to speak to people for Jesus'. The sermon of the German-Egyptian guest preacher at the Sunday services held to celebrate the church's success in moving to its own premises was of the same tenor: 'The Bible says: 'What has one to do day by day? To declare His name among the nations day by day. Where are the nations? Here are some. But most of them are not here. They are on the street, Germans, Vietnamese, Koreans, Chinese, Arabs, Bulgarians and others. The Bible says: Go and declare that God lives. You have to do many sacrifices. . . . Do you want to sacrifice something to God? Give Him people He could save. Save the people of God!'

To provide evidence of the power of God to the people of Oststadt, the English-speaking church organized a great healing meeting in spring 2005, renting the ice hockey arena of the city and inviting speakers from a network of pentecostal preachers and missionaries. Since the implementation of such an event required considerable economic resources, Pastor Joshua tried to persuade the congregants to give generous donations, pointing out the missionary task of the church: 'We have to bring the light of God to the people of Oststadt.'

Pastor Mpenza also regards healing and miracles as evidence of the power of God. When asked about the reasons that have attracted the congregants to his church, he brought up his own experience: 'I used to be Catholic; my father was Catholic; my mother was Catholic. Before answering the question I will give you an example from my own experience; because it's the same question. Labelled as Catholic, I went to a pentecostal church. I heard the Word of God; and I heard nothing Catholic, Protestant or Orthodox in this Word; I just heard the Word of God. And I realized that this Word had changed my life. This word brought me to the straight and narrow. This Word educated me. And I have seen the illnesses that were in my body leaving. So, I told to myself: I am on the right track. That is why I stayed there. . . . I think this applies to the people coming to the church. . . . After having had experience they say: "we are doing the right thing" '. Nonetheless, his church does not focus on either healing or testimony, though testifying constitutes an integral part of the services, where congregants, from time to time, declare that they have been healed or have found employment with the help of God. Instead of putting emphasis on healing and miracles, the French-speaking church tries to attract local inhabitants of the city by mobilizing the church's main resource, the ability of its members to sing. So, 'within the frame of its evangelization work' the church organized a gospel concert in December 2003. The church's gospel choir performed with other invited choirs from neighbouring cities. As Pastor Mpenza put it, 'there is evangelisation by means of language, and there is evangelisation by means of music'. In short: both churches, despite the lack of

German linguistic knowledge of the congregants, succeed in finding ways to address the local non-immigrant population. The congregants make the city residents an offer that goes beyond the expectations a receiving society has from its immigrants. Actually, the offer of the congregants represents a reversion of the dominant expectations. The migrants are not to fit into the schemes conceived for them by German migration policy; instead the German population will acquire 'the citizenship of the pentecostal community'.[17]

Challenging the Ideology and Policy of 'Fortress Europe'

It is through this vision of the place of Christianity in the modern world that these Christians understand their relationship to Germany. The personal relationship to the Holy Spirit joins Christians wherever they are located into a mission of bringing Christianity to the world. The churches help the believers articulate a form of identity that links them not only to Germans, but also to the world beyond German borders. The national frame is too narrow for these global players. As André Droogers has pointed out: 'The language miracle of the first Pentecost is more than a metaphor: Pentecostals behave like cultural polyglots. Whether or not the nation-state will survive the globalisation process, Pentecostals will not allow themselves to be constrained by national boundaries. They preach their own model of a world society, and give it substance within their own communities'.[18]

The rejection of the nation-state as a frame of reference by the two churches entails a challenge to the legitimacy of political decisions of these states. In a time of increasing restrictions on immigration to Europe, the churches provide legitimacy to transnational movement and claim rights to Germany. They preach that their movements represent God's will that can benefit refugees as well as those who are indigenous to Germany. Whatever German and European politicians claim, in Pastor Mpenza's eyes, the message of the Bible is clear: 'Every place whereon the soles of your feet shall tread shall be yours' (Deut. 11.24). It is about a promise of God to his followers: 'For ye shall pass over Jordan to go in to possess the land which the LORD your God giveth you, and ye shall possess it, and dwell therein' (Deut. 11.31). 'It is no accident that you are in Germany', he said once addressing the insecurity of his congregants, some of whom are waiting for a decision on their application for asylum for years while others are afraid of suddenly receiving a deportation letter from the authorities. 'I have seen people, who were older than me and who also wanted to come to Germany, but they have not come. I have acquaintances that had power and money. But they have not come to Germany. You should not be the slave of humans but of God'. 'The life of the Christian is not easy', Pastor Mpenza says again and again. But however challenging Christian life is, if the congregants live according to God's will, they should not have any doubts about whether or not they are on the right track. The Bible provides evidence of the difficulties immigrants meet in a strange world as well as the way to overcome them. Similarly, Pastor Joshua repeatedly makes reference to biblical migrants. Once he referred to Daniel who was 'in a strange land like you and me and never gave up. He only paid attention to what God said. He practiced effective prayer'. Then you 'will speak and it will come to pass'. 'Nothing will be impossible. You can climb to any height'. A short time ago the message in the English-speaking church was linked to the need of the congregants for German passports, legal residence papers, and marriages to Germans. Increasingly, the miracles promised include jobs and education, but in all cases Oststadt and Germany are envisioned as parts of a terrain in which God, not the German state has dominion. Pastor Joshua did not leave any doubt about this during a sermon: 'The landlord of our premises had asked me, where I would find the money for the monthly rent. I told him, Oststadt belongs to my father, my God'.

Conclusion

The congregations of the African immigrants have their own agenda; an agenda targeting not only immigrants but also the German population; an agenda challenging prevalent perceptions of immigration and the corresponding policy. The congregants do not accept being part of Germany in the taken-for-granted terms of nationality but still make claims to become part of the societies, in which they live. Past migration studies tend to cast all patterns of migration settlement into the same mode arguing for a model of assimilationism, cultural pluralism or transnationalism. In fact, there are multiple pathways of incorporation and many forms of being a transnational. The pathway we discussed in this article emphasizes connections to the locality of residence, Germany, and beyond but not in a mode that stresses regional, national or ethnic identities. It cannot be understood as simple integration into a 'political community'. Instead it is a form of 'belonging' within a global claim. Churches like these challenge, in particular, the assumptions of migration studies, in which migrants' religions are often described as defensive, restrictive and closed ideologies that stabilize the migrants against the background of their traumatic experiences of migration. On the one hand, the members of the churches are mostly 'foreigners', refugees or in-marrying immigrants who face the particular problems of strangers in a strange land.

On the other hand, they do not regard themselves as immigrant organizations or immigrant churches but as Christians who serve an ever-living and world spanning God. And God has nothing to do with national origins or culture. In their daily activities, the churches work within the tension of this contradiction. Their message provides the congregants with moral support and optimism, while their institutional connections and personal experiences offer them a way of identifying themselves within the new locality and create a sense of mission with regard to the indigenous population that gives them both voice and authority.

Notes

1 All names of persons and locations in this article are fictitious.
2 For a fuller version of this argument in the context of the theoretical debate on religion and migration, see Karagiannis, Evangelos and Glick Schiller, Nina, 'Contesting Claims to the Land: Pentecostalism as a Challenge to Migration Theory and Policy', *Sociologus: Journal for Empirical Social Anthropology*, 56(2) (2006).
3 Bade, Klaus and Bommes, Michael, 'Migration und politische Kultur im "Nicht-Einwanderungsland" ', in: Bade, Klaus and Münz, Rainer (eds), *Migrationsreport 2000, Fakten – Analysen – Perspektiven* (Bonn: Bundeszentrale für politische Bildung, 2000). 163–204; Heckmann, Friedrich, 'From Ethnic Nation to Universalistic Immigrant Integration: Germany', in: Friedrich Heckmann and Schnapper, Dominique (eds), *The Integration of Immigrants in European Societies. National Differences and Trends of Convergence, Forum Migration 7* (Stuttgart: Lucius & Lucius, 2003): 51–52, 74.
4 Treibel, Anette, *Migration in modernen Gesellschaften: Soziale Folgen von Einwanderung, Gastarbeit und Flucht, Grundlagentexte Soziologie* (Weinheim und München: Juventa Verlag, Second edn, 1999), 152.
5 Ibid. and 61–62.
6 Radtke, Frank-Olaf, 'Fremde und Allzufremde: Zur Ausbreitung des ethnologischen Blicks in der Einwanderungsgesellschaft', in: Wicker, Hans-Rudolf, Alber, Jean-Luc, Bolzman, Claudio, Fibbi, Rosita, Imhof, Kurt and Wimmer, Andreas Wimmer (eds), *Das Fremde in der Gesellschaft: Migration, Ethnizität und Staat* (Zürich: Seismo, 1996): 337–40.
7 Hoffmann-Nowotny, Hans-Joachim, *Soziologie des Fremdarbeiterproblems. Eine theoretische und empirische Analyse am Beispiel der Schweiz* (Stuttgart: Enke, 1973); Esser, Hartmut, *Aspekte der Wanderungssoziologie. Assimilation und Integration von Wanderern, ethnischen Gruppen und Minderheiten. Eine handlungstheoretische Analyse* (Darmstadt; Neuwied: Luchterhand, 1980). Esser's rational choice approach has shaped German migration sociology. For a brief recent summary see Esser, Hartmut, 'Ethnische Kolonien: "Binnenintegration" oder gesellschaftliche Isolation?', in: Hoffmeyer-Zlotnik, Jürgen H. P. (ed.), *Segregation und Integration: Die Situation der Arbeitsmigranten im Aufnahmeland* (Mannheim: Verlag Forschung Raum und Gesellschaft, 1986), 106–17.
8 Treibel 1999: 137.
9 Looking for criteria for the 'social rootedness' of the immigrants in Germany, the civil servants of the German naturalization authorities turn their attention to the migrants' participation in German associations, while the membership in migrant

associations is met with less enthusiasm (Leggewie, Claus, 'Integration und Segregation', in: Bade, Klaus and Münz, Rainer (eds), 2000: 97). In the 1980s, the issue of whether migrant organizations promote integration or segregation inspired great controversy in German sociology (see Elwert, Georg, 'Probleme der Ausländerintegration, Gesellschaftliche Integration durch Binnenintegration?', *Kölner Zeitschrift für Soziologie und Sozialpsychologie 34* (1982): 717–32; and Esser 1986). Mainstream migration sociology in Germany has generally accentuated the contributions of migrant organizations to segregation. For a short discussion of the issue in Germany, see Jungk, Sabine, 'Soziale Selbsthilfe und politische Interessenvertretung in Organisationen von Migrantinnen und Migranten – Politische Rahmenbedingungen, Forschungslage, Weiterbildungsbedarf', in: Informationszentrum Sozialwissenschaften und Landeszentrum für Zuwanderung NRW (ed.), *Migration und ethnische Minderheiten. Sozialwissenschaftlicher Fachinformationsdienst, 1* (2001): 7–15.

10   Wimmer, Andreas and Glick Schiller, Nina, 'Methodological Nationalism and Beyond: Nation-State Building, Migration and the Social Sciences', *Global Networks*, 2(4) (2002): 301–34.

11   Taking into consideration that the lack of a political incorporation concept for immigrants in Germany has been due to the long-lasting 'hope' of the German policy makers that the guest workers would return to their country of origin – a hope corresponding to the doctrine that 'Germany is not an immigration country' – it is not surprising that there is no political incorporation discourse concerning the refugees at all.

12   Bade and Bommes 2000: 184.

13   The German policy makers disregarded the fact that after the recruitment stop of 1973 and in view of the lack of an immigration law the right of asylum was the only open way to migrate to Germany apart from the family reunion and some additional exceptions (ibid.: 185).

14   'The structure of this abnormalization of life becomes visible in the comparison with expectations of what is considered normal in welfare states like the Federal Republic. The orientation to and compliance to the requirements for the participation in various societal functional spheres – such as work place or appropriate qualifications for the labour market, familial security, adequate language skills etc. – constitute a pattern of normalized life that is institutionalized and supported through welfare state benefits. Deviations from this pattern provoke irritation . . . In the case of refugees we talk about abnormalization of life because the measures introduced by the State since the early 1980s were targeted at making such an independent life permanently impossible. For we can construe the political regulative endeavours towards immigration to Germany at Federal and state levels as an effort to limit the social inclusion of these immigrant groups [. . .] to what is unavoidable for living' (Bade, Klaus, Bommes, Michael, Karagiannis, Evangelos, and Koch Ute, 'Migration und kulturelle Differenz in Gemeinden: Eine historisch-systematische Untersuchung. Bericht' (Osnabrück: Institut für Migrationsforschung und Interkulturelle Studien, 2001, *unpublished* manuscript), 150).

15   The regulations on the right of asylum seekers to work in Germany have repeatedly changed. Since 2001 asylum seekers are allowed to work after their first year

of residence in Germany. However, before an asylum seeker can accept a job the labour office has to check whether unemployed Germans or EU citizens could be considered. In a city like Oststadt, where the unemployment rate is constantly higher than 20 per cent this means that asylum seekers have no chance to find a job.

16 The close relation between Pentecostalism and images of modernity has been often pointed out by various scholars, cf. Cortén, André and Marshall-Fratani, Ruth, 'Introduction', in: Cortén, André and Marshall-Fratani, Ruth (eds), *Between Babel and Pentecost. Transnational Pentecostalism in Africa and Latin America* (Bloomington IN: Indiana University Press, 2001), 1–21; Marshall-Fratani, Ruth, 'Mediating the Global and Local in Nigerian Pentecostalism', *Journal of Religion in Africa, 28* (1998): 258–315; Meyer, Birgit, ' "Make a Complete Break With the Past": Memory and Post-Colonial Modernity in Ghanaian Pentecostalist Discourse', *Journal of Religion in Africa, 28*(3) (1998): 316–49; Maxwell, David, ' "Delivered from the Spirit of Poverty?" Pentecostalism, Prosperity and Modernity in Zimbambwe', *Journal for Religion in Africa, 28* (1998): 350–73.

17 Van Dijk, Rijk, 'From Camp to Encompassment: Discourses of Transsubjectivity in the Ghanaian Pentecostal Diaspora', *Journal of Religion in Africa, 27*(2) (1997): 154.

18 Droogers, André, 'Globalization and Pentecostal Success', in: Cortén, and Marshall-Fratani 2001: 54.

Chapter 21

Colonial Politicization of Religion: Residual Effects on the Ministry of African-Led Churches in Britain

Dapo Asaju

The Spirit of Colonialism is Still Rife in Nigeria

This chapter reviews the religious consequences of the 1884 Berlin–Congo Conference on the Partitioning of Africa, in relation to the politicization of religion by the British Colonial Government, using Nigeria as case study. It discusses the far-reaching implications of these, for religious peace in the country and the effects on the ministry of Nigerian-led diasporic Churches in Britain. The General Act of 26 February 1885 resulting from the Berlin Conference under the leadership of the German Chancellor Bismarck, focused in its first five sections on trade and commerce, tainted with political governance. In its sixth section, it veered into partial religious interest:

All the powers exercising sovereign rights or influence in the aforesaid territories bind themselves to watch over the preservation of the native tribes, and to care for the improvement of the conditions of their moral and material well-being and to help in suppressing slavery, and especially the slave trade. They shall without distinction of creed or nation, protect and favour all *religious* [emphasis mine], scientific, or charitable institutions and undertakings created and organized for the above ends, or which aim at instructing the natives and bringing home to them the blessings of civilization. Christian missionaries, scientists and explorers with their followers, property and collections, shall likewise be the object of special protection. Freedom of conscience and religious toleration are expressly guaranteed to the natives, no less than to subjects and foreigners.[1]

The above statement outlines the priorities of the colonial powers in their relation to Christian missions. Mission was not their primary emphasis. The European explorers that paved the way to opening up Africa to the world for exploration, had first and foremost commercial interests at heart, not necessarily to civilize the people; they already had long history of African civilization predating European missions.[2] In the Act of 1885, missionary endeavour was put at the same level with trade and scientific concerns while there was no special commitment to Christian evangelism over and above respect for the protection of other religions which Christianity was to encounter on the mission field. However, such respect for other religions was particularly limited to Islam and not generally extended to the indigenous religion of the ethnic identities in Nigeria.

It is notable that the advance of Islam in sub-Saharan Africa was another form of religious colonization. The Jihadists who took the North, forcibly subjugated the people and replaced their culture and indigenous religion with a totalitarian form of Islam. Up to date, most parts of Northern Nigeria have been officially declared as 'Shariah'-governed states, alongside with a long-standing, traditional Islamic Emirate governing system; this, in spite of the constitutional declaration of the Nigerian state as secular. Viewed from this perspective, we argue that Western colonialism was not the first form of colonization in parts of Africa. When British Colonial authorities conceded exclusive religious autonomy to Muslim Northern Nigeria, it was actually submitting to another form of colonialism; a structure that was to reverberate much later in the post-colonial era.

The spirit of 'colonialism' is still rife in Africa (albeit in disguise). Ethno-religious sentiments and structures established by the two colonial models subsist and are still being used as political tool for the continued manipulation and exploitation of the African people by former colonial masters and their surrogate African agents. These continue to serve the overall hidden interests of the Western colonial powers, as the colonies have not really been fully given-up by the West. Through remote control of governments, the use of debt burden and the imposition of stringent economic conditions through the IMF and World Bank, most of Africa remain impoverished and a tutelage of the West.

The most permanent mark of colonialism is linguistics. When Africans meet at international conferences, they are compelled to speak the different languages of their former colonial masters; English, French, Spanish, Belgian and Portuguese. Translations exist in these colonial languages; but not in Swahili, Akan, Yoruba, Igbo or Hausa. The basic identity of the Africans is wounded by the damaging and subjugating traces of colonial mentality.

Prior to the 'September 11' terrorist attack on the World Trade Center and the Pentagon in United States of America in 2001, the secularized and post-modern West had underestimated the relevance of religion in local and international politics. Centuries of influence by the renaissance, secularism and post-modernity coupled with scientific and technological developments, had relegated religion to the backspace of private life, whereas in parts of the developing world, particularly the Two-Thirds world, there had been a gradual build-up of the significance of religion as a tool in modern international politics. In an era of globalization, the West is now compelled to reckon with this fundamental dynamic. Behind many suicide bombings and terrorist attacks in the Middle East for instance, can be found traces of religious fanaticism; thus religion becomes a potent vehicle for the expression of popular protest and for propagation of a variety of socio-political objectives. The international community is currently in search of solutions to the consequences of religious terrorism for world peace, security and stability.

In a way, the colonial powers now apparently experience a backlash of their sowing religious polarization which they pursued among the colonies. The colonies are striking back, partly through massive immigration into Europe. Some employ religious sentiment to perpetrate violence and terrorism as vengeance for what they regard as inappropriate identification of the West with Christianity and its support for Israel. It is, for instance, still the view of the Muslim world that the colonial powers are serving the interests of Christianity; consequently rejecting the perceived evils of colonialism, Christians often suffer antagonism by non-Christian communities. Often, the former questionable actions of the West are visited on present Christian communities, because Muslim fanatics regard the West as synonymous with Christianity. For example, when the USA army attacked Afghanistan in 2001, Muslims in Kano, Nigeria killed some Christians and destroyed a number of churches. A similar reaction was recorded in Pakistan. The reality is that the West is now a post-Christian society. Therefore the assumption that former colonial powers still support Christian missions is erroneous. In contemporary times, the terrorist emergency in the West has also cast cloud on the Black communities in Britain and worsened the racist behaviour against Africans in diaspora because every black man on the street, irrespective of his religious faith, can be a suspected criminal or terrorist. This fundamental discrimination negatively affects the mission endeavour of immigrant African missionaries.

British Colonial Restriction on Early Christian Mission

The British colonial authorities found in religion a veritable tool for controlling the colonized people of Africa, one reason being that many Africans are incurably religious. Bolaji Idowu states that for instance, the Yoruba people are 'in all things religious'.[3] Even in the 'diaspora', religion and culture remain vitalizing elements for the sustenance of the African people under slavery, apartheid rule and similar suppression. Joel Edwards, Jamaican-Born general director of Britain's Evangelical Alliance remarks rightly that 'When Christians from the Caribbean and Africa move to Europe, they bring with them habits of the heart. African churches are some of Britain's biggest and fastest growing. So many immigrants have joined that more than half of London's practicing Christians are non-white. If you go to a foreign country, you are cut off from your own country. Church can be a great source of solace'.[4]

Islamic colonizers around the tenth century employed religion to subjugate the Northern people of Nigeria. The British found it also easy to use Christianity to control the South. When previously they took Northern Nigeria before the amalgamation of both Northern and Southern protectorates, policy shifted to wooing the religious sentiment of the volatile Muslim North, through their Emirs. This indirect ruling system served administrative convenience and resulted in the politicization of religion for political ends. Christian missions and the missionaries had to suffer for it. Here we find a contradiction in the British colonial policy. Christianity could be used to pursue colonial interest where it suited the authorities but it could be sacrificed for other preferred interests. This trend was to affect the nation's political fabric up to today. In the wake of renewed religious attacks on Christians by Muslim fundamentalists in Kano in May 2004, the Pentecostal Fellowship of Nigeria placed an advertisement into a Newspaper, containing the following excerpt:

> In the aftermath of the persecution which the Church has had to face in the North within the past few months, we traced the background of this challenge to the remote and immediate and came to the following conclusions: That from the hindsight of the British game plan and for obvious reasons of the will to continue to subjugate Nigeria under her influence, the colonialists bequeathed a legacy of religious partiality at the official corridors which to date has dictated the norm and egos of Islamic adherents as if Islam could eventually assume a National religion, irrespective of the constitutional provision for secularity of the Nigerian state.[5]

The reference to British colonial politicization of religion above is indicting. It relates to the 'Pledge' (agreement) entered into by Lord Frederick Lugard the then British Colonial Governor General, in 1900: The Government will in no way interfere with the Mohammedan religion. All men are to be free to worship as they please. Mosques and prayer places will be treated with respect by us.[6] Subsequently the Colonial Governments Certificate of Occupancy to the Church Missionary Society (CMS) gave details of the restrictions to evangelize the North:

> In towns and villages or quarters of towns and villages which are Mohammedan or predominantly Mohammedan . . . Not to preach at all in the vicinity of mosques or in or near markets or other places to which the public particularly resort, and not to preach in or near other public places except in so far as the Emir or Head Chief or Native Authority may, through the Resident give his consent thereto nor after any such consent shall have been withdrawn and Not to carry out house to house witnessing among the Mohammedans residents for purposes of missionary propaganda except in compounds at which previous indication has been given that such a house visiting would be welcomed generally by the people of the compound.[7]

Every effort made by mission authorities to reverse this position failed. Missionaries were thrown out of Zaria under humiliating conditions while the Colonial Government refused to protect them. A letter by Dr Miller to his wife illustrates one such event:

> Your letter reached us one day's journey from Kano, on our way back to Zaria. We were turned out of Kano, and after six years waiting and the four and half months marching, tramp, tramp, sleeping at night in hurts, bush, upon desert, night after night, at least we reached our destination so longed for, only to be kicked out. You cannot think what it meant. And now we are turned out of Zaria and are practically fugitives, without home and living from day to day, never knowing what the next will bring.[8]

Crampton[9] gives further evidence for the attitude of British Colonial authorities to missionaries in the nineteenth century's Mission to the North. He showed that rather than aid the missionaries, the government actively enacted policies that prohibited missionaries from carrying out mission work in the Muslim-dominated areas of the Nigerian protectorate. Lord Lugard, the first Governor General turned down requests by missionaries led by Bishop Herbert Tugwell for permission to remain in Zaria after the Muslim Emir ejected them from the ancient city without cause other than as Muslim communities, they wanted nothing to do with Christianity. The secret agreement which Frederick Lugard entered into with the Northern Muslim Emirs not to allow missionaries to operate in their domain, laid the dangerous foundation which pervades until today, that the Muslim North must enjoy a closed door to Christian evangelism, and see itself as an exclusively Muslim society. This attitude that prevented Christian mission works in the North for many decades until the 1950s and 1960s when under the military rule, some Christian presence became established in parts of the North. So, virtually all Christian missions in the North are contemporary, except for the Evangelical Church of West Africa (ECWA) which succeeded the Sudan Interior Mission (SIM), the tenacious champions of the Hausa Mission after CMS, efforts were aborted by the colonial authorities. The North still operate the Emirate system by which the powerful Emirs act as Islamic rulers.

The Colonial government generally was known for using divide-and-rule policy in the governance of their respective subjugated colonies. Nigeria was no exception. The North was favoured in political tutelage and governance. British Colonialists handed over power to the North, which in return provided rulers of the country for the larger part of the period of the country's independence. Since the First Republic in 1960, the North has operated the penal codes of Shariah Islamic jurisprudence alongside the English Common Law. By this they enjoy a unique privilege, later taken for granted when in 2001 most

Northern states unilaterally declared themselves Islamic States, adopting full 'Shariah' as their major jurisprudence. Christians' protest against the adoption of 'Shariah' was met with wanton killing of the protesters. The crisis in Kaduna led to the death of more than two thousand people, mostly Christians. In Bauchi, according to the *Human Rights Watch World Report 2002,*

> In July and August, violence broke out between Christians and Muslims in Tafawa Balewa in Bauchi State, apparently in response to the introduction of Shariah there. In September, more than 1000 people were estimated to have been killed in violence between Muslims and Christians in Jos, Plateau State.[10]

This report also observed the response of the international community to this violent development.

> The United States, United Kingdom and other Western governments continue to view Nigeria as a key ally in Africa in the 'war against terrorism', especially in view of its large Muslim population. These political considerations led to a reluctance to criticize Nigeria's human rights record. Overall, foreign governments remained silent in the range of serious human rights abuses taking place in Nigeria, with the exception of the sentences of death by stoning under 'shariah', which were widely condemned at the international level, by government officials, parliamentarians and non-governmental organizations in several world regions.[11]

Another massacre of 73 Christians occurred on 24 February 2004 at Yelwa, Plateau State. 'What began as a mere cow theft snowballed into a gruesome massacre of some 73 Nigerians in a single day in Yelwa, Shendam Local Government area of Plateau State. Mostly women and children, 35 of them were herded into a church and slaughtered like rams.'[12] In addition to this, three major churches in the town were destroyed (Catholic, Deeper Life Bible Church and Church of Christ). Similar incidences were re-enacted in surrounding areas in April and May 2004 (claiming more than two thousand lives). This forced the Federal Government to declare a State of Emergency in Plateau State for 6 months. Akintola, an outspoken Islamic proponent in Nigeria states in 'A New Islamic Renaissance' that, 'Like the 19th century "Jihad" in the North, the new desire of the Muslims in many parts of the world today, is to revive the pristine glory of Islam. It is the fervent belief of Muslims that in "shariah" lies the solution to all problems facing the world today.'[13]

Politicization of religion in Nigeria is also manifested in various other forms. Examples are the government appointments into choice political offices, and the adoption of Nigeria as member state of the Organization of Islamic Conference (OIC) despite the constitutional declaration of Nigeria as Secular State.[14]

Religion has become a major campaign issue during elections and getting a reliable census has become problematic because of claims of majority by adherents of the two contending religions, Christianity and Islam. Nigeria's foreign policy has been influenced by the religious perspectives of particular leaders at a given point in time. For example during the regional government system, the Muslim North remained opposed to Israel and pro-Arab, while the Christian East openly identified with Israel and pro-West. It was so openly pronounced that the then Prime Minister, Tafawa Balewa cautioned that 'It will be the end of happiness in this country when religion is brought into politics.'[15] Nigeria has already arrived at this situation. Calls by ethnic nationalities for a Sovereign National Conference to discuss and redesign Nigeria have been prevented by Government. The country is restive as the democratic experiment suffers persistent jerks. This emergent current of agitation and instability involves and affects both Nigerians at home and in the Diaspora. It also affects the nature, configuration and ministry of Nigerian Churches in Britain.

Effects on Nigerian-Led Churches in Britain

In this section, I will depend upon the findings of my own field research, attending some Nigerian-led Churches in London, Milton Keynes and Birmingham in Britain, as a Visiting Fellow in the Theology Department of Birmingham University, between January and June 2003. The following Nigerian-led Churches were observed: The Kingsway International Christian Church, London, led by Mathew Ashimolowo; the Christ Chapel International Church in South London, led by Tunde Joda; The Jesus Everlasting Foundation Ministry in Camberwell London, led by Samson Olomo; The Liberty Church, in Turnpike Lane London, led by Segun Johnson; the Christ Apostolic Church Birmingham led by A. Adedoja and the Redeemed Christian Church of God, Birmingham, led by M. Alake. My study reveals that there is a constant trend of maintaining the dominant composition of their respective Nigerian mother churches. In most Churches, the members are simply those who had belonged to these churches while they were at home in Nigeria. Their styles of worship were the same as in Nigeria, without due effort to contextualize worship pattern in the cultural milieu of Britain and among the indigenous people. Only in three of these churches were two or three Britons found and these were married to Nigerians. The implication of this is that the much talked about 'African Mission to Europe' is not yet a success unless the Europeans who supposedly are being re-evangelized are reached and converted. Operating Nigerian Churches in western territories do not necessarily indicate mission in the diaspora.

Anthony Reddie[16] attributes the origin and prominence of some African–led churches to the social need of immigrants to create safe and inclusive spaces where they can reveal their authentic selves. This functions as a solution to the cultural dissonance experienced by many of them as they struggle to reconcile two differing or opposing cultural situations or contexts. This struggle involves setting values relating to faith, culture and spirituality. In this sense may I add that some Nigerian-led Churches in Britain seem to have arisen as the continuation of traditional religious norms among Nigerians who regard Europe as an alternative space to relocate their format of Church ministry. My observation of some churches like the Redeemed Christian Church of God in London and Birmingham show no particular difference from their sister churches in Nigeria. No visible attempts are noticed in adapting to European culture to make their worship suitable to the indigenous British.

The failure of African churches in Britain to integrate the indigenous population into their membership is, on the one hand due to their inability to create relevant space for white members. In this sense, the nature, tempo and rhythm of their songs and music are a departure from familiar Western Church music. Bad time management, that is, too long church services are offensive to the white's sense of time discipline and economy. On the other hand, the indigenous people themselves are either scared to join these churches out of fear to be identified with the negative mental image of blacks (especially with regard to criminality), or they fall prey to the common racial prejudice. This is where also in Europe, the spirit of colonialism comes in. Nahashon Ndung'u repeats the old feeling:

> Long before the colonization of Africa by the European powers, the African personality had already suffered a great blow through the slave trade . . . It is however interesting to note that the Church in Europe was silent when millions of Africans were undergoing the agonies of slave trade. Failure to condemn the slave trade showed that the church shared the view that Africans belonged to an inferior race not befitting the biblical understanding of human beings.[17]

Many whites are yet to be convinced that the Africans, wherever they are found, have anything worthwhile to offer. They have little respect for the Africans and are not comfortable to stoop to the level of mixing with blacks in or be led by them in church. Consequently from my various visits to Nigerian-led churches the average proportion of white membership is in the region of 5 percent . This of course is not limited to the church context alone. In the social context, it is manifested in what Dilip Hiro described as 'The White flight'[18] namely the exodus of the white middle-class from black housing areas. This situation has turned some erstwhile mixed communities into virtually all black or all-Asian ones.

Roswith Gerloff rightly notes that 'The historical ignorance and cultural arrogance of Western Christians rendered churches which are part and parcel of world Christianity as "sects" and "cults" . . . '[19] On the other hand according to Gerloff, 'Black churches in Britain came into being out of a necessity, to serve in the first instance their own cultural and spiritual constituencies; nevertheless they themselves often displayed features bound up with the legacy of adaptation and a colonial mission and did not engage in genuine partnership.'[20] She claims that the link for partnership and networking between black and white churches in Britain, requires more than technical management but must arise from a spiritual foundation. Bongani Mazubiko agrees with the above in the following comments: 'For several years I lived in the West. Looking at the Church in England and Germany . . . the most persistent problem I perceive, rightly or wrongly, is that taint of arrogance among the older cultures. The worst part is that this arrogance is not just cultural but religious, which is such a big tragedy.'[21]

Hence the same 'tragedy' which arose from persistent effects of colonialism in Nigeria affects the impact of Nigerian-led Churches in Britain in the following ways. Perhaps the greatest problem confronting the African-led churches in Britain is the 'dependency syndrome', where churches have to seek financial grants from British churches as well as take advantage of the British Charity system. In Britain, churches are classified under registered Charity organizations. They draw some financial benefits from government and enjoy not only tax exemption but claim tax refund from the contributions of their members. This has been abused by churches who collect huge sums in forms of tithes and offerings from their congregation only to fund personal projects or invest in commercial ventures. The largest black-led church in Britain, the Kingsway International Christian Church in London, was embargoed and put under investigation for a period of time by the British Government on suspicion of fraudulent practices. The vital question is why blacks always expect grants from whites, as if they are unable to support themselves? The cause is traceable to the residual effects of colonial mentality. John Gatu, a Presbyterian minister in Lusaka, Zambia expresses the protest against this trend succinctly:

> We cannot build the Church in Africa on alms given by overseas Churches, nor are we serving the cause of the Kingdom by turning all bishops . . . into beggars . . . for Africa has money and personnel . . . let mission be the mission of God in the world, not of the West to the Third world.[22]

Gatu's views are correct. Churches in Africa are usually very rich. Some of their leaders live in affluence both at home and abroad, although in some cases, in contrast to the status of their suffering members. The same also affects African Churches in Britain. Many of their members consist of settlers who struggle daily at low paying jobs, burdened with huge bills and barely making ends meet. It is only recently, that through the increased influence of prosperity theological teachings, black Christians have begun to aspire educationally and professionally, making strides in business investment and changing the mental picture of Africans by whites, as poor, wretched and a low class race. This process of transformation is only just gathering momentum. The colonial mentality and ego-defeat is gradually wearing away. When it does, the African minister in church might become able to confidently impact the host community in Britain.

The British Colonial Government's official restriction of missionary activities in Northern Nigeria, partly borne out of the 'divide-and-rule policy', must be seen as basically responsible for the wide-spread religious dichotomy and consequent politicization of religion in Nigeria, which also accounts for persistent religious conflicts and disunity among Nigerians in the diaspora. Consequently, African-led churches in Britain carry over the ethnic mentality of religious and denominational characterization as it operates in Nigeria. These church leaders in Britain come almost entirely from the Southern parts of Nigeria, either from the Yoruba or Igbo ethnic stock. Notably, most of the members of their congregation consist of former immigrants from the same ethnic group as the church founder or leader. Hausas from the North, for instance, have no known Christian leader in Britain, since the Colonial government prevented the early evangelization of the Hausa people on a large scale. In other words, colonial influence on missions led to the prominence of denominationalism and ethnic partitioning, which have continued to influence the character and structural configuration of Nigeria-led churches in Britain.

The emergence of African-led churches in Europe has been propelled dominantly by Pentecostalism, which typifies the model of most diasporic churches. Although Britain, through the CMS along with the Wesleyan (Methodist) Mission pioneered Mission to West Africa and planted seed which later blossomed in Nigeria, the British parent churches have drastically declined. However, of much interest is the fact that these parent Anglican or Methodist churches have not felt obliged to open pastoral space to Nigerian priests to let Africans join them in large numbers. If this had been so, the African evangelical churches would have enriched the older denominations and been in the best position to reach white congregations with the message of a 'reverse' mission from Africa to Britain. It is notable for instance, that there are about 18 million Anglicans in Nigeria alone. Yet during my Fellowship at Birmingham University, it took me 6 months as an Anglican priest from Nigeria to be issued a license to officiate in any Anglican congregation in Britain. Any such applicant must receive the license of the Archbishop of Canterbury before any other bishop could issue same. By the time my license was ready, I had completed my Fellowship and returned home, never having an opportunity to officiate or preach in 'my own' Anglican Church in Britain. This is an illustration of the unwelcome stance of some British churches towards African priests. Unlike the typical African open welcome to any priest in visiting collar, black priests, even bishops, are easily snubbed and unwanted in many British churches. Yet these persistent feelings of racial superiority and colonial underrating of black churches as noted by Andrew Walls will hold the key to the survival and growth of the Church in contemporary times:

> Taking it as a whole, . . . the Missionary Movement has changed the face of Christianity. . . . The most remarkable feature of this transformation has been in the African continent, minimal in Christian profession when the missionary movement began, but now, when so much of the West is in the post-Christian period (loss of faith), Africa is moving to the position where it may have more professing Christians than any other continent.[23]

Hence, we submit that there is an urgent need for a theology of reconstruction that refines and re-defines the mission of the church in a global context, and also leads to effective mission work by diasporic churches. This necessitates a paradigm shift by African Churches in the diaspora from their dominant African acculturated outlook to a much wider European/global emphasis that accommodates the values, psychological and cultural ethos and norms of their indigenous host communities.

A Theology of Reconstruction

The proliferation of churches with the rise of Pentecostalism, as well as African Instituted Churches (AICs), has introduced a counterbalancing current to the continuing denominationalism of the mainline churches. The Pentecostals and Aladuras came as a challenge to the spiritual dormancy and lack of evangelical focus of these churches. They swept the Nigerian Christian landscape with spiritual revival. Most of their converts were not from 'pagans' but from the established European denominations. They were liberal in their doctrines, allowed easy access to priesthood even for women, encouraged vibrant styles of worship, permitted the use of spiritual gifts such as 'glossolalia' and prophecy; contextualized the Christian faith in terms of African culture through songs, music, use of the vernacular, calling on the names of God, traditional dressing and church paraphernalia. In short, the emergent new religious movements were a subtle protest to colonial imperialism operating in the church. The Christian field is an all-embracing show in Nigeria today, but hence also witnesses stiff competition between the various groups and denominations. With such churches as the 'Church of God Mission' formerly led by late Benson Idahosa; Redeemed Christian Church of God led by Enoch Adeboye; the Deeper Life Bible Church led by William Kumuyi, the Winners Chapel, led by David Oyedepo; The Redeemed Evangelical Church led by Mike Okonkwo, among the Neo Pentecostals, there is no more one particular brand of Christian expression dominant in Mission. But even these groups are not devoid of foreign influence as well, especially by the North American style of Pentecostal, charismatic Christianity which emphasizes Health and Wealth as well as Holiness theologies.

It is this kind of Nigerian Christianity above that the immigrants into Europe brought along as they settled as traders, students, missionaries or asylum seekers among foreign communities. When we therefore speak of Nigerian-led churches, we refer to two basic groups: first, there are Nigerians who are ordained priests of the mainline Churches such as the Anglicans, who have come to Britain, in the hope to work in the church which once was brought to their homeland, into which they were born and baptized. The second group are the leaders and members of various independent churches including Pentecostals and the AICs who, out of desire for a spiritual base, established branches of their home churches to cater for the spiritual needs of members overseas. This category is most prominent.

The colonial effects on Nigeria-led churches in Britain can be summarized in the following way:

1. The timidity to evangelize the indigenous people in their own, environment borne perhaps out of an inferiority complex based on racial suppositions. This is complemented by the assumption that whites will not come to church because of the long years of secularism and materialism.
2. The racial discrimination by the white population which prevents them from worshipping with blacks, intensified by their fear of security, or alienation by strange patterns and styles of worship, songs, dance and the language used in Nigerian-led churches.
3. Satisfaction of Africans about establishing congregations made up exclusively of people who had belonged to the same group as at home.
4. The continued replication of denominational affiliation abroad of churches established by missionaries under colonial influence, back in Nigeria.
5. As in the case of Nigerians who are ordained priests in the Anglican Church, their difficulty is to integrate into the Church of England as fully acknowledged ministers. Such involvement of Anglicans from Nigeria could have enabled the evangelical revival in the Nigerian Anglican Church (the largest Anglican community in the world), to impact the large numbers of Anglicans in Britain. Is it not an irony that the Church of Nigeria is growing, whereas the Church of England is declining. Hence I submit that the unpreparedness of the British church to open up to positive and salvaging influences from Africa, Asia and Latin America is due to the resilient feelings of colonial and racial superiority. There may be hope that with the wave of charismatic renewal taking place within the mainline churches (e.g. through the Alpha Course), and prayer groups, there can be an interface between British Christianity and the African approach. It is also hoped that these new forms and communities will no longer be seen as foreign spiritualities but as settled minorities within the larger British frame.

Conclusion

In conclusion, Nigerian-led Churches in Britain as in other parts of Europe need to re-examine their mission strategies and to formulate strategies for modifying their worship pattern to suit the cultural tendencies of the British communities. They also need to focus their evangelistic messages to relevantly address the issues of crime, loneliness, fear of the unknown, new diseases, emptiness of spiritual life, Christian education in schools, the dangers of the debate on inclusivity and of religious hatred, the secularist bent of government and almost total dislocation of Christianity in the official European Union, and the new dimension of terrorism and the need for the West to rediscover its Christian identity. Above these regarding, the spiritual dimension, African Christian Mission in the diaspora should provide alternative answers to the growing quest for alternative Spiritualities by an increased number of Europeans, and respond to the explorations into witchcraft and the Harry Porter craze. Christian missionaries must now return to the basic and simple delivery of the gospel message of the teachings of Jesus Christ and his apostles, to the authority of scripture and to the moral and ethical tenets of Christianity. As the church fails to address these issues, Christianity appears to be dead, irrelevant, out of date, and tacitly implicated in compromises. The African Church in the diaspora must remind people in Europe constantly of the reality of evil, the inevitability of death and the limitations of scientific accomplishments, material achievement and the irrelevance of rational positions on spiritual issues when death comes to a person. As an example, the future as well as Christ's 'parousia', together with the eschatological events which appear to play out in the contemporary world, are issues which African missionaries in the diaspora could highlight and discuss to make an impact on their British (or European) counterparts.

Notes

[1] See file://A:\The-Conference-(1885).htm (viewed 12 April 2003)
[2] See 'European Crusades, Christianisation and Colonialism', File://A:\West%20 Africa.htm (viewed 12 April 2003)
[3] Bolaji Idowu, *Olodumare-God in Yoruba Belief* (London: Longman & Co., 1968), ix.
[4] Joel Edwards, quoted in *Time* Magazine 16 June 2003, 27.
[5] Public advertisement paid by the Pentecostal Fellowship of Nigeria, signed by 18 leaders of Nigeria's largest Pentecostal Churches. See *Punch*, 13 June 2004.
[6] 'Proclamation of the Protectorate of Northern Nigeria'1900, in: CMS Archive, Birmingham University, G3 A9 L2.
[7] '"Restriction on public preaching and house to house visitation," 9 June 1931, CMS Archive on Northern Nigeria mission', in: CMS Archive, Birmingham University, G3 A9 L2 (1921–1934).
[8] Letter of Dr Miller to Mrs Miller, 13 May 1900, in: *Hausaland Mission* CMS Archive, G3 A9/6 (1901), 1–12.

[9] Eric P. T. Crampton, *Christianity in Northern Nigeria* (Ibadan: Daystar Press, 1980).

[10] *Tell* Magazine, 21 March 2000, 12.

[11] http://hrw.org/wr2k2/africa8.html

[12] *Tell* Magazine, 15 March 2004, 21.

[13] Ishaq Akintola, *Sharia in Nigeria* (Ijebu Ode: Shebiotimo Pub. 2001), 98.

[14] Constitution of the Federal Republic of Nigeria 1979, Section 10 (7).

[15] Dapo F. Asaju (ed.), *The Concept of Nigeria Unity* (Ilorin: Mobolaju Pub. 1989), 56.

[16] Anthony Reddie, 'Singing the Lord's Song in a Strange Land' *Black Theology in Britain,* 4(2) (May 2002): 186.

[17] Nahason Ndung'u, 'Towards the Recovery of African Identity', in: E. A. Obeng and Mary Getui (eds), *Theology of Reconstruction* (Nairobi: Acton, 1999), 258.

[18] Dilip Hiro, *Black British, White British: A History of Race Relations in Britain.* London: Grafton, 1991.

[19] Roswith Gerloff, 'Pentecostals in the African Diaspora', in: Allan Anderson and Walter J. Hollenweger (eds), *Pentecostals after a Century* (Sheffield: Sheffield Academic Press, 1999), 71.

[20] Ibid.: 79.

[21] Bongani A. Mazubiko, 'Towards a Dialogical Understanding of Mission and intercultural practice of the Christian Church', in: Roswith Gerloff (ed.), *Mission is Crossing Frontiers* (Pietermaritzburg: Cluster Publications, 2003), 204.

[22] Quoted in M. E. Uka, *Missionaries Go Home?* (New York: Peter Lang, 1987), 191.

[23] Andrew Walls, *The Missionary Movement in Christian History* (Edinburgh: Orbis Books, 1996), 85.

Chapter 22

The Implication of Mission from a Black Seventh-day Adventist Perspective, with Reference to Britain, the Caribbean and Africa

Herbert Griffiths

The way in which Seventh-day Adventists (SDA) execute the church's mission in today's post-modern society is distinct from 20 or even 10 years ago. This is particularly true in the case of Britain, which is now a multicultural society, with many facets of religion and religious organizations, each demanding a voice. Together with the challenge of secularism, economic and social factors, the Adventist church in Britain is forced to apply new methods in mission that is similar to those used in the Caribbean and Africa to enable the church to keep in touch with the community it wishes to serve. In this the SDA church in Britain is not unique but it is reflecting a shift in mission approach that has already taken place in other parts of the world, particularly in the two-thirds world countries, where economic and social conditions influence the type of mission the church is engaged in. The result of which is a network of community developments that have been established by lay-members of the church to address the needs of the local people.

Reasons for Mission

The SDA church's motive for mission can be summed up under a consortium of reasons. These fall broadly under three categories: the example of Jesus, the needs of people in the community and Christians who understand mission to lead people to know God and to have a better outlook in life generally. How this is done in practice varies from one culture to the next. In common with other Christian denominations, the SDA church's motif for mission derives from the Scriptures, especially from the life and work of Jesus. This one factor has always shaped the church in its mission outlook, and in directing people to Jesus Christ as the Son of God, who is the giver of grace. To many SDA, Jesus Christ is known as the provider, the encourager, the hope builder and sustainer, and the chief justice and arbitrator, as a result of their personal experience with him.

Jesus has placed in all who accept him the capacity to have a genuine love for humanity. Therefore Christ's active love in individuals motivates and empowers them to fulfil his mission at home and abroad. The SDA denomination's actual understanding of mission will, however, determine the nature and extent of its activities in the community it serves. It will project one of two images – either the church's organizational philosophy, or Christ's selfless love and care. In the first instance the church is protecting itself and its interests from outside influences; in the second the church breaks down barriers in order to reach various people in the community.

Understandably, the apostle Paul not only counselled and encouraged Christians in his own days, but influences the church today and that of the future to have and reflect the attitude of Christ when he argued; 'you should look not only to your own interests, but also to the interests of others. Your attitude should be the same as that of Christ Jesus' (Ph. 2.4–5 NIV). The church should feel and have compassion as Christ did for those around him who are suffering and are in a disadvantaged position in society. The mission of the church should therefore not be seen as a response of obedience to a command, but as a result of the grace of God as experienced by the members. There should be active involvement on the part of the church in each locality in relieving and the opening up of opportunities for both individuals and community developments. The mission of the church is to look after the needs of others, as Christ would do. This being the case the church should be seen as impartial in its dealing with people, communities or issues that they are confronted with daily.

According to Calvin Rock,[1] Adventists redefine the concept of their function in society through the employment of three biblical models: (1) the Israel of God; (2) the reform ministry of Elijah; (3) the work of John the Baptist. Each of the models reflects an important aspect of the self-image of the church. The Israelites were God's special people, chosen by God to function as the means through which other nations would acknowledge and worship him as the true God. Adventists through this model perceived themselves as propagators of God's truth. This model reinforces the idea of uniqueness. The Elijah model represents images of boldness in the period of apostasy. The role of John the Baptist as the forerunner of Jesus Christ provides for the SDA Church a dual directive: (1) of preparing the world for the imminent return of Christ, and (2) the call to reform in matters of diet and dress. The model, however, that has most greatly influenced and shaped the self-image of the SDA Church are the three angels' messages found in Rev. 14.6–12.[2] These angels observed by the prophet flying over the earth with the warning of Christ's imminent return, the fall of the old system, and the judgment, are believed by Adventists to typify the three-fold message, which they preach.

Adventists sustained by a clear vision of their special end-time message are enabled to remain loyal and mission-driven in their activities. Members are encouraged to participate in the mission programme through various training workshops and seminars that are provided in their local congregations. Additionally, once a month Adventist congregations provide mission-oriented programmes. These are designed to motivate members to be active in mission. The writings of Ellen G. White, the founder and prophet,[3] continue to be an authoritative source of truth that provide guidance, instruction, and correction for members of the SDA church, to fully support the involvement of every member in mission activities.

The majority of Adventist believers during the formative years were drawn from various religious communions. Inevitably differences in the interpretation of Scriptures created problems, causing difficulties in deciding on the direction of the church. The greatest difficulties the organization faced in its early days were how to transmit its self-image into a tangible working model without being labelled as a legalistic and fanatical religious group. Such descriptions would be in opposition to the self-image as God's people (the remnant), as the core of its mission was to rescue people from apostasy back to worshipping the true God. With the words of Michael Pearson:

> They believe that Adventism will be the refuge of all true believers in the midst of public opprobrium, and hostility from secular and ecclesiastical monoliths. The 'remnant' will be the focus of the last battle in 'the great controversy between Christ and Satan', immediately prior to the advent. That is not to say that salvation is thought to be available only within the Adventist church, . . . Rather, it is held that Adventism is, . . . the grit in the oyster around which the pearl of the remnant church will be formed. Such a self-understanding demands above all else that the Adventist church be preserved inviolate to perform its vital role.[4]

The avoidance of such a dilemma was achieved though careful studying of the Scriptures and following the instructions of Ellen G. White. Both leaders and members accepted Ellen G. White's writings as authentic; her writings provided the necessary parameter for the development of Adventist mission. Today the SDA church is a conservative Protestant Christian worldwide communion of over twelve million members. It operates hospitals, publishing houses, food factories, schools and universities, and is involved in development and relief work. Its primary focus is the transmission of the gospel mainly accomplished through the vehicle of local SDA congregations. The entire membership is committed to the over-all mission and contributes an average of ten percent of earnings (tithes) to the organization.

The SDA Church and Global Mission

In common with other Christian denominations, the SDA church is a mission-conscious denomination. Its missionary endeavours are recognized and accepted worldwide by other Christian bodies and by national governments. Different cultural groups have been reached with the primary purpose of establishing churches in their local and regional communities together with schools, hospitals and health care centres. Adventists are proud of their record of achievement; they have established themselves in more than two hundred countries and areas of the world as recognized by the United Nations.[5] They have a strong growth rate of 5–6 percent a year, with a membership of over 11.5 million in July 2000.[6] It is projected that the world membership by year 2005 will be over 15 million. Accessions to the World church membership in 1999 totalled 1.09 million. This represents the highest total ever achieved in a single year in the history of the SDA church.[7] With a continuously high accession, world church membership passed twelve million in 2001, with 55 percent of the total number of members living in less affluent countries such as Africa, South America and the Caribbean.[8] In 1950, there was one Adventist for every 3,300 people in the world, while in comparison the figure in 1975 was 1:1,480, and in 2000 1:519.[9] Reflecting on the growth of Christianity, Russell Staples states:

So rapid has been the growth of Christianity in the two-thirds world that the demographic center of gravity of Christianity has shifted from the Northern to the Southern Hemisphere, from the richer to the developing nations, and from the older to the younger churches.[10]

The two-thirds world, now the focus of SDA missionary activity, has become the church's greatest human resource. The church has succeeded in establishing Christian communities and has been instrumental in establishing various institutions such as educational and healthcare facilities, media centres, publishing houses and food industries. Nyaundi, commenting on the practicality of Adventism in Africa, stated that Adventist community services operate model farms which grow a variety of vegetables, and teach simple trades to school-leavers, preparing them for self-employment: 'Non-monetary assistance such as food, clothing, helping to build homes, and helping the sick with their daily chores is also given. . . . The SDA church . . . is also involved in projects concerned with community water supply, sanitation, basic healthcare, child immunization, and ante-natal clinics'.[11] In this way Adventism in Africa is creating favourable conditions, which ensure the church's presence and relevance in the community.

In 1990 the SDA world church adopted a global mission strategy, which focused mainly on church planting. Global mission was different in two ways from previous strategies, as John Dybdahl, in 'Adventist Mission Today–Taking the Pulse', explained:

Earlier evangelistic/mission programs emphasized number of baptisms. Different church entities were encouraged to baptise a target number of people. . . . Secondly, the emphasis moved from counting countries, that is, geopolitical entities, to people–unreached people. The churches planted were to be placed where there were none before.[12]

Under global mission the world was divided into 5,000 ethno linguistic or demographic segments of one million each in order to focus on people and regions where there was little or no Christian presence. This was a shift of paradigm from proselytizing to an intercultural understanding of mission.[13]

Another major change that has taken place in Adventism is the 'Tentmaker' or Global Partnerships programme. This concept is taken from Paul's support of himself in his mission work by the practice of his trade of tentmaker. Tentmakers are self-supported, and are not paid workers of the church as missionaries. They are either employed with a company or they become self-employed. These volunteers are trained in mission and they are able to enter countries or regions within their own country where regular foreign missionaries would not be able to go. For example, there are areas of the world where 60 percent of the world's population are Buddhist, Hindu, and Muslim.[14] These areas pose challenges to the SDA church as well as to other Christian denominations.

The Church's Mission and Socio-Political Issues

The SDA church leadership, after abstaining from socio-political involvement, has now undergone change in favour of the church becoming engaged in facing and helping to resolve some of the socio-political issues of the wider society. This was brought out in the address of Jan Paulsen, president of the SDA world church, to Adventist leaders at the headquarters in Silver Springs, USA, on 7 October 2002. The issue of the church addressing socio-political matters needed to be discussed, as previously the church has understood itself as 'politically neutral':[15] The 'remnant church' was to maintain its self-image of preparing people for Jesus' coming.[16] So Paulsen's' address signalled a new development in the church's attitude to global mission to reach various people in society that would otherwise be left out. The SDA church, Paulsen said, should be active in social justice, and not only in humanitarian aid and in the establishment of new churches.

Sensing the needs within the various world communities, and the issues confronting the SDA church and Christianity on a whole today, Paulsen challenged SDA church leaders and members to be more engaged with the everyday concerns of the societies in which they live. The 'broad and comprehensive' nature of the church's mission responds to people's 'everyday pain'. Addressing this issue he stated that:

We would fail as a church if we become indifferent to the suffering of this world, or become so wholly 'other—worldly' in our thinking that we are insensitive to the suffering of humanity, and cannot be bothered. For this is the world in which we also live.[17]

The SDA church has been active in mission, but it has in the past been particularly selective in its areas of missionary involvement, focusing on humanitarian aid, education, health and planting new congregations. In its involvement in these areas, the church has avoided some of the socio-economic challenges in societies that have surfaced in many parts of the world. These areas, as undesirable as they may be, or as unwilling as members may be to get involved, should also be part of the mission of the church. In spite of the political and cultural tensions that exist in some areas of the world, for example, in Africa and the Caribbean, the church has got a role to play.

The Church cannot detach itself from being a voice for the poor, refugees and the disenfranchised minorities in society. Getting involved in these and many other areas will consolidate the church's mission agenda, making it 'broad and comprehensive'. In this comprehensiveness of mission are elements that directly challenge the assumption of those in the past that the success of mission lies only in producing 'converts' and 'building up the church'.[18] Challenges confronting Adventists today demand that broader and flexible outlooks on mission are adopted in order to reach the every day needs of people. Therefore,

> It is right that as a church we should care about the secular community, care about those with health problems, whether AIDS or other ailments. It is right that we should be a delivery system for an education which is placed in very particular life-style values which are not generally available elsewhere. But it is also right that the church whether in Africa, in Asia, or in the islands of the Pacific yes, even much closer to where most of us live should have a greater part to play. It is right that as a community of faith we should also be a mouth-piece for the poor whose number is ever increasing, for the refugees who come to us in waves asking for . . . one more chance to build a life for their children. It is right that we should be a mouth-piece for other disenfranchised minorities.[19]

Addressing the issue whether the SDA church should take a stand within the political arena as a mouthpiece for 'disenfranchised minorities', is an historical move in itself. There has always been within the Adventist movement a strong 'antipathy to politics'.[20] Members in general always felt that this was an area they should avoid. But with the growing number of people suffering in society from hunger, poverty and injustice, there is now also increased appeal for the church to get involved. Because a person that is persistently deprived of basic material needs and political rights, is also a person deprived of much of self- respect, dignity and will. Paulsen realizes that it is not possible for Adventists as a denomination to continue to avoid these issues, if it is to fully participate in Christian mission to 'reach out' and meet people's needs wherever they are.

Black Caribbean Adventist Mission and the SDA Church in Britain

Before the arrival of African Caribbean's in the United Kingdom, British Adventists had already established educational, health and publishing institutions. Missionary endeavours focused on proselytizing. But all this produced little or no growth for the British SDA church. The White administrators were just struggling to keep the British Adventist church membership at an appropriate and acceptable level. The opposite can be said regarding the development and growth of Adventism in the Caribbean. From the arrival of Adventism, part of the African population that was taken to that region as slaves accepted Adventist teachings and values. They saw that there were similarities between their African traditions and Adventist principles. For example, Adventism was a 'lifestyle' religion, meaning that members should follow the examples of Jesus in their daily living, by helping the needy in their community. In Adventism the African was able to practice their 'oral tradition' from their African heritage. They were encouraged to communicate with their family, friends and neighbours about their faith.

African Caribbean Adventists were not aware of the decline in the British church membership before their arrival. Many were surprised to find that Adventism was not developed and well known, and that the majority of British SDA congregations had small memberships compared with the large scale of Adventism in the Caribbean. Take for example the SDA church in Jamaica.[21] In 1995 the smallest of three conferences, Central Jamaica Conference (CJC), with a population in its territory of over 1.08 million, had 65,385 members in 228 churches. Comparing CJC with the Welsh Mission, the smallest territory in the British Union of Seventh-day Adventists with a population of over 3.7 millions in 1995 in its territory, which had only 443 members in twelve churches, demonstrates the difference in scale.[22]

African Caribbeans brought their concepts and strategies of mission with them to Britain. They continued to be active in door-to-door witnessing, sell SDA magazines and books, talked easily with their work colleagues and neighbours about their beliefs; and also studied the Bible with friends and people they met and who showed an interest in knowing the Bible. They also supported evangelistic meetings hosted by the Adventist church. One can observe that Black Adventists from their arrival in Britain took ownership of the missionary activities in similar ways that they did in the Caribbean. Missionary outreach was no longer the sole responsibility of pastors and the few white members who participated in it from time to time, but it became the responsibility of Black lay-members and the whole church. This was a reversal of roles within the indigenous SDA church organization and its English membership. Before the arrival of Black Adventists, Britain was sending missionaries to the Caribbean and Africa, but now British Adventists had become the recipient of two-thirds world missionary activities.[23]

This reflects the larger picture of a paradigm shift in global mission of the church internationally. This shift in global mission is an extension of the type of projects churches are actively engaged in, both in the Caribbean or Africa, as they are compelled to respond to the social, educational and economic needs of the community. However, these types of missionary activities clashed with the self-image and concept of White British Adventism. For Black Adventists arriving in Britain during the 1950s and 1960s, the mission of the Church was the central point of their being. But what African Caribbeans found in White British Adventism was, that mission had become a side-section of the church's activity, something that was therefore almost peripheral, and something to which a few people had a special calling, but which did not really concern all members. In general, many members saw the fulfilment of the church's mission as the responsibility of the pastors and other paid employees to 'save souls for Christ'. In contrast, drawing on their Caribbean experience, Black Adventists in their day-to-day involvement in missionary activities, illustrated that the church's mission was every member's responsibility so that they would reach out into the wider community. They believed that 'all who receive the life of Christ are ordained to work for the salvation of their fellow men'.[24]

From the arrival of African Caribbean Adventists in Britain in the early 1950's to well into the nineteen nineties, their missionary activities focused mainly on evangelism, building up the membership and establishing new congregations. This method, used widely in the Caribbean, was also a great success for the British SDA church which largely grew. By 1990, however, it also became apparent for Black Adventists that new concepts and strategies were needed to be relevant to Britain's multicultural population. Local congregations began to re-evaluate their missionary strategies, and additional methods were initiated.

In analysing the trends in mission in today's British SDA church, there has been an increase in the establishment of day schools and nurseries, evening/weekend schools, the opening of day centres for the elderly and the unemployed, and feeding projects for homeless persons under this black influence. These projects are reaching the practical needs of individuals in the community. But now, these initiatives are not only applied by Black SDA congregations, but large majority White SDA congregations are also participating in these new missionary activities. This gives a good idea of the way Black members have impacted on the organization and are fulfilling the task of mission in today's multicultural society.

A recent survey shows how Adventist members in Britain now see the primary objective of mission for the SDA church in their locality. That there is a need to include the following: reach the un-churched White and ethnic group communities; mix with other denominations; make the gospel real and relevant to people.[25] These three areas of mission are of particular concern and are completely relevant to the Adventist church in Britain. Reaching the unchurched English and people of other cultures in Britain is very necessary, if the Adventist church is to stay relevant and survive the twenty-first century.

Lastly, members as they discovered the need for the SDA church to make the gospel relevant to the lives of secular-minded people in modern society, now also recognize that methods and practices used previously by the church are not reaching the majority of the populace. Therefore Adventists need to recognize that new strategies and methods must be developed to contact those whom they are still failing to reach. How the SDA church deals with these new developments in mission, will determine the type of church it will become in the twenty-first century. Will it be one that meets the needs of the whole community? For the SDA church to adequately do this, it has to become ecumenical and in some way to cooperate with other denominations at both local and national levels to devise workable solutions. An example of this in the Caribbean is demonstrated in different denominations joining together to oppose the increase in crime in neighbourhoods such as in Kingston Jamaica.[26] Turning to Britain, working in partnership with other denominations is appropriate, if only because within British Adventism a considerable number of SDA congregations conduct their weekly worship services in other denominations' buildings; so the mechanisms for such cooperation are well in place.[27] On the other hand, if the SDA church should prefer to stay insular, this would not be in the best interest of both the church and its mission development, as it would isolate Adventists from other Christian denominations.

For the SDA church to continue to reach out successfully, it requires a strategy that will enable it to understand the different issues that are particular to the community it wishes to serve. Without this understanding, interest or concern, those who proclaim the gospel will have 'little interest in the conditions in which people find themselves'.[28] It is essential for Adventists to be aware that the core of Christian mission is to be interested in the conditions that people find themselves in. God demonstrated this by sending his own son to live with humankind. This became the basis on which Jesus, in speaking to his disciples, was able to say in Jn. 20. 21, 'As the Father has sent me, I am sending you'. These words of Jesus have motivated Christian groups and organizations in every generation to participate in mission.

Notes

[1] Rock, Calvin, 'Institutional Loyalty Versus Racial Freedom: The Dilemma of Black Seventh-day Adventist Leadership', PhD dissertation, May 1984, University Microfilms International, Ann Arbor, MI: 5–6.

2 Rev. 14. 6–12: 'And I saw another angel fly in the midst of heaven, having the everlasting gospel to preach unto them that dwell on the earth, and to every nation, and kindred, and tongue, and people, saying with a loud voice, Fear God, and give glory to him; for the hour of his judgment is come: and worship him that made heaven, and earth, and the sea, and the fountains of waters. And there followed another angel, saying, Babylon is fallen, is fallen, that great city, because she made all nations drink of the wine of the wrath of her fornication. And the third angel followed them saying with a loud voice, if any man worship the beast and his image, and receive his mark in his forehead, or in his hand, the same shall drink of the wine of the wrath of God, which his poured out without mixture into the cup of his indignation; and he shall be tormented with fire and brimstone in the presence of the holy angels, and in the presence of the Lamb: and the smoke of their torment ascendeth up for ever and ever: and they have no rest day nor night, who worship the beast and his image, and whosoever receiveth the mark of his name. Here is the patience of the saints: here are they that keep the commandments of God, and the faith of Jesus'.

3 Ellen G. White is recognized as the 'Lord Messenger'. See *Seventh-day Adventists Believe: .A Biblical Exposition of 27 Fundamental Doctrines* (Washington, DC: Ministerial Association, General Conference of SDAs, 1988), 216.

4 Pearson, M. *Millennial Dreams and Moral Dilemma* (Cambridge: Cambridge University Press, 1990), 23.

5 Haloviak, Bert, 'Archives and Statistics', *Adventist Review* (Hagerstown: Review and Herald Publishing Association, 20–27 July 2000): 26.

6 Thompson, G. Ralph, 'Occupy Till I Come', *Adventist Review* (Hagerstown: Review and Herald Publishing Association, 2 July 2000): 8.

7 Ibid.

8 Adventist News Network Bulletin, 2 October 2001, available at: http://www.adventist.org/news.

9 Office of Archives and Statistics, *Seventh-day Adventist World Church Interesting Facts and Figures* (Washington, DC: General Conference of SDAs, September 2001).

10 Staples, Russell L. 'Historical Reflections on Adventist Mission', in John L. Dybdahl (ed.), *Adventist Mission in the 21st Century: Adventist Mission Today – Taking the Pulse* (Hagerstown: Review and Herald Publishing Association, 1999), 26–35.

11 Nyaundi, Nehemiah M. *Religion and Social Change: A Sociological Study of Seventh-day Adventism in Kenya* (Sweden: Lund University Press, 1993), 153.

12 Dybdahl, John L. (ed.) 1999: 21–22.

13 Gerloff, Roswith, 'Adventisten II: Missionen der Adventisten', in *Religion in Geschichte und Gegenwart (RGG4), 4. Völlig Neu Bearbeitete Auflage, Band 1: A–B* (Tübingen: Mohr-Siebeck, Sept 1998), 129–30.

14 This area of the earth is called the 10 × 40 window. The name is taken from the area's northern and southern boundaries – 40° southern and 10° northern latitude. The region stretches from Africa in the west to Japan in the east. This window touches parts of 82 countries in northern Africa, Asia, Europe and the Asia-Pacific Rim.

15 Pearson 1990: 23.

16 Understandably, the church's reluctance to get involved in the political arena derived from their 'understanding of Bible prophecy, particularly those recorded

in the books of Daniel in the Old Testaments and Revelation in the New Testaments. Adventists believe that in the 'last days', some Christian denominations will join force with the civil authority, which will result in the passing of laws that will demand that every Christian denomination conduct their worship on the same day'. See for example Dan. 7 and Rev. 12.17; 13.12, 14, 16.

17 Paulsen, Jan, paper presented to World Church executive committee members (Silver Spring, MD, 7 October 2002), 1: available at: http://www.adventist.org/news/specials/annual_council_2002/paulsen_opening.html.
18 Dorr, Donald, *Mission in Today's World* (New York: Orbis Books, 2000), 16.
19 Paulsen 2002: 3.
20 Theobald, Robin, 'The Politicization of a Religious Movement: British Adventism under the Impact of West Indian Immigration', *British Journal of Sociology*, 32(2) (June 1981): 204, reasons that Adventists antipathy toward politics derives from the denominations eschatological belief that politics will play a vital role in the series of events which precede Christ's second coming. Politics signifies for Adventists the world of wrangling politicians, Sabbath legislators, . . . who will eventually act against Christians including Adventists.
21 For administrative purposes the SDA church divided the country into three administrated regions that is referred to as conferences; they are East, West and Central Jamaica conferences. Adventists apply this management structure not only in Jamaica and the Caribbean, but within the countries they operate. In Britain there are two conferences and three missions. England is divided into two Conferences – North and South; Ireland, Scotland and Wales comprise the three missions. This structure was in place before the arrival of African Caribbean to Britain from the 1950s.
22 Griffiths, Herbert, 'The Impact of African Caribbean Settlers on the Seventh-day Adventist Church in Britain 1952–2001', Unpublished Ph.D Thesis, 2003, University of Leeds, 114.
23 Ibid.: 279.
24 White, Ellen G. *The Desire of Ages* (Mountain View: Pacific Press Publishing Assoc., 1940), 822.
25 Griffiths 2003: 280.
26 Adventist News Network Bulletin, 12 August 2003.
27 Griffiths 2003: 6–7.
28 Bosch, David J. *Transforming Mission: Paradigm Shifts in Theology of Mission* (New York: Orbis Books, 2001), 7.

Chapter 23

Kimbanguism as a Migrants' Religion in Europe

Aurélien Mokoko Gampiot

For the past few years, many African Christian religions whose presence had so far remained unnoticed in Europe have initiated actions which tend to draw the attention of the media and scholars from various backgrounds. Kimbanguism stands out among these religions due to its wide membership and its focus on identity and community. The purpose of this paper is first to trace Kimbanguism back to its genesis in order to better describe its present features; then to relate and analyze the modes of integration of Kimbanguist believers in European societies.

The Birth of Kimbanguism

Kimbanguism owes its name to Simon Kimbangu, a Congolese Baptist catechist, born around 1889 according to most scholars, but on 12 September 1887 according to the Kimbanguist believers. His home village was N'Kamba, near the Baptist mission of Gombé Loutété in the southwestern quarter of the then Belgian Congo (now the Democratic Republic of the Congo), where he was educated. Married and father of three boys, Kimbangu became a catechist in 1918. The same year, he began to hear the voice of Christ ordering him to convert his fellow countrymen. But Kimbangu resisted the calling until 6 April 1921, when his miraculous healing, in the name of Jesus, of a dying young woman, Nkiantondo, initiated a movement of spiritual awakening among the Congolese people. This act of healing was followed by many others: several people were raised from the dead, blind people recovered sight, mutes began to speak and paralytics to walk. But Kimbangu's prophetic action quickly took on new meaning and a new orientation: In his 'apostolic' circuits, he not only healed people, but also preached against witchcraft, offered moral principles and stigmatized the colonial order. What has remained to this day of his teachings against colonial domination is his famous sentence: 'the White man shall become black and the Black man shall become white', as retained by oral tradition and the proceedings of his trial by Belgian colonial authorities.

Kimbangu's action spurred three types of reactions, first, that of his African brothers and sisters, for whom he was a hero who awakened their political and spiritual conscience. For his experience, which was first and foremost a personal one, kindled his countrymen's faith: people crowded to him from the two banks of the Congo River and from Angola to listen to him, consequently renouncing witchcraft and forsaking their fetishes.[1] At a more political level, Simon Kimbangu's teachings made them aware of a number of actual problems, arousing all the social dissatisfaction of the Congolese people who suffered from oppression, poverty, and the absence of any black inventions that might compete with those of white people. Kimbangu thus appeared as a liberator whose mission was to bring peace, prosperity and happiness, but also a more efficient form of science than that of the European colonists. His audience rapidly increased, for his preaching was that of a nationalist, but also that of a black man who had become aware of the gap in progress and differences separating Blacks and Whites. The awareness of the colonial situation became an impulse for a nationalistic and anti-colonial movement, not only among the Congolese from the Belgian Congo, but also among the people from the French Congo and Angola. In the wake of Balandier and Jaffré, many scholars observed in it the first signs of twentieth-century Congolese nationalism, expressed in national as well as racial terms.[2]

Second, Simon Kimbangu's teachings also provoked the reaction of missionaries and colonial observers living in the Belgian Congo, who either doubted the reality of his healing powers or backed his action. The negative interpretation eventually influenced the colonial authorities and resulted in a political reaction.

Third, on the political platform, Simon Kimbangu's prophetic action drew the attention of the Belgian colonial authorities. He was arrested, along with 37,000 families of followers who were deported and banished to other parts of the colony. But the movement continued underground under the leadership of Kimbangu's wife Muilu Marie, when in 1959 Kimbanguism became a Christian church, officially recognized by the Belgian government and admitted into the World Council of Churches. However, Simon Kimbangu himself did not witness this official recognition of his movement, as he had died in October 1951 after 30 years of imprisonment.

This is how Kimbanguism, born from the consequences of the colonization and Christianization of the Congolese people, became a syncretic church based on the re-interpretation of the Christian message handed down by colonial missionaries. The point here is to understand the development of the faith after Simon Kimbangu's death.

Contemporary Kimbanguism

In order to properly depict contemporary Kimbanguism, it is necessary to give an account of its sources of inspiration, its conception of Black identity, and the succession crisis the church is currently confronted with.

The three sources of Kimbanguist faith

Adding to the response to the colonial situation described by such scholars as Balandier, contemporary Kimbanguism draws from three sources: the Bible, the inspired hymns, and the messages of the spiritual leader Papa Diangienda (Simon Kimbangu's youngest son). Kimbanguists hold the Bible as the only holy book. Shortly before being arrested, Simon Kimbangu himself recommended reading the Bible regularly and under all circumstances.[3] But the Bible is re-read through a prism offered by Diangienda, who, emptying it of its Western content, involved the believers in a process of critical re-interpretation of their ethnic self-representation.[4]

Next to the Bible are what the Kimbanguists themselves call the 'inspired hymns'. These are the messages received from God or the angels by 'inspired' persons. The latter, chosen by God Himself, regardless of gender, age, ethnic origin, nationality or education, are used as instruments of God's will for the purpose of conveying messages to the wider Kimbanguist community, to Christendom at large, or even to the whole of humankind. Simon Kimbangu himself initiated the practice when he was challenged by Rev. Jennings,[5] who doubted the reality of his calling. The first stanza of his first hymn, as transmitted by oral tradition, sounds like a guideline given to the believers:

Sing the angels' hymns / You shall receive all the nations / This is Jesus' ultimate promise / Don't lose sight of this.

These hymns render multiple themes, announcing Christ's Gospel, emphasizing souls to be saved, the glory of the next world and, above all, the issue of Blackness. They can be classified into three categories: revelation of past events, awareness of present events, foretelling of the future or prophecy. They can be lamentations, songs of praise, teachings or threats, warnings or even ultimatums.

Finally, the prophetic messages of His Eminence Diangienda Kuntima represent the third source of Kimbanguist theology. The youngest of Kimbangu's sons, born in 1918, he was the first spiritual leader of the church, from its official recognition until his death in July 1992.[6] His messages, which are all speeches and sermons, constitute the very basis of Kimbanguist theology. His words, held as sacred and integrated into the interpretation of both the Bible and the inspired hymns, have become the community's voice and collective memory. Like the inspired hymns, they reveal the past, decipher and give meaning to the present, and foretell the future. The bulk of these messages shape the redefinition of Black identity as it is accomplished by the Kimbanguists.

How Kimbanguists reconstruct Black identity

The Kimbanguist identity is both a religious and a racial one, because being a Kimbanguist believer is inseparable from the consciousness of one's Blackness. A Kimbanguist is always considered as a person whose self-definition is shaped in terms of Black identity and membership to the church. But Black identity is construed as negative in the Kimbanguist set of beliefs, whereas Kimbanguist identity is seen as positive. This form of self-awareness clearly appears in the inspired hymns and in Diangienda's messages and re-reading of the Bible. As a matter of fact, Kimbanguist identity is a complex structure. It rests on several pillars. The first of which are, on the one hand, the ancestors Adam and Eve who are held to have been black, and on the other hand, a set of three territories comprising, first, Africa the motherland; second, the so-called 'three Congos' (Congo-Kinshasa, Congo-Brazzaville and Angola) which were home to the ancient kingdom of the Kongo (corresponding to the Bakongo ethnic group's linguistic area, to be distinguished from the Congos as nation-states carved by European powers) and are seen as the landmarks of the world; and lastly the Holy City of Kimbanguism, that is, N'Kamba, Simon Kimbangu's native village, considered to be both heaven on earth and the cradle of humankind, the very place where God created Adam.

In addition to these tenets, the Kimbanguist church has beliefs of its own: in Simon Kimbangu as the incarnation of God the Holy Spirit and of the mystery of the Holy Trinity (he and his youngest son Diangienda Kuntima are believed to be the same person, namely the Holy Spirit, while his other two sons, Kisolokele and Dialungana, are believed to be respectively God the Father and God the Son, as revealed in inspired hymns); in the Kimbanguist church as universal and chosen by God; and in a new, positive Black identity as opposed to the present one, supposed to bear the stigma of a curse. The curse on black people is believed to be proven by the absence of black inventions in the technological and scientific fields, the oppression they are still forced to bear from the dominant Other, and also by witchcraft, which is still wreaking havoc in the two Congos and Angola and is considered as the real nature of the Original Sin. Yet, the Kimbanguist vision of the future announces that black people will eventually be liberated from their alienation: They will create totally new inventions, will gain rehabilitation in the eyes of the whites, and will resume their initial status, – that of the forebears Adam and Eve before they committed the first sin. The Kimbanguists actually atoned for the Original Sin, and are now living in the hope of a new status for black men and women. However, this has not stopped their church from undergoing a severe crisis.

The succession crisis

For the past few years, Kimbanguist life has been dominated by a succession crisis which began with the death of Dialungana, Simon Kimbangu's second son, in August 2001. For clarification's sake, the Kimbanguist hierarchy is twofold: On the one hand, there are the pastors, deacons and deaconesses, and catechists; on the other hand there are the members of the biological lineage of Simon Kimbangu. The latter authority was born spontaneously, from the faith and speculations of a number of believers, who have regarded Kimbangu's descendents (children, grandchildren and great grandchildren) as sacred persons to varying degrees, at the expense of members of the clergy. But in October 2002, the Kimbanguist clergy held an extraordinary general meeting in N'Kamba with the purpose of reconsidering the official texts and principles of the church as they had been published in 1963. This meeting resulted in the writing of 63 'resolutions' reasserting the role of the clergy and ranking the descendents of Simon Kimbangu only as counsellors of the new spiritual leader (Simon Kimbangu Kiangani) whereas the latter's 25 cousins had already designated themselves as spiritual leaders, claiming to be on an equal footing with him as heirs to Simon Kimbangu's legacy.

Such proceedings were approved by the official spiritual leader, Simon Kimbangu Kiangani (Dialungana's eldest son and the eldest male grandchild of the founder) and have thrown the church into unprecedented turmoil. The N'Kamba resolutions are being boycotted by both a number of believers who perceive them to be a move of the clergy to get rid of the authority of the Kimbangu family, and by the cousins of the spiritual leader who have started a schism from the official church named the Church of Jesus Christ on Earth by his Special Envoy Simon Kimbangu (EJCSK). Their official slogan now is '*vingt-six égal un*' (26 equal one) meaning that Kimbangu the Holy Spirit can manifest himself only in the unity of his descendents.

This crisis affects the EJCSK wherever it is established, in Africa as well as in Europe, where it has been existing since the 1970s. However, the price Kimbanguist migrants have to pay is to have to practice their faith in an environment that does not favour its expression.

Kimbanguist Immigration in Europe

The Birth of Kimbanguism in Europe: Switzerland, France and Belgium

In Europe, Kimbanguist Congolese immigration has a particular status insofar as it initially consisted entirely of students. In the 1970s, a group of Kimbanguist students coming mostly from the Congo-Brazzaville and the then Zaire, finding themselves dispersed in several European countries (France, Great Britain, Switzerland, Belgium, France, Germany, Portugal, Spain etc.), decided to meet in Paris to celebrate Christmas, at the instigation of the first deputy spiritual leader Charles Kisolokele Lukelo (Simon Kimbangu's eldest son), who was then in Switzerland for a medical check-up.[7]

This is how the International Kimbanguist Circle (CIK) was born. Its primary goal was to liaise between the migrant Kimbanguist students in Europe (especially those living in France, Belgium and Switzerland) as well as with the authorities of the EJCSK in Zaire. Furthermore, the CIK was meant to provide the Kimbanguist church with an official structure in Europe, so that it might legally organize worship in the countries where Kimbanguist presence was noticeable. The Kimbanguist students living in Europe were suffering from spiritual dearth, worshipping in mainline Protestant or Roman Catholic churches next to elderly people rather than youngsters, listening to sermons in which pastors and priests seemed to go out of their way to avoid addressing key issues of Christian morals, such as sexual freedom which for the Kimbanguists was literally a taboo. The CIK, whose aim also was to provide these students with a structure for worship, was greatly helped in April 1978 by the visit of a 250-strong delegation of pastors, choir members, members of the Kimbanguist brass band (FAKI) and other officials from Brazzaville and Kinshasa. The French Protestant Federation, under the leadership of its President, Rev. Jacques Maury (now retired), and the community of the Deaconesses of Versailles, helped the CIK to apply for and gain legal recognition in France. For the first time, an African-born and African-created church had succeeded in setting up in France under the French principle of secularity, that is, as a religious association. This example was followed by Kimbanguists living in Belgium, Great Britain, Switzerland, Germany, Spain and Portugal. The point here is to understand how Kimbanguist migrants live their faith in Europe, within social environments that are hardly favourable to its full expression.

Kimbanguist faith and community expression in Europe

The integration of Kimbanguist believers in European social contexts also depended on the help of mainline Protestant or Roman Catholic churches. Certain missionary priests or pastors who have lived in Africa are familiar with Kimbanguism which they discovered in its home contexts, and consequently they offer Kimbanguist migrants a warm welcome, allowing them to worship in their churches or temples. But it is worth noting that the recognition of the EJCSK by the World Council of Churches has also facilitated its religious inclusion in Europe, although the relations between the two bodies are tense at present, due to the Trinitarian controversy.

But the expression of Kimbanguist faith in Europe is also confronted with hostile attitudes such as racism and the religious indifference of the host societies, which hamper the integration of Kimbanguist migrants into these societies. In this matter, the tactics used by Kimbanguists to circumvent the obstacles to their inclusion into the host societies appear to be in keeping with their community logic. The Kimbanguist community, similar to other community networks, constitutes a coherent micro-society, in which solidarity works as a fundamental value. Confronted with the indifference and lack of knowledge displayed by the host society, all the barriers put up to prevent the new migrants' positive reception are circumvented by the process of their inclusion into the micro-society. The church aims at promoting mutual aid between the migrant believers, by organizing visits to the sick church members in hospitals, and to the families mourning a departed relative, collective contributions for the repatriation of the dead to their home countries or the weddings of its members.

Religious services also allow the group to reconstruct its identity as a specific religious body, establishing places of reunion in four main locations: Paris and surroundings, Brussels and surroundings, Geneva and London. Groups of Kimbanguist believers regularly travel across the European Union, crossing and re-crossing the borders to celebrate a religious holiday or a wedding, or attend a funeral.

Kimbanguist faith holds as a sacred place any visible space that bears witness to the lives of Simon Kimbangu, his wife Muilu Marie and their three sons. Anything bearing their imprints is considered to be sacred. Apart from N'Kamba which is their Holy Land, Kimbanguists also rank among their sacred places the courthouse of Mbanza-Ngungu, where Simon Kimbangu was sentenced to death, and the prison where he served his life sentence in Lubumbashi, and Lutendele, located on the bank of the Congo River (200 km from Kinshasa) where the Kimbanguist Divinity School was built. This is a place where, according to Kimbanguists, Simon Kimbangu, in chains, was thrown into the river by the Belgian colonists; but as he was an extraordinary person, he stood upon the surface of the water and walked to a cave where he left his foot- and fingerprints, which to this day serve as material evidence of his divine power. There are many other holy places in the Kimbanguist religious landscape; the point here is to show that Kimbanguist faith including the double dimension of time and space, the migrant believers' religious practice is oriented to their home countries. For instance, certain Kimbanguist families make pilgrimages to their home countries and set their prayer schedule by the time zone of their home country, instead of that of the host country: Believers are recommended, but not morally obliged, to pray at the following hours: 6.00 am, 10.00 am, noon, 3.00 pm, 10.00 pm, midnight and 3.00 am. In Europe, people put their clocks forward or back following regulations of their governments, heads of state or European authorities. Because their church's principles emphasize submission to the political authorities, many Kimbanguists abide by the daylight saving time switch dictated by the authorities, as far as working time, school time and administrative procedures are concerned, but they prefer praying by the time zone of their home countries, which implies a one- or two-hour difference.

This peculiarity of sacred time is reinforced by the fact that the authorities of the host countries do not let Kimbanguist believers freely access the places they hold to be holy on European soil, namely, the Brussels and Geneva hospitals where Charles Kisolokele and Joseph Diangienda, the first and last sons of Kimbangu, passed away. On 8 July 2001, all the Kimbanguists living in Europe gathered in Geneva, where they commemorated the ninth anniversary of Diangienda's death, and a small group of officials went into the hospital room where he, to put it in the Kimbanguist way, 'left his physical body'. The date of 17 March 2002, the tenth anniversary of Kisolokele's death, was the occasion of a grand celebration in Brussels, where all the believers living in Europe gathered in the presence of twelve of the 26 grandchildren of Simon Kimbangu. Again, a small group of people was admitted into the hospital room where Kimbangu's son had departed.

In such instances, Kimbanguist faith faces the resistance of the host societies, whereas in their home countries, the spot where Paul Dialungana died on August 16, 2001 is already listed among the official holy places of the EJCSK. His death, related in a conscious parallel with the death of Jesus on Mount Calvary, is said to have taken place on a hill situated between N'Kamba and Kinshasa. Yet, in the context of migration, Kimbanguist faith finds itself disturbed: A prophetic and messianic church in a non-national environment raises a territorial question that never occurs in their home countries, where all the holy places are freely given to the church by the governments. Such is for instance the case of the courthouse where Kimbangu was tried and the prison where he was kept: Both were given to the church by the Zaire government and turned into places of worship and pilgrimage.

As regards the daily practice of their faith, Kimbanguists in Europe have to deal alternately with two value systems, regulated either by tradition (i.e. the original religious values) or by modernity (i.e. the values that are socially established in the host countries). The experience of Kimbanguist migrants, as it appears from the many interviews I conducted with them, and my own sociological observations, consistently reveals these dialectics at work between the two value systems.

The issue at stake is the following: How are Kimbanguists able to live their faith according to Christian morality in societies which, among other factors, have been fundamentally shaken by the counter-culture movements of the 1960s? To understand the meaning assigned to Christian morality by modern European societies, it is necessary to locate it in the problematics of de-christianization. Europe has progressively seen its moral code transformed in the wake of social evolution, as has been noted by the French philosopher Jean-Claude Guillebaud.[8] This observation, together with many others, mirrors the widespread attitude of rejection of the moral codes formerly regulated by the churches. Thus it is logical that there should be a discrepancy with the Afro-Christian minorities, among them the Kimbanguist group, settled in Europe with morals as their top priority. Being a Kimbanguist believer in Europe implies leaving the Congolese societies, where values are upheld by traditional as well as religious moral codes, and where the emergence of individualism is hampered by hierarchy, tradition and collective conscience, and living in European societies where socially established values seem to boil down to individual conscience, equality (instead of respect for authority) and moral laxity. Therefore, individual and collective behaviors of Kimbanguists on European soil are subjected to a dual tendency; on the one hand, they keep an eye on their traditional religious moral code, and on the other hand, they follow the necessary agenda of adaptation to their new social environment. In fact, the individual integration of each Kimbanguist believer proves to be a very ambiguous process. While the integration process is already underway, it is still curbed by a variety of ethnic or racial barriers, such as the selective reception of migrant workers into the economic spheres of the host societies (qualified jobs being reserved for the nationals), socio-economic exclusion which is often coupled with the racism and discrimination they perceive, and finally the lack of knowledge of Europeans about Kimbanguism. These are the many obstacles to their integration in Europe.

Yet, all things considered, Kimbanguism has more to gain than to lose from its migratory situation in Europe, because it is an essential financial source for construction of the EJCSK in the Democratic Republic of the Congo. The church has no other financial help than the collective effort of its members, hence the Kimbanguist migrants represent an essential asset which it greatly depends upon. But with regard to Europe, Kimbanguism has less chances of success. How can such a church attract European followers, when Europeans not only reject institutionalized religions and opt for more customized forms of spirituality, but also seem to reappraise African identity exclusively in terms of dance, drums, the phantasm of exotic sexuality or even witchcraft, all of which are strictly forbidden by Kimbanguism?

The traditional expression of the Kimbanguist church is threatened by both the religious indifference of the host societies and by their lack of knowledge about this particular religion. Consequently, two categories of Kimbanguist believers emerge: On the one hand, there are those who lose their faith and embrace the social constraints of the countries where they live; and on the other hand, there are those who voluntarily reject the socially established code and remain confined within the limits of their own community. Feeling rejected and unknown, the latter in search of hope and solace turn to the internal cohesion of the community, which, although shaken by the succession crisis, comes out reinforced by its migratory situation in Europe.

Notes

[1] The Jesuit Father Van Wing himself recognized this in the following passage: 'When Simon Kimbangu, recognized as a saviour of his people, imposed the destruction of the Nkisi, he was obeyed, not only by his conscious followers, but

by entire populations which had no direct contact with either him or his disciples'. Van Wing, Jan, *Etudes Bakongo II: Magie, Sorcellerie et Religion* (Brussels, Bruges: Desclée de Brouwer, 1959), 168. – The lawyer Jules Chomé stressed that 'such reforms could not but cause a drastic change in Blacks' social life. If the administration or the missions had tried to impose them, they would have met with uncontrollable resistance. Simon Kimbangu is obeyed by his followers. In the villages he has won over, all the wives of polygamous husbands but one have been sent back to their families. The ceremonial drums, indispensable accessories of the forbidden feasts, have been destroyed'. Chomé, Jules, *La Passion de Simon Kimbangu* (Paris: Présence africaine, 1959), 15. Both translations by Cécile Coquet.

[2] Balandier, Georges, *Sociologie Actuelle de L'afrique Noire, Dynamique Sociale en Afrique Centrale* (Paris: Presses Universitaires de France, [1955] 1991), 427.

[3] Simon Kimbangu said: 'The Holy Spirit has revealed to me that the time had come to give myself up to the authorities. . . . I shall leave you with nothing else than the Bible. Read it in any circumstance of time or place, and never fail to put into practice God's commandments', quoted in Diangienda Kuntima, Joseph, *L'histoire du Kimbanguisme* (Kinshasa: Editions Kimbanguistes, published jointly by the Editions du Soc in Lausanne/Switzerland, 1984), 82. Translation by Cécile Coquet.

[4] 'Resorting to the Bible allows for utopian constructs and the belief in a salvation of the Black race under the guidance of its prophets, who are the founders of the churches', Balandier 1991: 425. Translation by Cécile Coquet.

[5] A missionary called Jennings, seeing that the choir surrounding Simon Kimbangu sang exclusively Baptist hymns, walked up to him and challenged him thus: 'So Jesus, who gave you the power and strength to raise people from the dead, has so deprived you of hymns that you have to resort to ours?' Instead of answering him, Simon Kimbangu made a few steps aside from the crowd and prayed unobtrusively. A moment later, he came back and taught the choir members a totally new hymn. It was the first Kimbanguist hymn. Since that time, Kimbanguists had hymns that are exclusively their own. Diangienda 1984: 45. Translation by Cécile Coquet.

[6] Diangienda Kuntima was first succeeded by his elder brother Dialungana, until the latter died on August 16, 2001, and then by Dialungana's son Simon Kimbangu Kiangani, who was nominated in October 2001.

[7] The Kimbanguists themselves, reflecting on the fact their history is rooted in three countries (the former Belgian and French Congos and Angola), say that the emergence of Kimbanguism in Europe was in a way 're-enacted' in three European countries – Switzerland, France and Belgium – under the control of Kisolokele.

[8] 'In a mixture of hope and arrogance, audacity and folly, playful exuberance and moralistic ideologies, a vast libertarian thrill coursed through all the industrialized societies from 1964 to 1973. From Japan to California, from old Europe to young America, the same insurrection against authority, social taboos, constraints and carnal pessimism mobilized a young generation that suddenly could not bear the 'old order' any longer. Within the span of a few years, a whole construct of collective representations and their judicial trappings was profoundly shaken. Thirty years later, the system is totally destroyed'. Guillebaud, Jean-Claude, *La Tyrannie du Plaisir* (Paris: Seuil, 1998), 45–46. Translation by Cécile Coquet.

Chapter 24

The Position of African Christians
in the Netherlands

Alle G. Hoekema

This report describes the current situation of migrants, particularly African Christians, in the Netherlands. Before we discuss several of the problems and challenges faced by these African Christians, various statistics are presented. Because Dutch government policy on migrants and refugees is hardening, their problems will probably increase in the future. It should be borne in mind that some of the figures given here are likely to change in the near future.

Statistics

It is very difficult to establish how many non-western migrants there are in the Netherlands, let alone the total number of non-western migrant Christians. The official government statistics distinguish between first- and second-generation 'immigrants' (the former born outside the Netherlands, while the latter, although born in the Netherlands, have a mother and/or father who was/were born outside the country). In 2005, according to these official data, out of a total of some 16 million inhabitants, there were almost 1.7 million non-western immigrants in the Netherlands. Of these, 295,000 (first-generation) and 215,000 (second-generation) persons did come from Africa, making it a total of 510,000 migrants from Africa. However, as no fewer than 315,000 (168,000 first-generation, plus 147,000 (second-generation) of these migrants are from Morocco and almost 16,000 (first- and second-generation combined) are from Algeria, or Tunisia,[1] the other 179,000 come from other African countries.[2] People who are still in the process of being admitted as immigrants, and those whose request has been declined but who are unable or unwilling to return and have remained unregistered in the country, are not included in these figures. Nobody knows exactly how large the latter category is.[3]

The following are the seven largest groups of migrants from Africa:

Somalians	21,733 (First and second generation)	15,083 (First generation only)
Cape Verdians	19,966	11,537
Ghanaians	19,108	11,977
Egyptians	18,528	10,982
South Africans	16,180	8,901
Angolans	11,601	9,285
Ethiopians	10,292	7,147[4]

These groups are followed by migrants from the Democratic Republic of Congo, Sudan, Nigeria and Sierra Leone; each group comprising 6,000–8,000 migrants (first-and second-generation totals).

Each of these groups has a different background. Almost all the migrants from Somalia came to the Netherlands for political reasons, mostly between 1992 and 1994.[5] In general, their social, cultural and economic position is difficult; also, the hardening government policy is aimed to let them return to Somalia. May be these are the main reasons, why their totals decreased rather dramatically during the most recent years (from almost 29,000 in 2002 to less than 20,000 in 2006); quite a few Somalians, who hold a Dutch passport, in recent years moved to the United Kingdom (Birmingham, Leicester). The Cape Verdians have been here for several decades; the first arrived in the early 1970s, for economic reasons. Many of them live in or around Rotterdam; they work as seamen or construction workers, or in the cleaning, hotel, or catering industries.[6] Most of them are Roman Catholic. Over 30 per cent of the migrants from Ghana and Nigeria live in Amsterdam South-East (the Bijlmer district); they started arriving in the Netherlands in the 1980s. Especially the Ghanaians are metamorphosing from a 'migrant community' into an 'ethnic minority'. The Egyptian migrants, too, had economic reasons to come, and most of them make a good living here. The Ethiopians and Eritreans are political asylum seekers, and life is hard for many of them. The South Africans are, of course, a special category: Some of them are white (conscientious objectors and those who re-migrated for economic reasons), while most others are black (political refugees who have stayed and other, recent immigrants).

Kathleen Ferrier – who until 2001 was coordinator of SKIN (see below) – recently estimated that there are about 800,000 non-western migrant Christians in the Netherlands; this group includes Catholics (who may well form the majority), Orthodox, Protestants, Pentecostals, and members of independent churches. This number may be slightly inflated.[7] However, since Ferrier does not indicate which definition of 'migrant' she uses, it is difficult to determine her figures. Similarly, it is not easy to establish the number of African Christians present in the Netherlands. Assuming that some 60 per cent of African migrants are Christian, there are roughly 100,000 Christians from Africa in the Netherlands, not including unregistered and undocumented persons.

African Churches: Categories[8]

Migrant Christians in the Netherlands fall into one of three categories, namely:

Roman Catholics

Most come from a Portuguese- or French-speaking area. They may well form the majority of migrant Christians in the Netherlands. The Roman Catholic Church strives to integrate migrants into Dutch parishes. Till recently the pastoral care for all migrants (including those from Eastern Europe) was delegated to a special secretariat, the 'Cura Migratorum'. Now this has become a task of the dioceses itself.[9] Migrants belonging to a higher social stratum often succeed in joining an existing Dutch-speaking parish. For many, however, that is impossible, for cultural, social, and linguistic reasons. Research in Rotterdam has shown that while many Catholics from Africa join a Pentecostal or an African Independent church, others become alienated from the church. Some of the reasons given for this are that the liturgy of the Catholic Church in the Netherlands, that the perception of the faith are different from what was experienced in Africa, and that some prominent Catholic leaders in especially Congo and Angola cooperate, or used to cooperate, with corrupt, dictatorial rulers.[10]

Orthodox Christians

Most come from Egypt or Ethiopia/Eritrea. Research carried out ten years ago indicates that some 1,500 Egyptian Copts had contact with their church, although only 300 of them attended church services regularly in one of the six or seven cities in which Copts congregate. According to the same research, many Ethiopians have lost contact with their church. A few thousand persons, including Rastafarians from Jamaica, are members of the Ethiopian Orthodox church, with some 500 forming its active nucleus. J. H. Sommer, who carried out the above-mentioned research, stated that he expected this number to increase, because some years before a priest had been sent to serve this church, and his arrival probably would attract other Ethiopians.[11] There are also small evangelical groups of Christians from Egypt, Ethiopia, and Eritrea.

Other migrant Christians

Some belong to old, established migrant groups (e.g. the Église Wallonne, which originated during the 80-year war between the Netherlands and Spain, when French Protestants took refuge in Holland), others to churches with a strong Protestant tradition (e.g. the Moluccan and Indonesian churches, and the Scots International Church in Rotterdam, which attracts many Africans), and yet others to independent, mainly international churches. Many West African Christians fall into the last-mentioned category. Some of them belong to an international (Pentecostal) network, while others have joined an independent congregation, such as The True Teachings of Christ Temple, which was founded in the Netherlands as a house community in the early 1980s.[12] There are many churches of the latter kind in Amsterdam (especially in the South-East district), where there are at least 75,000 Christian migrants, including possibly 10,000 Ghanaians.[13] Over 40 independent, African-led congregations meet in the Bijlmer neighborhood; at least 25 of them use Twi in their services along with English. In addition, there are several French- and Lingala-speaking congregations.[14] Many African churches have been founded in other parts of Amsterdam and in other main cities. Rotterdam, where there are several old seamen's churches and Asian churches (e.g. the strong Chinese missions and the Pakistani, Indonesian and Iraqi congregations), also has many African churches.

Networks

Besides their own local, international and ethnic networks, there are at least two inter-church networks in which African churches participate. One of these is SKIN ('Samen Kerk in Nederland'), in which 54 migrant churches and Christian groups work together. Around 35 of these member groups have an African background. SKIN performs several roles: It acts as the groups' platform within the larger society; it provides contact with white churches and organizations; it initiates discussions about practical problems and tries to find solutions to them, if necessary with government officials; and it encourages theological and social discussions about current, relevant matters.[15] SKIN collaborates with the main Protestant Church ('Protestantse Kerk in Nederland', formerly 'Samen-op-Weg kerken') as well as with, for example, the National Council of Churches and the Netherlands Missionary Council.

The second network is GATE ('Gift of Africa to Europe', formerly 'Gospel of Africa to Europe'), an organization mainly comprising independent and evangelical African churches active in the field of evangelization in Europe. GATE collaborates with several mission organizations in the Netherlands, coordinates activities in the above-mentioned field, and inspires many participants. Locally, various African churches and groups collaborate by means of a loosely organized council or network.

Problems and Challenges

Many of the problems faced by migrant churches – and especially the African-led churches – are of a practical nature. One such problem is finding an affordable place in which to congregate. In Amsterdam South-East, many churches meet in former parking garages near or beneath huge apartment blocks. To get to these churches, one has to walk past unpleasant, graffiti-covered concrete walls. Unfortunately, the local government is not very co-operative on this point because of its policy of separation between Church and State.[16] White churches are reluctant to offer space in their buildings, for instance during the afternoon. There are a few church buildings which accommodate a number of congregations, such as the Nieuwe Stad church in Amsterdam South-East. No fewer than eleven groups congregate in this beautifully structured building, which has several halls around a covered 'market' place.[17] The construction of another church building which can host a number of 'migrant churches' is on its way.

A second problem is language. Many migrants have difficulties learning Dutch, partly because it was not their original intention to stay here, and partly because they (and their pastors) live almost entirely within their own subculture – which does not facilitate integration. A third problem is that the Dutch government sometimes denies a visa to pastors from abroad, and sometimes even expels them, at the expense of congregations in which such a pastor functions as the key figure. A fourth problem is the increasing racism and xenophobia in Europe – and that includes the Netherlands, where such sentiments have been intensified by the politics of the spiritual heirs of the late Pim Fortuyn, who was murdered in May 2002, and by the brutal murdering, in 2005, of the film maker Theo van Gogh by a Dutch Muslim with a North-African background. All this has led many Africans (Ghanaians and others) to move temporarily to another country, such as Italy. Also, new, stricter immigration laws are making life extremely hard for many Africans, and the prospects for many of them are dim. It is feared that many who cannot or will not return to their home country, but are not eligible for a residence permit, will join the underground army of homeless urban nomads. Finally, the contacts between migrant churches and indigenous churches need to be improved. Often, white churches are to blame for the lack of contact, although some migrant churches have a tendency to be too insular.

As to this last-mentioned problem, there are, fortunately, some signs of hope. A few years ago, SKIN and the Netherlands Missionary Council organized a multicultural Kirchentag ('Churches' Day') in Amsterdam, and at a smaller scale a follow-up event took place in The Hague. Such gatherings are instrumental in improving mutual relations. Also, a local and practice-oriented variant of a large international, scientifically grounded project of the Vrije Universiteit (Free University) in Amsterdam to bring together Bible study groups from many cultures, seems to be working well in The Hague. Hopefully, this example will be followed elsewhere.

Migrant churches also face challenges. Some African churches have taken the lead in providing a shelter for drug addicts, teenage mothers or women who have become victims of prostitution and/or of traffickers in women. By doing so, they set an example to other, white churches and open channels of contact. Three years ago, reverend Tom Marfo, pastor of The House of Fellowship, received an award named after the Netherlands' first female cabinet minister, Dr Marga Klompé. Unfortunately, the most recent legal measures of the Dutch government (February 2004) seem to be endangering his welfare work. The social and religious work of other black pastors has been highlighted in national TV programs or in long newspaper articles. Many African churches function as a safe social meeting place for unregistered migrants. Some churches have good contacts with Dutch lawyers, some of whom provide free legal advice. All in all, it can be said that many migrant churches practice a holistic approach in which spiritual and physical healing and the well-being of individuals is considered important. In this process of healing, the believing community is essential. Christianity is a matter not of a certain doctrine, but of a lifestyle determined by discipleship of Jesus. Here, white Christians are starting to learn from their black brothers and sisters.

Several migrant churches are gradually beginning to understand that, in due time, it will be necessary to have pastors who can rely not only on their personal charisma, but also on their theological knowledge, preferably with an African flavor. The Hendrik Kraemer Institute and the NBI (Netherlands Bible Institute, now part of a large college, Windesheim), both of which are located in Utrecht, offer special preparatory courses for those wishing to enroll at a regular vocational school of theology. Here, the language problem forms a serious barrier. The Vrije Universiteit offers a Master's program in which members of migrant churches can participate; a parallel program in English is being considered. So far, however, only a few individuals have enrolled; most are from Moluccan churches and other Asian communities, although one or two do have an African background. The Pentecostal Tyndale Seminary provides courses in English. Such theological training is also necessary to enable African churches to start a real dialogue with the white churches and with white society at large.

A few years ago, several articles in *Trouw* (a daily newspaper) have expressed an over-simplified fear that the so-called neo-conservatism of the churches of 'the South' (i.e. mainly Africa) will eclipse the achievements of the Enlightenment within the established white churches.[18] Unfortunately, the pastors and theologians of African churches did not feel called or were unable to respond to, and to possibly contradict, the opinions expressed in such newspaper articles. Yet, this will become increasingly necessary. Moroccan and Turkish

Muslims are now able to articulate their position in the debate on a multicultural society in our country, as politicians, novelists, actors and columnists; here, however, sub-Saharan Christians – with the exception of a few politicians who do not emphasize their Christian background – lag behind.

Finally, it may well be time to reconsider the term 'migrant churches'. Many respected mainline churches have migrant roots, but have long been accepted as recognized minorities, for example the Lutherans, the Huguenots, and – partly – the Mennonites. Therefore, it is understandable that leading African Christians insist that what should be emphasized is not their being African – that is, not the cultural, even exotic, aspects of their churches – but the fact that they are permanent minority churches in the Netherlands with a contextual theology equally as valuable as the traditional western theology. Also, a shift can be noticed towards truly 'International churches', which are not only multi ethnical, but also open to indigenous Christians.[19]

Notes

[1] Figures from Centraal Bureau voor de Statistiek (CBS), Voorburg/Heerlen, 2006, www.statline.cbs.nl. A large majority of the second-generation migrants have two parents who were born outside the Netherlands.

[2] In 1995, CBS estimated that there were almost 70,000 persons from sub-Saharan Africa in the Netherlands. See Ter Haar, Gerrie, *Halfway to Paradise. African Christians in Europe* (Cardiff: Cardiff Academic Press, 1998) [1998 a], 73.

[3] Estimates vary between 45,000 and 115,000. Half of these persons are from Turkey or Morocco, while 10,000–40,000 have their origins in a politically unsafe asylum country. See: www.fundamenteel.nl/NietGeregistreerden. Gerrie ter Haar 1998: 117, states that most estimates (in around 1997) vary from 60,000 to 100,000 undocumented persons, most of them living in the urbanized, western part of the country (the 'Randstad'). In a recent report it is estimated that between 40 and 50 per cent of the migrants belonging to Christian communities in the Bijlmer district of Amsterdam, are undocumented persons. Euser, Hans; Goossen, Karlijn; De Vries, Matthias; Wartena, Sjoukje, Migranten in Mokum. *De Betekenis van Migrantenkerken voor de Stad Amsterdam* (Amsterdam: Vrije Universiteit, 2006), 96.

[4] Until 1993, when Eritrea became an independent state, Eritreans were counted as Ethiopians. According to CBS statistics, in 2005 there were 867 Eritrean migrants in the Netherlands.

[5] Mohamoud, Abdullah, 'Somaliërs: overleven in een ongemakkelijke omgeving', in Ineke van Kessel and Nina Tellegen (eds), *Afrikanen in Nederland* (Amsterdam/Leiden: KIT/Afrika Studiecentrum, 2000), 133–45. In 2003, a Somalian immigrant – Ayaan Hirsi Ali – became a member of parliament for the conservative-liberal Volkspartij voor Vrijheid en Democratie (VVD). In connection with the migrant policy, her blunt and critical statements about gender inequality within Islam, about Mohammed, and about the backward attitude of religious people in general have aroused quite a lot of debate, in both parliament and society at

large. Together with the film maker Theo van Gogh she made a widely discussed and by many people repudiated film 'Submission', about the rights of Moslem women. The film led to the violent death of Van Gogh. Ayaan herself resigned from parliament in May 2006 to join a neo-conservative think-tank in Washington, the American Enterprise Institute.

6 Strooij, Henny, 'Eilanden aan de Maas: De Kaapverdische gemeenschap van Rotterdam', in Ineke van Kessel and Nina Tellegen (eds) 2000: 43–60. João Varela – a Cape Verdian – has been a member of parliament since 2001, representing the new, right-wing party LPF (Lijst Pim Fortuyn). In a way, this shows that the interests of migrants who have lived here for quite a time differ from the interests of those who arrived later. In Rotterdam, there is a separate Portuguese-speaking parish for the Cape Verdians; however, there is also a Protestant congregation which maintains contact with the Church of the Nazarenes.

7 Ferrier, Kathleen, *Migrantenkerken. Om Vertrouwen en Aanvaarding* (Kampen: Kok, 2002).
Hoekema, Alle and Van Laar, Wout (eds), *De wereldkerk op een km2. Migrantenkerken in Rotterdam/ The World Church on One km2. Migrant Churches in Rotterdam* (Utrecht: Netherlands Missionary Council, in cooperation with Netherlands Mennonite Mission Council, 2004), 30. Her estimate is based on unofficial statistics from the Roman Catholic Church and the SKIN organization. Not only must a distinction be made between those who are only nominally Christian and those who in some way or another are active in one of the many churches, but it is also unclear how many unregistered migrant Christians there are and how many 'migrants' have a western background. Therefore, the Roman Catholic missiologist Frans Wijsen (quoted by Euser, Hans, Goossen, Karlijn, De Vries, Mathias and Wartena, Sjoukje (et al.) *Migranten in Mokum. De betekenis van migrantenkerken voor de stad Amsterdam* (Amsterdam: Vrije Universiteit, 2006), 34 mentions the figure of 640,000; he departs from the supposition that most non-western people in one way or another remain religiously active. Other estimates are close to Wijsen's figures. Kathleen Ferrier was the coordinator of SKIN from 1995 to 2001; she was subsequently elected to parliament as a member of the Christen Democratisch Appèl (CDA).

8 See for these categories the comprehensive volume edited by Jongeneel, J. A. B., Budiman, R. And Visser, J. J., *Gemeenschapsvorming van Aziatische, Afrikaanse, Midden- En Zuid-Amerikaanse Christenen in Nederland. Een Geschiedenis in Wording* (Zoetermeer: Boekencentrum, 1996) and also Ferrier 2002: 33–41.

9 See for recent developments as to Roman catholic migrants: Castillo Guerra, J., Wijsen, F. and Steggerda, M., 'Een gebedshuis voor alle volken. Kerkopbouw en kadervorming', in *Rooms Katholieke Allochtonengemeenschappen* (Zoetermeer: Boekencentrum, 2006).

10 Maaskant, Judith, 'Afrikaanse katholieke Pinkstergelovigen in Rotterdam', *Wereld en Zending* 28(4) (1999): 37–44 [1999 a]; and Maaskant, Judith, *Afrikaans en katholiek in Rotterdam: Waar Kerk je Dan?* (Catholic University of Nijmegen: KUN, 1999) [1999b].

11 Sommer, J. H., '"Waar de Nijl uitmondt in de Noordzee...." Koptisch en Ethiopisch orthodoxe christenen in Nederland', *Religieuze Bewegingen in Nederland* 28 (1994): 37–78; Ferrier 2002: 74–86.

[12] The True Teachings of Christ Temple is one of the earliest and largest African churches in the Netherlands. It was founded by Rev. Daniel Himmans-Arday in the early 1980s, and now has hundreds of members. This church has been researched by several scholars. By far the best-known studies about this church and about African migrant churches in general have been performed by Gerrie ter Haar 'Afrikaanse kerken in Nederland', *Religieuze Bewegingen in Nederland 28* (1994): 1–35; Idem, 'Strangers in the Promised Land. African Christians in Europe', *Exchange 24*(1) (1995): 1–33 [1995 a]; Idem, 'Ritual as Communication: A Study of African Christian Communities in the Bijlmer District of Amsterdam', in Jan Platvoet and Karel van der Toorn (eds), *Pluralism and Identity. Studies in Ritual Behaviour* (Leiden: Brill 1995), 115–42 [1995 b]; Idem, (ed.), *Strangers and Sojourners. Religious Communities in the Diaspora* (Leuven: Peeters, 1998); and Idem, 'The African Diaspora in Europe: Some Important Themes and Issues', 37–38, and Idem, 'African Christians in the Netherlands', 153–71 in 1998 in note 2 above; 'Afrikanen in Nederland: Een Inleiding', in Ineke van Kessel and Nina Tellegen (eds) 2000: 11–41; 'Tot genezing geroepen. Een Ghanese dominee in de Bijlmer', *Wereld en Zending 3*(2) (2001): 35–43. Other valuable resources are Jongeneel, Budiman and Visser (eds), whose work will be updated in the coming years, and (for Amsterdam South-East) De Jonge, Jan, 'Halverwege de hemel'. In: Euser (ed.), *Religieuze kaart van Amsterdam-Zuidoost* (Amsterdam, 1994), 2006, and Droogers, André; Van der Laan, Cornelis; Van Laar, Wout (eds), *Fruitful in this Land. Pluralism, Dialogue and Healing in Migrant Pentecostalism* (Zoetermeer: Boekencentrum, 2006).

[13] Source: Euser *et al.*, ii 2006: 37–40.

[14] Van den Broek, A.P. Ieder hoorde in zijn eigen taal, (Amsterdam: Raad van Kerken in Nederland/SKIN, 9th edition, 2004); this directory contains the addresses and other data on almost all churches and Christian groups in the Netherlands which use foreign languages. It is regularly updated and can be obtained through SKIN (Koningin Wilhelminalaan 5, 3818 HN Amersfoort, The Netherlands).

[15] See www.skinkerken.nl. SKIN publishes a quarterly newsletter. Some ethnically European churches are also members of SKIN, for example the EKD, a Spanish Protestant Church, and several seamen's churches – which is why SKIN does not call itself a 'migrant churches' organization. Large differences between several member churches and groups mean that it is not always easy to have an open discussion about certain hot theological and ethical issues.

[16] Surprisingly, the present mayor of Amsterdam (Job Cohen) has a positive attitude regarding the role of religions in the process of integrating cultural minorities in the city, as does one of his aldermen, Aboutaleb (a Muslim with a Moroccan background). Many other politicians, however, prefer the absolute separation of society and religion. Nevertheless, a new round of discussions started recently about the (positive) role of religion in the Dutch society.

[17] Source: Van den Broek 2004.

[18] Ton Crijnen in *Trouw,* July 25: 2003, and Hester Haarsma, 'Met elkaar leven valt vies tegen', *Trouw*, September 5: 2003.

[19] See Euser 2006: 29.

Chapter 25

An Ecumenical Challenge at the Beginning of the Twenty-first Century: Koinonia vs. Convivence

Benjamin Simon

Presenting the Problem

Those who take part in a pentecostal worship service of an African Initiated Church (AIC) in the diaspora are acquainted with a form of singing, praying, and praising God which is unusual in the European tradition. How would those who before have never encountered African worship react to the 'noises' and sounds of this event? This is one reason why many African churches and congregations in the diaspora in Europe are encountering prejudice and fear. These traditions, rites, and customs are different from the Western pattern of worship service so that Europeans prefer to withdraw rather than to approach. The strange noises, which emerge from their parish hall on Sundays, motivate few Europeans to look for personal contacts with African Christians.[1] Whatever is strange to their minds remains strange! There is no empathy and certainly no common celebration. Only in rare cases, we find ecumenical interaction between the hosting European congregation and the African Church.[2] One of the reasons for this, which we want to pursue, is the lack of structure in concrete ecumenical encounters. This has to do with the highly abstract handling of present ecumenical ecclesiology.

There is a great need for a model of ecumenical coming-together that allows unity in pluriformity and paves the way to a living ecumenical encounter. The following contribution therefore tries to elaborate new ways for worldwide church development, that is, how the ecumenical movement (local as well as global) approaches all the new challenges in the African Christian community; for example, the pentecostal movement as part of the African Christian community.

Ecumenical Movement Quo Vadis? Following the Tracks of the Koinonia Model[3]

The plurality of the African Initiated pentecostal churches in the diaspora in Europe, and their many shapes of ecumenical interaction, require an ecumenical model which may form the basis for a common ecclesiology of equality, embracing all denominations. In the ecumenical movement of recent decades, many ecclesiological models have been discussed, tried out, and put aside. In almost every decade the ecumenical movement drew upon a renewed model for its unity. Some examples were an organic union, the conciliar community, the unity in reconciled difference, the community of communities, the community in solidarity[4] and, at last, the model of koinonia. The special merit of the koinonia model is that it cannot be simply subsumed under other models of union.[5] It allows different denominations to hold on to their individuality.

I begin with explaining the history and the approach of the Koinonia model such as developed by the former General Secretary of the WCC, Konrad Raiser. After calling the churches to visible unity in foregoing important WCC declarations (World Assembly in New Delhi 1961, Uppsala 1968, and Nairobi 1975), the World Assembly in Canberra 1991 risked another attempt to turn the vision of a united world church into a reality. Since the declaration at Canberra, 'The Unity of the Church as Koinonia: Gift and Vocation',[6] the koinonia model gained constant importance during the nineties. This declaration begins with the saving will of the triune God for all creation and humanity, and the place and task of the church as the foretaste, sign, and servant for God's reconciling and unifying action.[7] It introduced the term Koinonia, in order to put the unity of the church into context of God's all-embracing plan.[8]

Two years later at the 'Faith and Order' assembly in Santiago de Compostella, Konrad Raiser introduced the koinonia model as a central subject: 'On the way to all-embracing Koinonia (1993)'.[9] In this assembly, it was particularly the representatives of the Roman Catholic Church and the Pentecostal Churches which took part in it in a very active way. One goal of the assembly was the development of an image of visible unity as intended in the Canberra declaration. The hope was to see more clearly which steps on the way to visible unity still needed to be taken which obstacles had to be overcome.[10]

Lastly, alongside with these two assemblies, the 'Charta Oecumenica' (1989)[11], chapter 2, 'On the way to visible community of the churches in Europe', referred to the koinonia model. In drafting this, the Council of the European Bishops Conference (CCEE) and the Conference of the European Churches (CEC) took a responsible role. The new aspect, brought in by koinonia was that the image of the 'unity' among the churches as an institutional realisation was to be replaced by a shift to the image of 'community'. The classical New Testament passage proving the unity of the church is found in Jesus' farewell speech in Jn 17, 21. His most central concern is shown in his prayers for the Oneness of all believers: believers should be one with the father and the son, as the father and the son are one to testify to God in the world, so that the world may believe that God sent Jesus. This Oneness between father and son and between the believers and the father does not express similarity but solidarity, that is, the close connection of those who are different.[12]

Beside Jn 17, Paul's letter to the Ephesians is mentioned as the decisive basis for all ecumenical statements on the unity of the church.[13] The mission of unity encountered in Ephesians relates to the basic contradiction between Gentiles and Jews as manifest in the early church from the very beginning. Jesus has torn down the separating walls between those 'inside' and 'outside' by the sacrifice of his own body (Eph. 2.14). Paul consequently uses the language applied by baptismal sermons (opposites such as 'dead-alive', 'once-now'):

> But now in union with Christ Jesus, you who once were far off have been brought near through the shedding of Christ's blood. Thus you are no longer aliens in a foreign land, but fellow-citizens with God's people, members of God's household (Eph. 2.13–19 NEB).[14]

Having stated this, however, we should not ignore that koinonia is only one of the many New Testament images applied to the church. Besides the New Testament quotations just mentioned, many other images and metaphors for 'church' are utilised.[15] We mention as examples denotations such as 'people of God', 'body of Christ' or 'temple of the Holy Spirit'.[16] Also the term 'Ecclesia' is a New Testament image, meaning the called-out people. Each image inspired by the gospel, puts forward a very specific aspect and context of community, and thus produces a certain meaning. Using koinonia underlines the together-ness of the believers.[17] From this angle Konrad Raiser was able to bring community to the fore in the ecumenical movement, and able to speak of a life in relationship (*Leben in Beziehung*).[18]

Five aspects of the koinonia model are of central importance:[19]

1. The model of koinonia views the unity of the church as a community of believers that has its origin in God, and to this end a Trinitarian theology is developed. The community grows and lives out of the fact that people, through faith, have communion with the triune God who himself is living in the union of three persons open to humankind.[20] It is this Trinitarian model which motivates the faithful on their path to a visible church.
2. The model of koinonia allows all denominations grounded in the New Testament to participate in it. Into consideration are taken not the tensions or schisms of past history but the New Testament vision of 'koinonia', which is older and more basic than all dogmas of the churches.
3. Choosing the model of koinonia, all believers have the chance to hold on to the one church yet maintain their differences. In contrast to previous ecu-menical concepts the idea of 'union' with its tendency to establish institutional unification does not play a primary part. Instead we speak of a community in which all augment each other or in the words of Konrad Raiser, 'The church and its unity are relational and not understood first of all as institutional and dogmatic'.[21]

4. The model of koinonia takes into account the ongoing character of the unity of the church and therefore takes seriously the community of local, regional and international relationships. Every congregation represents the church of Jesus Christ. The unity of the church is an ongoing process, which is quite different from many rigid models discussed in the ecumenical movement before.

5. A last aspect of the koinonia model underlines the relationship between ecclesiology and ethics. Faith and action belong together in the New Testament's testimony to unity. Konrad Raiser quotes in this context the metaphor of stewardship (Eph. 2.19-22). Fellow lodgers are equal yet different; fellow lodging includes full participation of all the tenants in the house.[22]

From here the question arises whether the koinonia model can be put into practice; this means in our context, especially taking into account the diasporic African Initiated Churches and their patterns of ecumenical interaction. Ecumenical co-operation requires a constant involvement with other cultures and denominations and demands, what I would call, an 'intercultural flair'. The pluriformity of churches on a global as well as a local level cannot be described any longer by traditional denominational distinctions. Even the young churches, which grew out of Western missions, developed their own shape of being Christians, transcending all denominational associations.[23] This new type of Christianity, which can cut through all denominations, comes mostly from pentecostal churches of an African expression and origin. In order to create an ecumenical relationship between different cultural and traditional congregations and churches, it is very important to look for new ways and new ecclesiological models.[24]

From here, even the koinonia model looks rather like a static model which – with its normative dogmatic aspects – does not give much support for the ecumenical forms of lively interaction in the practice of pentecostal churches, especially of an African approach. Numerous programs of the WCC today find less public interest than many secular initiatives with clear-cut public profiles. Christians might still be engaged in this.[25] But this lack of public interest – which the members of the Commission for Faith and Order try to address – could be removed if the ecumenical movement would engage in a more pragmatic philosophy.

Convivence – A New Way into the Ecumenical Future?[26]

At the beginning of the twenty-first century, on the way to a church that does not flatten the pluralism of diverse confessional structures and their particularities, we need a pragmatic ecclesiological model which does engage with the necessities and problems of those involved in it; an ecclesiological model which offers precise steps in the process of ecumenical togetherness. The worldwide 'oikumene' needs a model which does not, by one-sided moral appeals, feel obliged to share with others, but which gives directions to the challenges of getting along together in church and society, in particular in culturally diverse communities.

From the foregoing, especially with the rapid growth of young churches all over the world – mostly of the pentecostal type – it becomes evident that ecumenical interaction has to look for a 'hermeneutic of the stranger'. This 'hermeneutic of the stranger' may be a help on the way to a visible community where Western Churches and AICs encounter each other, especially in a diasporic situation. The missiologist Theo Sundermeier distinguishes four levels in his 'Hermeneutics of the Stranger'.[27] These are of great benefit for the ecumenical interaction of Western churches with AICs in the diaspora. Sundermeier uses here the notion 'stranger' as a geographical and cultural term of distinction. It points to a person who arrives from outside of one's own area and carries another cultural mark.[28] This stranger may be even a member of the same religion. The emphasis lies here on cultural and traditional difference.

Following are Sundermeier's four levels:

(i) Perception from Distance. Here the task is to see how the 'stranger' presents him- or herself and what he/she is like. His first encounter with the church has to be without evaluation and has to keep a certain distance. The distance grants an overview. This first step has to be taken in the wider ecumenical movement as well, wherever congregations and churches enter into an ecumenical interaction. Theologically, it is the command 'not to make images' (Ex. 20,4). The image interdiction underlines the necessity of getting rid of any image, which has a hold on us and to be open to any new encounter, in this context, meeting strangers without prejudice.[29] This means in daily practice encountering AICs among us without prior judgement by taking part in their rites and worship services several times. Likewise, one should, from a certain distance, be open to the different and often strange customs and theologies.

(ii) Participatory Observation. This method, which has been used in field research since Malinowski,[30] serves the second level in ecumenical encounters. Participant observation is not a one-way street, but a mutual happening between Christian communities. The reciprocal exchange contributes to cross-fertilization. In this process, dealing with experiences of difference is practised. In doing so, every church is allowed to keep its identity. Mutual visits of sister congregations must not lead to a mixing-up of the churches; rather, the two congregations stimulate one another by their cultural and theological differences. Thus the cornerstone for ecumenical togetherness may be placed.

(iii) (Partial-) Identification. The third level is to encourage not to give up one's identity. On the contrary, every person involved in the ecumenical interaction brings in his or her experience and character into it. This sometimes happens in symbolic language, which may cause difficulties in the encounter. Ecumenical partners always have to keep in mind problems of translation[31] in the existing differences. Very often symbols impede understanding even if their attempt is to make understanding easier.[32] The knowledge of the symbols and the ability to translate help us to understand the life-conditions of Africans in the diaspora. To speak with Paul Ricoeur: 'The symbols make us think!' They encourage the person who loves the 'oikumene' to employ an empathetic procedure. Such empathy enables us to develop sympathy and may become the foundation for partial identification without giving up one's own identity in the ecumenical discourse.

(iv) Convivence. On the fourth level, the 'hermeneutics of the stranger' comes to fruition. The experience of a strange culture – even if it is not a strange religion – can now be translated into one's own terms, and the symbolic language may be interpreted correctly. So the convivence, which is the goal of all xenological and intercultural hermeneutics, is well founded and enacted. The term 'convivence' stems from the South American Theology of Liberation. It has been disseminated during the last two decades and now denotes a life lived in devotion, which includes experience, practise, aspects of individualism and collectivism, participation and exchange.[33] Although the term 'convivence' has been mostly used for the dialogue of religions, Theo Sundermeier utilised it also for the ecumenical getting-together, as the notion includes a certain degree of compatibility possible to make use of it in both directions. It not only gives us the chance to keep the one '*familia dei*' before our eyes but also God's worldwide creation. 'Convivence' empowers intra-religious as well as inter-religious communities.

There are three pillars, which support the model of convivence: First of all, convivence may be characterised as a helping community. There are the neighbours who help and assist each other in everyday life. There is no feeling of being excluded. Convivence gives us a feeling of protection and acceptance. Second, convivence describes a learning community. Nobody just learns, nobody just teaches, because knowledge born from experience is as significant as learning by studying. During the mutual exchange, both sides relate to each other and gain their 'being-subject' back.[34] There is no teaching subject or learning object. Since this may not be allowed in repressive societies or hostile environments, it is in the church that the model of convivence as the learning community of those, who learn together and from each other, can come into existence.[35] Third, convivence may be envisaged as a festive community. Festivity breaks through the routine of every day life and manifests itself as a quite different truth. In transcending limits it enables the cultural stranger to find an entry into the community. Thus it may be regarded as the gate to community.[36] Celebrations and festivity are ways of first contacts with ecumenical forms of interaction between denominations belonging to various cultures.

The Necessity of a Paradigm Shift
in the Worldwide Ecumenical Movement

Looking at worldwide developments in ecumenical interactions at the beginning of the twenty-first century, the issue of change of paradigm in ecumenical theology arises. This certainly is the case when we look at the latest ecumenical challenge caused by the growth of the pentecostal movement and its origins in the black tradition.[37] In this context it makes sense to use the term 'paradigm'. This is to put equal weight on the koinonia model as on the convivence model. In colloquial language the term paradigm is strictly used as an 'exemplary case' or as a 'typical example of'. But here 'paradigm' can also be used as 'frame of reference' which is a standard for any activity of the human spirit.[38]

The origin of the term 'paradigm' lies with the American philosopher Thomas S. Kuhn[39] who used it in the fields of theory of science and history of science. His intention was to show that the progress in science might happen in small steps or in great revolutions.[40] A new idea developed and in time this fresh idea found more and more acceptance. When a new paradigm develops, it becomes a kind of 'canon' for further valuable and efficient concepts. In our context, I do not apply the term paradigm in such an all-inclusive definition as Kuhn. I want to use it rather as a frame of reference. If we use the term paradigm as a frame of reference in present ecumenical interaction, we can also use the koinonia model correctly as a paradigm for the ecumenical theology of the past decade.

During the last decades there were many opinions pronounced which evaluated the model of koinonia in a rather critical way. Lukas Vischer, former Chairman of the Commission on Faith and Order critiqued it already in Canberra 1991.[41] After a short positive evaluation, he questioned many aspects out of which I present here only three relevant to our subject.

1. The model of koinonia does not reflect the crisis-prone situation of the world and humanity and of the task of the church conscious to be a sign of solidarity and community. The conciliar process of justice, peace, and the preservation of creation corrected in some way this position.[42]
2. The World Assembly in Nairobi 1975 developed the concept of a conciliar community. However, this sadly has been given up in the ensuing years: The visionary aim of a universal council of all churches was replaced by the demand for conciliar structures.
3. Since the scriptures of both the Old and New Testaments do not present a uniform ecclesiology, it is superfluous to look there for a biblical concept of unity. Rather the process to which the New Testament testifies has to be continued and adequate forms of community have to be found for today.

Besides Vischer's critique, the objections raised by Erich Geldbach seem to be a great help. Geldbach spoke – not without ironic connotations – about koinonia as the 'new holy word of the ecumenical movement'.[43] The goal of his investigation was to explore the meaning which koinonia (the communion-ecclesiology) gained in bilateral discourses between the Roman Catholic Church and other denominations. He discovered the following argumentative structure: First of all a Trinitarian basis is being presupposed. From here the sacramental character of the church as tool of God's salvation is deduced. The central focus of the church then is the Eucharist. With reference to the structures of koinonia, also Lukas Vischer remarked that koinonia belongs to a static framework, which is displayed in many local churches. At the top of these is the bishop and the association of bishops as heads of churches finally requires a primate.

As soon as the discourse about the communion of churches approaches this point, the ancient controversial topics of how to understand ministry and authority come up again. Geldbach concludes that the communion-ecclesiology ultimately underlines the Roman Catholic demand for a primate. In doing this it becomes a 'hermeneutical principle of submission'.[44] There is much polemic energy in these conclusions, but certainly the koinonia model does not help resolve the old controversial issues between the confessions. The following critical points touch on almost on any subject essential for the koinonia model when it postulates progress or even means of solution:

- The search for overcoming the conflicts within the WCC.
- The possibility of speaking of different levels of community.
- The search for a biblical foundation of unity.

This critique of the koinonia model also applies to the worldwide propagation of the Pentecostalism. Here, the ecumenical movement increasingly encounters structures culturally and denominationally different from those of historical Christianity. The Koinonia model is not able to do justice to this new situation.

The Koinona Model: Unacceptable for Present Developments

A look into the New Testament meaning of koinonia reveals two focal points, first togetherness of the believers and second sharing within the Christian community.[45] These two basic ways of Christian communion are the centre of ecumenical interaction. But how do we put them into practice? The koinonia model does not render any help how to proceed in concrete situations. How can togetherness and sharing be practised? This challenge is especially highlighted by the new ecumenical arrivals just outside our own front door: Equal partnership cannot come into existence as long as 'sharing' is nothing but a one-way traffic. 'Life in community' ('Leben in Gemeinschaft', Raiser) is not substantiated nor realized, as long community is not given priority.

Furthermore, the sharing on moral grounds encouraged by the koinonia model, and geographically and culturally practised within the north–south axis, is not longer acceptable. Ecumenical interaction starts from local levels and requires an ecclesiological model feasible for welcoming strangers in spite of cultural differences, and (very often) because of lack of historical denominational criteria. The Canberra declaration uses the koinonia model for finding unity in the sacramental life of the church, as we have seen above:

> The Unity of the Church as koinonia: Gift and Calling: The Unity of the church in which we are called is a koinonia given and expressed in . . . a common sacramental life entered by the one baptism and celebrated together in one eucharistic fellowship.[46]

But what about ecumenical interaction among those churches which are 'non-sacramental', that is, those which do not place the sacraments into the centre of their spiritual life? This applies especially to the pentecostal churches of the southern hemisphere.

The question is highly significant today. The New Testament term koinonia as the central term of the oikumene appears to be overcharged and not feasible to describe the given ecclesiological pluralism? In my opinion this model does not resonate with the practical life of the ecumenical movement. Certainly it is not a pure coincidence that in the New Testament period an abundance of images and metaphors for 'ecclesia' did arise.[47] The biblical authors did not limit themselves to only one variant of New Testament ecclesiology. This would have meant to give one cultural expression preference over others. It would have limited and cut to pieces the rich pluralism of biblical images and metaphors.

The Convivence Model as Departure
to a New Ecclesiology

The ecumenical movement by employing the koinonia model tries permanently to look out for what it should do. Much more helpful it would be to look out for what is actually happening, or what can already be found. The model of convivence aims at this. Its point of departure is the situation at hand! To put it differently: The koinonia model may be seen as an ecumenical approach from above which is quite contrary to how all young churches in the southern hemisphere think and live! The convivence model starts as an ecumenical approach from below, very close to these new movements.

Therefore to overcome the restrictive metaphor of koinonia and to obtain a new distinctive ecumenical profile[48] a real change of paradigm of mission and theology within the WCC is necessary. This necessity arises most urgently not least when faced with the fast-growing AICs which meanwhile are dispersed all over the world. The 'oikumene' needs a new frame of reference in the third millennium that is not to rely on one single biblical model of the church but rather follow the suggestions of Lukas Vischer and the pluralistic mentality of the New Testament for building adequate structures for the ecumenical community today. Convivence rests on the three pillars of sharing, of learning from each other, and of celebrating together. These give the churches and congregations the opportunity to put the theory and experience of intercultural interaction into practice.

Yet, the three pillars of sharing, learning and celebrating can also lead to a division of the secular and the religious realm. This would certainly contradict the holistic intents of convivence and the concept of spirituality among African Christians. Both sides belong together. No sharing, learning, or celebrating can take place inside the framework of the church if it does not also occur in everyday life and vice versa:

- 'Sharing' refers to the everyday social being-together the same as to the sharing among brothers and sisters. This is true in pastoral and in eucharistic settings where people may count on reciprocal help in the secular world as in the church.
- 'Learning from each other' refers to both intercultural and theological learning. The partners may first get acquainted with each other on the artistic or the culinary level, yet this can lead to spiritual and religious reconciliation. To learn from each other deepens empathy so necessary for coming together.
- 'Celebrating together' may take place in a profane setting or in a worship-service. Feasts are a part of our human condition. They contribute decisively to any ecumenical interaction.

In contrast to the koinonia model, convivence is freed from preconceived guidelines and therefore open to all kinds of procedures. It accepts what it encounters as cultural and denominational divergences but respects the remaining differences. Convivence does not embark on simply smoothing over controversies. On the contrary, it encourages the ecumenical partners to assert their identities and not to sacrifice themselves to a model of uniformity.[49] Contrary to a binding model of community, which promotes long duration, includes strict guidelines and tries to reconcile all differences, convivence does not aim at a unanimous voice. Convivence has a participatory dimension and thus expresses an ongoing process and always falls back on life as the foundation of every coming-together (con-vivere). So convivence is able to develop a new ecumenical ecclesiology. By making use of the hermeneutics of the stranger, it seems leading to an adequate paradigm for ecumenical interaction at the beginning of the new century. With this, Ecumenism is on the right way towards a visible shape of the worldwide Christian community.

Notes

[1] See my plea for the term 'African Christians' and the discussion with the position of Ter Haar, Gerrie, *Halfway to Paradise: African Christians in Europe* (Cardiff: Cardiff Academic Press, 1998), in Simon, *Benjamin, Afrikanische Kirchen in Deutschland* (Frankfurt am. Main: Otto Lembeck, 2003).

[2] Cf. Simon, Benjamin, '. . . damit sie alle eins seien – Afrikanische Pfingstler und Ökumene' in Christoph Dahling-Sander, Kai M. Funkschmidt, and Vera Mielke (eds), *Pfingstkirchen und Ökumene in Bewegung* (Frankfurt am. Main: Otto Lembeck, 2001), 138–57.

[3] Cf. Raiser, Konrad, *Ökumene im Übergang: Paradigmenwechsel in der ökumenischen Bewegung?* (München: Kaiser, 1989).

[4] See 'Auf dem Weg zu einer umfassenden Koinonia: Botschaft der 5. Weltkonferenz in Santiago de Compostela für Glauben und Kirchenverfassung', *Ökumenische Rundschau 42* (1993): 476–79, 53.

[5] Raiser, Konrad, 'Modelle kirchlicher Einheit: Die Debatte der siebziger Jahre und die Folgerungen für heute', *Ökumenische Rundschau 36* (1987): 195–216.

[6] '"Die Einheit der Kirche als Koinonia: Gabe und Berufung", ÖRK, Erklärung der Vollversammlung von Canberra 1991', *Ökumenische Rundschau 40* (1991): 180–82.

[7] Cf. Ökumenischer Rat der Kirchen (ed.), *Auf dem Weg zur Koinonia im Glauben, Leben und Zeugnis* (Genf: WCC, 1993): 14.

[8] Ibid.

[9] Cf. WCC (ed.), *Fifth World Conference on Faith and Order, Santiago de Compostela: Message Sections Reports, Faith and Order Paper Nr. 164* (Genf: WCC, 1993).

[10] Ökumenischer Rat der Kirchen 1993: 17.

[11] 'Entwurf einer Charta Oecumenica für die Zusammenarbeit zwischen den Kirchen in Europa', *Materialdienst 50* (1999): 95–96.

[12] Cf. Käsemann, Ernst, *Jesu letzter Wille nach Johannes 17* (Tübingen: J. C. B. Mohr, 1967), 101.

[13] See especially Eph. 4, 1–6.

[14] Raiser 1989: 158.

[15] Cf. Minear, Paul, *Bilder der Gemeinde. Eine Studie über das Selbstverständnis der Gemeinde anhand von 96 Bildbegriffen des Neuen Testaments* (Kassel: Oncken Verlag, 1964). Minear mentions 96 ecclesiological pictures and metaphors all coming from the New Testament.

[16] Cf. Roloff, Jürgen, 'Die Bedeutung des Gottesvolkes – Gedanken für die neutestamentliche Ekklesiologie', *Glauben Lernen 2* (Heft 1) (1987): 33–46.

[17] WCC 1993: 15.

[18] Raiser, Konrad, 'Neue theologische Ansätze in der ökumenischen Diskussion', in Christoph Dahling-Sander and Thomas Kratzert, *Leitfaden Ökumenische Theologie* (Wuppertal: foedus, 1998), 28–36, here p. 30.

[19] See for the following: Die Einheit 1991; Auf dem Weg zur Koinonia 1993; Auf dem Weg zu einer umfassenden Koinonia 1993.

[20] Meyer, Heinrich, *Ökumenische Zielvorstellungen* (Göttingen: Vandenhoeck u. Ruprecht, 1996), 81.

[21] Raiser 1998: 32: 'eine Gemeinschaft [. . .] die die Kirche und ihre Einheit relational (sieht) und nicht in erster Linie institutionell oder dogmatisch versteht'.

[22] Raiser 1989: 160.

[23] Cf. Feldtkeller, Andreas, 'Ökumene, Missions- und Religionswissenschaft. Eine Verhältnisbestimmung', in Dahling-Sander und Kratzert (eds), *Leitfaden Ökumenische Theologie* (1998): 37–43, here p. 38.

[24] Here I disagree with Dahling-Sander, Christoph, 'Auf dem Weg zur sichtbaren Gemeinschaft?', *EMW – Informationen 123* (2000): 25. He sees in the koinonia model a profitable theological criteria for the theological co-operation between churches and congregations of different languages and origin.

[25] Ökumenischer Rat der Kirchen 1993: 14.

[26] Cf. Sundermeier, Theo, 'Konvivenz als Grundstruktur ökumenischer Existenz heute', in Volker Küster (ed.), *Konvivenz und Differenz* (Erlangen: Erlanger Verlag, 1995), 43-75. The term 'Konvivenz' comes from Latin American liberation theology and focuses on the way of Christian togetherness. Sundermeier introduced that term in Mission Theology and in the Dialogue of Religions.

[27] Sundermeier, Theo, *Den Fremden Verstehen. Eine Praktische Hermeneutik* (Göttingen: Vandenhoeck und Ruprecht, 1996).

[28] Ibid.:12.

[29] Ibid.: 224.

[30] Cf. Schmied-Kowarzik and Justin Stagl (eds), *Grundfragen der Ethnologie. Beiträge zur gegenwärtigen Theoriediskussion,* Second edn (Berlin: Dietrich Reimer, 1993).

[31] Cf. Sundermeier, Theo, 'Verstehen und Übersetzen als Grundprobleme missionarischer Existenz', in Wolfgang Günther (ed.), *Verstehen und Übersetzen. Beiträge vom Missionstheologischen Symposium Hermannsburg 1999* (Hermannsburg: Missionsverlag, 2000), 11–34.

[32] Sundermeier 1996: 168.

[33] Cf. Schoenborn, Ulrich, *Gekreuzigt im Leiden der Armen. Beiträge zur kontextuellen Theologie in Brasilien* (Mettingen: Brasilienkunde-Verlag, 1986), 45.

[34] Sundermeier 1996: 190–91.

[35] Sundermeier 1995: 43–75, here p. 48.

[36] Cf. Assmann, Jan, 'Der zweidimensionale Mensch: Das Fest als Medium des kollektiven Gedächtnisses', in Assmann, Jan (ed.), *Das Fest und das Heilige* (Gütersloh: Gütersloher Verlag, 1991), 13–30.

[37] Hollenweger, Walter J. *Charismatisch-pfingstliches Christentum. Herkunft, Situation, Ökumenische Chancen* (Göttingen: Vandenhoeck und Ruprecht, 1997).

[38] Eberhard Jüngel mentioned these ideas at a Symposium in Tübingen; cf. Raiser 1989: 53.

[39] Kuhn, T. S. *Die Struktur wissenschaftlicher Revolutionen, 2. revidierte und um das Postskriptum von 1969 ergänzte Aufl.* (Frankfurt am. Main: Suhrkamp, 1978).

[40] Cf. Enns, Fernando, 'Ökumenische Theoriebildung. Was tun eigentlich Ökumeniker?', in Dahling-Sander und Kratzert (eds) 1998: 13–27, here p. 26.

41 Cf. Vischer, Lukas, 'Ist das wirklich die Einheit, die wir suchen? Zur Erklärung der Vollversammlung des Ökumenischen Rates der Kirchen in Canberra: Die Einheit der Kirchen als Koinonia: Gabe und Berufung', *Ökumenische Rundschau 41* (1992): 7–24.

42 Scherzberg, Lucia, 'Das Koinonia-Konzept des Ökumenischen Rates und der Gemeinschaftsbegriff', *Ökumenische Rundschau 2* (2002): 157–66.

43 Geldbach, Erich, 'Koinonia. Einige Beobachtungen zu einem ökumenischen Schlüsselbegriff', *Ökumenische Rundschau 44* (1993): 73–77, here p. 73.

44 Ibid.: 77.

45 Cf. WCC 1993: 15.

46 Gassmann, G. and Radano, J. A. (eds), *The Unity of the Church as Koinonia. Ecumenical Perspectives on the 1991 Canberra Statement on Unity. A Study Document requested by the Joint Working Group between the Roman Catholic Church and the World Council of Churches* (Genf: WCC Publisher), 1993, 2.

47 Cf. Minear 1964.

48 Cf. Ökumenischer Rat der Kirchen 1993: 14.

49 Cf. Simon 2003.

Chapter 26

The 'Program for Cooperation between German and Foreign Language Churches' and African Churches in the Rhein-Ruhr-Region: Developments from 1999

Ursula Harfst

Introduction

This report was presented to the African Diaspora conference in September 2003. Rewriting it in 2006 for publication, meant a total reexamining of the whole situation of migrant churches and the relationship between them and the (so-called) German main line churches which has been very fluid.

A Short Look Back

In April 1998, the 'Program for Cooperation between German and Foreign Language Churches' was started by the United Evangelical Mission (UEM). UEM 'is an international missionary communion which currently consists of 34 member churches in Africa, Asia and Germany. The objective is the communion in mission and reciprocal assistance in implementing missionary tasks. The United Evangelical Mission is the successor to the Vereinigte Evangelische Mission which, as a German missionary organisation, was itself established in 1971'.[1]

The purpose of the program was to evaluate which kind of migrant churches existed, what kind of cooperation would be possible and what kind of support these churches would need. The pioneering coordinator of this work was Claudia Währisch-Oblau, a pastor of the Protestant Church in the Rhineland (Evangelische Kirche im Rheinland, Landeskirche). She described the goals of the program as:

> Assist immigrant churches to establish a visible presence within the context of German church and society; help German churches to understand and

appreciate the movement of reverse mission that is taking place through the presence of immigrant congregations; – develop projects of common/inter-cultural evangelism.[2]

Soon also the following tasks of the program became clear: 'support migrant churches to form formalized net-works'[3]; offer seminars and education for pastors and church leaders from migrant churches as well as common meetings for pastors and members of German- and so-called foreign-language congregations to share the faith and foster a better understanding. Germans and migrant Christians together prepared almost all of these seminars and meetings.

Observation and Evaluation of the Program

In 2003 the program's database contained 390 migrant churches and congregations in the Rhein-Ruhr-Region of Germany, of which 177 were African. In March 2006, there were 190 African churches out of 431 known local churches.[4] Actually the categories 'migrant church' or 'foreign-language church' show only one of their characteristics. They all celebrate worship in at least one other language than German and many of their members have a background of migration. But regarding denomination, culture, members' time of stay in the country, education and social status, there are big differences between the various churches. So we, employees of the program, as well as members of the churches who work with this program, always deal with the question, whether it is suitable to see the 'foreign-language churches' as one monolith group.

The project's vision is that of an intercultural church, of One Body in Christ. We recognize the desire from both sides to be one church. But there is also the strong hope within migrant churches to be accepted as they are. Migrants need to meet and celebrate worship in languages and under cultural and theological conditions close to those in their home countries. Unity with the German churches and society cannot imply becoming like the Germans, but to determine their place, task and form of community in their own ways. What comes into existence are 'Zwischenwelten': worlds in-between.

The Structure of the Program

Research, individual case-work, education and information, and political involvement are the main of the project. The work of the program grew and so did the number of employees. The staff in 2003 included three pastors, one in a full-time position and two part-timers. Claudia Währisch-Oblau still coordinates the program. From 2002 to 2005, she was assisted by Ursula Harfst. From 2002 to 2005, Gotthard Oblau led the training course 'Church in an intercultural context' (Kirche im interkulturellen Kontext – KIIK) for pastors and church leaders of all kinds. All three pastors were paid by the Evangelical Church in the Rhineland. Unfortunately, the future of the program is uncertain. While the two part-time pastors' contracts ended in 2005, Claudia Währisch-Oblau will leave the program in 2007. How the work will continue is not yet certain. But UEM and the Evangelical Churches in the Rhineland and of Westphalia recognize the significance of migrant churches and the importance of the work of the program.[5]

Raising Awareness in the German Church

Over the past years, the awareness of the existence of migrant churches has grown on all levels within the German churches and the knowledge about them has widened considerably. For example, compulsory courses on ecumenism for pastors in training of the Protestant Churches in Rhineland and Westphalia now include teaching units about cooperation with migrant churches. Ecumenical committees within church districts regularly ask for information about migrant churches and initiate contacts and cooperation with them. The church leadership has also become more aware of their situation. German churches have begun to allow input from migrant churches into their own reflections. For example, a working group was installed within the Protestant church of Westphalia to start thinking about its own profile. One question regarding this new profile has been whether the church desires to stay white or rather become multiracial. So the committee on Ecumenism and Mission established a subcommittee which now reflects on how to cooperate with these congregations. Another example is a major study undertaken by the Protestant Church of the Rhineland, in the context of re-considering its profile, which mentions the 'increasing importance' of migrant churches for mission in Germany.[6]

In January 2003, the constitution of the Evangelical Church in the Rhineland was changed by its Synod. In addition to the given geographical parish system, there is now the possibility to establish non-geographical parishes. This grants migrant churches the chance to apply to become units within this church. The migrant congregations, as full members of the Church in the Rhineland, will then have all rights. They will also be required to accept not only being part of a Protestant denomination but all its rules and laws, such as full university studies as a requirement for pastors. Up to now only one church started the process of becoming a full member. For other congregations reflections about a special cooperation are underway.

In Addition, the theological input and the visibility of migrant churches is rising. Representatives of migrant churches have participated in mission events of German churches like ProChrist[7], Christival[8] and Missionale[9]. Church members took part in programs and pastors led seminars. For example, on 1 April 2006, the Korean Pastor Dr Yong Joon Choi, Hanbit Evangelische Kirchengemeinde, Köln and the Ghanaian Pastor Edmund Sackey-Brown, Lighthouse Fellowship,

Mülheim an der Ruhr taught at the Missionale in Cologne about: 'The mission-minded church strategies in building a multicultural ministry'.

On the regional level, interest is increasing in many places. For instance, in Duisburg, the committee for Ecumenism often explores ways to bind the German and the foreign language churches together. Worship services of 'foreign-language' churches are visited, common services are celebrated, pastors of migrant churches are invited to meetings of the German pastors, and plans are made to invite migrant representatives to the annual synods. In 2006, seven Synods of regional church districts named representatives for local work and contact. Pastors of migrant churches often meet together with these representatives in Duisburg, Cologne and other cities to discuss theological and social issues and to plan common events such as joint services and participation in events of a migrant church or the Protestant church district. In Wuppertal and Cologne the possibility of establishing International Church Centres in the inner city together with migrant churches has been explored, but did not work out yet.

More Openness to Mutual Theological Learning and Discussion

Since 2003, the Protestant Church in the Rhineland has opened several of its seminars for the continuing education for its own pastors to pastors of migrant churches. Together with an African, a Nepali and two Korean pastors, I took part in the seminar by Professor Manfred Josuttis entitled 'Counselling in the Power of the Coming One'.[10] I was struck by the seriousness and the mutual interest in such a mixed group. The input of the migrant pastors was fantastic and very well received by the Germans. The comment of Professor Josuttis was: 'When I told you my ideas which sound crazy to many (for example, expelling the power of grief by the power of God), they were immediately supported by the experience of you, friends from foreign-language churches'. The migrant pastors also confirmed their gratefulness for having been able to participate in such a seminar. They learned about German theology and practice, received deeper insights in the faith, spirituality, life and work of German pastors, and had the chance to share their own knowledge and experience. In November 2003, a seminar on Biblical hermeneutics was organized by the Protestant Church in the Rhineland. Three migrant Pentecostal pastors were invited to share their understanding of Eph. 6.10–20, and how they live out the struggle with powers and principalities in their environment.

Acceptance of Migrant Churches

For the many migrant churches who want to cooperate with the Protestant churches in 2000, the so-called list-process was started. As members of this official list the churches are accepted as ecumenical partners by the Evangelical

Churches in the Rhineland and of Westphalia. The process strengthens their position with the German churches and the state, and it connects them with each other.

In 2006, out of 431 foreign language churches with evangelical, pentecostal and charismatic backgrounds in North Rhine-Westphalia, 134 congregations have been accepted to the recognised list. The criteria for acceptance have been jointly developed by representatives of migrant churches and these two Protestant churches.[11] This list was first published by the United Evangelical Mission on 24 January 2001, and is being updated in January each year.

All churches on this list are invited to meetings which take place at least once a year. At these assemblies, information about the work of the program is provided and a committee of representatives is elected which continues the work between meetings and also decides which churches are accepted on the list. The meetings begin with a common service and a common lunch is provided. A regular feature is discussion among the diverse language groups. Here problems and ideas are shared and finally brought to the plenary and committee. This committee of elected representatives of the so-called 'list-churches' and representatives of the two mentioned German churches meets regularly to discuss issues of mutual interest . Here many of the following ideas were born and put into practice:

1. The recognized list of churches was passed to the 'Ausländerbehörde' (office for resident foreigners) in North Rhine-Westphalia. That made it easier for members who live under travel restrictions (e.g. asylum seekers) to more easily obtain travel permits within Germany and to obtain visas for pastors coming from abroad.
2. All German prison chaplains were informed that they should assist migrant pastors with prison visitations. One pastor felt that he is now treated with respect, and that the whole procedure of entering the prison had been simplified.
3. For these congregations acknowledged as ecumenical partners, it is easier to find venues in facilities of German congregations – against fears by the German people-congregation to receive a 'sect', which often is their first question.
4. Meanwhile, there have been many contacts with the 'Ausländerbehörden'.

In 2003, a meeting between representatives of migrant churches, the UEM program, the Protestant churches, and high-level officials of the Interior Ministry of the State of North Rhine-Westphalia resulted in an agreement which will give asylum seekers much more freedom to travel in church affairs, and which will make it easier for pastors without recognized academic qualifications to obtain a visa to work in Germany. We see now even a willingness to allow asylum seekers to change their status to obtain a 'pastor's visa', if either their own congregation or other church organizations pay them a decent salary.

Building Networks

An important outcome of this process is the foundation of the 'Association of Christian Migrant Churches' (ACMK) in North Rhine-Westphalia in June 2003. Forty-eight congregations of different descent and ethnicity (all members of the list) decided to establish this association in order to gain strength by unity and to speak with one voice to the government and the boards of the so-called mainline churches. They hope for better understanding with and acceptance by the German Protestant churches. They support the ecumenical cooperation between German and 'foreign-language' churches. The association also plans to join the Association of Christian Churches in North Rhine-Westphalia ('Arbeitsgemeinschaft Christlicher Kirchen'). Membership in the latter has so far been denied to churches which only applied individually. In 2006, the ACMK was formally and legally established. Now it is in the process of organizing itself, handling the denominational and ethnic differences, defining its specific goals and tasks and increasing its membership.

Training Course for Pastors and Leaders of Congregations Called 'Kirche im interkulturellen Kontext' ('Church in an Intercultural Context')

In 2000, pastors from 'foreign-language' churches voiced the urgent need for a training program specifically targeted at their churches. This program needed to provide more knowledge and insight into German culture, history, theology and ways of thinking, as well as deeper knowledge about the Bible and tools for intercultural evangelism. Available theological training programs in Germany were seen as unsuitable, too long, and too expensive. Therefore, a ten-weekend training course for pastors and leaders of migrant churches was jointly developed by pastors and teachers of these churches, the coordinator of the program Währisch-Oblau, and Burkhard Weber, the director of Johanneum Bible School, a free organization within the German Protestant churches. Four courses are already completed. Teachers with German as well as immigrant backgrounds have taught the classes (in 2001/2002, 3 teachers from abroad compared to 13 from Germany; in 2004/2005, 4 from migrant churches and 15 from Germany). The second course and the following have been opened for German participants who are interested in intercultural theological dialogue and church work to make it a truly intercultural program.

The participants learn from each other, grow spiritually and develop a fellowship which overcomes cultural and denominational barriers. In March 2006, the fifth course commenced with thirteen participants from six countries.

Barriers and Difficulties

German representatives sometimes complain that it is difficult to cooperate with people from migrant churches. When they invite them, there seems to be a lack of interest in common events. This is also true in reverse: When 'foreign-language' churches invite the Germans, they seldom follow. The problem may be language barriers or different styles of how to proclaim the 'Good News'. On both sides there is mistrust and lack of respect about whether the partners can be considered to be real Christians. Some German church officials still tend to regard migrant churches as too traditional or even fundamentalist, not having gone through the process of 'Enlightenment'. Some migrant churches consider the German churches to be dead or not committed enough. In future, we have to work on these problems from both sides.

It is still true that 'very few [migrant] Protestant congregations own or rent premises big enough to hold a worship service there'.[12] Still, most migrant churches are regarded as paying 'guests' in church buildings. Often they have to move or cancel their allocated time when the 'host' – congregation needs the rooms. Still, disused church buildings are sold for such huge sums that migrant churches do not have the resources to buy or rent them. Church buildings belong to individual congregations, and they mostly sell the property to the highest bidder because they need the money to continue their work. A solution that has been suggested is a special fund set up by the territorial church to meet these problems. But it seems unlikely that this suggestion will be soon put into practice. Alternatively, regional church districts, the Synods of the congregations in one city or area could support the migrant churches in their coming-together with local German congregations. Even today, German congregations tend to complain about the noise and dirt caused by their migrant 'tenants', and often solve problems simply by ending the contract. In some such cases, the co-workers of the program were able to mediate and help the congregations to understand each other better.

Unfortunately, only 40–50 per cent of the 'list-churches' participate in the annual meetings mentioned above. There is still mistrust toward the German churches and also disappointment and anger. People think that the German churches could do more to accommodate them. On the one hand, this may be true. On the other hand, their power – especially in relation to the government – is often overestimated by many Christians from abroad.

Some Observations Regarding
African Churches

For the staff of the program, it is easier to criticize the German church, as the evaluation has been done by German pastors. We want to be supportive of migrant churches. But what can the staff do regarding problems between and within their own ranks? Within African churches there is the strong will to build common organizations or associations to become stronger and support each other. But denominational and cultural differences, and also reservations about each other, often hinder cooperation. The staff of the program here tries to support self-organization, if asked to do so. The number of African churches appears to be increasing rapidly. In a city like Düsseldorf, one can find more than 20 African churches. On the one hand, there is regret about the splitting and the conflicts. On the other hand, the total number of members increases with the rising number of congregations. Another problem surfaces soon for African churches. What is going to happen to the children and youth of the second and third generation? They live in two different cultures. They are bilingual, speaking both German and the language of their families. They will express their faith in ways that are different from those of their parents. For them or their children, worshiping in, for example, Twi will seem old-fashioned, exotic or boring. Means have to be explored how they can live their faith in a way which fits their situation.

Our Vision

We dream of an intercultural church where people of all nations and colours will serve God together. We dream of a church without barriers: a church which resembles the colourful body of Christ within this world. We hope and we pray that the body of the Church of Christ in Germany will become colourful and attractive for all kinds of people. May the Holy Spirit inspire the different churches so that they become a living sign of God's love in the world.

Notes

[1] http://www.vemission.org/english/index.html?/english/info/index.html 08.06.2006.
[2] Währisch-Oblau, Claudia, 'From Reverse Mission to Common Mission. . . . We hope! Immigrant Protestant Churches and the "Programme for Cooperation between German and Immigrant Congregations" of the United Evangelical Mission', *International Review of Mission, LXXXIX*(354) (July 2000): 467–483, here p. 467.

[3] Ibid.: 477.
[4] Source UEM Database: accessed on 24 March 2006; available at: http://www.vemission.org/fileadmin/Dateien/Arbeitsbereiche/Fremdsprachige_Gemeinden/08-03-12liste.pdf.
[5] In June 2006 the synod of the Church in the Rhineland passed a resolution to provide 100,000 € per year for a work with and of migrant churches; the new concept of this engagement is still to be developed by the church board. http://www.ekir.de/ekir/dokumente/ekir2006ao-ls-ds01spar-und-struktur-vorschlaege.pdf 12.06.2006: 41–42.
[6] Evangelische Kirche im Rheinland (ed.), *Auf Sendung. Mission und Evangelisation in unserer Kirche*, Düsseldorf 2002, 23–24.
[7] A big, televised evangelism event run by Evangelicals from both the territorial and the free churches.
[8] A Christian youth congress which drew more than 30,000 participants in 2002.
[9] An annual meeting of several thousand members and pastors from many churches in Rhineland and Westphalia who want to strengthen evangelism within their churches.
[10] 30 June 2003–4 July 2003, 'Seelsorge in der Kraft des Kommenden' in Rengsdorf.
[11] Währisch-Oblau 2000: 477, 481. The criteria are: sharing the faith in Jesus Christ (following the basis of the World Council of churches), commitment to ecumenical cooperation with German- and foreign-language churches, organisational stability, willingness of the pastors to participate in courses of continuing education and the two written recommendations.
[12] Währisch-Oblau 2000: 474.

Index

Calata, James 90

Calvary Ministries (CAPRO) 175

Cameroon 13, 80, 81, 85, 170, 171, 173, 178, 179, 254, 272

Canada 21, 87, 88

Carey, Lott 79

Carey, William 78

Caribbean 1, 84, 87f, 208–16, 282, 293–300, 303fn

Cassirer, Ernst 105

Catholic, Catholic Church, Catholicism 9–17, 22, 43, 51–7, 76–82, 86f, 130, 146, 158, 182, 194–204, 208–13, 236, 272, 284, 309, 315f, 321fn, 324, 330

Celestial Church of Christ (CCC) 16, 41, 128, 130–5, 137

Cerullo, Morris 184

Chad 13, 171f

charismatic churches/movements 140–2, 92, 116, 167–231, 290, 340

Charismatic Evangelistic Ministry (CEM) 198, 199

charismatic renewal 168–269, 172, 182, 185–90, 192–207, 209

see also Christianity

Cherubim and Seraphim movement/ churches 16f, 41

Chidester, David 99

Chikerema, James 55

Chilembwe, John 81

Christ Apostolic Church (CAC) 30fn, 41, 128–35, 137fn, 210, 285

Christ Army Church 41

Christian Association of Nigeria (CAN) 41

Christian Missionary Foundation (CNF) 175f

Christian Council of Nigeria (CCN) 41f

Christian Institute 58

Christian Student Social Movements of Nigeria (CSSM) 174–6

Christianity and Africa 2–4, 10–12, 14, 16, 21, 23–4, 34, 45–7, 55, 63–4, 68, 70–1, 74–5, 84, 94, 105, 186, 253, 296

and Catholicism 11–12, 14–15, 43, 56, 198–9, 201

and Protestantism 12, 14–15, 43

'Church in an Intercultural Context' (KIIK) 337, 341f

Church Missionary Society (CMS) 12, 14f, 89, 282f, 288

Church of God in Christ (CoGiC) 127, 225–7

Church of God Mission (International) 38, 171, 182, 289

Church of Jesus Christ on Earth by His Special Envoy Simon Kimbangu (EJCSK) 308–12

Church of the First Borns 182

Church of the Lord/Aladura (CLA) 38, 41, 127–35

Churches of the Spirit 4, 208–9, 211, 213–15, 217, 219

Colley, William W. 79

colonialism, colonial 9f, 13–17, 23, 33, 47, 50–61, 63–75, 80f, 82, 86–93, 97–106, 114f, 124, 126, 134, 140–4, 248–58, 279–91, 304–6

Colonso, Harriette 142

Conference of African Churches in Switzerland 42

Congo xii–xiv, 1, 3, 4, 13, 15, 35, 37, 50, 52, 57, 60, 81–4, 87, 92f, 148, 219, 212, 266, 272, 304–16

conversion, converts 10, 12, 16, 45, 51, 52, 66–8, 72, 76–7, 79, 81, 97–109, 119, 140, 144, 158, 174, 181, 183, 190, 195, 213–16, 243, 250, 253, 259, 261fn, 285, 298, 304

Coptic, Copts 24, 316

Council of Christian Communities of an African Approach in Europe (CCCAAE) 42, 212

Crane, William 79

Crowther, Samuel Adjai 21, 42, 88f

Crummell, Alexander 89

Dahomey 13, 255

Daneel, Marthinus 59, 215

Daniels, David 225